The New Generations of Europeans

Demography and Families in the Enlarged European Union

The International Institute for Applied Systems Analysis

is an interdisciplinary, nongovernmental research institution founded in 1972 by leading scientific organizations in 12 countries. Situated near Vienna, in the center of Europe, IIASA has been producing valuable scientific research on economic, technological and environmental issues for over three decades.

IIASA was one of the first international institutes to systematically study global issues of environment, technology and development. IIASA's Governing Council states that the Institute's goal is: *to conduct international and interdisciplinary scientific studies to provide timely and relevant information and options, addressing critical issues of global environmental, economic and social change, for the benefit of the public, the scientific community and national and international institutions.* Research is organized around three central themes:

- Energy and Technology
- Environment and Natural Resources
- Population and Society

IIASA is funded and supported by scientific institutions and organizations in the following countries:

Austria, China, Czech Republic, Egypt, Estonia, Finland, Germany, Hungary, Japan, Netherlands, Norway, Poland, Russian Federation, Sweden, Ukraine, United States of America.

Further information: http://www.iiasa.ac.at

The European Observatory on the Social Situation, Demography and Family 1998 to 2004

The European Observatory on the Social Situation, Demography and Family was a multi-disciplinary network of independent experts established and funded by the European Commission. Between 1998 and 2004 the Austrian Institute for Family Studies (ÖIF) coordinated the Observatory.

The European Observatory had a national expert in each of the then 15 member states of the European Union. These experts monitored and reported on political, demographic and socioeconomic changes and how these influenced the social situation and the family.

This book, *The New Generations of Europeans: Demography and Families in the Enlarged European Union*, summarizes the insights from the research of the Observatory.

Further information: http://europa.eu.int/comm/employment_social/eoss/

This publication is based on articles and contributions presented during the closing conference of the European Observatory on Demography, the Social Situation and Family that took place from 27 to 28 September 2004. The Observatory was entirely funded by the European Commission. However, the reports and contributions in the present publication do not necessarily reflect the opinion or position of the European Commission, the Austrian Institute for Family Studies or the International Institute for Applied Systems Analysis.

Population and Sustainable Development Series

The New Generations of Europeans

Demography and Families in the Enlarged European Union

Edited by

Wolfgang Lutz, Rudolf Richter and Chris Wilson

IIASA

EARTHSCAN

London and Sterling, VA

First published by Earthscan in the UK and USA in 2006

ISBN-13: 978-1-84407-351-1 paperback
ISBN-10: 1-84407-351-3 paperback
ISBN-13: 978-1-84407-352-8 hardback
ISBN-10: 1-84407-352-1 hardback

Typesetting by Ingrid Teply-Baubinder
Printed and bound in the UK by Bath Press, Bath
Cover design by Yvonne Booth

For a full list of publications please contact:

Earthscan
8–12 Camden High Street
London, NW1 0JH, UK
Tel: +44 (0)20 7387 8558
Fax: +44 (0)20 7387 8998
Email: earthinfo@earthscan.co.uk
Web: **http://www.earthscan.co.uk**

22883 Quicksilver Drive, Sterling, VA 20166-2012, USA

Earthscan is an imprint of James & James (Science Publishers) Ltd and publishes
in association with the International Institute for Environment and Development

A catalogue record for this book is available from the British Library

Library of Congress Cataloging-in-Publication Data

The new generations of Europeans: demography and families in the enlarged European
Union / Wolfgang Lutz, Rudolf Richter and Chris Wilson (editors).
    p. cm.
  ISBN-13: 978-1-84407-351-1 (pbk.)
  ISBN-10: 1-84407-351-3 (pbk.)
  ISBN-13: 978-1-84407-352-8 (hardback)
  ISBN-10: 1-84407-352-1 (hardback)
    1. Europe–Population. 2. Family–Europe. 3. Fertility, Human–Europe. I. Lutz,
Wolfgang. II. Richter, Rudolf, 1952- III. Wilson, Christopher, 1956-
HB3581.A3N494 2006
304.6094–dc22, 2006001115

Mixed Sources
Product group from well-managed
forests and other controlled sources
www.fsc.org Cert no. SGS-COC-2121
© 1996 Forest Stewardship Council

Contents

List of Acronyms

ACC13   Thirteen acceding and candidate countries to the EU, prior to 1 May 2004
10 acceding (Cyprus, Czech Republic, Estonia, Hungary, Latvia, Lithuania, Malta, Poland, Slovakia, Slovenia)
3 candidate (Bulgaria, Romania and Turkey)

ANOVA   Analysis of variance between groups

BiB   *Bundesinstitut für Bevölkerungsforschung* (German federal population research institute)

CAPI   Computer-Assisted Personal Interviewing

CC   Candidate country

CC3   Three candidate countries (Bulgaria, Romania and Turkey)

CEE   Central and eastern Europe

CEECs   Central and eastern European countries

CYRCE   Circle for Youth Cooperation in Europe

EC   European Community

EQLS   European Quality of Life Survey

ESS   European Social Survey

EU   European Union

EU15   The 15 member states of the European Union prior to 1 May 2004: Austria, Belgium, Denmark, Finland, France, Germany, Greece, Ireland, Italy, Luxembourg, Portugal, Spain, Sweden, The Netherlands, United Kingdom.

EU25   The 25 member states of the European Union at 1 May 2004: Austria, Belgium, Cyprus, Czech Republic, Denmark, Estonia, Finland, France, Germany, Greece, Hungary, Ireland, Italy, Latvia, Lithuania, Luxembourg, Malta, Poland, Portugal, Slovakia, Slovenia, Spain, Sweden, The Netherlands, United Kingdom.

EURODAC   Community-wide system for the comparison of fingerprints of asylum applicants and illegal immigrants

FATE   Families and Transitions in Europe

FI   First instance

FFS	Fertility and Family Surveys
FPA	Family Planning Association (United Kingdom)
GDP	Gross domestic product
GDR	German Democratic Republic
GNP	Gross national product
GP	General practitioner
HCSO	Hungarian Central Statistical Office
HFA	Health for All
HIV/AIDS	Human Immunodeficiency Virus/Acquired Immunodeficiency Syndrome
HWF	Households, Work and Flexibility
INE	*Instituto Nacional de Estadística* (Spanish national statistical institute)
IOM	International Organization for Migration
IPPAS	International Population Policy Acceptance Survey
IQV	Index of Qualitative Variation
ISCED	International Standard Classification of Education
LDC	Less-developed country
MAC	Mean age at childbirth
MDC	More-developed country
MEDA	Middle East and Mediterranean
MISSOC	Mutual Information System on Social Protection (in the European Member States and the European Economic Area)
MPG	Migration Policy Group
NAFTA	North American Free Trade Agreement
NATO	North Atlantic Treaty Organization
NGO	Nongovernmental organization
NIEPS	Network for Integrated Population Studies
NMS	New member states
NRR	Net reproduction rate
OASIS	Old Age and Autonomy: The Role of Service Systems and Intergenerational Solidarity
OECD	Organisation for Economic Co-operation and Development
PAYG	Pay as you go
PLN	Polish unit of currency (zloty)
PPP	Purchasing power parity
PPS	Purchasing power standards
PRI	Population Research Institute
pTFR	period Total Fertility Rate
RRR	Refugee recognition rate
STDs	Sexually transmitted diseases

TCFR	Total cohort fertility rate
TFFMR	Total first female marriage rate
TFR	Total fertility rate
UN/ECE	United Nations Economic Commission for Europe
UNDP	United Nations Development Programme
UNESCO	United Nations Educational, Scientific and Cultural Organization
UNHCR	United Nations High Commissioner for Refugees
UNICEF	United Nations International Children's Emergency Fund
WHO	World Health Organization
WTO	World Trade Organization

Part I
Introduction and Overview

Chapter 1

Introduction

Wolfgang Lutz and Chris Wilson

Europe's future will be built by its citizens, but who will those citizens be? How numerous, how healthy, how long-lived? How many children will they have? What kind of families will they live in, and what are the main challenges to their social cohesion? During its six-year mandate from 1999 to 2004, the European Observatory on the Social Situation, Demography and Family endeavored to answer these and similar questions. At a final meeting in Brussels in September 2004, the Observatory's experts provided summary papers of discussions on the various topics—fertility, living arrangements, migration and health—each of which had been the theme of one of its annual seminars. Those summary papers, which are reproduced as chapters in this publication, not only represent the personal views of the authors on the questions posed above but are also based on extensive empirical analyses and discussions with input from all European Union (EU) member countries.

To speak meaningfully about the future, we need to understand the present and the past. To grasp where Europe is heading, we have to see where we are today and how we got here. All forecasting is subject to uncertainty, but demographic patterns are often more predictable than many other social and economic phenomena. Many of the people who will shape Europe's future are alive today. Thus, we already know a good deal about Europe's future generations. In this introduction, we sketch out some of the key elements of Europe's demographic landscape and provide an overall context within which the detailed contributions that make up the rest of the book can be viewed.

1.1   The New Generations of Europeans

In his recent book, *The European Dream*, bestselling author Jeremy Rifkin, an American, contrasts the American dream of 200 years ago with the European dream of today. He writes:

> The European dream emphasizes community relationships over individual autonomy, cultural diversity over assimilation, quality of life over the accumulation of wealth, sustainable development over unlimited material growth (Rifkin, 2004, p. 3).

> The fledgling European dream represents humanity's best aspirations for a better tomorrow. A new generation of Europeans carries the world's hopes with it (Rifkin, 2004, p. 8).

Whether or not the world is looking to the coming generations of Europeans for inspiration, there is no doubt that Europe itself should be greatly interested in who those future Europeans will be.

Who then constitutes the new generations of Europeans? In a demographic sense, the question is easy to answer. Those who are young today and those who will be born over the coming years (plus the young adults who may still enter Europe as immigrants) will form the active adult population that will shape Europe over the coming decades. As for those who are already alive—the children of today—we already know how many there are, what kind of families they live in and what education they are receiving. We also know to some extent what their attitudes, preferences and orientations toward the future are. Of course, we know that many of these attitudes and attributes will change with age and that the young Europeans of today will see the world somewhat differently once they have grown up. But research has shown that many important objective characteristics—education being a particularly significant one—as well as preferences and general attitudes tend to be surprisingly stable along cohort lines. In other words, what is formed and shaped in childhood and young adulthood tends to be a key determinant of what people do and think throughout the rest of their lives. This stability of cohort characteristics can give us a valuable framework within which to study the coming generations.

Before we embark upon the more specific topics discussed in this volume, it may be worth looking critically at another word in its title, namely, the notion of *Europeans*. Who are we? Do we consider everyone holding the passport of an EU member country (or possibly any European country) to be European? Or do we define European identity as applying to all the people who live more or less permanently within European borders, whether or not they hold the citizenship of a European country, including past and future immigrants? As we shall see,

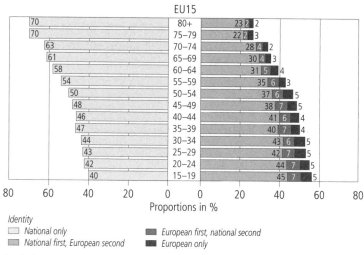

Figure 1.1. Age pattern of identity for EU15 from Eurobarometer.

Note: Calculations by Isolde Prommer (International Institute of Applied Systems Analysis, Austria).

Source: Eurobarometer 46.0 (1996).

different chapters in this volume will apply different definitions, depending on what the specific research question is. Irrespective of these definitions, we can go further and ask how European the Europeans are. To be called a European, should there be some sense of European identity in addition to a strictly national identity?

Figure 1.1 presents data from a 1996 Eurobarometer survey in which respondents were asked whether they identify themselves as (i) nationals of their country (with no sense of being European); (ii) nationals first and Europeans second; (iii) Europeans first and nationals second; or (iv) Europeans only. Not surprisingly, a very small fraction (ranging from 1 percent in Finland to 8 percent in France) called themselves 'only European,' whereas the largest group (ranging from 29 percent in Luxembourg to 65 percent in Sweden) called themselves 'only nationals.' The group of those seeing themselves as 'nationals and Europeans' is around 50 percent in France, Italy, Luxembourg and The Netherlands and between one-quarter and one-third in most other countries. But perhaps of greater interest here are the differences not among countries but according to age. Are young Europeans more European than older ones? *Figure 1.1* clearly shows that indeed they are. For all countries taken together, a majority of the population above the age of 45 feel 'national only,' whereas below that age this group becomes a minority. There is a very clear, almost linear pattern showing that the younger the respondents, the more European-minded they are and that the older the respondents, the more national-minded they are. Assuming that the question of national versus European identity is one of the attitudes that remain rather stable over the life course, we can infer from this pattern that the future generation of Europeans is also likely to have more of a European identity.

Speaking of Europeans as persons living within the European Union raises another ambiguity. The EU has been expanding its territory and population over time through the accession of additional countries. This specific feature of EU evolution is the focus of this volume; indeed, the accession of ten new member countries in 2004 was the main reason for focusing on the next generations of Europeans, especially as, in all likelihood, EU expansion will not stop at 25 member countries. How then should this book deal with the fact that there may be many future Europeans, living or yet to be born, in countries that are not members of the EU today? As we cannot foresee which countries will join the EU at what point in the future, the only feasible solution is to limit the discussion in this book to the 25 current EU member countries—a pragmatic choice for a volume in which a number of chapters exclusively address issues of the ten 'new' member countries that joined in 2004. On the one hand, this structuring of chapters along 'old' and 'new' member country lines may seem arbitrary from a substantive perspective (there is no clear dichotomy in terms of demography and family forms). On the other hand, however, this 15 to 10 split reflects an institutional reality of the EU and of its Observatory in that until 2004 only scientists from the 'old' EU15 were represented in the Observatory. Were a similar book to be written five years hence, such distinctions would hopefully be obsolete.

The process of EU enlargement has another noteworthy demographic aspect. In comparisons between Europe and the United States, attention is often drawn to the fact that while the American population is rapidly expanding, European population growth is stagnating, with actual shrinkage expected in the future. We can observe that the total population of the EU increased from 376 million in January 1999 to 381 million in January 2004. This increase of 5 million or just 1.3 percent over five years compares with a population increase in the United States of 22 million (from 271 to 293 million) or 8.1 percent over the same period. This rapid population growth is expected to continue because of higher fertility and immigration levels in the United States than in the EU. Over the next 20 years the American population is likely to increase by another 20 percent, while the longer-term projections foresee a likely decline in population size for Europe. However, for the European Union as a political entity and common market, the population size increased by 20 percent overnight on 1 May 2004—an increase that will take the United States two decades to achieve. This strategy of averting population decline by expanding the European Union may well have a similar effect to traditional population growth (when it comes) in terms of the positive economic effects of increased market size. Over the next 50 years we expect the population of the United States to increase by another 50 percent. Following the same expansive strategy, the EU, which is expected to have negative natural growth, would have to include not only Turkey and the Balkans but also Ukraine and even Russia to keep pace with such growth. But as will be discussed below, changes in population size are in many respects less relevant than changes in age structure, which are hardly affected by the accession of new countries.

1.2 Age Structure and Fertility Change

The composition of a population plays a decisive role in its future economic and social development. Thus, consideration of age structure is the best point of departure when considering likely future trends. Demographers conventionally call their favorite graphs of age structure 'population pyramids,' a pair of horizontal bar charts with the youngest ages at the bottom and the oldest at the top and males and females on either side of the central axis. A population's past experience of mortality, migration and fertility is written into its age structure. Of these three processes, fertility is especially important. The impact of changes in mortality is spread out over many age groups, whereas the effect of fertility change is all concentrated at the base of the pyramid. Migration has so far played a fairly small role in determining Europe's age structure, simply because it has been a much smaller phenomenon than fertility or mortality. Over the last half century, the net inflow of migrants into the 25 countries that now make up the EU (EU25) has probably been between 10 and 15 million people. Over the same period more than 300 million babies have been born in the EU25. Even now, with net migration into Europe at a historic high and fertility lower than ever before, the annual total of births in the EU is around four times the annual number of immigrants. Thus, past fertility trends play a key role in determining age structure.

The broad picture of long-term, age-structure change in Europe can be seen in the three panels of *Figure 1.2*. These show the population pyramids for the EU25 in three given years: 1965, 2003 and 2030 (based on projections by the Council of Europe [2005]). The impact of fertility change is dramatic. In 1965, at the peak of the baby boom, Europe's population was growing steadily, and each cohort of babies was larger than its predecessors. Although the deficit in births during the two world wars is apparent, the overall shape in 1965 does indeed look rather pyramidal. In contrast, in 2003 after almost four decades of declining fertility, the population pyramid looks more like a pentagon, with each new cohort of babies being smaller than the one before. In the 1960s, 70.4 million babies were born in the EU25; over the ten years from 1993 to 2002, the number was 48 million. To express this change in the number of births per woman (the total fertility rate): on average, women were

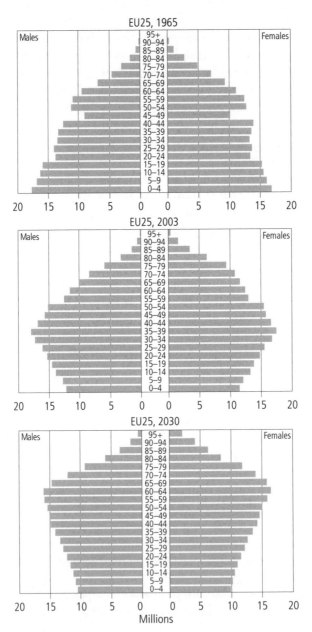

Source: Council of Europe (2005).

Figure 1.2. EU25 age structure in 1965, 2003 and 2030.

having 2.66 children in 1965 and 1.46 children in 2002. A further way of thinking about the impact of fertility change is to consider intergenerational replacement. Roughly 2.1 children per woman are needed to ensure that a cohort of women is replaced by another cohort of the same size in the next generation. In 1965 fertility was about 125 percent of the replacement level; in 2003 it was about 70 percent. A simple comparison of cohort size confirms the current situation. As the average age at which women have their children is roughly 30, we can gain a fair estimate of recent replacement by comparing the number of women aged 30–39 with the number of girls aged 0–9. In 2003, 34.2 million women had been replaced by 23.6 million girls—70 percent replacement.

The population pyramid for 2030 is, of course, to some degree based on assumptions. However, when trends have been regular for long periods, they provide a strong basis for forecasting what lies ahead. Moreover, just as past trends in fertility have shaped our current age structure, so age structure constrains future population growth. This is the phenomenon known as demographic momentum. A population that has been growing, like that of Europe in 1965, tends to keep on growing for some decades, even after fertility falls below the replacement level. This is because Europe in 1965 had a large number of children and young adults. As these young people grew up and reached childbearing age, these large cohorts inevitably produced a relatively large number of babies, even if fertility per woman was very low. In contrast, small cohorts, such as those born in Europe over the last 20–25 years, cannot produce a future baby boom of comparable scale to that of the 1960s simply because there will be far fewer potential mothers in, say, 2030 than there are today. We are thus very unlikely to see a new surge in births, even if fertility per woman rises considerably. In fact, the Council of Europe's projections do assume an increase in fertility per woman over the coming decades, but this is not enough to offset the rapidly shrinking cohort sizes, with the pyramid becoming progressively top-heavy.

While there are certain broad similarities in demographic patterns today across Europe—for example, fertility is below replacement level everywhere—there are also marked differences among countries. To keep matters simple, it helps to consider three groups of countries within which the impact of fertility change has been generally similar. One group is the eight states of eastern and central Europe that joined the EU in May 2004 (Czech Republic, Estonia, Hungary, Latvia, Lithuania, Poland, Slovakia and Slovenia). A second group comprises four countries in southern Europe (Greece, Italy, Portugal and Spain), while the third is made up of seven countries from northern and western Europe (Denmark, Finland, France, Ireland, The Netherlands, Sweden and the United Kingdom). For the sake of simplicity, we refer to these groups as the Eastern-8, Southern-4 and Northern-7. Each of these groups has had a distinctive history of fertility change, principally to do with when and how completely the baby boom ended and was replaced by the baby bust. Fertility in the Northern-7 fell rapidly from 1965 until about 1980 but then roughly stabilized at values not far below replacement level (1.7–1.8). In the Southern-4 fertility fell later (1975–1990) but reached much lower levels and has stabilized at about 1.2–1.3 for the last ten years. Fertility in the Eastern-8 was close to or above replacement level until the collapse of the old Communist system and then fell to very low values. Today it is similar to the levels seen in the Southern-4. It is perhaps still too soon to say how permanent the fertility fall in eastern and central Europe will be, but as it is now a feature that has been present for over a decade, it seems reasonable, on balance, to assume that fertility there will remain similar to that of southern Europe. The other six member states of the EU mostly have fertility histories that lie somewhere between the three groups shown here. These differences in the timing and extent of fertility decline have left their mark in very different age structures.

The three panels of *Figure 1.3* show the current population pyramids for the Northern-7, Southern-4 and Eastern-8. The more radical nature of fertility decline in southern Europe (since the mid-1970s) and in eastern and central Europe (since 1990) has left them with far more constricted bases to their age pyramids than countries such as France or the United Kingdom. In the seven northern countries, the first years of the baby bust in the 1970s saw the number of births fall (the number of those aged 20 to 29 is clearly lower than those aged 30 to 39). However, fertility has roughly stabilized since then, producing a broadly flat-sided base to the pyramid, in marked contrast to the very narrow base in southern and eastern Europe. Comparing the size of the 0–9 age groups with the 30–39 age groups again provides an approximate indication of intergenerational replacement in recent years. In the Northern-7, 11.7 million women aged 30 to 39 have produced 9.5 million daughters now aged 0 to 9 (i.e., 80 percent replacement). In the Southern-4 a slightly smaller number of women aged 30 to 39 (9.5 million) have produced far fewer daughters (5.5 million) or less than 60 percent replacement. In the Eastern-8, 4.7 million women have had 2.7 million daughters (also below 60 percent replacement). A further point is also evident in *Figure 1.3*: to some extent, the very low fertility of southern Europe has been disguised thus far because the baby boom cohorts were moving through the childbearing ages. The largest age groups at present are the 25–39 age groups. In the coming decades, however, the much smaller cohorts born since the mid-1980s will be at reproductive age. Unless these cohorts (currently aged 0 to 19) have substantially higher fertility than their parents, the number of births in countries such as Italy and Spain will shrink even more rapidly in the future than it has to date. In sum, while there are some broad similarities in age-structural changes across Europe, the differing fertility histories of the various regions mean

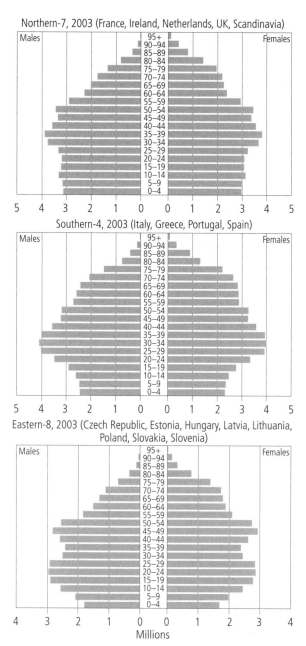

Source: Council of Europe (2005).

Figure 1.3. Age structure, 2003, in three parts of the EU: Northern-7, Southern-4 and Eastern-8.

that the future impact will be much greater in southern Europe than in France, the United Kingdom or Scandinavia.

1.3   Aging, Fertility and Migration

From reading discussions of demographic issues in the media, including many generally serious publications, one could easily gain the impression that the future aging of European society is an impending disaster of almost apocalyptic proportions. Amid the hyperbole it is easy to lose sight of the fact that aging is both inevitable and in certain respects desirable. All populations that have long life expectancy and low long-term rates of population growth will experience aging. The only ways of avoiding aging are to downgrade health care or to have substantial and continuing population growth. Most Europeans prefer long lives to short, in the main want few children and do not wish there to be an endless population increase; thus, demographic aging can be seen as a logical consequence of these preferences. Indeed, it could even be judged as a measure of our achievement in extending life. However, while aging is an inevitable and global phenomenon, Europe will experience a form of 'superaging' in the middle decades of this century; the baby boom cohorts are very large, and their aging will greatly exacerbate the problems that aging usually generates. What should be the response of European societies in view of these changes? The most sensible goal is to attempt to stabilize the base of Europe's population pyramid. If each birth cohort is substantially smaller than the one before, as has been the case for the last 40 years, then it will be very hard in the long run to sustain the economic bases of our present social systems. However, this policy goal is more easily stated than realized.

To some extent, immigrants can fill gaps in the age structure caused by low fertility. A shortfall in births in 1980 can, in principle, be made up for by recruiting migrants aged 25 in 2005. (And most migrants are young adults, generally aged 15 to 35.) A rough approximation of the number of migrants needed for such a balancing act to work can roughly be gauged with reference to the replacement level of 2.1 children per woman. In the EU over the last ten years, fertility has been a little over 1.4, or at only two-thirds replacement level. For the cohorts born from 1995 to 2005 to be as large as the cohorts of their parents, one migrant would need to be recruited for every two births. This is a much higher ratio of migrants to hosts than has ever been observed for a sustained period in any large country, let alone for an entity of 450 million people. In countries such as the Czech Republic, Italy or Spain, where fertility is 1.2 or less, the need for migrants to top up the deficient cohorts would be even greater. Coping with migration on such a scale may be possible, but it would require a radical change in policies and attitudes.

Moreover, the long-term effect of this alternative depends not just on the scale of the immigration but also on how many children the migrants have. The logic of intergenerational replacement applies to migrants just as much as to the native-born. As migrants grow old, unless they replace themselves more effectively than the native-born population, they too do not solve the problems of aging. Only if migrants have higher fertility than their hosts will they help alleviate the consequences of aging. From this point of view, it is clear more or less everywhere that the fertility of migrants tends to converge with that of the host population. The speed of convergence varies among migrant groups and cultural settings, but assimilation occurs sooner or later. In addition, low fertility is becoming a global phenomenon, so that even migrants from high-fertility countries may soon have fertility well below the replacement level. In short, migration cannot be regarded as a one-off solution to the problems caused by aging. In so far as migration can help matters, it can do so only if there is a continuing large stream of immigrants, and large numbers of migrants with a non-European cultural background will cause challenges in terms of integration and future social cohesion in Europe.

1.4 Aging and the Economy

Not surprisingly, changes to the age structure of the magnitude that will be seen in Europe over the coming decades will have large-scale economic effects. It is important to realize, however, that aging per se is not necessarily a problem. The difficulty arises because Europe's social and economic institutions are not set up to cope with it. Particular attention has been focused in recent years on the issue of pensions and other age-related welfare benefits; a consideration of these institutions shows the ways in which society is likely to need to adapt in order to cope with aging. Europe's welfare state regimes were mostly created in their present form in the 25 or so years between the end of World War II and the first oil shock, and the institutions put in place reflect the character of the economy and society at that time. However, taking a long-term view, we can see that this was a most unusual period. The baby boom led to a substantial population increase, and economic growth was at record levels. Between 1948 and 1973, the gross domestic product (GDP) per head in continental western Europe grew by more than 5 percent a year. This was far higher than ever seen before or since for a sustained period, the long-term trend being about 2 percent a year. The pensions and welfare state systems that we have today were based on the assumption that both the population and the economy would continue to grow rapidly. Only now, fully 30 years after this assumption ceased to be true, are governments slowly coming to terms with the changes needed to make Europe's welfare state systems sustainable at a time when neither the population nor the economy is growing rapidly.

While attention to the impact of aging has tended to focus on the costs involved, especially pensions, what matters in a more general sense is the size of the labor force. Pensions and other welfare benefits represent a form of claim on the stream of wealth being created by the people who are at work. Thus, it is the relative size of the working and nonworking populations that is most relevant. All other things being equal, the low fertility of recent decades implies a marked shrinking of the working-age population over the next 25 years. The impact will, of course, be greatest in the countries where fertility has fallen most. Barring some miraculous discovery of a way of returning to rapid productivity gains, there are essentially only two ways in which the impact of this shortfall of workers can be mitigated. First, the proportion of the population actually engaged in paid employment (and thus paying taxes) can increase. Second, more workers can be imported through immigration. Neither of these two policy choices is universally popular. The former option involves persuading more women to work (especially in southern Europe) and delaying retirement for both sexes. Such changes may be just as controversial as advocating large-scale immigration.

1.5   Meeting the Challenges of the Future

A well-known cliché on the theme of population asserts that demography is destiny. This is wrong. To a substantial degree we can still choose our future. However, demography does impose strong constraints on the range of feasible options. Taking these constraints into account is the basis for all sound planning for our shared future.

So how will future generations of Europeans meet the challenges that lie ahead? To gauge this we need to assess the various dimensions of Europe's current demographic and family regime. Each of the chapters that follow takes on one of those dimensions for detailed scrutiny. The chapters are organized into thematic sections. Part I deals with overall demographic trends and their relationship with social and economic constraints. Part II investigates fertility trends in detail. Part III considers family forms and living arrangements. Part IV examines the often-controversial topic of international migration. Part V focuses on health and mortality. To end the book, Part VI considers future challenges for research and policy. The chapters reflect the diversity of scientific approaches embraced by the Observatory. Some chapters are theoretical, others empirical; some are comparative, others case studies. This diversity gives the reader a flavor both of the many dimensions of demographic and social change in Europe today and of the styles of scientific investigation used to understand that change. Each of the substantive parts (II to V) consists of three chapters, the first providing an introduction to the subject and examining trends in the 'old' EU of 15 members, the second dealing with trends in the new member states and the third considering likely future trends. Given the unavoidably uncertain nature of the future, the authors of the third chapter in each section were given more scope for speculation and kept their contributions somewhat briefer than the more detailed discussion of recent and current trends.

This introduction is Chapter 1. In Chapter 2 Constantinos Fotakis and Fritz von Nordheim provide an overview of the social situation in Europe in 2004. As they note, the future will pose many challenges to the future generations of Europeans, and meeting such challenges will require full use to be made of the high human and social capital that all European countries possess. The fertility section begins with Chapter 3 by Juan Antonio Fernández Cordón who considers trends in childbearing and emphasizes that any policy attempting to increase fertility must be embedded in a wider set of social policies. In Chapter 4 Zsolt Spéder examines the relationship between childbearing and attitudes in a number of both 'new' and 'old' member states. As he points out, while many of the post-Communist societies of eastern and central Europe seem to share many attitudes, there are profound differences between, for example, Italy and Finland. The enduring nature of many of these national attitudinal differences may well have important implications for future fertility and family patterns. The issue of what we can sensibly assume about future fertility levels is taken up in detail by Wolfgang Lutz in Chapter 5. Reviewing the main theories of fertility, he points out that there is no consensus as to what can be expected and that a great deal of uncertainty about future fertility trends still exists.

Part III of the book deals with family forms and the various transitions of early adult life. In Chapter 6 Giovanni B. Sgritta relates demographic patterns to differences in the nature of the welfare state regimes in the different parts of Europe. His evidence suggests that the very low fertility of southern Europe is closely linked to the specific character of the social and economic institutions found in those countries. This too suggests that low fertility is likely to be a structural feature of life in countries such as Italy for the foreseeable future. Chapter 7 by Siyka Kovacheva examines the nature of early adult life in a group of member states, both 'new' and 'old', and relates family formation decisions to economic and social changes. The need for family-related policy to be formulated in the wider context of social and economic institutions is clearly shown. The third chapter on family forms is Claire Wallace's consideration of future trends in Chapter 8. She paints two scenarios for Europe's future: flexibility and inclusion on the one hand versus polarization and exclusion on the other. As she notes, both features already exist, and future cooperation and social policies will determine which will dominate Europe's future.

Migration, especially immigration, is possibly the most contentious issue facing Europe and forms the focus for Part IV. Johannes Pflegerl reviews trends in the EU15 over recent decades in Chapter 9. As he concludes, immigration has the potential to play a major role in the development of human capital in Europe, but taking advantage of this potential remains controversial in many countries. In Chapter 10 Dušan Drbohlav looks at migration trends in the new member states, making specific policy recommendations to maximize the potential benefits and minimize the drawbacks of migration. Chapter 11 by Catherine Wihtol de Wenden examines the broad outlines of migration and its relationship to Europe's labor markets and other economic institutions. As she concludes, immigration will play an increasingly important role in shaping the identity of Europe in the coming decades.

Part V of the book focuses on health and mortality. Hans-Joachim Schulze in Chapter 12 provides a model linking the decisions of individuals and families to the wider environment of the health-care system and policy. The family, he notes, plays a crucial role in prevention and care and must be taken into account in all health systems. Chapter 13 by Christoph Sowada focuses on one health system, that of Poland, to provide a detailed case study of how demographic, economic and political forces work to shape the development of a health system and the benefits it provides. The health-related section concludes with Chapter 14 by Robert Anderson, whose discussion of future developments in the health sector provides a valuable EU-wide perspective.

Part VI consists of two chapters, one dealing with possible innovations in research on demographic issues and the second addressing the policy responses to demographic change. In Chapter 15 Jan H. Marbach investigates the links between civic society and the family that could provide important insights for future research. The European model of development, with its joint emphasis on economic growth and social cohesion, depends fundamentally on strong civic institutions. The varying character of social capital around Europe provides important insights into the social resources that individuals and families can draw upon to solve the problems of day-to-day living. Finally, in Chapter 16 as a stimulating epilog to the detailed discussion of the book's other chapters, Landis MacKellar provides a thought-provoking résumé of the issues at hand. He offers three dilemmas that Europe must resolve: i) the status of the young must rise, but the voting power of the old is strong; ii) the Lisbon Process is on a collision course with the European social model; and iii) Europe needs immigrants but does not want them. Framed in these stark terms, it is clear that Europe's future generations face a challenging time. The insights provided by the contributions to this volume give us some idea of how they may meet the challenges ahead and shape Europe's future.

References

Council of Europe (2005) *Recent Demographic Developments in Europe 2004*, Strasbourg, France: Council of Europe Publishing, January.

Eurobarometer 46.0 (1996) *Personal Health, Energy, Development, and the Common European Currency*, Zentralarchiv für empirische Sozialforschung, Cologne, Germany, October–November.

Rifkin, J. (2004) *The European Dream*, New York, USA: Penguin Books.

Chapter 2

The Social Situation in the European Union, 2004

Constantinos Fotakis and Fritz von Nordheim

2.1 Introduction

Each year the European Commission's Directorate General for Employment and Social Affairs issues a publication that describes the social situation in the European Union (EU) and, among other things, provides a prospective view of population trends across the European Union that indicates challenges and opportunities for economic and social welfare. On 1 May 2004 a very significant enlargement of the EU took place; this chapter focuses on the impact on EU social conditions of the expansion of the European Union's borders to include ten new member states: the diversification of social conditions, the increased number of policy challenges and, to help member states address these challenges, the greater opportunities for economic growth within an enlarged EU.

2.2 The Demographic Portrait

Following EU enlargement, nearly three-quarters of the population lived in six of the 25 member states, namely, France, Germany, Italy, Poland, Spain and the United Kingdom, while the remaining one-quarter were distributed among 19 member states with small to very small populations (*Figure 2.1*).

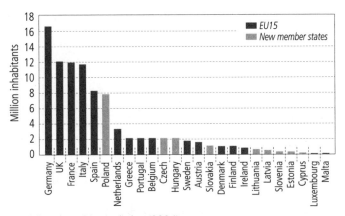

Source: Eurostat demographic statistics (2004).

Figure 2.1. Total population of EU25 member states at 1 January 2002.

Enlargement has not changed the EU's aging process. Though the populations of the new member states (NMS) are presently somewhat younger and longevity is lower, fertility levels will quickly bring them close to the EU15.

It is the swing in fertility levels from baby boom to baby bust that has been the main driver of sudden demographic change. For the last decade the average fertility rate in the EU25 has remained below 1.5, which is almost 30 percent under the replacement ratio. Migration inflows have become the main driver of population growth in the EU, as even the new member states progressively shift from being sending to receiving countries.

Rapid population aging is certain to be a dominant trend in EU25 demographic developments in the coming decade (2010–2020), and aging is set to continue and intensify over the subsequent two decades (*Figure 2.2*).

The trend foreseen after 2010 toward a contracting active population and an expanding retirement population will intensify the need to reform economic and social policies. The prospect of a shrinking working-age population implies that future economic growth will increasingly depend on productivity gains made through human capital development and increases in physical capital. Europe's ability to improve the quality of its human capital will steadily become a more critical parameter for growth in gross domestic product (GDP) (*Figure 2.3*).

The next five years represent the last part of the demographic window of opportunity before a rapid process of aging begins. To prepare for aging, efforts must be intensified to increase employment and raise the age of exit from the labor market.

At the 2001 Lisbon Summit, European leaders committed themselves to an agenda of economic reform aimed at 'making Europe the most competitive knowledge economy in the world by 2020.' The changes this entails are often referred

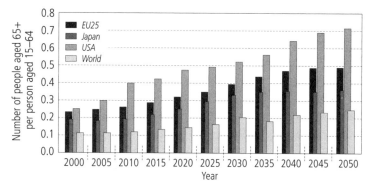

Source: For EU15 Eurostat (2000) demographic projections (baseline scenario). For all others, United Nations World Population Prospects (2002 revision) (medium variation).

Figure 2.2. Old age dependency ratio (number of people aged 65+ per person aged 15–64) forecast to 2050.

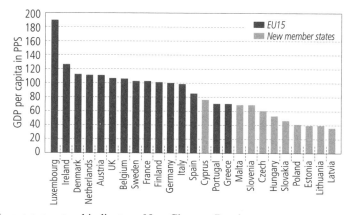

Source: Eurostat structural indicators, New Chronos Database.

Figure 2.3. GDP per capita in purchasing power standards (PPS), 2002 (EU15 = 100).

to simply as the Lisbon Agenda. Meeting the Lisbon policy objectives related to employment growth and the modernization of social protection, as well as promoting the economic and social integration of immigrants, will be crucial to the EU's ability to handle the challenges. The social and economic implications of the aging of the European population, while serious, may become manageable if the right policy measures are taken in time.

2.3   Living Conditions

Although the EU population rose by 20 percent on 1 May 2004, its GDP increased by only 4.5 percent; national and regional income disparities thus widened, accentuating the need to promote social cohesion in the EU. Socioeconomic differences between the EU15 countries and most of the new member states are particularly pronounced. Moreover, during the 1995–2002 period, income gaps, while narrowing significantly among countries and regions in the EU15, widened among the new member states.

While significant progress toward social cohesion was observed in the EU15 over the last decade, enlargement will set new challenges in that area. Income in 82 regions of the enlarged EU, accounting for 31 percent of the total population, will be below 75 percent of the EU25 average. Two-thirds of people on below-average incomes live in the new member states and represent some 95 percent of their population. Only Cyprus, Malta, and metropolitan areas of the Czech Republic, Hungary and Slovakia show levels of GDP per capita (in purchasing power standards [PPS]) comparable to EU15 standards.

Relative levels of poverty in the new member states tend to be moderate in comparison with those of the EU15, although they have increased over the last decade. The lower living standards observed in most of the new member states are mainly a question of insufficient income in absolute terms (*Figure 2.4*). People's opinions on the quality of life vary greatly between EU15 countries and the new member states, which further reinforces this view: 88 percent of citizens in the EU15 are satisfied with their quality of life compared to 65 percent of citizens in the new member states. Using an absolute poverty level defined as an income of less than two US dollars per day, it can be seen that in five of the eight new member states of central and eastern Europe (CEE), more than 2 percent of the population are living in absolute poverty.

Consumption patterns across the enlarged EU reflect not only income differences but also the availability of goods and services. During the 1990s there was a general trend in the EU15 countries toward an increased proportion of the household budget being spent on housing and a corresponding drop in the proportion attributed to food. This is not the case in the new CEE member states, where food remains the largest expenditure category, largely because of lower income levels. In terms of digital technology, a larger percentage of the population possess a mobile phone for personal use in the EU15 countries (70 percent) than in the new member states (44 percent), with similar trends also observable for Internet usage. In addition to reflecting income and relative cost differences, the digital technology figures also reflect differences in infrastructure across the enlarged EU, implying that reducing the gaps in access to new technologies would require both improvements in household income and investments in infrastructure.

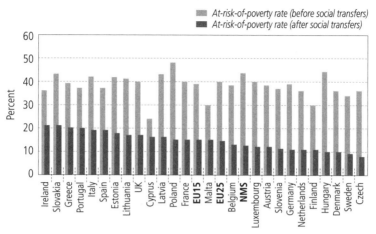

Source: Eurostat New Chronos Database.

Figure 2.4. Population of the EU25 member states (2001) at risk of poverty: Rates before and after social transfers.

2.4 Social Protection Reforms

Comparisons of social protection provisions and social and civil dialog in the new member states and the EU15 document a range of differences but also reveal many similarities. Many of the problems observed in the new member states in central and eastern Europe stem from the pre-1990 and transition periods. Across the board, the ability to achieve changes and deliver on reforms has often been constrained by inadequate administrative and social governance capacities. There is still a substantial gap in some of the new member states in terms of civil society support structures and social partnership. These difficulties cannot be defeated overnight, but the progress made in adopting the voluminous legal framework required for EU membership, the *acquis communautaire (acquis)*, indicates that, with time, they will be accommodated within the range of variations in EU15 countries.

Reforms in the organization of pensions and health care have opened the way for improvements. The new member states share the same interest as EU15 member states in securing the EU pension objectives of adequate benefits, higher employment, later retirement and the effective regulation and sound management of pension funds. In the area of health care, despite progress made, improvements are still seriously impeded by the low relative level of health-care spending (roughly 25 percent of EU15 levels measured in PPS).

2.4.1   Social and civil dialog

While, from an institutional perspective, social dialog is better consolidated at EU level than ever before, it has become more precarious as an empirical reality in the workplace after enlargement. Industrial relations and social dialog are areas where enlargement presents a particular challenge. The new member states are still in the process of establishing a fully fledged system of industrial relations. Social dialog is much less developed than in the EU15 countries, and the social partners currently find it difficult to fill the economic and social governance role that the European social model assigns to them. Yet, amid all differences in size and character, there are also important similarities between these new member states and the EU15, particularly when one considers the large variations within the latter. Such similarities can, for example, be found in trade union density and direct collective agreement coverage. The EU will have to support the new member states of the CEE in their effort to develop lively and efficiently functioning industrial relations built on social dialog.

Core civil society capacities influence the overall economic, social and political performance of a country. Studies from the early 1990s find the extent of civic-mindedness of members of a society, the prevalence of social norms promoting collective action and the degree of trust in public institutions to be less developed in transition economies and, furthermore, confirm that there are correlations between these phenomena and economic growth.

Recent studies document that the gaps among current member states in social participation have narrowed (*Figure 2.5*). Yet civil dialog as part of social policy governance also depends on the extent to which general participation transforms itself into relevant nongovernmental organizations (NGOs) and on the capacities of government. From that perspective there is little doubt that civil society forces and the potential for civil dialog in most of the new member states need to be further developed.

2.4.2   Diversity and the fight against discrimination

With EU enlargement, ethnic diversity will increase as a result of higher internal migration and because of the minorities in the new member states (e.g., the Roma and Russian minorities). EU15 member states have identified the danger that discrimination may hamper socioeconomic integration and inclusion of ethnic minorities (i.e., that it will lower social cohesion and economic growth). In the new member states, where the traditional resources for addressing discrimination issues have been substantially weaker, there is a growing public awareness of the need to act which, in combination with the new policies established through the adoption of the *acquis*, can become a driver for improvements.

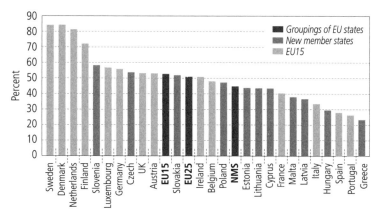

Source: Ten NMS: Eurobarometer (May 2002); EU15 countries: Eurobarometer (1998).

Figure 2.5. Civic participation in the EU25 (percentage of people who participate in at least one organized activity, e.g., charity, religious activity, cultural activity, trade union, sport, environmental).

Disability policies in the new member states are often oriented toward segregation rather than mainstream action across all policy areas. Moreover, although quota systems are prevalent, there appear to be major problems with their practical enforcement. Disability policies in these countries are only now beginning to move away from the old-style 'protectionist' policies based on medical models of disability and marked by the prevalence of institutionalization and sheltered employment.

2.5   Conclusion

The scale of challenges arising from the EU enlargement in 2004 is particularly large. But the experience from former accessions of countries with a GDP markedly below the EU average (e.g., Greece, Ireland, Portugal and Spain) confirms that major improvements in the social situation can be achieved through concerted and sustained efforts at national and EU level.

In these efforts, there are a number of achievements and relative advantages that the new member states can build on:

• The underlying human capital potential in the new member states is encouraging, as the states can build on good overall levels of educational attainment.

- That several new member states have been able to introduce advanced pension and health reforms in the midst of economic and political turmoil also demonstrates an ability to tackle difficult reforms that can be applied in the further process of change.
- Moderate levels of relative poverty in most new member states indicate that there is a fair degree of national social cohesion and that social protection schemes are having a sizable impact; these can be an important asset for successfully tackling the challenges of economic modernization and globalization.

On the basis of these opportunities and the considerable progress in the *acquis*, the ten new member states—with the support of EU policies—could become an important driver of economic growth and social improvement in the enlarged European Union.

Finally, in terms of the implications of this review of social and economic trends for demography, there are, first and foremost, still considerable differences, especially in living standards but also in many other aspects of socioeconomic organization, between the 15 'old' members of the EU and the ten newcomers. Moreover, the eight formerly Communist states of central and eastern Europe share a specific social and economic inheritance from the days of a rigidly planned economy. While convergence is likely to reduce east–west differences in the long term, the new member states are at present sufficiently similar to each other, and sufficiently different from the EU15, to justify the two groups being studied as separate entities.

Part II
Fertility Trends in an Enlarged European Union

Chapter 3

Low Fertility and the Scope for Social Policy: Understanding the Context

Juan Antonio Fernández Cordón

What will happen to a Europe that can no longer assure the renewal of generations? What will happen to an ageing Europe?

How can we explain the decline in fertility and the persistently low fertility rates? What do the fertility differentials between Member States actually mean?

How, and under what circumstances, can public policy impact on fertility, when it is too low? (Bagavos and Martin, 2001, p. 3)

3.1 Introduction

Fertility in Europe has long been viewed as an issue that falls exclusively within the private domain. In recent years, however, the continuing low birth rate has prompted some scholars and policy makers to consider if social policy can have a legitimate role in influencing personal decisions regarding fertility. The synthesis report of the annual seminar of the European Observatory on the Social Situation, Demography and the Family, 'Low Fertility, Families and Public Policies,' held in Seville in September 2000, summarizes some of the fundamental questions about the future of fertility in Europe. In addressing these topics the papers presented were far from alarmist, thus in my opinion contributing to a better understanding of the reasons for low fertility and making useful revisions to the tools available to governments seeking to influence fertility. Indeed, conclusions were broad and rather optimistic in the sense that they recommended mainstreaming fertility-related policies into the entire range of social policies.

Much of what is known in detail about the determinants of fertility in Europe comes from a series of surveys carried out in the 1980s and early 1990s: the Fertility and Family Surveys (FFS), promoted and coordinated by, inter alia, the Geneva-based Population Activities Unit of the United Nations Economic Commission for Europe (UN/ECE). This project, which aimed to shed light on fertility matters, was one of the most ambitious ever conceived. Only a few months before the European Observatory annual seminar in Seville, the FFS Flagship Conference, 'Partnership and Fertility—A Revolution?,' held in Brussels, considered the results of this comparative research project. Professor David Coleman, in his closing address, expressed a rather pessimistic view of the progress made to date by including among today's remaining challenges in demography the need 'to explain the variation of fertility in developed countries over time and space, especially the very low fertility which has persisted now for years in some countries.' In a similar vein, Dirk van de Kaa asked in his opening address if low fertility is 'post-modern and beyond the action of Governments' (cited in Macura and Beets, 2002, pp. 13–16).

At the beginning of 2004 the European Population Forum, held in Geneva, had a session entitled 'Childbearing and Parenting in Low Fertility Countries: Enabling Choices,' in which there were lengthy discussions about the political status of the low fertility issue (is it really a problem in a world of job scarcity and concern about reproductive health and access to proper contraceptive means?) and about the need to protect individual rights, especially those of women. From among the Forum's conclusions, I will reproduce only one: 'Low fertility is clearly a major policy concern for the region and an increasing number of governments are addressing the issue but no conclusion was reached on how to resolve it' (European Population Forum, 2004, p. 33).

It seems, putting all this together, that there is a general recognition of the problem but no obvious answer. An examination of the extensive bibliography on the matter shows that the scientific community is not at present in a position to offer clear-cut options for specific policy measures (see, however, McDonald [2000]). What we do know is that in most European Union (EU) countries low fertility is a long-standing situation that will have unpleasant consequences for the sustainability of the social protection system and that its causes are far from clearly understood, which raises fundamental doubts simply about the opportunities for addressing it—doubts that result in the lack of a clear policy response.

We must at least assume that low fertility is a definite problem for the Europe of today, and I would argue that it should be considered as a major issue for social policy. To ascertain why the level of fertility is so important for our future, I will first focus on the main changes that have occurred over the last few decades and on some future prospects. The recent course of fertility will have definite consequences for the volume and structure of the population to come; I will use population projections based on a moderate fertility recovery to show what impact should be expected on the growth rate and age structure of the future European (EU15) population and thus on the social protection system and the labor market. Some problems also have to be faced as a result of recent changes in the formation and dissolution of families and conditions of childbearing that are closely associated with the new fertility pattern. Most of the explanations for low fertility are related to general changes in society that involve the family, but do we know enough about the causes of the fertility decline to derive some efficient policy measures? This will lead us back to the initial question of why concern over low fertility should be embedded in present European countries' social policies.

3.2   Facts and Prospects

3.2.1   The path to low and very low fertility

In the early 1930s almost all western and central European countries were reproducing at below-replacement level:[1] *'never before* in history have there been such *enormous changes* in fertility behavior *in so many societies* as took place in the 20th century'[2] (Frejka and Ross, 2001, p. 247). More than one-half of the world's population now lives in countries with a below-replacement fertility level. Low fertility, however, does not appear to be a problem specific to the European Union or developed countries; nor should it be seized upon as a temporary phenomenon that could reverse itself at some time in the future.

Following World War II the secular fertility decline was interrupted in most western countries by a period of increasing fertility known as the 'baby boom.' In the EU15 high fertility rates were maintained until the mid-1960s but have since fallen everywhere, although with important country differences in terms of the extent and tempo of the decline. In the 15 countries of the EU15 taken as a whole, the average number of children per woman aged 15 to 49 (total fertility rate [TFR]) fell from a maximum of 2.72 in 1965 to a minimum of 1.42 in 1995, a decline of 46 percent in 30 years; after a small recovery, it reached 1.5 in 2002 (Eurostat, 2004a). In 2002 not a single country in the EU15 reached 2 children per woman. Only Ireland (1.97) and France (1.89) came close to the mythical figure. Other countries were very far from it, especially Spain (1.25), Italy (1.26) and Greece (1.25). Changes during this period have completely transformed the relative positions of

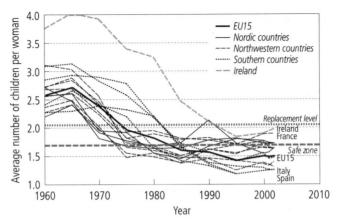

Source: Eurostat (2004a).

Figure 3.1. Total fertility rate in countries of the EU15, 1960–2002.

European countries. Nordic countries have registered a modest fertility decline, as have France and the United Kingdom. All these countries had close to average fertility at the beginning of the period of decline. The southern countries, which scored the highest fertility rates around 1965 (with the exception of Greece), and also Austria and Germany, have reached, after a very sharp decline, the lowest levels in the EU15 (*Figure 3.1*). Northern, central and western countries of the EU15 have never experienced levels of fertility as low as they are now in the southern countries.

There is some evidence that a new era has begun. Although fertility remains at very low levels in some countries, it is no longer declining in the EU15, having apparently been stabilized at about 1.4 to 1.5 since 1995. There may even be some signs of a modest recovery of the TFR, but to date the increase is very small compared with the huge fall since the mid-1960s (Eurostat, 2004b).

The demographic consequences of sustained very low fertility are clearly enormous. McDonald (2002) points out that at the Total Fertility Rates currently prevailing in the very low fertility countries of the EU15, a stable population[3] decreases at the rate of 1.5 percent per annum, which means that after 100 years it will fall to less than 25 percent of its original size. In contrast, with a TFR of 1.9 (the current level in France), the annual rate of decline is only 0.2 percent, and after 100 years the population will maintain 82 percent of its size. It is clear that small changes in fertility have major effects on the size of the future population and that all subreplacement situations should not, therefore, be considered as equivalent. The potential impact of the fertility level is very high but can be fully perceived only in the long term. In the short and medium term, the consequences of the present age structure and of decreasing mortality will be crucial, especially for population aging.

On the other hand, the possible counteracting effects of increasing immigration, increasing labor force participation rates and increasing productivity could prevent some of the population aging effects and labor shortages, but only if fertility remains in the upper part of the below-replacement level (McDonald and Kippen, 2001). According to this view, countries of the EU15 could be divided into a group of moderately low fertility (those with a TFR above 1.7) and a group of very low fertility (those with a TFR below 1.5). According to recent trends, countries in the 1.5–1.7 range may be considered as being in transition from one group to the other. McDonald and Kippen (2001) consider the TFR 1.7–2.0 range as a safe zone in the sense that both population decline and population aging are manageable within it; they further believe that very low fertility countries (below a TFR of 1.5) constitute a major problem. The idea of a safe zone is interesting because it stresses the limits of policies aimed at offsetting the consequences of low fertility rather than acting on the fertility level—what we may call adaptive policies. In that sense, a better overview could be obtained by associating the TFR level with an indicator of a country's capacity for implementing adaptive policies. I will return to this issue later.

Considered as a whole, the EU15 region is well below the safe zone, but as policies related to the level of fertility are implemented at national level, what probably matters more are the wide differences among the countries. As shown in *Figure 3.1*, only France and Ireland are clearly within the safe zone. Countries like Denmark, Finland, The Netherlands and the United Kingdom, however, are on the edge of the 1.7 limit. The group of very low fertility countries includes all the southern countries (Portugal being in the upper limit) plus Austria and Germany. This group, already a large one, also contains a majority of the countries of the new EU25.

3.2.2   Delayed childbearing and cohort fertility

Almost since the beginning of demographic analysis, there has been an ongoing debate about the relative status of period fertility measures (TFR being the most commonly used) and cohort fertility measures (total cohort fertility rate [TCFR] is the equivalent of TFR for cohorts). Recently, the debate has become more intense and has even, at times, reached the fields of politics and policy making. There is no doubt that the cohort point of view widens our knowledge of the course of fertility, and important methodological innovations have recently been introduced in this area to help correctly appraise changes in the current fertility measures. The most important question, for its practical outcomes, is to ascertain what part of recent fertility decline results from changes in the timing of births (tempo effects). If tempo effects have indeed had a significant impact on recent period fertility decline, an increase in the total fertility rate is to be expected in the future, as this indicator underestimates the 'true' cohort fertility[4] when births are delayed.

During the first part of the secular fertility decline, mainly characterized by the reduction in large families, the mean age of mothers at the birth of their children declined in all the central and western countries until 1975 and in the southern countries until 1980. Since then, the mean age at childbirth (MAC) has been increasing in all EU15 countries. This increase summarizes important shifts in the age structure of fertility, in particular, the fall in fertility in women below 30 because of delayed first and second births (especially important in the southern countries) and a certain increase in fertility in women over 30. By 2002 the MAC had reached 29.4 years in the EU15 as a whole but was over 30 in Italy and Spain.

For the youngest cohorts that have not yet ended their reproductive life, the possibility of a future recovery in postponed births still exists. Past experience of older cohorts, however, shows that a full recuperation has never happened. In all EU15 countries the completed fertility of the 1930 cohort exceeded the replacement level (except for a slight difference in Luxembourg). In contrast, the 1963 cohort attained replacement level only in Ireland (2.27), barely attained it in France (2.06) and was well below replacement in Italy and Germany (1.58) and Austria and Spain (1.66) (Eurostat, 2004a) (*Figure 3.2*). Although the recent fertility decline will translate into lower cohort fertility, the postponement of births in the young generations could significantly explain the present very low fertility levels. The estimates of cohort completed fertility show a rather moderate decline in the more recent cohorts that have completed their fertility, when compared with the recent sharp decline in annual fertility rates. The gap between moderately low fertility countries (those above 1.7) and very low fertility countries (below 1.5) appears mostly in the younger cohorts (here, only up to those born in 1963). In the central and western countries, completed fertility declined at a very low pace in cohorts born after 1950, with even a small upsurge in some countries. In Germany and Italy the decline continued at a good pace, the latest cohorts with completed fertility having reached between 1.5 and 1.6. As births are still being delayed, it seems probable that younger cohorts who are still of reproductive age will not reach the lowest levels of the fertility experienced in more recent years. The recent fertility increase experienced in all countries of the EU15 (since 1998) should be considered, in part, as an effect of births previously delayed. What distinguishes some very low fertility countries like Italy or Spain is the persistently low fertility of young cohorts.

Union formation and dissolution have also undergone important changes in the last three decades, with a decrease in the number of marriages, increasing divorce rates and the emergence of new forms of unions (Billari, 2004). Since 1970 the annual number of marriages in the EU15 has dropped by 600,000 (a 25 percent de-

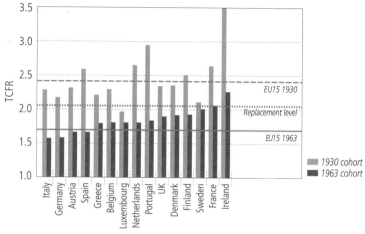

Source: Eurostat (2004a).

Figure 3.2. Cohort fertility, 1930 and 1963 cohorts, countries of the EU15 (ordered by TCFR in 1963 cohort).

cline). The gross marriage rate[5] has declined from 7.9 per thousand to 4.9 per thousand (Eurostat, 2004a). At the same time, the mean age at first marriage of women went up from 23.2 years in 1970 to 27.7 in 2002 (Eurostat, 2004a)—evidence that the reduction in the number of marriages was more intense among the younger generations.

In 1970 the total marriage rate,[6] a more elaborate period measure formally similar to the total fertility rate, was close to 1 in almost all EU15 member countries, indicating a high frequency and increasing precociousness of marriages. The decline of marriage among youth first affected Scandinavia and then extended to other countries. The total marriage rate fell to 0.57 in 1995—a 40 percent decline and the strongest-ever fall in peace time (Cliquet, 1991). The total marriage rate stabilized during the decade 1985–1995 (1980 in Denmark) at levels between 0.55 in France and 0.77 in Portugal and has increased in some countries (not the southern countries) since 1995. In the EU15 region, the mean age at first marriage has increased by 1.2 years, while the total marriage rate has remained at an almost constant level, providing evidence that the increasing marriage rate of women over 30 is to some extent compensating for the still-declining marriage rates of the younger age group.

The effects of marriage timing represent a complex phenomenon associated with the evolution of consensual unions from mostly premarital to increasingly lasting unions. In 2002 the mean age at first marriage was almost identical in France and Spain (28 years), with Italy (27.4 years) close behind. As consensual unions are far more frequent in France, however, it is difficult to establish a sound relationship between the fall in marriage rates and the decline in fertility. At the heart of the problem lie the recent changes in the proportion of births outside marriage.

One of the most striking facts about recent fertility trends is the considerable increase in the proportion of births outside marriage. This type of birth represented 5.6 percent of total live births in the EU15 in 1960, 6.8 percent in 1975 and 30.2 percent in 2002 (Eurostat, 2004a). In spite of a general tendency toward increasing proportions in all countries, there are still large differences among countries. In Sweden the majority of births are now outside marriage (56 percent in 2002). In other countries like Denmark (44.6 percent in 2002), France (43.7 percent in 2001) and the United Kingdom (40.6 percent in 2002) such births have reached very high proportions. At the other end of the scale, only in Italy (9.7 percent in 2000) and Greece (4.3 percent in 2001) do births outside marriage remain at low levels. Greece seems to be an unusual case in the EU15, especially as it is also one of the two or three countries of lowest fertility. In Spain births outside marriage increased very slowly until 1995 (11.7 percent), but the proportion of these almost doubled in eight years (22 percent in 2002), according to the Spanish national statistical institute (*Instituto Nacional de Estadística* [INE]).

When comparing period fertility in the EU15 countries, we can see that most of the differences are accounted for by differences in the proportion of births outside marriage. The fraction of the TFR based on marital births[7] shows a higher convergence among countries. In 2002, countries like Austria, Denmark, Finland, France, Germany, Portugal, Spain and the United Kingdom were in a narrow range of 0.9 to 1.1 (*Figure 3.3*). In contrast, differences in the fraction of the TFR based on births outside marriage have clearly widened, especially since the mid-1980s (*Figure 3.4*). In France and the United Kingdom, for instance, births outside marriage remained at a more or less constant proportion until 1980–1985 and then increased rapidly. This shift is associated with an important change in the nature of consensual unions, which are increasingly considered as a normal situation for the childbearing-age population and credited with prospects for stability that are similar to those of marriage. This process has not yet been completed either in countries of low fertility, such as those of the south, or in Austria and Germany.

It has been usual to explain the low proportion of births outside marriage in the southern countries by cultural specifics, in particular, the still-strong influence of the Catholic Church. One argument against this view is the complete homogeneity found in opinions and attitudes concerning new family forms and behaviors when comparing the southern countries to the rest of the EU15 countries. Moreover, recent developments in Ireland and Spain reinforce reasonable doubts about the relevance of cultural factors. Ireland, a leading Catholic country, has seen the proportion of births outside marriage rise from 1.6 percent, the lowest level in the EU15 in 1960, to 31 percent in 2002 (Eurostat, 2004a), showing the speed with

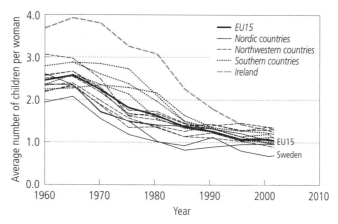

Source: Eurostat (2004a).

Figure 3.3. Total marital fertility rate (births within marriage) in EU15 countries, 1960–2001.

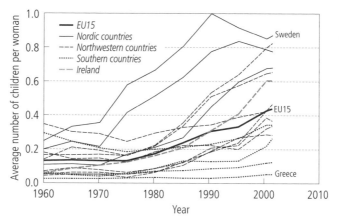

Source: Eurostat (2004a).

Figure 3.4. Total nonmarital fertility rate (births outside marriage) in EU15 countries, 1960–2001.

which a convergence process can take place if adequate material conditions are met, even if institutional changes are slower. The case of Spain, with over one-fifth of births outside marriage, also shows that traditions and religious norms are no longer dominant among youth.

Briefly stated, the decline in fertility in the EU15 countries can partly be seen as the continuation of a secular trend, temporarily interrupted by the baby boom. The theory of the first demographic transition included the idea of a stable final state of equilibrium, with replacement-level fertility corresponding to very low mortality rates. This has obviously not happened in modern societies, and there is no indication in recent trends as to how low fertility can go.

Golini (1998) has tried to infer an absolute minimum based on both theoretical and empirical considerations, arriving at a TFR of about 0.75; but even if proved right, his hypothesis is not very helpful, as differences between countries are persistent and there is no indication at all of a general convergence to very low levels. Livi Bacci (2001) prefers to consider a range of possible variations for the future— between 1.4 and 2.1 for cohort completed fertility—which he claims is consistent with the long-range fluctuations experienced in the past. But his multifaceted arguments have not convinced everyone, and because the range is so broad, the problem of very low fertility is not emphasized. The question as to how low fertility can go would, in fact, seem to be a dead end. We have no grounds for estimating a minimum fertility level, and even if we had, it would be of little use in policy making.

Recent fertility trends in western developed countries, especially those of the EU15, do, however, show evidence of some common features, like delayed childbearing and an increase in the proportion of births outside marriage, as well as the persistently striking differences among countries of low fertility, a number of which are in the 1.2–1.4 range.

In its 2003 population projections,[8] Eurostat (New Chronos Database) developed three different scenarios for future fertility. The stable TFR value projected in 2050 is 1.42 in the low scenario, 1.67 in the base scenario and 1.94 in the high scenario. On a long-term basis, a stable TFR is equivalent to the cohort completed fertility. Thus, according to Eurostat, the EU15 will never reach replacement level, although in the high scenario, fertility will be in the safe zone above 1.7. In the base scenario, which must have been considered the most probable one at the time the projections were prepared, the TFR in 2050 almost equals the level of completed fertility in the most recent cohort of 1963. The low scenario falls into the range of very low fertility situations. All in all, Eurostat's view on future fertility is rather a pessimistic one. This impression is confirmed when the projection for each member country is considered (*Figure 3.5*).

Only in the high scenario does the final value (in 2050) of projected TFR exceed present cohort fertility levels (except in Ireland, for which a decrease is expected in any case). According to this projection, the present relative position of member countries will remain basically unchanged for the next 50 years—a very unreliable statement. Demographic projections are still a very coarse prediction exercise, and few of the recent methodological innovations relating to tempo and quantum effects and few of the country specifics seem to have been included in the fertility scenarios.

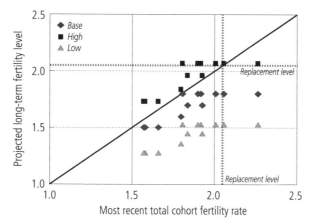

Source: Eurostat, New Chronos Database; Eurostat (2004a).

Figure 3.5. Eurostat projection scenarios: A view of future fertility.

Before turning to the causes for low and very low fertility as a basis for action, I will briefly analyse the impact of recent trends and the projected fertility level on the EU15 population and their consequences for some key social and political issues. The data for the future will be based on the high Eurostat projection scenario for two reasons. First, the high scenario hypotheses for fertility and immigration are closer to recent demographic trends than the other two. Second, it will serve to show more convincingly that, even in the event of a more favorable future, some problems related to population aging remain ahead of us.

3.2.3 Why does a low fertility level matter?

The level of fertility should be considered as an important component of the future of European societies. The European social model relies heavily on intergenerational solidarity, which means, in practice, that the adult population takes care of children and youth by raising them in the family, paying for their personal expenses and contributing with taxes to public expenditure dedicated to children and young people (for example, education and health). When today's young people reach working age, they will be expected to repay their debt by taking care of the older nonworking population. While grown-up children may still be expected in our societies to care for their own dependent parents, this no longer includes economic and health support, as retired people receive their pensions based on contributions made by the employed population and health expenses are funded by the general taxation system. All other conditions remaining equal, any changes in the relative importance of the receiving and contributing groups will affect the functioning of the system. This will happen, in particular, if the adult population ceases to generate a sufficiently young population.

In fact, the continuity of the system is based on two conditions that were fulfilled when it was initially implemented but have changed considerably in recent times: an increasing population (or, at least, a nondecreasing population) and the predominance of families with sufficient caring capacity. In a nondecreasing population ratios between significant age groups are maintained over time and social benefits can easily follow the progress of employment and productivity. When the population increases (i.e., when the generation of the children outnumbers the generation of the parents), the system allows for a rare combination of sufficient benefits and reduced contributions, making everybody happy and unconcerned for the future. That was precisely the situation in many European countries during the 1960s.

The second condition, although it is closely related to population changes and its importance is becoming increasingly clear these days, is mentioned less frequently. The new forms of families that are emerging are experiencing more difficulties not only in caring for elderly dependent relatives without increased help from the social protection system but also in having and raising children without some sort of support. This is not a temporary change but based—like the search for gender equality and the spread of education—in the deep-rooted social and economic changes that have opened the way for women to enter the labor market.

Population changes are determined by three components: mortality, fertility and migration. I deal mostly with fertility in this chapter, but a word is needed about mortality. The continued increase in life expectancy in the countries of the EU15 has determined, and will continue to determine, important variations in the age structure of the population. Future progress in life expectancy[9] will mostly benefit the elderly, as has been the case in recent years, thus increasing the size of the elderly population and intensifying population aging. From the individual point of view, it will mean more years lived in retirement and as a dependent. The consequences are different depending on the type of protection system in operation. In a pay-as-you-go system, the load on the contributing population will increase unless a reduction in expected benefits is imposed on retired people. Slowing the increase in life expectancy would be a way of reducing population aging, but fortunately such a policy will not even be considered. On the contrary, a good part of public policies and investments aim to increase the duration of life in good health and economic conditions.

The case of migration deserves special consideration, as it has become a de facto substitute for fertility. Demographers in general share the belief that, in the future, increasing immigration will not replace increasing fertility to prevent

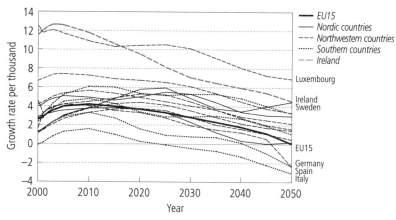

Source: Eurostat, New Chronos Database.

Figure 3.6. Population annual growth rate in EU15 countries. Projection 2000–2050: high scenario.

long-term population decline and aging, although its contribution in the short and medium terms could be considerable.

European (EU15) population has been, and will continue to be, characterized in the future by three main features: decreasing growth, increasing immigration and demographic aging.

3.2.4 Decreasing population growth

During the last four decades the EU15 population has been growing at a decreasing pace (from 8.6 per thousand in 1960–1964 to 2.9 per thousand in 1985–1989), but the tempo changed in the nineties, stabilizing the rate at around 4 per thousand (Eurostat, 2004a). According to recent demographic projections, the EU15 will remain close to zero population growth during the next 25 years. Of course, these are only projections that could prove wrong depending on changes in future immigration flows and the level of fertility.

In Eurostat's high scenario, EU15 population growth will continue at a decreasing rate that will turn negative by 2045 (*Figure 3.6*). In this scenario the countries with the lowest growth rates will be Italy (with a negative growth rate from 2023), Spain (negative from 2040) and Germany (negative from 2045).

3.2.5 Increasing immigration

Current population growth in the EU15 is mostly due to immigration. Natural growth (difference between births and deaths) decreased in all the member countries from 7.9 per thousand in 1960–1964 to 0.8 per thousand in 1995–1999 (ten times less). Germany, Italy and Sweden then experienced negative growth rates. Since 1995, however, because of the moderate fertility recovery, the decreasing trend has stopped. Nevertheless, Germany and Italy, and now Greece, show negative natural growth rates.

In contrast, immigration net flow has continuously increased, from 0.6 per thousand in 1960–1964 to 2.8 in 1990–1995 and 3.3 in 2001 for the EU15 (Eurostat, 2004a). More than 80 percent of total population growth in the EU15 is due to immigration. This proportion is higher in the southern countries, which combine lower fertility and higher immigration flows. Germany and Italy are both countries where immigration offsets the negative natural increase and allows for a modest population growth.

3.2.6 Increasing population aging

Persistently low fertility increases the imbalance between the young and the older generations, with the latter additionally benefiting from mortality reduction. Low fertility is not the only factor of population aging; mortality could become the dominant factor in some developed countries, but fertility is the only factor that may eventually be reversed. On the other hand, when country differences are being evaluated, the role of increased life expectancy in the aging process is less important than the fertility level because there are no extreme differences in mortality inside the EU15. Population aging also depends on the population momentum (i.e., its capacity to grow because of previously high fertility resulting in the presence of relatively large young cohorts). Southern countries have benefited from this in recent times, but its importance is reducing and it will eventually reverse.

Population aging is already a fact in all EU15 countries. The proportion of the young population has been declining for more than three decades in all countries. In the EU15 the proportion aged 0 to 19 years has decreased from 32 percent in 1960 to 22.4 percent in 2003. At the same time, the elderly group (60 and over) has increased from 15.5 percent in 1960 to 22.2 percent in 2003. During this period the working-age population (20 to 59 years) slightly increased its weight in the total population (from 52.7 to 55.4 percent) as a result of previous high fertility rates (Eurostat, 2004a).

There are considerable variations in population aging among the EU15 countries because of their differing recent demographic history. Not surprisingly, the proportion of young population is lower in the southern countries and in Germany, where fertility has remained at very low levels—in some cases for the last 20 years. The highest proportions of young population are found in Ireland, the last country to enter the fertility decline, in France, with stable moderately low fertility (always above the safe zone) and in the United Kingdom, also with above-average fertility

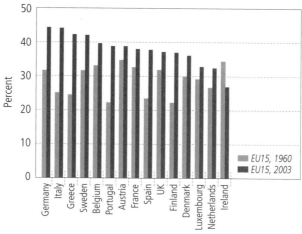

Source: Eurostat (2004b).

Figure 3.7. Elderly dependency ratio (ratio of 60+ to 20–59 population) in countries of the EU15, 1960–2003.

rates. The proportion of people aged 60 and over is also higher in Italy, Germany, Greece and, to a lesser extent, Spain (which, with the exception of Ireland, had the highest fertility level before the beginning of the decline). Population aging increased from 1960 to 2003 in all countries, but—as is happening with the fertility level—the relative position of countries has now reversed. Three of the four southern countries are among the five most aged countries (with Belgium and Germany). Ireland is, for the time being, the only exception, as it is still the country with the youngest population in the EU15 (Eurostat, 2004a).

The elderly dependency ratio[10] increased from 29.3 percent in 1960 to 40 percent in 2003, indicating that the weight of the elderly dependent population[11] supported on average by each person of working age has increased by one-third. The actual ratio between dependents and contributors is different because not every person over 60 is retired and not every person of working age is actually employed, but the elderly dependency ratio is a good indicator, especially when changes are being considered over time. Other factors affecting the real dependency ratio are the progress of productivity and the level of pensions.

In all countries (except Ireland[12]) the elderly dependency ratio increased between 1960 and 2000, but most significant are the countries' divergent trends (*Figure 3.7*). All these recent trends will continue in the future, even in the most favorable Eurostat population projection (high scenario), which includes a fertility recovery that in 2030 will reach a thereafter-constant total fertility rate of 1.94 (EU15) and net immigrant entries of almost one million per year from 2010 onward.

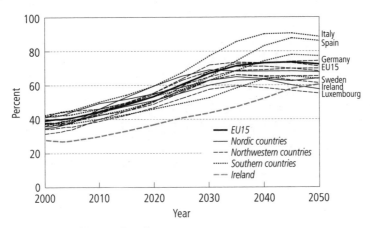

Source: Eurostat, New Chronos Database.

Figure 3.8. Elderly dependency ratio (ratio of 60+ to 20–59 population) in EU15 countries. Projection 2000–2050: High scenario.

According to the high scenario, the elderly dependency ratio will increase continuously in the EU15, reaching a maximum of 73.3 percent in 2045 (an 88 percent increase). The dependency ratio will more than double in the southern countries of Italy (90.5 percent), Spain (87.6 percent) and Greece (77.8 percent), while the Nordic countries will be in the lower range, with the minimum in Denmark (57.6 percent) (*Figure 3.8*).

This ratio is considered a fundamental component of the pension system equilibrium. Part of the southern countries' demographic disadvantage can be expected to be offset by an increase in their labor force participation rates, especially those of women, which are at present lower than in western and northern countries. Nevertheless, a tremendous gap will exist between these regions of the EU15 if the demographic future resembles the recent past. The general policy of real convergence among member countries will have to consider the demographic factor as an important distortion factor. Will it be possible to base convergence on identical economic indicators while there is a clear divergence in the demographic basis for some fundamental elements of public expenditures? Not in the absence of policies aimed at demographic convergence that should be assumed at the European level.

One of the most relevant features of the future population will be the increasing number and proportion of the very old (over 80 years) who are more subject to a loss of or reduction in their personal autonomy. Although the problem is partly an economic one it is mainly demographic, as these individuals require personal services. At present, care of older dependents falls mostly on the family, especially on women, but immigrants are also playing an increasing role here. In the future,

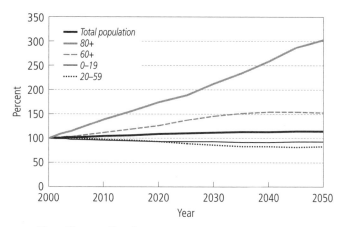

Source: Eurostat, New Chronos Database.

Figure 3.9. Relative increase of various EU15 population age groups. Projection 2000–2050: High scenario (2000 = 100 for each group).

the caring capacity of families will be reduced because of decreasing household size, increasing female participation in the labor force and the growing residential autonomy of the elderly. When older persons (especially women) lose their partner, they tend to live on their own—a situation that is preferred by both old persons and their relatives but makes caring a more complicated task, especially in large cities and with adult children increasingly living far away.

According to the Eurostat 2003 base projections, the population aged 80 and over will triple by 2050, while the population aged 60+ will increase only by 50 percent and the total population will remain practically at its present volume (a 14 percent increase in 50 years). The young and working-age population will decrease slightly during that period (*Figure 3.9*). In 2050 the very old population will represent over 11 percent of the total EU15 population, reaching above 14 percent in Italy and 12 percent in Austria and Spain.

Comparing the three Eurostat scenarios, we find only small differences in aging indexes projected in 2050: the proportion of the population aged 60 and over will vary from 32.9 percent (high scenario) to 36.6 percent (low scenario), and the proportion aged 80 and over will vary between 10 and 11.1 percent. The dependency ratio will reach 77.8 percent in the low scenario and 72.3 percent in the high scenario (*Figure 3.10*). This rather surprising view of the future shows the dominant influence of the present age structure (which results from past demographic trends) and stresses the very long-term effects of demographic factors.

Basic trends in population aging do not change with the fertility and immigration levels of the high scenario. The rather small differences between extreme

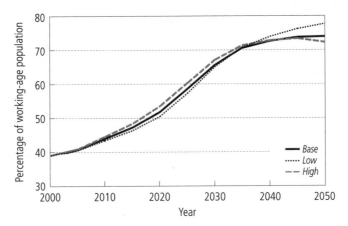

Source: Eurostat, New Chronos Database.

Figure 3.10. Old age dependency ratio (ratio of 60+ to 20–59 population) in three projection scenarios: EU15, 2000–2050.

scenarios, if compared with the increase during the projection period, are obtained at the price of a strong increase in population, mainly because of projected immigration flows of almost 42 million in the high scenario (only 14 million in the low scenario), with fertility never reaching the replacement level. Increasing immigration or fertility always means an increase in total population. In fact, the number of elderly people is much higher in the high scenario (141 million in 2050 as against 112 million for the low scenario); thus, more funding for pensions, health and social services will be needed if this turns out to be true. The advantage lies in the larger working-age population, which also means that more employment is needed. One possible way of resolving this issue can be briefly stated: to ease the problems caused by aging we need to create more jobs that can be filled by immigrants. If this view is taken, economists should determine what the driving forces for job creation could be in the new context of an increasing demand for personal services and a growing number of immigrants.

3.2.7   Could immigration solve the problem?

A question that has attracted much attention in recent years is what size of immigrant flows would be necessary to offset the present demographic trends that are leading to declining population and increasing age? Is it possible to compensate for the fertility decline by increasing immigration?

A much-debated United Nations document (United Nations, 2000) has shed new light on the matter. Its basic conclusion is that the number needed varies tremendously according to the demographic objective. To prevent population decline, the EU15 would need around 47 million net immigrants during the 2000–2050 period; and almost 80 million would prevent a drop in the working-age population. The last objective considered in the UN document, that of keeping a constant elderly dependency ratio (in other words, that immigration should total 674 million or more than double the present EU15 population), is clearly out of reach.[13] With this, the authors were clearly demonstrating that immigration could never be considered as a realistic solution for preventing the impact of population aging on the basic generational equilibrium.

This does not mean that immigration has no positive effect and that population aging is unavoidable in the future with or without immigration. Its long-term dimension will essentially depend on the future course of fertility. That is why, within the EU15, the southern countries and Germany will be the most affected unless a complete reversal of the course of fertility takes place—a possibility not foreseen in Eurostat projections. It would be advisable for Eurostat to produce more frequent population projections, taking into account the more recent demographic changes, and also to produce specific scenarios for each member country.

3.2.8 Knowledge and action

We have briefly reviewed fertility trends and their expected consequences for future declining population growth and increasing population aging. Some of these effects are expected to be a feature of the new demographic regime in post-transition countries. Low mortality rates, even with above-replacement-level fertility, mean a higher proportion of elderly people in the population and that the progress of life expectancy will increase population aging even more in the future. We have to learn to live with the new age structure, and some adaptive policies need to be implemented to cope with it. This should be the first objective of social policies.

3.2.9 Adapting to population aging

The most important challenges that such policies need to address are labor shortages, imbalances in the fiscal equilibrium of pension systems and increasing demands for care from elderly dependents. In all these fields the demographic factor is only one of the components; adaptive measures will also need to be directed at other factors. The support capacity of the working-age population could be improved by increasing the labor force participation rate, which will also help to prevent labor shortages. How possible it will be to increase activity rates will depend on the country, but in all countries such a step will chiefly depend on increasing the female participation rates. These rates are much lower on average in the southern countries—although no longer for the younger generations. The massive and permanent presence of women in the labor force is at the core of important social changes, and low fertility is very much related to the way society deals with those changes. Further increases in female participation rates will, however, intensify the importance of reconciling work and family life, and any course of action aimed at improving compatibility between employment and childbearing will help solve the problem of labor shortages in the future.

Another often-mentioned adaptive policy is to increase productivity. Certain conditions are needed if this is to be turned into an increase in the support capacity of the working-age population. First, not all of the productivity increase should be compensated for by a reduction in labor demand (this could be tempting in the event of a reduction in the labor supply). Second, distribution of productivity gains should not be made available to the retired population through automatic increases in their pension because if pensions are indexed on wages, productivity gains will have no effect. Some other adjustments are possible, including delaying the retirement age or modifying pension schemes—measures that have been widely discussed in recent years. To say the least, introducing such changes is politically difficult.

The increasing demand for public support for the care of elderly dependents results from the increased number of very old persons experiencing reduced personal autonomy and from the decreasing care capacity of families. The latter is related to the new situation of women who have traditionally assumed, and still assume, the main burden of care in the family. Reconciling caring for an elderly dependent and working is a situation with which an increasing number of women—and families—will be faced.

All adaptive policies have in common the need to make real choices among society-wide priorities when assigning public resources and, more generally, to define the desired model of society. These matters have no technical solution. They belong to the political sphere and have to be decided through the appropriate channels and mechanisms in our democratic societies.

3.2.10   Reproduction: The need for a new social contract

Fertility has not—as previously supposed—reached a single stable equilibrium level in countries that have completed the demographic transition. There is no visible mechanism for stopping the fertility decline at some stage in the future, and we find a wide range of situations in post-transition countries, with almost all having fertility below replacement level and some of them very far from achieving replacement level. What is our understanding of the factors that influence the fertility level at this moment in time? Is there anything that can be done to maintain fertility at least somewhat closer to the replacement level?

When dealing with the problem of low fertility, the old and more-apparent-than-real distinction between pronatalist measures and family policies must be avoided. There is now a general agreement about protecting and respecting rights and choices when implementing policies affecting childbearing, and there is also enough evidence that any other approach is basically ineffective. Low fertility should be considered as a symptom of problems in the family and of a lack of social and cultural adjustments to the new situation of women, in particular, working mothers.

Pronatalism has become an archaic concept, no longer applicable in current circumstances. The main precondition for pronatalist measures was the existence of a traditional reproduction model (a male-breadwinner-headed family). These measures acted by seeking horizontal equity between different sizes of family and influencing the cost of children for all or specific categories of families in special circumstances. Today, analysts credit this type of traditional measure with a very moderate positive effect (Gauthier, 1996) or even a total lack of effectiveness (Ditch [2000], quoted by Bagavos and Martin [2001]). At the Seville seminar, McDonald (2000) also quoted Demeny (1997, p. 10) who stated that societies facing depopulation must move 'from the domain of ordinary economic calculus to the domain of political economy, from redistributive jockeying to agreement on fundamental changes in the constitutional contract that sets the rules of societal interaction.'

The dominant theoretical approach to recent family changes is the second demographic transition,[14] a theory first proposed by Lesthaeghe and van de Kaa and later developed by them and others (see especially van de Kaa [1987] and Lesthaeghe [1995]). The theory describes, and supposedly explains, the progress of cohabitation, lone parenthood, childbearing outside marriage and low fertility—all changes that parallel a retreat from marriage and sexual restraints. One of the central ideas of this approach is that economic progress frees populations from worries about material needs and allows for enlightened and self-realizing behavior.

One should expect that so praised a framework (see Coleman [2004]) would have very clear responses to the main demographic problems that Europe is facing today: why is fertility so low and why is it lower in some places than others? But, quite surprisingly, this is not the case.

According to Coleman (2004) it would be logically necessary, given the underlying theory, for populations that score highest on postmaterialistic, ideational responses to have lower fertility levels, but the relationship is the reverse. Lower fertility is found in countries considered less advanced in the transition process, not only the southern countries of Europe but also Germany, Japan and South Korea. In fact, we may just consider that there is no empirical evidence of a relationship between a country's degree of postmaterialism (an indicator of its position in the transition process) and the period level of fertility (*Figure 3.11*).

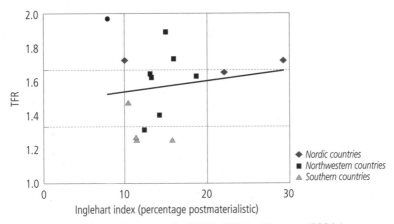

Sources: Inglehart Index in Cuyvers *et al.* (2003); TFR in Eurostat (2004a).

Figure 3.11. Relationship between postmaterialism and fertility level in countries of the EU15 (circa 2002).

The second transition theory does not offer a clear view of what the ultimate stage of the transition will be. Many authors have pointed out that even if other forms of union are emerging and consolidating, marriage is still the dominant form in almost all countries and that, in some countries, marriage rates have recently increased. On the other hand, the fact that consensual unions are less favorable to fertility must be merely a transitory effect that will disappear when this type of union spreads and is adopted as a normal way of living together with the same prospects for stability as marriage.[15] The increasing proportion of births outside marriage, something that can already be observed in Sweden and progressively in other countries, could be a good indicator of this change. One of the problems with the second transition theory is that it does not allow for changes in the concepts themselves: when consensual unions acquire all the essential features of marriage and, in particular, deserve the same social acceptance, transition from marriage to consensual union would lose some of its sociological importance. The same could happen with births outside marriage, a prospect that could be of great importance for the future of fertility and will contradict the predictions of the theory.

Among other leading commentators, Livi Bacci (2001) points to the dual nature of children. They are a private good (for their parents) and also a public good, necessary for the sustainability of the social protection system and for the economic functioning of society in general. Possibly similarly inspired, McDonald (2002) stresses the contradiction between (i) the market rationale, where employers have no interest in the family status of their workers and favor free, risk-averse persons that maximize their utility to the market and (ii) the private world of the family, where altruism is a necessary ingredient. The world of the market economy and the private world of the family are considered separate. McDonald (2002) sees the logic behind this in the sense that the market economy is implicitly based on the persistence of separate male and female roles. As a result of this contradiction, and as childlessness increases and first and second births are delayed, fertility will tend to be low.

That children are also a public good is not a new feature, and the existence of the market economy is scarcely new either. What has really changed is the reproduction model, formerly based on a male breadwinner, connecting with the production sphere of the market, and a female carer, in charge of reproduction, connecting only with the distribution sphere of the market. The model changes when both members of the family are expected, even compelled, to participate in the labor force. This change is partly due to the demographic transition, which has reduced the maternity and housework burden on women, while women and girls have gained better access to education. Changes in the economy, with the growing importance of services, have also contributed to the entry of more women into the labor force and induced them to stay there. In sum, the working mother personifies a real social revolution. Not only has society not yet adapted to such a change but, as McDonald (2002) argues, the new market economy may be exacerbating the situation for the working mother.

What is wrong is not the new model: women have gained an autonomy that they previously lacked, marriage is no longer their only fate (nor that of men) and there is also more freedom in the relations between the sexes. What does cause problems is the lack of social and cultural changes that should have accompanied the new model. The division of labor inside the family has not yet been adapted to the new situation. The time schedule of social and economic activities has not sufficiently changed. Business hours, working hours, even school-opening hours have not been adapted to suit the working mother (or, for that matter, the working father). And last but not least, the dominant worker model is still the male worker, not only free of family responsibilities but with the support of a wife or mother expected. Working women have had to adapt to this model and, as working was initially considered to be their own personal choice, to cope with their household tasks without much assistance from their partners.

The passage of women from the home to the labor force has not caused the same kind of problems associated with the flow from the primary sector to the other two sectors. Until now the costs implied by this transfer have been assumed by women themselves—and with the increasing perception on the part of the family that women's contribution to the family is essential, even though domestic tasks and caring activities are shared unequally between women and men. Thus, in the absence of adequate societal support policies, the cost is transferred to society—one of the strategies women use to succeed in a labor market that does not consider their personal and family situation is to stop having children or to limit their number.

It seems that, even in today's world, there are strong reasons for people wanting to have children. All existing surveys indicate that only a small minority plans to remain childless and the number of desired children is consistently higher than the actual number of children. The question does not seem to arise, at least for the moment,[16] as to why people wanting to have children are not having them.

Women's entry into the labor market has occurred progressively with relatively little change in the workplace. Women's participation in the labor force has now ceased to be considered a personal choice and has become a necessary contribution to family income. That explains why the problem of reconciling work and family has been seen as a gender equity problem, with policies and actions favoring an equal share of caring and domestic tasks—a legitimate and necessary objective but one that has not gone beyond the private world of the family and has not, apparently, concerned employers or governments. At present, the idea is gradually emerging that female participation in the labor force is a major problem that concerns the whole of society, and some public policies are being implemented to reconcile work and the family, with 'strong conclusions about the effectiveness of work–family support resources in maintaining fertility rates' (McDonald, 2002, p. 15). To date, however, the market and most employers have remained largely unconcerned with the problem, maintaining a model of labor relationships that has little connection with current social reality.

The attempts by women and families to transfer part of the work–family compatibility burden to society—to the state in the form of adequate public support policies and to employers in the form of more work flexibility and greater equality between men and women—have been of limited success in both the family and the workplace in a context of unemployment and labor instability. Changes in the labor market may encourage employers to adopt strategies aimed at attracting and keeping their employees by offering more appropriate working conditions for working mothers and fathers. As mentioned before, increasing female participation would entail increasing the number of working mothers. Their availability will, however, depend on the existence of adequate policies of work–family support.

The general objective of increasing the employment rate in the EU member countries stated in the Lisbon Summit of 2001 could, in future, attract more attention to differences in the extent of family support in each country. In some countries, especially in southern Europe, the lack of adequate support measures could be a serious drawback to adapting the labor supply to a sustained increase in employment.

The conflict between the still-private model of reproduction and the public model of production by the market is at the heart of persistent low fertility. Bridging the gap between them will be a long-term but unavoidable and urgent process. The need for a new social contract has already been noted here. It is an ambitious program that should inspire every single measure aimed at solving the low fertility problem.

3.2.11 The specifics of very low fertility

With characteristic directness, McDonald (2002, p. 2) has noted:

> The important theoretical question is what are the features that distinguish post-transition countries and subgroups with moderately low fertility rates from those with very low fertility.

But this is not just a theoretical question; an important objective for public action would be to detect and correct the factors causing very low fertility.

The dominant theoretical framework mentioned above has reached an impasse when dealing with very low fertility countries. Taking the southern countries as an example, it is clear that on the one hand, the alleged cultural specificities accounting for the lagging behind of these countries in the second transition process could not explain that—against all reasonable expectations—they should show the lowest fertility rate. On the other hand, the very idea of cultural specifics that are negatively associated with the usual indicators of postmodernism has to be revised.

Coleman (2004, pp. 21–22) refutes the idea of common European solutions, based on the argument that a wide variety of national problems require their own individual policy responses. He argues that the low-fertility countries of southern Europe have a greater resemblance to the low-fertility societies of Asia, while the countries of northwestern Europe are closer to the 'English-speaking world overseas.' To support his statement, he describes the southern countries as manifesting 'familist-traditions, rejection of "second demographic transition" behaviour, low female workforce participation rate, high unemployment and rigid labor regulations.' It is not difficult to show, taking Spain as an example, how these much-repeated beliefs are far from present reality and dynamics. Rejection of second-transition behavior does not follow from the recent increase in births outside marriage (now over 21 percent), nor from the fact that one-third of marriages end in divorce,[17] nor from the continuous increase in single-parent families. Low but rapidly increasing female workforce participation conceals the more significant differences between the younger generations, which are already at comparable levels to other western European countries, and the older generations, which have extremely low participation rates, a situation accounted for by the short period that has elapsed since the changes began (around 1985). And how do the rigid labor regulations fit with the fact that Spain is the country with the highest percentage of nonpermanent jobs in the EU15?

By insisting on offering cultural explanations that simply do not match the facts, we are barred from an understanding of the situation of southern countries that could lead to more-effective policy actions.

All the changes described by the second transition theory are at work in the southern countries of Europe, with understandable lags in their recent entry into the process of change that, of course, are partly due to what is happening in their particular cultural context. But opinions and attitudes in the south concerning family changes are rapidly converging with those of the rest of Europe and, in some cases, are ahead of them. It may be true that we sometimes find a mismatch between attitudes and actual behavior. For instance, women in Spain are more enthusiastically modern in values concerning the family than women in several northwestern European countries. When comparing Spaniards and Britons, Catherine Hakim (2003) chooses to believe that the Spanish data are affected by a 'political correctness bias,' but of course one may also consider other possible explanations like the lack of access to convenient child care or noncooperative attitudes in male partners (Tobío, 2004).

Very low fertility situations have to be analysed in the context of the common features of social evolution of European countries described by the second demographic transition theory. We have seen that moderately high levels of fertility are congruent with the theory inasmuch as the new forms of union will replace marriage and an increase in births outside marriage will take place. This process is lagging behind in the countries of low fertility. As researchers we have to detect the obstacles that prevent the developments that have already occurred in other countries. For southern countries two main drawbacks could account for a good part of the difference in fertility levels: the situation of young adults and of working mothers.

In Spain and Italy the increasing delay in entering active and reproductive life by the young generations is freezing their social integration. Their behavior is closely related to the economic situation (labor market) and the housing situation, even though certain cultural factors make life easier for the younger generations and their families. This delay is doubtless having a strong impact on family formation and on first births. The labor market situation may improve in the near future for demographic reasons, but in a country like Spain the most important issue at present is the housing market where price increases have made it practically impossible for young people to have a home of their own.

Spain is a country where working mothers receive strong support from their own mothers (the children's grandmothers), which explains why their labor force participation rates are lower than in other countries but still high in relation to the lack of public support. This situation is possible because mothers currently working belong to the first generation of women aiming to stay in the labor force and their mothers are part of the last generation of women that lived according to the old male-breadwinner model (Tobío, 2001). These special circumstances will not be repeated in future generations.

Working mothers are now prepared to accept some sacrifices, as they have the feeling that they are making history, but their example prevents others who are less prepared for such efforts from having children. Surveys on the caring strategies of working mothers show the difficulties of the task in a nonsupportive context (Tobío 2002) and how it affects their willingness to have more children.

3.3 Conclusions

Concern about low fertility (and its consequences) is spreading in the European Union. All member countries have below-replacement levels of fertility, which means a potential population decrease in the absence of immigration. At present, immigration represents 80 percent of the total population increase in the EU15. The most important consequence of low fertility is population aging with all its implications for the sustainability of the social protection system and the equilibrium of the labor market.

The fertility issue should be embedded in social policies in a threefold strategy. The first objective would be to implement adaptive measures to face the unavoidable population aging associated with post-transition demographic features of low mortality and low fertility. The second objective would be to act on the work–family relationship to adjust to the new reproduction model based on the two-earner family and the emergence of the working mother. Work–family reconciliation is the one essential dimension of this strategic objective that should also involve employers. The third objective is to deal with situations of very low fertility by removing country-specific obstacles affecting the fertility level.

The type of adaptive measures chosen will depend on political choices and could be strongly influenced by European political philosophy, shared by all member countries. Acting on the work–family relationship would require a new social contract, as it affects every dimension of our lives. In that case, common causes should lead to common measures in the EU15—measures able to take into account differences in each country's situation in the process of social and demographic changes.

Notes

1. Their net reproduction rate (NRR) was below 1. The NRR measures the number of daughters of reproductive age per woman, taking into account the combined effect of fertility and mortality.

2. The emphasis is mine.

3.   A stable population is a long-term model showing that a population with constant mortality and fertility rates has a constant growth rate and constant age structure.

4.   The total cohort fertility rate is the average number of children born to women of a given cohort (usually a generation defined as those born in the same year) during their reproductive age span.

5.   Average number of marriages in total population.

6.   May be considered as the average number of first marriages per woman aged 15 to 49 *in a given year*. If age at first marriage is declining, both young and older cohorts will have high marriage rates, thus increasing the total first marriage rate which could be even higher than 1.

7.   Obtained by multiplying the TFR by the proportion of births in the marriage.

8.   Eurostat's 2004 projections were not available to the author at the time of writing.

9.   The Eurostat population projection high scenario, used here, foresees a life expectancy of 87 years for women and 83.7 years for men in 2050.

10.   A very common index of population aging, calculated by dividing the 60+ population by the 20–59 population.

11.   Economic (pensions) and, for the very old, personal dependency.

12.   In 1960 Ireland had an above-average elderly dependency ratio because its working-age population was smaller percentage-wise than in other countries, despite its proportion of the 60+ age group being the lowest in the EU15.

13.   David Coleman (2004) has pointed out the case of South Korea, where the equivalent of the whole world population would be needed to achieve this goal.

14.   I agree with Livi Bacci (2001) that demography suffers from an inflation of 'transitions' used as a synonym for 'change.'

15.   Marriage stability has been reduced in recent times, as shown by the divorce rate level (Council of Europe, 2002).

16.   Marriage stability has been reduced in recent times, as shown by the divorce rate level (Council of Europe, 2002).

17.   Author's estimate based on latest number of legal separations and annual number of marriages.

References

Bagavos, C. and Martin, C. (2001) *Low Fertility, Families and Public Policies. Synthesis Report*, Paper presented at the Annual Seminar of the Austrian Institute for Family Studies, Vienna, Austria, 'Low Fertility, Families and Public Policies,' held 15–16 September 2000, Seville, Spain.

Billari, F. (2004) *Choices, Opportunities and Constraints of Partnership, Childbearing and Partnering: The Patterns in the 1990s*, Solicited background paper presented at the United Nations/Economic Commission for Europe, 'European Population Forum,' held in Geneva, Switzerland, 12–14 September.

Cliquet, R.L. (1991) 'The Second Demographic Transition: Fact or Fiction?' *Population Studies*, no 23, Strasbourg, France: Council of Europe.

Coleman, D.A. (2004) 'Facing the 21st Century. New Developments, Continuing Problems,' in Macura, M., MacDonald, A.L. and Haug, W. (eds) *The New Demographic Regime: Population Challenges and Policy Responses*, New York, USA and Geneva, Switzerland: United Nations, pp. 11–43, See http://www.unece.org /ead/pau/epf/epf_ndr.htm/ accessed in December 2005.

Council of Europe (2002) *Recent Demographic Developments in Europe*, Strasbourg, France: Council of Europe.

Cuyvers, P., Schulze, H.-J., Künzler, J. and Hooghiemstra, E. (2003) *Eurobarometer 59, Partners on Fertility and Division of Housework/Child Care in the European Union*, Report for the European Commission (DG V), The Netherlands: Amsterdam; Germany: Würzburg.

Demeny, P. (1997) *Policy interventions*, Paper presented to the Expert Group Meeting on Below Replacement Fertility, held at the Department of Economic and Social Affairs, Population Division, United Nations, New York, 4–6 November.

Ditch, J. (2000) *Fee, Fi, Fo, Fum: Fertility, Social Protection and Fiscal Welfare*, Paper presented at the Annual Seminar of the Austrian Institute for Family Studies, Vienna, Austria, 'Low Fertility, Families and Public Policies,' held 15–16 September, Seville, Spain.

'European Population Forum' (2004) of the United Nations/Economic Commission for Europe, held 12–14 September, Geneva, Switzerland, See http://www.Population action.org/issues/globalinitiatives/ICPD/documents/EPF_FinalReport.pdf/ accessed in December 2005.

Eurostat (2004a) *Statistiques de population 2004*, Luxembourg: Communautés Européennes.

Eurostat (2004b) *Premières estimations démographiques pour 2003. Statistiques en bref, Thème 3, 1/2004*, Luxembourg: Communautés Européennes.

Frejka, T. and Ross, J. (2001) 'Paths to Subreplacement Fertility: The Empirical Evidence,' *Population and Development Review*, **27** (Supplement): 213–254.

Gauthier, A.H. (1996) *The State and the Family: A Comparative Analysis of Family Policies in Industrialized Countries*, Oxford, UK: Oxford Clarendon Press.

Golini, A. (1998) 'How Low Can Fertility Be? An Empirical Exploration,' *Population and Development Review*, **24**(1): 59–74.

Hakim, C. (2003) *Models of the Family in Modern Societies: Ideals and Realities*, Aldershot, Hampshire, UK: Ashgate.

Lesthaeghe, R. (1995) 'The Second Demographic Transition in Western Countries: An Interpretation,' in Mason, K.O. and Jensen, A.-M. (eds) *Gender and Family Change in Industrialized Countries*, Oxford, UK: Clarendon Press, pp. 17–62.

Livi Bacci, M. (2001) 'Comment: Desired Family Size and the Future Course of Fertility,' in Bulatao, A.E. and Casterline, J.B. (eds) *Global Fertility Transition*, New York, USA: Population Council, pp. 282–289.

Macura, M., and Beets, G. (eds) (2002) *Dynamics of Fertility and Partnership in Europe. Insights and Lessons from Comparative Research*, vols 1 and 2, New York, USA: United Nations.

McDonald P. (2000) *The "Toolbox" of Public Policies to Impact on Fertility—A Global View*, Paper presented at the Annual Seminar of the Austrian Institute for Family Studies, Vienna, Austria, 'Low Fertility, Families and Public Policies,' held 15–16 September, Seville, Spain.

McDonald P. (2002) *Low Fertility: Unifying the Theory and the Demography*, Paper prepared for Session 73, Meeting of the Population Association of America, held 9–11 May, Atlanta, GA, USA, See http://eprints.anu.edu.au/archive/00001113/ accessed in December 2005.

McDonald P. and Kippen, R. (2001) 'Labor Supply Prospects in 16 Developed Countries, 2000–2050,' *Population and Development Review*, **27**(1): 1–32.

Tobío C. (2001) 'Working and Mothering. Women's Strategies in Spain,' *European Societies*, **3**(3): 339–371.

Tobío C. (2002) 'Conciliación o contradicción, cómo hacen las madres trabajadoras en España,' in *Revista Española de Investigaciones Sociológicas*, **97**:155–186 [in Spanish].

Tobío C. (2004) 'Review of Models of the Family in Modern Societies: Ideals and Realities, by C. Hakim,' *British Journal of Industrial Relations*, **42**(3): 563–587, September, See http://ssrn.com/abstract=584211/ accessed in December 2005.

United Nations (2000) *Replacement Migration: Is It a Solution to Declining and Ageing Populations?* New York, USA: United Nations Department of Economic and Social Affairs, Population Division.

van de Kaa, D.J. (1987) 'Europe's Second Demographic Transition,' *Population Bulletin*, **42**(1): 1–58.

van de Kaa, D.J. (2002) 'Is Low Fertility Post-Modern and Beyond the Action of Governments?' in Macura, M. and Beets, G. (eds) *Dynamics of Fertility and Partnership in Europe: Insights and Lessons from Comparative Research*, vol 1, New York, USA: United Nations, pp. 13–16.

Chapter 4

Childbearing Behavior in the New EU Member States: Basic Trends and Selected Attitudes

Zsolt Spéder

4.1 Introduction

In the eight new European Union (EU) member states of the former eastern bloc, childbearing behavior has changed radically as a result of the rapid societal changes—or more precisely, changes of gear—that took place from 1990 onward. The family model that had emerged and prevailed during the Communist era disappeared quite quickly after the transformation of the political, economic and institutional regimes of the former Communist countries—a transformation that can be characterized as 'catching-up modernization' (in German, *nachholende Modernisierung*) (Zapf, 1996; Adamski *et al.*, 2002).

The new member states (NMS) of the EU planned to (re)establish the functioning institutional configurations of the west. If, however, social action and decision making are constrained by structural factors, then it can be assumed that, after a transition period, the former Communist countries will take over the family model prevailing in the west. However, although there have been profound changes in the demographic regimes in western Europe since the 1970s, usually referred to as the 'second demographic transition' (Lesthaeghe and Surkyn, 2004), it is debatable

59

whether this transition can be characterized as homogeneous. Thus, if different family models do exist, which models will spread? And what kind of influence will the 'inheritance' of the Communist institutional setting—the 'legacies' of the 40 (or 70) years' experience of the Communist system—have in the formation of any new model? Moreover, can we assume that the structural factors that are shaping social reality in the former Communist NMS today will lead to the same or similar models as occurred years before in the west? And, to formulate an even more current question: are there any new influences in the NMS after and as a result of their accession to the European Union?

Of course, changes have occurred and continue to occur—and not just because of structural features. The systemic transformation has led to cultural shifts, a redefinition of the importance of different life domains, a balancing of freedoms and obligations and the emergence and/or triumph of, for example, individualization and consumerism. Nonetheless, can one be really sure that during the pre-1990 period there were no changes in the cultural and values systems in the eight NMS? What kind of gender values existed during the period of full female employment, for example, and did they evolve? Or from another perspective: can one really assume that values diffused in line with institutional changes, or should a time of disorganization (Philipov, 2003) and/or inertia be assumed?

Naturally, this chapter cannot aspire to give a definitive answer to questions that have been discussed widely in recent literature (Lesthaeghe and Moors, 2000; Macura *et al.*, 2000; Kotowska and Jozviak, 2003; Philipov and Dorbritz, 2004). It will be a more limited undertaking, namely, *to illustrate a number of features of the fertility behavior and family-related attitudes of the younger generation in the new member states.* This description will be incomplete in that I will refer to Cyprus and Malta, two of the ten new member states, only rarely, for two main reasons. First, there is much less data available for these two countries. Second, I will be emphasizing the system dependence of social action and decision making, and those two Mediterranean countries did not undergo the same type of changes as the former Communist NMS. However, I am aware that fertility change has been enormous in the last decade in Cyprus and Malta.

The main focus of this chapter is to show selected characteristics of childbearing behavior in the eight new member states. As, numerically speaking, the objective indicators (total fertility rates, nonmarital childbearing, nuptiality) are well known, I will turn, after a brief description of these, to the more subjective components of childbearing. In the case of 'open societies,' where there are growing opportunities and greater options available for the achievement of life goals, it is vital to understand values, attitudes and intentions if the possible future trends are to be discerned. The desired number of children, for example, is a well-known subjective indicator of fertility. Thus, after discussing the family size planned by young women in the new member states, I will turn my attention to more indirect attitudes—those influencing the 'societal climate' for fertility. First, I will discuss the partnership forms and family relations that are endorsed or disapproved of; then, I will look at some aspects of the value placed on children.

In my analysis I use three types of data. For the description of basic trends, I use the latest available data of the European Council. To describe young women's fertility plans, I use Eurobarometer data from 2001–2002. For the description of family-related attitudes, I use the data of the International Population Policy Acceptance Survey (IPPAS) carried out after 2000 in several countries. The second round of the International Population Policy Acceptance Survey is the result of international cooperation led by the German Federal Institute for Population Research (the *Bundesinstitut für Bevölkerungsforschung [BiB]*) in Wiesbaden. The survey was executed and financed by the participating countries, and the comparative dataset was produced in the course of the project, 'Dialog—International Population Policy Acceptance Study: The Viewpoint of Citizens and Policy Actors Regarding the Management of Population Related Change,' funded by the European Commission. I must mention one more thing before beginning my analysis, and this relates to comparisons. To understand the specific features of childbearing behavior in the NMS, it is important to look at the 'old' EU member states. To simplify the comparison with the 15 'old' states I have chosen three different countries from the pre-2004 EU: *Austria*, representing a continental country; *Finland*, representing a Nordic country; and *Italy*, representing a southern or Mediterranean country. Naturally, the lack of data availability limited my selection, but my wish to show the internal differences of the 'old' countries played a role in deciding which countries should play the reference role. (In this study I will sometimes refer to these countries as EU15 countries.)

4.2 An Overview: The State of Fertility and Partnership Formation in the New EU Member States

The variability of the period Total Fertility Rate (pTFR), the indicator that shows 'actual' childbearing behavior in a country at a given point of time, is rather small in the new member states. In the eight former Communist NMS in 2002, the difference between the lowest (Czech Republic, 1.17) and the highest (Cyprus, 1.49) is just above 0.3, and in the eight NMS in 2002 it falls within a range of 0.2 (*Figure 4.1*). Compared with the EU15 countries, the new EU member states tend to be among the lowest fertility countries (Kohler *et al.*, 2002). It is well known that the 'lowest-low' level is greatly influenced by postponement of childbearing (i.e., women starting their fertility career at a later age) (Bongaarts and Feeney, 1998; Kohler and Philipov, 2001). The formula proposed by Bongaarts

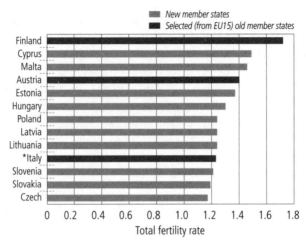

Figure 4.1. Total fertility rate in the new EU member states (NMS) and selected EU15 countries, 2002.

Note: *2001 value.
Source: Council of Europe (2002).

and Feeney, as well as providing estimates of the completed fertility rates (Frejka and Sardon, 2003), predicts the increase in the pTFR that can be expected if postponement stops, although to date, no country has shown a significant increase. Furthermore, it would be misleading to assume that a change in fertility behavior is related only to the mean age of first childbearing, which is the implicit assumption in the Bongaarts–Feeney formula.

The character of the change in childbearing behavior is well documented. After the societal transformation began, people started postponing the decision to have a child and, to date, have had fewer children (Lesthaeghe and Moors, 2000; Macura *et al.*, 2000; Kohler and Philipov, 2001). The scale of the change is extraordinary, the pTFR falling by nearly one child in several countries. The decrease of the pTFR in the NMS was clearly as remarkable as in the 'old' EU15 countries of western Europe. (*Figure 4.2* describes the changes in pTFR in 13 countries.) Taking into account both the decrease and the fertility level, we find a greater homogeneity in the NMS today than one and one-half decades ago.

We cannot, however, find homogeneity in the share of nonmarital births (*Figure 4.3*). In two of the three Baltic countries (Estonia and Latvia), the share of nonmarital births is around 50 percent, while in most of the countries the ratio falls between one-fifth and one-third, and in two below 15 percent. The percentage increase between 1990 and 2002 also shows the dissimilarity among the countries (*Figure 4.4*). In Poland the increase was 8 percent; in Estonia and Lithuania more

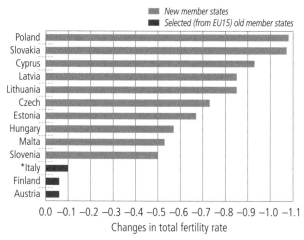

Note: *2000 value.
Source: Council of Europe (2002).

Figure 4.2. Changes in total fertility rate in the new EU member states and selected EU15 countries, 1990–2002.

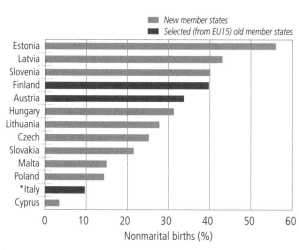

Note: *2000 value.
Source: Council of Europe (2002).

Figure 4.3. Percentage of nonmarital births in the new EU member states and selected EU15 countries, 2002.

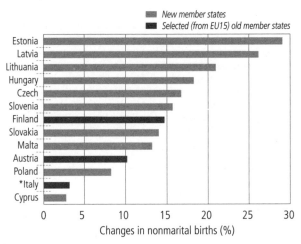

Note: *2000 value.

Source: Council of Europe (2002).

Figure 4.4. Changes in nonmarital births in the new EU member states and selected EU15 countries, 1990–2002.

than 25 percent. As mentioned, the homogeneity in the most recent pTFR is the result of quite different developments. Note that both a high and a low level of nonmarital births can characterize (transient) lowest-low fertility.

The increase in nonmarital births highlights the modifications that have taken place in partnership formation and the different pace of changes in fertility decline. Detachment from marriage and childbearing is unambiguous in many of the new member states. Increased cohabitation is responsible for the increase in nonmarital births; but it is also assumed that much of the cohabitation will turn into marriage after a while or is itself due to childbearing. The most recent data support this assumption: in Hungary, for example, about three-fifths of nonmarital births occurred during cohabitation.

The status and the size of the change in the total first female marriage rate (TFFMR) reveal the importance of partnership formation, as pointed out in recent literature (Lesthaeghe and Moors, 2000; Philipov and Dorbritz, 2004). The TFFMR in the NMS is at an historic low: in six countries it is lower than in Austria, which has the lowest level of the three EU15 reference countries (*Figure 4.5*). In eight of the ten NMS, however, it is lower than in Finland and Italy. The level of the TFFMR is higher only in Cyprus and Malta as compared to the selected EU15 countries.

Regarding the *changes* in the TFFMR since 1990, Cyprus, with an increase, is clearly an exception, and only in Slovenia is there a very moderate change, as also occurred in the EU15 reference countries (*Figure 4.6*). In the remaining NMS

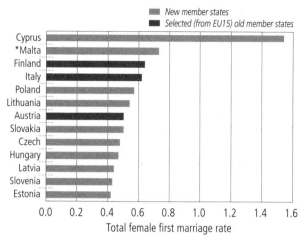

Note: *2001 value.
Source: Council of Europe (2002).

Figure 4.5. Total female first marriage rate in the new EU member states and selected EU15 countries, 2002.

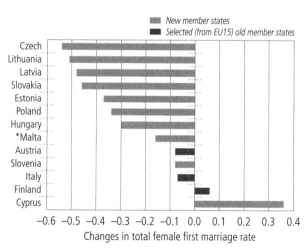

Note: *2001 value.
Source: Council of Europe (2002).

Figure 4.6. Changes in total female first marriage rate in the new EU member states and selected EU15 countries, 1990–2002.

the TFFMR basically halved during the period analysed. The decrease was most remarkable in the Czech Republic, Latvia and Lithuania. Hungary, on the other hand, showed a less dramatic change, but its starting position in 1990 was different. The differing extent of the decrease in the TFFMR resulted in quite a high homogeneity, with the TFFMR varying only in a very narrow age range in the eight former Communist NMS in 2002. Of course, postponement of first marriage, which characterizes the countries analysed, distorts the TFFMR (Philipov and Dorbritz, 2004).

In the NMS countries, if young adults do not marry, are they really cohabiting? The data from the second round of the IPPAS carried out under the Dialog project, as mentioned above, give an overview of the living arrangements of young adults. The survey provides data for five of the eight former Communist NMS, namely, the Czech Republic, Hungary, Lithuania, Poland and Slovenia. The data from the three selected EU15 countries are also integrated into the dataset. We can thus examine two types of living arrangement:

1. The partnership relationship, where we distinguish four categories: staying single; cohabitation; marriage; and other arrangements; and
2. Household composition, where we distinguish five categories: living alone; living as a couple; living as a couple with children; one-parent household; and other arrangements.
   (The 'other arrangements' category mainly covers young adults living with parents.)

Our interest here is in the share of those cohabiting and those living alone who are not in a permanent partnership. The small size of the sample in some countries meant that a broad age range had to be defined for the young adults (18–34) and that the responses of men and women had to be combined. Naturally, there are gender differences regarding partnership, but these are disregarded for the sake of the analysis. Around one-half of the persons aged 18–34 live alone, and the other one-half are in some sort of partnership (*Table 4.1*). The differences among the countries are quite remarkable, although in most the proportion varies around 50 percent. Only 31.9 percent of Lithuanian young adults live alone and have never been married, while the corresponding figure in Hungary is 47.3 percent and in Slovenia, which has the highest ratio in the NMS, 52.5 percent. The variation among the three EU15 countries selected is noteworthy. In Italy nearly two-thirds of the young adults live alone and have never been married, while in Austria and Finland, the equivalent proportion is well below 50 percent.

Regarding the increase in nonmarital births, the ratio of those cohabitating is significant, especially in relation to those living within marriage. The difference

Table 4.1. Partnership status of young adults, aged 18 to 34.

Partnership status	Czech Republic	Hungary	Lithuania	Poland*	Slovenia	Austria	Finland	Italy
Single	45.7	47.3	31.9	49.6	52.5	45.2	41.5	64.0
Cohabitation	7.8	8.7	5.3	–	15.5	16.1	30.8	3.4
Marriage	40.5	41.3	52.8	49.0	30.3	35.0	25.4	31.2
Other (divorced)	6.0	2.7	10.0	1.4	1.7	3.7	2.3	1.4
Total (%)	100.0	100.0	100.0	100.0	100.0	100.0	100.0	100.0
(N=)	(356)	(939)	(454)	(1792)	(534)	(671)	(1031)	(1670)
Cohabitation /marriage	0.19	0.21	0.10		0.51	0.46	1.21	0.11

Note: *Denotes slightly different answer categories.
Source: International Population and Policy Acceptance Survey, own calculations.

Table 4.2. Household composition of young adults, aged 18 to 34.

Household composition	Countries					
	Lithuania	Czech Republic	Hungary	Slovenia	Finland	Austria
Living alone	7.6	5.3	3.1	3.9	23.2	13.7
Couple	6.9	8.4	8.9	5.6	29.4	10.6
Couple with children	43.3	32.0	33.2	27.0	27.2	34.9
Single parent	2.5	2.0	1.2	0.6	1.6	3.6
Other	39.7	52.3	53.6	62.9	17.6	37.2
Total (%)	100.0	100.0	100.0	100.0	100.0	100.0
(N=)	(436)	(356)	(941)	(538)	(1041)	(699)

Source: International Population and Policy Acceptance Survey, own calculations.

in the distribution of current partnerships between marriage and cohabitation is enormous among the countries: in Italy, Lithuania and Poland the ratio of those cohabiting is almost negligible; in the Czech Republic and Hungary the ratio is around the one-fifth mark; in Austria and Slovenia the proportion is around one-half. Finally Finland, a Nordic country, can be found at the other end of the scale, with more young adults cohabiting than living within marriage (*Table 4.1*, last row). All these differences are logical when the variation in the sphere of nonmarital births is taken into account.

Table 4.2 illustrates that in most countries, being single does not mean living alone. Finland is a clear exception, and Austria also has an above-average ratio of singles. In the former Communist NMS the ratios are clearly below 10 percent, indicating that most of those young adults had not yet married and, having no coresidential partnership at the time of the interview, were living with their parents.

The ideal way of showing the association between partnership forms and types of birth (marital, cohabiting or single parent) would be through a comparison of the country-specific ratio and the change in the ratios over the last decades. As such figures are not available, a similar association is shown—that between the

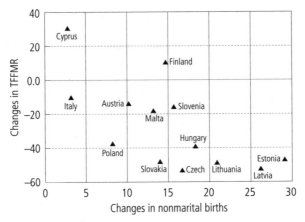

Source: Council of Europe (2002).

Figure 4.7. Changes in total female first marriage rate and nonmarital births in the new EU member states and selected EU15 countries, 1990–2002.

change in TFFMR and the change in the ratio of nonmarital births (*Figure 4.7*). The association is clear and of a negative character: the greater the decrease in the tendency to marry, the more the proportion of nonmarital births increases.

To sum up, the NMS are rather homogeneous with regard to fertility (as measured by pTFR). But this homogeneity seems to be the result of different developments and the varying pace of change in fertility decline. Differences did emerge, partly because of the variety of living arrangements (the varying importance of marriage and cohabitation). It was surprising to note that clear differences in living arrangements can produce very similar fertility regimes; and finally, a well-known fact could once again be corroborated, namely, that as far as family formation is concerned, there is remarkably more heterogeneity among the 'old' European countries than among the NMS countries.

4.3 Fertility Preferences of Young Adults: Total Number of Anticipated Children

Fertility outcomes result from interwoven structural conditions (e.g., labor market structures, economic necessities, child-related policy regimes and structural uncertainties) and the ideational or cultural climate (e.g., values, attitudes, normative beliefs, plans and wishes). These form—in tandem—the actual childbearing behavior (Lesthaeghe, 2002). Putting aside this duality for the sake of the analysis, I will concentrate on the ideational environment of fertility development, in other words, on the planned number of children and on attitudes toward basic partnership forms and selected 'child-specific' family forms. It is known that plans, wishes and attitudes can only partly influence childbearing behavior and also that predictions based on individuals' plans are sometimes likely to fail. I believe, however, that in modern societies, such plans are characterized by increasing options, by a greater variety in pursuable life goals and by an increasing freedom of choice, all of which result from the growing importance of individual decision making. Consequently, the intentions and plans of individuals, and their determinants, should be studied more carefully, especially where the focus is on future development. In other words, fertility can increase only if individuals are ready to incorporate children—and a given number of children—into their life plan. In that sense, in an atmosphere of growing diversity and in a situation where there is nearly perfect contraception, a high enough *intended* number of children and a positive attitude toward children are both prerequisites for fertility reversal.

The total number of anticipated children is a central concern in fertility research (Bumpass and Westoff, 1970; Goldstein *et al.*, 2003; Fahey and Spéder, 2003). Although there are reservations about intentions and attitudes being able to help predict future developments, supporters of this approach believe that provided suitable concepts and carefully chosen measures are used, research on ideational components can contribute to a better understanding of childbearing behavior and thus help predict future development (Fishbein *et al.*, 1980). Most recently it has been shown that the German-speaking countries have experienced the 'emergence of sub-replacement norms' fertility (Goldstein *et al.*, 2003, p. 14). Regarding the NMS, and especially the former Communist countries, the following important question should be addressed: has the long-lasting, very low fertility situation decreased the fertility intentions of young adults? Or, to put it another way, is there any sign of adjustment (upward) in fertility plans in the eastern European countries? Naturally, it would be preferable to answer such a question using longitudinal data (Bumpass and Westoff, 1970), but cross-sectional data can also give some insights.

The figures for the mean expected family size and the distribution of young adults according to the number of anticipated children can be shown using Eurobarometer data from the ten EU candidate countries for 2001 (*Table 4.3*). Because of the small sample and the very similar answers of male and female respondents, the answers of men and women have been combined.

The total number of anticipated children (existing and planned) of young adults varies around the value of 2.0 in most of the countries. In six of the ten countries the number falls into the 1.9–2.1 band; in two further countries it is only slightly out of this age range. Two countries seem to fall out of the range: Cyprus is a clear exception with a value of 2.54, and in the Czech Republic the value of 1.82 is somewhat lower than 2.0. Naturally, intentions may never be fully realized, but the

Table 4.3. The mean total number of expected children (existing plus planned) and the distribution of young adults (aged 18 to 34) regarding the number of anticipated children, by country, in 2001.

Countries	Total number of expected children	Number of children		
		0–1	2	3+
New EU member states				
Cyprus	2.54	5	49	40
Poland	2.14	17	60	23
Lithuania	2.09	21	61	19
Latvia	2.06	16	66	17
Hungary	2.05	18	62	20
Estonia	2.03	22	55	23
Slovakia	1.97	20	68	12
Slovenia	1.96	16	57	27
Malta	1.88	21	64	15
Czech Republic	1.82	27	60	14
Selected EU countries				
Finland	2.41	17	48	35
Austria	1.73	36	53	11
Italy	1.98	16	62	21

Source: Eurobarometer 59.2; Candidate Countries Eurobarometer (2002).

values indicated suggest that the aggregate fertility level could increase in the near future in the NMS countries. Naturally, it is difficult to forecast what level might be reached, but the prevailing intentions—around two children per woman—could be a basis for an increase in fertility. In the three selected 'old' EU countries the variation is much greater than in the NMS, the gap between Austria (1.73) and Finland (2.41) being 0.68.

The only comparable data for change over time for the countries analysed is for Hungary. In Hungary the Fertility and Family Survey indicated a level of 2.1 as a mean of total anticipated children among women aged 20–34 in 1992, and the very same level was found ten years later (2001–2002) in the survey 'The Turning Points of the Life Course' (see Spéder [2001] for the concept and methodology of the Hungarian survey). It is surprising but true that, at the aggregate cohort level, there was no change in the preferred number of children in Hungary and thus no sign of adjustment during the period of profound societal change (compare *Table 4.4*). Nevertheless, what has changed is the growing tension between the number of planned children and the number actually born.

It is also worth looking at the distribution of the total number of expected children according to the specific number of children. The two-child ideal seems to be the dominant form in all countries, and variation is due to deviation from this

Table 4.4. Women's planned and actual number of children, and the difference between them, according to cohort, in 1992 and 2001–2002.

Cohort	1992			2001–2002		
	Plan	Fact	Difference	Plan	Fact	Difference
20–24	2.1	0.5	1.6	2.1	0.4	1.7
25–29	2.1	1.4	0.7	2.2	1.1	1.1
30–34	2.1	1.8	0.3	2.2	1.6	0.6
35–39	2.1	1.9	0.2	2.2	2.0	0.2

Sources: For 1992, Hungarian Central Statistical Office (HCSO) Family and Fertility Survey. For 2001–2002, 'Turning Points of the Life Course,' Hungarian Demographic Research Institute, own calculations.

ideal. Both in the Czech Republic and Poland, 60 percent of the respondents intend to have two children. In Poland the share of respondents planning more than two children is quite high (23 percent), while in the Czech Republic those planning only one child is more widespread (27 percent). Based on the two Hungarian surveys mentioned we found that the popularity of the two-child norm has declined, while the one-child model and the three-or-more-child family model have become more popular. Thus, in Hungary the mean anticipated family size of 2.05 is due to a kind of pluralization of family ideals.

4.4 Attitudes of Young Adults Toward Family Formation and Childbearing in Selected Countries in the IPPAS Survey

The ideational climate that possibly influences childbearing decisions is quite extensive. Barber *et al.* (2002) showed, for example, how mothers' values and attitudes about the ideal number of children influence their daughters' decision about how many children to have and when. Preferences about different domains of life (especially work, leisure and family) or the importance given to career may also influence fertility decisions (Crimmins *et al.*, 1991).

The International Population and Policy Acceptance Studies dataset that will be used in the last section is very rich in attitudinal and value indicators concerning population trends, family issues, gender relations, how children are valued and family and work relations. In the last section of this analysis, selected variables will be used to illustrate the *ideational climate* surrounding family formation in the NMS. There will be an analysis of attitudes clearly linked to partnership (as the basic context for childbearing) and family type (as endorsed or disapproved of). Where data are available, all the NMS will be incorporated into the analysis, as will the three selected EU15 countries.

The exact wording of the question-and-answer categories can be found in the Appendix to this chapter. To facilitate understanding, only negative or positive assessment are included in the tables—the middle-ground 'neither good nor bad' or 'neither agree nor disagree' are not shown. I will, however, sometimes refer to this number as a 'neutral' or 'tolerating' opinion.

The influence of the ideational climate, the importance of attitudes, values and economic rationality is often mentioned but not yet fully understood, as Bernardi (2003) has pointed out. Social learning, reinforcing or rejecting models, 'social contagion' and normative control are social mechanisms influencing childbearing behavior. In the IPPAS survey, questions were asked regarding the evaluation of different demographic processes and family situations. Here, I take into consideration the positive and negative attitudes, the ideas regarding situations and the processes that were favored or rejected. I assume that positively assessed processes constitute a stimulating environment, as long as negatively assessed processes are rejected or discouraged. I make the assumption that in modern societies, where sanctions do not seem to be too strong, positive evaluation and ascriptions could have a stronger influence on behavior.

4.4.1 Attitudes toward partnership forms

The relevant literature suggests that living arrangements have an effect on child-bearing propensity (eg., Pinelli *et al.*, 2002). The single status is to a large extent incompatible with parenthood, and fertility is clearly lower in situations of informal cohabitation than among those living within marriage. If this correlation remains valid, then it is important to have a picture of the attitudes of young adults toward different kinds of demographic development and partnership forms, especially toward 'living alone' and 'cohabitation.'

Living alone and living single is clearly not a desired way of life in NMS countries. In all five former Communist NMS the vast majority clearly assess the 'increasing number of people living single' as a negative tendency, with less than 5 percent assessing it as positive (*Table 4.5; Table 4.8*, first column). It is in Hungary that the greatest rejection is observed, while in the Czech Republic and Poland, strong neutral minorities are found. Results of in-depth analyses about living single in Hungary point in the same direction: singles have not chosen this living arrangement, do not want to stay single but have not found a suitable partner. Moreover, they are not satisfied with their situation (Utasi, 2003). In the selected EU15 countries people are quite divided in their assessment. We find a very high disapproval of living single in Finland and Italy and a more neutral (neither good nor bad) attitude in Austria. Furthermore, there are minimal positive attitudes in Finland. Altogether, the ideational climate is definitely not positive with regard to the growth of singlehood.

Table 4.5. Opinion on the increasing number of people who live alone (aged 18 to 34).

Countries	Positively valued (endorsed)	Negatively valued (disapproved of)
New EU member states		
Poland	4.5	61.4
Czech Republic	4.3	59.0
Slovenia	3.7	75.4
Lithuania	0.9	79.6
Hungary	0.8	91.8
Selected EU countries		
Italy	14.6	75.8
Austria	10.5	48.6
Finland	1.0	73.5

Source: International Population and Policy Acceptance Survey, own calculations.

Table 4.6. Opinion on the increasing number of people who live together unmarried (aged 18 to 34).

Countries	Positively valued (endorsed)	Negatively valued (disapproved of)
New EU member states		
Czech Republic	37.5	10.1
Slovenia	35.0	17.4
Hungary	24.5	20.8
Lithuania	22.2	20.8
Poland	21.4	29.6
Selected EU countries		
Austria	37.0	12.9
Finland	25.9	19.0
Italy	22.6	24.5

Source: International Population and Policy Acceptance Survey, own calculations.

The evaluation of the *growing importance of cohabitation* is quite similar in the NMS countries investigated. The majority of young adults have a neutral assessment of the increasing number of people cohabiting: there is neither clear support nor a clear and strong disapproval, rather a *high degree of tolerance* toward cohabitation as an increasingly important partnership form (*Table 4.6*; *Table 4.8*, second column). Above-average support can be found in Austria, the Czech Republic and Slovenia, three neighboring central European countries. An evaluation of the decreasing importance of marriage fluctuates between negative and neutral positions in the countries analysed (*Table 4.7*). In Austria, the Czech Republic and Slovenia,

Table 4.7. Opinion on the declining number of marriages (aged 18 to 34).

Countries	Positively valued (endorsed)	Negatively valued (disapproved of)
New EU member states		
Slovenia	12.2	37.6
Czech Republic	11.7	29.8
Poland	9.1	46.4
Hungary	5.1	49.1
Lithuania	3.0	55.8
Selected EU countries		
Italy	29.0	51.8
Austria	13.5	26.3
Finland	4.7	41.0

Source: International Population and Policy Acceptance Survey, own calculations.

Table 4.8. Attitudes toward partnership relations (aged 18 to 34).

Countries	Living alone as a preferred living arrangement	Living in cohabitation tolerated	Marriage is not outdated institution	Marriage is the only (exclusive) basis for living together
New EU member states				
Slovenia	5.8	87.4	77.3	15.8
Czech Republic	4.5	78.2	82.1	11.1
Hungary	4.2	83.8	85.7	21.5
Poland	4.0	78.7	89.9	27.6
Lithuania	1.6	66.3	83.3	29.4
Selected EU countries				
Finland	4.6	87.2	81.4	9.8
Italy	1.2	N/A	80.0	21.5
Austria	N/A	89.6	70.5	14.3

Source: International Population and Policy Acceptance Survey, own calculations.

more young adults are neutral, while in Hungary, Italy and Lithuania, the ratio of those negatively assessing the decreasing importance of marriage is slightly higher.

Further analysis is needed of the assessment of partnership relations today. I intended to demonstrate that singlehood (usually associated with childlessness) in most countries is not a very positively evaluated living arrangement and that the distinctions and borders between cohabitation and marriage—both legitimate options in life and/or in the life course—seem to have become blurred. Cohabitation is, however, widely tolerated and neutrally assessed but not strongly desired. Marriage is not disapproved of; for the majority of female young adults marriage is not an outdated institution (*Table 4.8*).

Table 4.9. Opinion on the increasing number of childless people (aged 18 to 34).

Countries	Positively valued (endorsed)	Negatively valued (disapproved of)
New EU member states		
Poland	8.4	57.9
Czech Republic	7.9	57.8
Slovenia	4.1	77.9
Lithuania	3.3	76.8
Hungary	2.5	84.5
Selected EU countries		
Italy	24.5	57.1
Austria	10.4	60.7
Finland	5.2	61.1

Source: International Population and Policy Acceptance Survey, own calculations.

4.4.2 Attitudes toward different fertility regimes (family forms)

Our questions regarding the different fertility regimes covered three different scenarios: childlessness, one-child family and nonmarital childbearing. Young adults clearly *reject childlessness*. In most of the countries the level of positive evaluation with regard to growing childlessness is below 10 percent (*Table 4.9*). The ratio of neutral answers is between 20 and 30 percent, and the vast majority of respondents disapproved of the increase in childlessness. The highest disapproval can be found in Hungary, Lithuania and Slovenia (around four-fifths of respondents). In the other countries the rate of disapproval was around 60 percent. The assessment of childlessness is quite homogeneous: there is no clear sign of positive attitudes, and a tolerant attitude remains in the minority.

Nor is the *only child* model positively evaluated (*Table 4.10*). In most countries no more than one-tenth of young respondents positively evaluate the increasing number of children growing up without siblings. In three countries this ratio is below 5 percent. In Italy, where the questionnaire was different, with only three possible answer categories as opposed to five in the other countries, the ratio is around one-fourth. Comparing the new member states with the old ones, we find exceptions, general patterns and countries with very low levels of approval in both groups. The negative evaluation of the trends mentioned (disapproval) is generally around 50 percent, but in many countries it is much higher. We can conclude that there is no strong support for a one-child family, and little tolerance can be found of this family form.

The attitude toward *nonmarital births* is rather divided in the former Communist countries (*Table 4.11*). We find a clear rejection of the growing number of nonmarital births in Hungary (65.3 percent) and in Poland (53.3 percent). In the

Table 4.10.   Opinion on the increasing number of children being an only child (having no brother or sister) aged 18 to 34.

Countries	Positively valued (endorsed)	Negatively valued (disapproved of)
New EU member states		
Lithuania	9.4	45.6
Poland	8.9	49.3
Czech Republic	7.7	53.1
Slovenia	3.3	66.6
Hungary	1.9	74.9
Selected EU countries		
Italy	24.1	64.0
Austria	9.3	51.3
Finland	1.8	75.0

Source: International Population and Policy Acceptance Survey, own calculations.

Table 4.11.   Opinion on the increasing number of children born outside marriage (aged 18 to 34).

Countries	Positively valued (endorsed)	Negatively valued (disapproved of)
New EU member states		
Lithuania	12.4	23.8
Czech Republic	12.3	23.2
Slovenia	12.2	30.5
Poland	5.0	53.3
Hungary	3.3	65.3
Selected EU countries		
Italy	30.1	50.5
Austria	17.4	22.4
Finland	15.7	23.1

Source: International Population and Policy Acceptance Survey, own calculations.

other eastern countries (Czech Republic, Lithuania, Slovenia) a tolerant attitude is widespread. There are strong differences in attitudes in the selected EU15 countries. The trend is rather positively evaluated in Austria, tolerated in Finland and disapproved of in Italy. If we compare the attitudes with the prevalence of nonmarital births (see *Figure 4.3*), the differences in attitudes correspond to the share of nonmarital births.

Table 4.12. Feeling completely happy and satisfied just staying at home in modern society, females aged 18 to 34.

Countries	Agree	Disagree
New EU member states		
Lithuania	82.8	2.1
Poland	70.3	11.6
Czech Republic	69.3	9.0
Slovenia	62.5	13.0
Hungary	56.2	13.9
Selected EU countries		
Italy	79.4	20.6
Austria	54.8	25.4
Finland	29.9	33.6

Source: International Population and Policy Acceptance Survey, own calculations.

4.4.3 Value of children

For a preliminary glance at the cultural meaning of children in different countries, three indicators were selected from the IPPAS as measurements of the value of children. The selection is restricted, as some items were not identical in the questionnaire in all countries. The three components are as follows:

1. Happiness in modern society achieved only by staying at home with the children;
2. Satisfaction with the parental role as sole identity; and
3. Enjoyment of life (fun) with children.

A first look at the distribution of answers clearly shows that there is an overall positive attitude toward all the components of the value of children mentioned. However, the level of agreement and neutral assessment, but not that of the disagreements, vary according to countries and components.

Regarding the importance of *children and home as an exclusive source of happiness* in modern society (*Table 4.12*), in the former Communist countries, support for this statement varies from 56.2 percent (Hungary) to 82.8 percent (Lithuania), and overall there is a clear positive consensus. Variations can be found not in terms of disagreement but in terms of the proportion of neutral attitudes. In the selected EU15 countries the assessment is more varied, occurring mainly in the share of positive and *neutral assessments*. While in Italy four-fifths agree, in Finland the ratio of support is only 30 percent (*Table 4.12*).

Table 4.13. Being perfectly satisfied with life if you have been a good parent, females aged 18 to 34.

Countries	Agree	Disagree
New EU member states		
Lithuania	87.9	3.3
Hungary	84.0	2.7
Poland	80.0	5.5
Czech Republic	73.0	7.1
Slovenia	66.2	14.7
Selected EU countries		
Italy	97.8	2.2
Finland	47.2	28.9
Austria	–	–

Source: International Population and Policy Acceptance Survey, own calculations.

Table 4.14. Always enjoying life with children, females aged 18 to 34.

Countries	Agree	Disagree
New EU member states		
Poland	94.2	0.2
Lithuania	92.0	1.7
Hungary	87.1	1.7
Czech Republic	83.2	1.6
Slovenia	81.4	6.1
Selected EU countries		
Austria	76.5	8.3
Finland	50.3	20.0
Italy	–	–

Source: International Population and Policy Acceptance Survey, own calculations.

The *assessment of the parental role as a sole identity* in modern society differs once more among countries (*Table 4.13*). Strong support can be found in the former Communist NMS, and there is a strong gap between Finland and Italy. Strong disagreement can also be found in Finland and Slovenia. (Naturally, as far as this variable is concerned, one should be aware that the parental role is not offset against other possible roles in modern society.)

Enjoying life with children is assessed in mostly the same way in the countries under investigation (*Table 4.14*). In all former Communist NMS discussed here, more than 80 percent of the young adults enjoy their time with children, and in the three EU15 countries only in Finland is there a low level of agreement.

Thus, although mainly positive attitudes were found in the countries investigated with regard to the different components of the value of children, there are remarkable country-specific differences. If one compares the NMS with the selected

EU15 countries, one finds greater homogeneity in the former than in the latter. The attitudes of Austrian, Finnish and Italian young adults differ quite remarkably.

4.5 Summary: Some Remarks

The aim of this chapter was to give a brief account of basic fertility trends in the new EU member states and to deal in somewhat greater detail with one aspect of the determinants of fertility, namely, to describe selected attitudinal conditions of fertility decisions and (future) trends.

The current fertility situation of the countries is well documented in the literature; the relatively high homogeneity of the period fertility level and the heterogeneity of nonmarital births in the NMS countries were both stressed. It was also possible to state that diversity seems to be even greater among the EU15 countries. Additionally, it was found that although the former Communist NMS experienced the same societal transition during the last one and one-half decades, their fertility development—their path to low fertility—was not the same. Furthermore, the relationship between partnership formation and fertility was stressed somewhat more strongly, and it was pointed out that the transition is not yet over.

The second part of the chapter was based on the assumption that in modern societies, with the growth of opportunities and with social action increasingly being the result of individual decisions (Beck, 1986), subjective components (values, attitudes and intentions) are becoming more and more important. A high enough anticipated number of children is a prerequisite for fertility development; moreover, positive, supportive attitudes toward children in families and long-term partnerships can contribute (as a motivating belief and/or a normative control) to achieving the expected number of children. Naturally, the structural features of a society, such as the standard of living, labor-market security and child-related welfare programs and provision should be taken into consideration; nor, finally, must gender relations (facts and beliefs) be left out. It was not, however, possible to discuss all the components mentioned, only some selected measures. It was argued that the quite high level of expected family size together with the negative attitude toward child-poor families is a solid basis for expecting a slight reversal in fertility development in the NMS countries. However, it is still too soon to hazard any prediction of the actual timing and scale of any future changes in fertility.

Appendix

Attitudinal questions about partnership and family (IPPAS):

Opinion on:

a) The increasing number of couples who live together unmarried;
b) The increasing number of couples who decide to remain childless;
c) The declining number of marriages;
d) The declining number of births;
e) The increasing number of children being an only child;
f) The increasing number of persons who live alone; and
g) The increasing number of births among unmarried couples.

(*Answer categories*: 1: Excellent; 2: Good; 3: Neither good, nor bad; 4: Bad; 5: Very bad; *Italy*: only three codes)

Marriage and/or cohabitation, Agreement statements (three-category scale):

a) Marriage is an outdated institution.
b) It is acceptable for a couple to live together without intending to get married.
c) Marriage is the only acceptable way of living together for a man and a woman.

(*Answer categories*: 1: Agree; 2: Do not agree; 3: Neither agree nor disagree/no opinion)

Value of children questions: Agreement statements (five-category scale):

a) The only place where you can feel completely happy and at ease is at home with your children.
b) I always enjoy having children near me.
c) You can be perfectly satisfied with life if you have been a good parent.

(*Answer categories*: 1: Strongly agree; 2: Agree; 3: Neither agree nor disagree; 4: Disagree; 5: Strongly disagree)

References

Adamski, W., Machonin, P. and Zapf, W. (eds) (2002) *Structural Change and Modernisation in Post-Socialist Societies*, Hamburg, Germany: Reinhold Krämer Verlag.

Barber, J.S., Axin, W.G. and Thornton, A. (2002) 'The Influence of Attitudes on Family Formation Processes,' in Lesthaeghe, R. (ed) *Meaning and Choice: Value Orientation and Life Course Decisions*, The Hague, The Netherlands: Netherlands Interdisciplinary Demographic Institute, pp. 45–95.

Beck, U. (1986) *Risikogesellschaft*, Frankfurt am Main, Germany: Suhrkampf [in German].

Bernardi, L. (2003) 'Channels of Social Influence on Reproduction,' *Population Research and Policy Review*, **22**: 527–555.

Bongaarts, J. and Feeney, G. (1998) 'On the Quantum and Tempo of Fertility,' *Population and Development Review*, **24**: 271–292.

Bumpass, L.L. and Westoff, C.F. (1970) *The Later Years of Childbearing*, Princeton, NJ, USA: Princeton University Press.

Council of Europe (2002) *Recent Demographic Developments in Europe*, Strasbourg, France: Council of Europe.

Crimmins, E.M., Easterlin, R. and Saito, Y. (1991) 'Preference Changes among American Youth, 1976–86,' *Population and Development Review*, **17**(1): 115–133.

Fahey, T. and Spéder, Zs. (2003) *Fertility and Family Issues in an Enlarged Europe*, Dublin, Ireland: European Foundation for Improvement of Living and Working Conditions.

Fishbein, M., Jaccard, J.J., Davidson, A.B., Ajzen, I. and Loken, B. (1980) 'Predicting and Understanding Family Planning Behaviors: Beliefs, Attitudes and Intentions,' in Fishbein M. and Ajzen, I. (eds) *Understanding Attitudes and Predicting Social Behavior*, Upper Saddle River, NJ, USA: Prentice-Hall, pp. 132–147.

Frejka, T. and Sardon, J.-P. (2003) 'Fertility Trends and Prospects in Central and Eastern Europe: The Cohort Perspective,' in Kotowska I.E. and Jozwiak, J. (eds) *Population of Central and Eastern Europe: Challenges and Opportunities*, Warsaw, Poland: Statistical Publishing Establishment, pp. 91–116.

Goldstein, J., Lutz, W. and Testa, M.R. (2003) 'The Emergence of Sub-Replacement Family Size Ideals in Europe,' *European Demographic Research Papers*, **2**: 27, Vienna, Austria: Vienna Institute of Demography of the Austrian Academy of Sciences.

Kohler, H.-P. and Philipov, D. (2001) 'Tempo Effects in the Fertility Decline in Eastern Europe: Evidence from Bulgaria, the Czech Republic, Hungary, Poland and Russia,' *European Journal of Population*, **17**(1): 37–60.

Kohler, H.-P., Billari, F.C. and Ortega, J.A. (2002) 'The Emergence of Lowest-Low Fertility in Europe during the 1990s,' *Population and Development Review*, **28**(4): 641–680.

Kotowska, I.E. and Jozwiak, J. (eds) (2003) *Population of Central and Eastern Europe: Challenges and Opportunities*, Warsaw, Poland: Statistical Publishing Establishment.

Lesthaeghe, R. (ed) (2002) *Meaning and Choice: Value Orientation and Life Course Decision*, The Hague, The Netherlands: NIDI CBGS Publications, pp. 45–95.

Lesthaeghe, R. and Moors, G. (2000) 'Recent Trends in Fertility and Household Formation in the Industrialized World,' *Review of Population and Social Policy*, **9**: 121–170.

Lesthaeghe, R. and Surkyn, J. (2004) *When History Moves On: The Foundations and Diffusion of a Second Demographic Transition*, Paper presented at the 12th Biennial Conference of the Australian Population Association, 'Population and Society: Issues, Research, Policy,' held 15–17 September, Canberra, Australia.

Macura, M., Kadri, A., Mochizuki-Sternberg, Y. and Lara Garcia, J. (2000) 'Fertility Decline in the Transition Economies, 1989–1998: Economic and Social Factors Revisited,' *Economic Survey of Europe 2000, no 1*, New York, USA: United Nations.

Philipov, D. (2003) 'Fertility in Times of Discontinuous Societal Change,' in Kotowska, I.E. and Jozwiak, J. (eds) *Population of Central and Eastern Europe: Challenges and Opportunities*, Warsaw, Poland: Statistical Publishing Establishment, pp. 665–690.

Philipov, D. and Dorbritz, J. (2004) 'Demographic Consequences of Economic Transition in Countries of Central and Eastern Europe,' *Population Studies*, **39**, Strasbourg, France: Council of Europe Publishing, See http://book.coe.int/EN/ficheouvrage.php?PAGEID=36&lang=EN&produit_aliasid=1717/ accessed in December 2005.

Pinelli, A., De Rose, A., Di Gulio, P. and Rosina, A. (2002) 'Interrelationship Between Partnership and Fertility Behavior,' in Macura, M. and Beets, G. (eds) *Dynamics of Fertility and Partnership in Europe. Insights and Lessons from Comparative Research*, vol 1, New York, USA: United Nations, pp. 77–98.

Spéder, Zs. (2001) 'Turning Points of the Life Course. Concept and Design of the Hungarian Social and Demographic Panel Survey,' See http://www.dpa.demografia.hu/ accessed in December 2005. For article in Hungarian, see *Demográfia*, **44**(2–3): 305–320.

Utasi, Á. (2003) 'Independent, Never Married People in Their Thirties: Remaining Single,' *Demográfia*, special edition, **46**: 73–94, Budapest, Hungary: Demographic Research Institute.

Zapf, W. (1996) 'Die Modernisierungstheorie und unterschiedliche Pfade der gesellschaftlichen Entwicklung,' *Leviathan*, **24**(1): 63–77 [in German].

Chapter 5

Alternative Paths for Future European Fertility: Will the Birth Rate Recover or Continue to Decline?

Wolfgang Lutz

Over the last decade the European population has experienced rates of reproduction that are at historically unprecedented low levels. In the 25-member European Union (EU), the current generation of adults is being replaced by one that is less than two-thirds its size. As demonstrated in the introduction to the present volume, this low level of fertility will have significant and lasting effects on Europe's age structure and population size. The last two chapters have described in some detail how fertility rates have been changing over the past decades in different parts of Europe and shown that the trends are far from uniform across the continent. They have also discussed the social and economic factors that have been associated with these trends and the role of public policies in influencing them.

In this chapter we will focus explicitly on the future. We will try to look at the coming generation of Europeans: Europeans who have yet to start childbearing, some of whom, in fact, are still unborn. We will particularly try to assess how many are likely to be born over the coming decades. One section will argue that the social sciences have yet to produce a useful theory with the predictive power to anticipate future European fertility trends. Despite the lack of a general theory, however, some theoretical arguments suggest that, in certain cases, fertility rates will recover and, in other cases, continue to decline. We will discuss some of the most influential arguments that have been published in the scientific literature—six that suggest higher future fertility and eight indicating continued fertility decline.

5.1   The Lack of a Theory with Predictive Power in Post-Demographic Transition Populations

Explanations and projections of fertility trends in different parts of the world have been generally guided by the paradigm of demographic transition which assumes that after an initial decline in death rates, birth rates— after a certain lag—also start to fall. In this general form the model has received overwhelming empirical support in capturing the remarkable fertility changes that happened during the twentieth century.

The demographic transition began in the late eighteenth and nineteenth centuries in today's more-developed countries (MDCs) and spread to today's less-developed countries (LDCs) in the latter half of the twentieth century (Notestein 1945; Davis 1954; Coale 1973; Davis 1991). The conventional theory of demographic transition predicts that as living standards rise and health conditions improve, mortality rates first decline and then, somewhat later, so too do fertility rates. Demographic transition theory has evolved as a generalization of the typical sequence of events in what are now MDCs, where mortality rates declined comparatively gradually from the late 1700s, then more rapidly in the late 1800s to be joined, after a gap of up to 100 years, by declining fertility rates. Different societies experienced transition in different ways, and today various regions of the world are following distinctive paths (Tabah 1989). Nonetheless, the broad result was, and is, a gradual transition from a small, slow-growing population with high mortality and high fertility to a large, slow-growing or even slowly shrinking population with low mortality and low fertility rates. During the transition itself, population growth accelerates because the decline in death rates precedes the decline in birth rates.

Unfortunately, the demographic transition paradigm—although useful for explaining global demographic trends during the twentieth century and having strong predictive power in terms of projecting future trends in countries that still have high fertility—essentially has nothing to say about the future of fertility in Europe (Lutz, 1994). The recently popular notion of a second demographic transition is a plausible way of describing a bundle of behavioral and normative changes that took place recently in Europe, but it has little or no predictive power. In fact, the social sciences as a whole have yet to come up with a useful theory to predict the future fertility level of post–demographic transition societies. All that forecasters can do is try to define a likely range of uncertainty. As the fertility transition is irreversible, we are sure that the fertility rate will not go back to pretransitional high levels, say, to above a value of 3.0. There is no equally convincing argument about a lower bound, although many demographers tend to think that fertility is unlikely to fall below 1.0 for long periods. But where fertility will come to stay within such a range is very uncertain, and there is a real possibility that future fertility will show the strong fluctuations we have seen over the past decades. Hence, thinking in terms of a long-term stable level—as underlies the population projections of the United Nations and of many statistical agencies—may be the wrong way of thinking about the future.

5.2 Arguments in Support of Assuming Higher Fertility

(a) The homeostasis argument

The usual interpretation of the demographic transition theory is that an initial equilibrium between high birth rates and high death rates is disturbed by declining mortality which, in due course, triggers a fertility decline that will bring birth and death rates back into equilibrium at low levels. However, history has shown that fertility declines with all their irregularities and national particularities have not generally stopped at replacement level but have continued to decline further. The homeostasis argument would stress that this is simply an overshooting that will be reversed after some inevitable societal adjustments. Recently, this has been most explicitly expressed by Vishnevsky (1991) who does not see fertility levels as the sum of individual behavior but rather as one aspect in the evolution of a system that determines behavior. He believes that the development of the demographic system is directed by a proper, inherent goal. In the process of self-organization the system aims at self-maintenance and survival. For human beings at a certain stage of evolution, a new and higher goal is assumed to appear that goes beyond pure population survival, namely, one of maintaining homeostasis in the reproduction of the population, even in the face of considerable fluctuations in external conditions (Vishnevsky, 1991, p. 265).

It is difficult to test this hypothesis empirically because it does not specify the time horizon within which fertility rates would recover. In Lutz (1994) it was mentioned that the then recent fertility increase in Sweden, a forerunner of many other social issues, might possibly be seen as an example of such a homeostatic response. But since the early 1990s, fertility has declined in Sweden from 2.1 to 1.5. Another weakness of this argument is that nothing is said about the mechanisms and motivations at the individual level that should induce couples to have more children. It therefore remains a philosophical argument without predictive power. At that level, the homeostasis argument still seems a worthwhile consideration, although it is highly controversial and authors such as Westoff (1991) criticize the assumption of a 'magnetic force' toward replacement.

(b) Assumption of fertility cycles

Several views summarized under this heading have in common that they believe the present low level of period fertility to be just the bottom of a cycle and that the future will bring an upward trend. These views can be grouped into arguments with respect to the timing of fertility within cohorts and to intergenerational fertility fluctuations. The first argument was based on the observation that in many countries the recent declines in total fertility were accompanied by declines in the fertility rates of younger women. Hence, one could assume that the observed trends reflect only a delay in childbearing (the timing of fertility) and do not indicate a decline in the number of children a woman has over her life span (the quantum of fertility). As there has been much new writing on the tempo effect in recent years, this issue will be treated as a separate argument listed below as (e).

The other view of cycles focuses on intergenerational effects. Here, it is assumed that the fertility level of the parent generation is a determinant of their children's reproductive behavior. Best known in this context is the relative income hypothesis of Easterlin (1980). In short, this hypothesis assumes that fertility is determined by income relative to aspirations, with cohort size determining income: generation 1 has low relative income and low fertility; generation 2 grows up with low aspirations for wealth but, finding labor market conditions advantageous because there are few competitors, has a high relative income and high fertility; generation 3 is numerous and has high aspirations, and this results in low relative income and low fertility. Empirically, this model fits nicely to the United States baby boom in the 1960s and the subsequent fertility decline. But it is only half a cycle. A new baby boom has, thus far, failed to materialize. For other countries even the historical application fits less well. There are a number of conceptual problems, such as the fact that within a generation, fertility is unevenly distributed among families— some have many children, others only one (see discussion in Lutz [1989])—and the fact that women have children at different ages, which soon smoothes out any cycle. But even if this assumed mechanism is not a dominating factor for fertility trends, it may well play a role as one among several factors, with the other factors simply being more dominant for the time being.

(c) Fertility-enhancing public policies

The discussion about possible government policies that aim to increase the fertility level is as old as the discussion of the perceived negative influences of such policies. Fernández-Cordón has covered this issue extensively in Chapter 3. In short, both the political feasibility and the effectiveness of such policies are unclear at this stage. Any assessment is complicated by the fact that many social policies, ranging from labor laws to pension systems, have implications for childbearing behavior, even if they are not explicitly pronatalist or antinatalist. In its 2000 assessment of the state of our knowledge about future demographic trends, the United States National Research Council (2000, p. 107) gives a succinct summary:

> In various ways, industrial societies already provide various rewards, but using them to deliberately manipulate fertility is a sensitive issue, potentially involving substantial economic transfers, and likely to be contested. Whether such policies will be adopted in specific countries depends on the indeterminate outcome of political struggles that are difficult even to visualize at this time. Even if such policies were adopted, the fertility response would not be predictable.

There is little to be added to this statement except, perhaps, that over the past few years the public debate has become more heated. With the retirement of the baby boom generation (born in the early 1960s) finally appearing on the radar screen of social security and pension planners with their 25–30 year time horizon, the discussion has now gone well beyond the population-forecasting community. Economic policy groups at the highest level have started to give the demographic challenge top priority. A study by the European Banking Federation (2004), in which the chief economists of over 4,500 commercial banks in Europe highlighted the economic dangers of population aging, stated as the first of its three main recommendations: 'Increasing the birth rate is particularly important.' It is safe to expect this discussion to intensify over the coming years.

As for the tool box of policy measures that could influence fertility rates, there has recently been a new contribution in the proposal of tempo policies, that is, policies that aim not at the number of children that women have in the course of their life but rather at the timing of the births—this, in an attempt to prevent a further increase in the mean age of childbearing (see discussion later in this chapter). Lutz and Skirbekk (2004) have recently proposed that such tempo policies could be operationalized by reforming the education system to shorten the period of education—which typically precedes childbearing—and thus exert downward pressure on the mean age of childbearing while still enabling the same level of education. Such reforms are already under way in many countries for reasons unrelated to demography and, hence, could also be given a demographic rationale.

(d) National identity and ethnic rivalry

While macroeconomic concerns, such as the pensions gap, cannot be expected to influence individual reproductive behavior without public policy intervention, this may not be the case with the issue of national identity. Fears related to the ethnic composition of the population and ingroup–outgroup feelings can be powerful emotional forces that may directly influence individual reproductive behavior. In Lutz (1994) examples of this were found in Israel/Palestine, Northern Ireland and the Baltic states, where clear rivalry between two population groups seemed to be associated with higher fertility levels than might have been expected both from their socioeconomic standing and when compared with other populations. One could hypothesize that such fertility-enhancing ethnic rivalry could be spread to other industrialized countries, as migration establishes new ethnic minorities. But the empirical trends of the past decade have not confirmed this hypothesis. On the contrary, there are strong counterexamples, such as francophone Canadians, non-Hispanic Californians or Germans living in cities with a large Turkish population, all of whom have very low fertility and where evident ethnolinguistic rivalry is expressed by means other than fertility levels. Furthermore, the most recent demographic trends from the Baltic states show that the fertility rates of both ethnic groups—Russians and nationals—have fallen significantly. Hence, it looks unlikely that ethnic rivalry will become a significant fertility-enhancing force in Europe in the coming decades.

(e) An end to the tempo effect

Although demographers have long known that period fertility rates, such as the most often used total fertility rate (TFR), are distorted by tempo effects, it is only in recent years that more systematic attention has been paid to this phenomenon and that tempo-adjusted fertility rates have been proposed. The tempo effect refers to the fact that period fertility rates are artificially depressed at times when the mean childbearing age increases. It was estimated that, at the EU15 level, the measured fertility rate of around 1.5 children per woman would, in fact, be more like 1.8 if the increase in the mean childbearing age suddenly stopped (Lutz *et al.*, 2003). The close relationship between low period fertility and increasing mean childbearing age can also be clearly seen from trend data for the new member countries of central and eastern Europe. *Figure 5.1* shows that after decades of relative stability, the TFR began to decline steeply around 1990 at the beginning of the major political and economic transformations in those countries. *Figure 5.2* shows that this decline was associated with an equally sudden increase in the mean childbearing age. In other words, women in these countries had started to postpone childbearing. But even if they all postpone having children (and completed cohort fertility does not change), period fertility, which is currently depressed, will have significant and lasting effects on the absolute numbers of children born and will therefore represent a force toward population decline and accelerated population aging.

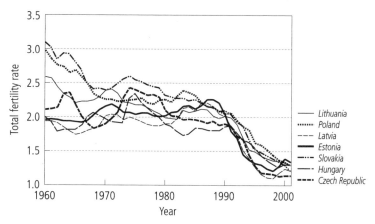

Source: Council of Europe (2003).

Figure 5.1. Central and eastern Europe, total fertility rate, 1960–2001.

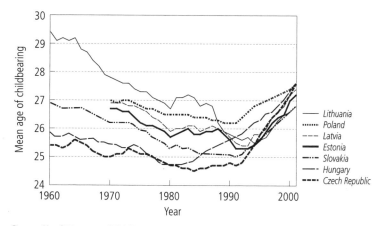

Source: Council of Europe (2003).

Figure 5.2. Central and eastern Europe, mean age of childbearing, 1960–2001.

This so-called tempo effect on fertility has recently received considerable attention in the demographic literature (e.g., Bongaarts and Feeney, 1998; Kohler and Philipov, 2001). It is based on the analytical insight that fertility is currently low in Europe for two different reasons. First, women are postponing giving birth, resulting in fewer births in the calendar years during which this delay happens (the tempo effect). Second, even after adjusting for this tempo effect, fertility is below replacement level (the so-called quantum of fertility). If women do not completely forego giving birth, delayed childbearing does not affect the total number of births

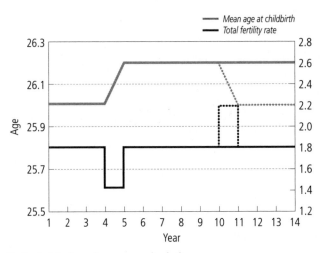

Source: Hypothetical data based on own calculations.

Figure 5.3. Illustration of the tempo effect in which an increase in the mean age of childbearing (gray line) in year 4 results in a depressed period total fertility rate (TFR) in that year. The dotted lines give the case in which the mean age decreases again and there is a positive tempo distortion.

women will have over the course of their lives (the cohort fertility), but it still lowers period birth rates as long as postponement continues. *Figure 5.3* illustrates this somewhat counterintuitive phenomenon graphically. Let the gray line be the mean age at childbearing which is constant until year 4, then increases by 0.2 years (roughly the annual increase currently experienced in Europe) over the fifth year and stays constant thereafter; the period fertility rate will then be lower in the fifth year (here 1.4 instead of 1.8) because some women who would otherwise have had their children in the fifth year waited until the sixth year. And in the sixth year the period fertility will be back to its old level if the mean age at childbearing is again constant at the higher level. It is important to note that this process will not, by itself, result in a compensatory higher period fertility rate in the later years unless the mean age falls again (as indicated by the dotted lines in year 10) and unless there is an inflated period fertility during this year.

In the context of tempo analysis, much of the demographic work to date has focused on estimating fertility rates that adjust for this tempo effect, seeing it as a disturbance that should be eliminated to enable a 'purer' fertility measure to be produced, namely, the tempo-adjusted total fertility rate. Lutz *et al.* (2003) turn this approach upside down and focus on the tempo effect, not as a problem to be ironed out but rather as a focus of interest that could provide a leverage point for possible attempts to influence the level of period birth rates, something we call tempo policies. Quantitatively, these show that at the EU15 level, a hypothetical end to postponement would bring the period TFR up from its current 1.5 level to 1.8, a development that over the coming decades would significantly moderate population decline and aging. Their scenarios also show that about 45 percent of the calculated population decline is due to the tempo effect. In terms of aging, they show that a continuation of the tempo effect for the next 10 to 40 years would imply the need for an additional 500 to 1,500 million person–years of workers to support the elderly population for the rest of the century, as compared to a no-delay scenario (hypothetical immediate end to the tempo effect). This clearly demonstrates that the changing age of childbearing represents a very important force in population dynamics in Europe and one that requires special attention.

In real life some of the postponed births will never take place; moreover, increases in the mean childbearing age tend to reduce the quantum of the fertility of the cohorts concerned. This can arise for various reasons, ranging from instability of partnerships to involvement in the workforce, but it is particularly due to the decline in fecundability (the probability of becoming pregnant) with age, a decline that accelerates for women after the age of 35. This tempo–quantum interaction is an important additional factor when studying the consequences of postponement for fertility rates.

Will the fertility-depressing effect of delays in childbearing continue in the future? Some countries where the mean childbearing age is already around 30 years, for example, France, The Netherlands and Spain, have recently seen a leveling off of the increase. But in many countries, particularly those of central Europe, the mean age at which women give birth is still much lower. If we assume some sort of social convergence in Europe, this would imply that some of these countries may well experience many more years of increasing age at childbearing and hence, a fertility-depressing tempo effect. And there are currently very strong social and economic forces in our society that exert pressure toward later childbearing. A few worth mentioning are the expansion of education, high youth unemployment and an increasingly competitive work situation for young people who do find a job.

But there is no doubt that at some point, postponement will have to come to an end, and at that point in time, period fertility rates would again increase to the level suggested by the tempo-adjusted fertility rate (1.8 instead of 1.4 in the above example), always assuming that the quantum of fertility did not decline further. Hence, several authors expect period fertility rates to recover somewhat over the coming years, particularly in those countries where the mean childbearing age is already rather high.

(f) Rock-bottom fertility

Finally, in the recent literature some authors have suggested that the fertility level we are seeing in today's countries of lowest fertility is probably the lowest we will ever see. This assumes that there is some minimal (rock-bottom) fertility level below which fertility rates will not fall (at least, not for long periods). Authors have made these assumptions for differing reasons. Sobotka (2004) has shown, based on tempo-effect reasoning, that in none of the countries with recent period fertility rates below 1.3 (lowest-low fertility) have the tempo-adjusted fertility rates fallen below that level. He thus concludes that at least in the near-term future, 1.3 seems to be a bottom level of fertility that is unlikely to be breached.

More substantive reasoning comes from the recent work of Foster (2000), who argues that there is a genetic predisposition toward nurturing behaviors that will always lead men and women to have children. She finds three intertwining groups of concepts in the motivation for parenthood that are clustered around the ideas of love, passing on genes and finding some meaning in life, in particular, (i) the desire to love and nurture a child and to create a family, (ii) the desire to have a stake in the future, to pass on one's own genes and those of one's partner and to live on in someone else and (iii) the desire to find a meaning and purpose in life beyond attaining individual educational, economic and career aims. If true, these arguments make it unlikely that human fertility will approach zero, although this kind of qualitative research cannot predict the level at which it will stop falling.

In a similar vein, Antonio Golini (1998) has speculated what might be the lowest possible level of cohort fertility. Simulating a case in which 20 to 30 percent of all women remain childless and the remainder have just one child, he comes up with the estimate of 0.7 to 0.8 children per woman as the lower bound for cohort fertility. But what guarantees are there that childlessness will not increase to above 30 percent? In former West Germany childlessness is already estimated to be above 40 percent for women with an academic education. In other words, it is very difficult to make the case for any specific level of fertility (other than zero) as a lower bound. And, as it turns out, some of these estimates are still substantially lower than those currently being experienced in the countries of lowest fertility.

5.3   Arguments in Support of Assuming Lower Fertility

(a) Trend toward individualism

According to the sociological theories of Tönnies (1887) and Durkheim (1902), the process of modernization is characterized by a transition from 'community' (in German, *Gemeinschaft*) to 'society' (in German, *Gesellschaft*). While community refers to a lasting and complete living together under a relatively stable structure, society means a mere proximity of persons who are independent of one another and is characterized by relatively open structures. In the process of transition, an increasing number of functions that used to be met by the family have now been taken over by anonymous institutions. This means not only an increase in equality and personal freedom but also in individualism, as well as a weakening of inter-personal bonds. Regarding the future of the family, Hoffmann-Nowotny (1987) assumes that the trend of increasing differentiation as well as multiple and partial integration will continue, especially for women. From a sociological point of view, he concludes that there is little reason to believe that the family as we know it can and will survive as the mainstream model for future living patterns. This view is not too different from the notion of the second demographic transition put forward by Lesthaeghe (1983) and van de Kaa (1987) to characterize a new phase of de-mographic behavior that expresses itself through a lower propensity for marriage, a higher instability of unions, increase in nonmarital fertility and lower total fertility.

Another psychological aspect of this supposed trend toward individualism is that men and women are increasingly reluctant to make decisions that have long-term consequences and that clearly limit their future freedom of choice. Moreover, the decision to have a child predetermines many choices for the subsequent two decades; once a child is born, second thoughts are impossible. If the trend toward greater mobility in all aspects of life were to continue, this could well mean fewer responsible men and women daring to become parents.

While there is little empirical basis for evaluating the validity of the presump-tions for the future described above, they do seem to be powerful arguments and plausible explanations for recent trends. If, in the future, this trend goes to an ex-treme, counterforces could be mobilized to compensate for some of the negative aspects of this. But a return to traditional patterns of community with their restric-tions on individual freedom is very unlikely. Most of the following arguments are more or less related to this general continued modernization argument, but they should be mentioned because they emphasize specific relevant aspects of it.

(b) Economic independence of women

One recent trend, often singled out as a dominant feature of societal change, is the increasing economic independence of women. Female participation in the labor force has been increasing steeply in virtually all industrialized countries over the last decades. The increase has been strongest in Scandinavia, where labor force par-ticipation is almost universal among adult women below the age of 50. Female ac-tivity rates in North America are not much lower; and in Italy over the last decades, female participation in the labor force has increased by more than one-third. One might expect such a fundamental change in the role and orientation of women with respect to economic activity to be associated with changing reproductive patterns, unless work and childrearing are fully compatible.

One must be cautious, however, when pointing to female economic activity as a major determinant of declining fertility. It may also be that the lower number of children desired by women motivates them to enter the labor force rather than stay at home, or there may be a joint driving force behind both trends. This is supported by the evidence that in several countries fertility rates have recently recovered, despite very high and still-increasing female participation in the labor force. The key question in this multifaceted issue seems to be how women can combine parenthood with participation in the labor market (e.g., Kiernan, 1991). This may be a decisive question for future European birth rates. While, even with flexible legal regulations and good child-care systems, career-oriented women on average will not have very large families, for more family-oriented women policies aimed at improving compatibility may make a difference.

More recent studies have pointed to the changing nature of the correlation between female employment and fertility across European countries. Engelhardt and Prskawetz (2004) have shown that, around 1985, this correlation changed from significantly negative to significantly positive, in other words, that higher female employment, over the past two decades, has been associated with higher fertility in Europe. This seems to be mostly a function of the dichotomy between high fertility countries that also have high female participation in the labor force (most strongly in France and Scandinavia) and the southern countries with low female employment and low fertility. In the latter countries, because of the conservative social norms and the associated compatibility problems, women still have to make a fundamental choice between pursuing a career or having a family. An increasing number of young women choose the former, thus bringing down the fertility rates. In France and the Nordic countries, women are more easily able to combine both.

(c) Instability of partnership

As mentioned above, marital stability has been declining almost universally in all industrialized countries. Part of the reason for this phenomenon clearly lies in the increasing economic independence of women, as discussed above. Women are no longer forced for economic reasons to stay in an unsatisfactory union if they earn an independent income. Another reason may lie in the general increase in mobility in modern industrialized societies and in a declining threshold in the level of dissatisfaction necessary to attempt to change conditions. Whatever the social and psychological reasons may be, a young couple today can count less on actually staying together for at least 20 years, the minimum time required for two parents to raise a child.

There is increasing evidence from empirical studies (Kiernan, 1992) that it is actually more harmful to children for their parents to separate than was assumed in the past, with adverse effects not only on social behavior indicators and intellectual performance but also on a child's happiness and feelings of security. Thus, responsible prospective parents, sensitive to the likely trauma of parental separation on children, may, if they have doubts about the stability of their partnership, decide not to have children. This is true of marriages and, even more so, of the increasing number of nonmarital unions, which, as indicated by statistical data, for example, in Sweden (Prinz, 1995), seem to have much lower stability.

One possible counterargument would be that remarriage (or the formation of a new nonmarital union) may actually be an incentive to have an additional child to strengthen the relationship between the new partners. Although this may happen in individual cases, empirical analysis on data for Finland, cross-classified by marital status and number of children (Lutz, 1993), show that although a slight effect of this kind exists, it is clearly not significant for total fertility.

(d) Consumerism and use of time

Commentators on the recent fertility decline often mention the increase in consumerism as a basic underlying cause. Under this form of materialism, people would supposedly prefer to invest in their own pleasures than in children; they would rather buy a new car than have another child; they would rather spend their time watching television than changing diapers. Underlying this view is the notion that having children is work and not fun. As pointed out by Keyfitz (1991), though couples in the past had to work harder and for longer hours to earn a living, they still found time to have plenty of children. The extra leisure time they have now, however, is not being spent in having children. If one defines having children as work, one must talk about the opportunity cost involved. In the words of Keyfitz (1991, p. 239): 'No one complains about the opportunity cost of having sex. Thus, to talk about the opportunity cost of children indeed highlights the problem of non-childbearing.' He suggests thinking of a work–fun continuum and trying to move childbearing toward the fun end of that continuum.

Whether or not childbearing, and especially childrearing, will become a more favored leisure-time activity of men and women will depend on the trade-offs between fun and burden. Some European cities already have more dogs than children. Obviously, the work–fun balance is more favorable for pets which are less of a commitment and, in the worst-case scenario, can always be given away. This argument clearly suggests that unless the burden of having children is diminished or the reward of having children is enhanced, the balance for childbearing will continue to be negative.

(e) Improving contraceptives

This argument is less concerned with changing values but works more at a mechanistic level. It can be demonstrated empirically that, in all industrialized societies, a significant number of children are born without being planned, either for that specific time period or at all. For unplanned children, demographers often distinguish between timing failure (premature pregnancy) and quantum failure (unwanted pregnancy). Both types could be reduced by more efficient contraceptive use; for the latter this would clearly imply lower fertility; for the former the issue is theoretically immaterial. In practice, however, one can assume that a certain fraction of the births categorized as timing failures might not have come about at a later point in time because of changing living conditions, such as, for instance, disruption of a union or a more demanding job. With respect to unwanted pregnancies, Westoff *et al.* (1987) estimate that for a number of countries of low fertility, completely efficient contraception would bring fertility rates down by somewhat less than 10 percent and would also make a significant contribution to bringing down the number of abortions.

Presently, we are still far away from a perfect contraceptive that requires no effort to use and has no negative side effects. An increasing number of women report being tired of using the pill, yet sterilization is not appealing to all (especially in continental Europe) because of its irreversibility. A hypothetical new 'perfect' contraceptive, without any side effects, that is taken only once and needs a procedure to reverse it for the woman to become pregnant, would certainly change the picture because in numerous cases of ambivalence and risk taking this would clearly inhibit pregnancy. Going to the doctor or not going to the doctor (as is the case now) in order to have a child would make quite a difference to future fertility levels.

(f) Declining ideal family size

Despite declining fertility rates over the past two decades, the ideal size of family desired by men and women, as collected in various surveys, showed a surprisingly consistent figure of well above two children on average in most countries. The discrepancy between high expressed preferences and actual low fertility has given rise to a family policy rationale that would help young couples have the highest number of children they want and thus contribute to raising the fertility rate. New surveys, however, have found that the ideal family size for young people may have started to decline in some countries. The most recent data from Eurobarometer suggest that in the German-speaking parts of Europe, the ideal family size stated by younger men and women may be as low as 1.7 children per woman on average. And in many other countries, the data show that the ideal family size for men and women aged below 35 is lower than for those above 35.

Goldstein *et al.* (2003) discuss the consistency and the credibility of these new findings which—if they are indeed indications of a new trend—will alter the current discussion about future fertility trends in Europe. Their paper also presents and discusses a plausible hypothesis to explain such a new decline; this assumes that through social learning the younger generations adapt their ideals to what they see as the reality of the generation above them, thus explaining the possible lag of 20 to 30 years between the decline in period fertility and the decline in ideal family size. If substantiated, this hypothesis could point to a spiral of further fertility declines in Europe.

(g) Density, pollution and other biomedical factors

In recent years there has been increasing collaboration between social scientists and researchers in the biological and biomedical fields concerning the possible physiological factors involved in the recent fertility decline. These studies have a broad range of possible mechanisms that cannot be adequately summarized here. There has been rather strong evidence that human fertility declines with higher population density (Lutz and Qiang, 2002) which, in a future of higher population density, would imply pressure toward lower fertility. Other studies stress the possible impacts of environmental pollution on sperm counts and sperm quality which in some countries seem to have reached alarmingly low levels (Skakkebæk *et al.*, 2001). There are arguments that smoking, stress and different kinds of pollution are already resulting in a higher degree of involuntary childlessness, particularly in cases where births have been postponed until an age at which biological fecundability is already starting to decline.

There does not seem to be any convincing evidence yet that pollution is indeed a factor driving the fertility decline, but the possibility cannot be dismissed when the future of fertility is being considered.

(h) Competitiveness associated with globalization

One final argument has to do with economic globalization and the associated increase in competitiveness at all levels. To be successful in a globalized economy, a young man or woman has to invest money in education, be very mobile (ready to move to different places at short notice) and be prepared to work late evenings and at weekends, if necessary. These last two conditions do not make it easy to maintain a stable relationship or to raise young children. Hence, modern economic conditions are sometimes characterized as being structurally unfriendly toward establishing a family. If they do not inhibit fertility completely, such conditions are at least a strong incentive to postpone childbearing and thus contribute to the tempo effect as well as to the risk of not being able to have children once working conditions are considered sufficiently established for a baby break to be affordable. As these forces of increasing competitiveness are likely to become even stronger in a further-globalizing world, they may become a powerful driver toward even lower fertility in the future. In fact, although the emphasis on globalization is novel, the idea that competition leads to low fertility goes back over 100 years to Dumont's (1890) notion of social capillarity.

5.4 Conclusions

This attempt to summarize some of the most important arguments that have been either around for a while or recently added to the discussions has deliberately abstained from weighing the positive and negative arguments against each other. That there are six arguments on one side and eight on the other does not necessarily mean that fertility is more likely to decline further than to recover. Weighing these factors clearly requires further analysis and must necessarily include a good deal of expert judgment. Yet, as outlined in Lutz (1996), such a judgment should not be based on the opinions of experts, who do not justify their views, but rather on a scientific assessment of the validity and the relative importance of different arguments, which then can lead to some ranking. This chapter tries to prepare the way for a more rigorous assessment and to show that there is, indeed, great uncertainty about the future course of fertility in Europe.

References

Bongaarts, J. and Feeney, G. (1998) 'On the Quantum and Tempo of Fertility,' *Population and Development Review*, **24**: 271–292.

Coale, A.J. (1973) 'The Demographic Transition,' in *Proceedings of the International Population Conference*, vol 1, Liège, Belgium: International Union for the Scientific Study of Population.

Council of Europe (2003) *Recent Demographic Trends 2002*, Strasbourg, France: Council of Europe.

Davis, K. (1954) 'The World Demographic Transition,' *Annals of the American Academy of Political and Social Science*, **237**: 1–11.

Davis, K. (1991) 'Population and Resources: Fact and Interpretation,' in Davis K. and Bernstam, M.S. (eds) *Resources, Environment and Population: Present Knowledge*, Oxford, UK: Oxford University Press, pp. 1–21.

Dumont, A. (1890) *Dépopulation et civilisation: étude démographique*, Paris, France: Lecrosnier et Babe.

Durkheim, E. (1902) *De la division du travail social*, second edition, Paris, France: Felix Alcan.

Easterlin, R.A. (1980) *Birth and Fortune. The Impact of Numbers on Personal Welfare*, New York, USA: Basic Books, Inc.

Engelhardt, H. and Prskawetz, A. (2004) 'On the Changing Correlation between Fertility and Female Employment over Space and Time,' *European Journal of Population*, **20**: 35–62.

European Banking Federation (2004) *Letter no 15* (July), Brussels, Belgium: The European Banking Federation, See http://www.fbe.be/ accessed December 2005.

Foster, C. (2000) 'The Limits to Low Fertility: A Biosocial Approach,' *Population and Development Review*, **26**(2): 209–234.

Goldstein, J., Lutz, W. and Testa, M.R. (2003) 'The Emergence of Sub-Replacement Family Size Ideals in Europe,' *European Demographic Research Papers, no 2*, Vienna, Austria: Vienna Institute of Demography of the Austrian Academy of Sciences.

Golini, A. (1998) 'How Low Can Fertility Be? An Empirical Exploration,' *Population and Development Review*, **24**(1): 59–74.

Hoffmann-Nowotny, H.-J. (1987) 'The Future of the Family,' in *Plenaries. European Population Conference 1987: Issues and Prospects*, Helsinki, Finland: Central Statistical Office, pp. 113–200.

Keyfitz, N. (1991) 'Subreplacement Fertility: The Third Level of Explanation,' in Lutz, W. (ed) *Future Demographic Trends in Europe and North America. What Can We Assume Today?* London, UK: Academic Press, pp. 235–246.

Kiernan, K. (1991) *The Respective Roles of Men and Women in Tomorrow's Europe: Human Resources in Europe at the Dawn of the 21st Century*, Paper given to Eurostat International Conference, held 27–29 November, Luxembourg.

Kiernan, K. (1992) 'The Impact of Family Disruption in Childhood on Transitions Made in Young Adult Life,' *Population Studies*, **46**: 213–234.

Kohler, H.P. and Philipov, D. (2001) 'Variance Effects in the Bongaarts–Feeney Formula,' *Demography*, **38**(1): 1–16.

Lesthaeghe, R. (1983) 'A Century of Demographic and Cultural Change in Western Europe: An Exploration of Underlying Dimensions,' *Population and Development Review*, **9**(3): 411–435.

Lutz, W. (1989) *Distributional Aspects of Human Fertility. A Global Comparative Study*, London, UK: Academic Press.

Lutz, W. (1993) 'Effects of Children on Divorce Probabilities and of Divorce on Fertility: The Case of Finland 1984,' *Yearbook of Population Research in Finland*, **31**: 72–80.

Lutz, W. (1994) 'Future Reproductive Behavior in Industrialized Countries,' in Lutz, W. (ed) *The Future Population of the World. What Can We Assume Today?* London, UK: Earthscan, pp. 267–294.

Lutz, W. (ed) (1996) *The Future Population of the World. What Can We Assume Today?*, revised edition, London, UK: Earthscan.

Lutz, W. and Qiang R. (2002) 'Determinants of Human Population Growth,' *Philosophical Transactions of the Royal Society B: Biological Sciences*, **357**(1425): 1197–1210, 29 September.

Lutz, W. and Skirbekk, V. (2004) 'How Would "Tempo Policies" Work? Exploring the Effect of School Reforms on Period Fertility in Europe,' *European Demographic Research Papers no 2*, Vienna, Austria: Vienna Institute of Demography of the Austrian Academy of Sciences.

Lutz, W., O'Neill, B.C. and Scherbov, S. (2003) 'Europe's Population at a Turning Point,' *Science*, **299**: 1991–1992.

Notestein, F.W. (1945) 'Population—The Long View,' in Schultz, T.W. (ed) *Food for the World*, Chicago, IL, USA: University of Chicago Press, pp. 36–57.

Prinz, C. (1995) *Cohabiting, Married, or Single. Portraying, Analyzing, and Modeling New Living Arrangements in the Changing Societies of Europe*, Aldershot, UK: Avebury.

Skakkebæk, N.E., Rajpert-De Meyts, E. and Main, K.M. (2001) 'Testicular Dysgenesis Syndrome: An Increasingly Common Developmental Disorder with Environmental Aspects,' *Human Reproduction*, **5**: 972–978.

Sobotka, T. (2004) *Postponement of Childbearing and Low Fertility in Europe*, Doctoral dissertation, Amsterdam, The Netherlands: Dutch University Press.

Tabah, L. (1989) 'From One Demographic Transition to Another,' *Population Bulletin of the United Nations*, **28**: 1–24.

Tönnies, F. (1887) *Gemeinschaft und Gesellschaft. Grundbegriffe der reinen Soziologie*, Darmstadt, Germany: Wissenschaftliche Buchgesellschaft [in German].

United States National Research Council (2000) *Beyond Six Billion: Forecasting the World's Population. Panel on Population Projections*, Bongaarts J. and Bulatao, R.A. (eds) Washington, D.C., USA: Committee on Population of the Commission on Behavioral and Social Sciences and Education, National Academy Press.

van de Kaa, D.J. (1987) 'Europe's Second Demographic Transition,' *Population Bulletin*, **42**(1): 1–58.

Vishnevsky, A. (1991) 'Demographic Revolution and the Future of Fertility: A Systems Approach,' in Lutz, W. (ed) *Future Demographic Trends in Europe and North America. What Can We Assume Today?* London, UK: Academic Press, pp. 257–270.

Westoff, C.F. (1991) 'The Return to Replacement Fertility: A Magnetic Force?' in Lutz, W. (ed) *Future Demographic Trends in Europe and North America. What Can We Assume Today?* London, UK: Academic Press, pp. 227–233.

Westoff, C.F., Hammerslough, R. and Paul, L. (1987) 'The Potential Impact of Improvements in Contraception on Fertility and Abortion in Western Countries,' *European Journal of Population*, **3**(1): 7–32.

Part III

Family Forms and the Young Generation in an Enlarged Union

Chapter 6

Europe's Coming Generations: The Influence of the Past

Giovanni B. Sgritta

What will Europe's coming generations be like? There is no firm answer. We can conjecture, but we cannot foresee future events. In a globalized, ever more uncertain world, the changes are so rapid and intense, and the interdependence of the processes so strong, that the possibility of predicting future directions remains ineluctably out of our reach. This does not mean, however, that we should abandon our attempts to understand. One thing is certain: the coming generations will—at least, partly—be the result of the past and the present: that is, they will be the children of the circumstances in which their grandparents and parents used to live and live today.

The world, and with it, Europe, will change—quickly or slowly, in one way or another. The inheritance of the past and the present will, however, inevitably affect the direction and rhythm of that change. It may encourage convergence toward a single model or it may keep the distances between European countries basically unchanged for some time to come: distances between, on the one hand, those countries that press hard on the accelerator of transition from youth to adulthood and thus hasten independence and, on the other hand, those that pave that transitional path with obstacles and difficulties and thus prolong the journey. Given the present condition of the European economy, and taking into account the impact of the enlargement from EU15 to EU25, the second hypothesis seems more probable at the moment, namely, the freezing of the differences. The ratifying strength of the European treaties and action programs certainly favor the other hypothesis. However, the processes underlying the differences among the member states regarding the formation of the new generations have distinct peculiarities, and the regulatory instruments within the mandate of the European Union (EU)— typically, family policies—are still rather ineffective, if not actually extraneous to the political agenda. And that would also favor the second hypothesis.

The purpose of this chapter is to review the family changes that have taken place in the EU15 in recent decades and to situate them in the wider context of social and economic transformation. As such, the chapter can be seen as both a review of demographic trends and an introduction to Europe's varied patterns of welfare state regimes.

6.1   From Past to Present

In traditional societies the formation of the new generations took place almost exclusively in the family and largely followed a pre-established timetable and benchmarks. The system left little room for externalities. The investment in children lasted a relatively short time, and the proceeds went to the exclusive benefit of the family. Training for an occupation took place within the household according to a rigid, gender-based division of labor. The successive phases of the life course also followed pre-established channels according to family needs. Childhood did not last very long: just the time necessary for learning vital survival skills and for the continuation of domestic and family activities. Adolescence, as a distinct phase of life, namely, a preparation for adulthood, scarcely existed.

With the advent of the industrial capitalistic mode of production, knowledge took its place alongside the other classic factors of production (land, capital, work). A new phase of the life cycle, adolescence, was now inserted between childhood and adulthood, during which the crucial knowledge required for doing a job in the market was acquired. As time went by, the cost of children grew. The interests of the family no longer related exclusively to the domestic sphere but to the needs of society in a wider sense. The repercussions of this were enormous. The economic significance of procreation changed radically. Parents continued to produce children but in ever fewer numbers and for reasons that were essentially non-economic. Externalities to childbearing became costs and benefits that were passed on to society at large. The family was no longer a self-sufficient unit. The welfare state partially replaced the welfare family, and the gap between family and societal behaviors grew accordingly. The interests of one and the other took different courses and were in part defined by the demarcation line between their respective and shared responsibilities.

Societies, however, are fluid entities. Thus, for a long time, no fundamental changes took place in the phases, or in the duration of the phases, of the individual's life cycle. The passage to adulthood continued to follow a relatively rigid and standardized model. The salient characteristic of the regime of transition to adulthood, which Galland (1986) has defined as 'settling down,' is that the final stages of the process follow one another in a relatively short time: you find a job, leave your parents' house, get married and have children—all in a handful of years. This model survived in Europe more or less until the end of World War II and in some countries, in southern Europe, for example, even longer. The most important changes were those that concerned the duration of education and the distinctions made between 'male' and 'female' careers. Starting from the mid-1960s, in fact, education levels rose rapidly all over Europe. This was quickly followed by a growth in female participation in the labor market and ever greater numbers of females taking to professions and activities that had been exclusively male preserves.

The transformations that took place in the meantime in the economic sphere and in political and state institutions had a decisive influence on the changes in the life course. For a certain period of time these changes mainly involved men; women felt them much less and sometimes not at all. The 'Fordist' society, based on mass production and the growth of industrial productivity, implied a separation between the different institutional spheres and thus a distinction between the activities that took place within the domestic sphere, which were the responsibility of women, and those that took place in the factory and the market, which were performed by men. The same can be said concerning the structures of citizenship. With the development of industry, in fact, the capitalistic system had to:

> . . . come to terms with subsistence needs that could not be satisfied in the labor market. This social configuration thus foresees both an extreme segregation based on gender membership and the establishment of an extended welfare state (Crouch, 2001, p. 56 [author's translation]).

The welfare state, in turn, was typical of the industrial society in that it perfectly mirrored the logic of the division of work between the spheres of the market and the family. Moreover, the patriarchal-type family relied on the economic and legal authority of the male head of the family, the only person employed in the labor market and thus the beneficiary of a wage that guaranteed the maintenance and, by derived right, the social security of its components—elderly people and children, who were considered dependent and inactive subjects, and women, who were entirely dedicated to domestic work and care activities (classified as private tasks and thus unpaid) and who were also unvalued in spite of their vital importance for the functioning of society.

Thus, for at least the first three post-World War II decades, the satisfaction of the primary needs of the great majority of European societies centered on the compromise between the three principal institutional mechanisms: the *labor market*, the *family* and the institutions of the *welfare state*. In an attempt to provide for the basic well-being of their citizens, European societies of the second half of the last century arrived at solutions that, although they had different stages and stresses, were basically similar. To reduce these solutions to their essentials: in work, and specifically in industry, full employment of the male population, with few variations on a national scale or among different countries, prevailed. Generally, work meant full-time work, and this continued for the whole life span until pension age. There were greater fluctuations in the employment rate of females, who were mainly occupied in the domestic sphere (Crouch, 2001). Education was increasing, especially at the secondary and tertiary levels. Social mobility in the course of a working career and between successive generations was also growing. On the whole, the younger generations enjoyed relative advantages in terms of education, income and work status in comparison with preceding generations.

Mid-century European societies also had widely similar features from the point of view of social protection. Although the differences among countries on this front were relatively wide in terms of guaranteed rights and the level of insurance cover, social insurance systems generally spread throughout European countries. On the whole, these measures aimed to ease the transition from the traditional to the industrial society, compensating the working classes to a certain extent for the uncertainties and problems created by the market. The prevailing expectation at the time was that the burden of providing for the satisfaction of collective and individual needs should fall to the public sector. Inadequate social intervention programs meant that such expectations were not always met. Nor did the programs adopted in individual countries necessarily present common characteristics. Yet, whether seen from the perspective of the measures adopted or in terms of the number and identity of the beneficiaries, the provisions introduced in the first decades after World War II without any doubt bear witness to the willingness to transfer responsibilities from the traditional institutions of family and kinship to the state. For over 20 years the way social citizenship was administered and the collective commitment to it exemplified this very specific vision of the social life.

Between 1960 and the mid-1970s, the trend of making spending on major social programs a percentage of gross domestic product (GDP) grew steadily almost everywhere—proof of the basic institutional convergence of the welfare state in European countries (Sgritta, 1994). In the same time span, expenditure quotas for the education, health and pensions sectors increased. The only exception was expenditure under the heading 'family benefits,' which decreased almost everywhere from the beginning of the 1970s in comparison with the previous decades (O'Higgins, 1988, pp. 214–215).

There is not much to add to what has already been said about the characteristics of the family of that period. The main elements were: 'the asymmetrical relation of the sexes to the occupation structure' (Parsons, 1954, p. 90); a limited variability in the panorama of living arrangements; high marriage stability and thus a low rate of divorce; a high predisposition among young people toward marriage and, on average, high levels of fertility; limited premarital cohabitation; and a low proportion of births outside marriage. Nevertheless, a certain variability had already appeared in this scenario of relatively coherent and homogeneous behaviors. To a large extent the differences were due either (i) to the level of industrial backwardness in the development of the economy of some countries and thus to the still-important role of the primary sector (for example, in Ireland, Greece, Portugal, Spain and, to a certain extent, Italy, where the age at marriage was therefore relatively higher) or (ii) to deep-rooted cultural and religious factors, that, as in the cases of Sweden and Denmark, showed themselves in greater family instability and higher levels of illegitimate births (Crouch, 2001, pp. 266–267). The situation in the European countries with regard to life course was also quite homogeneous then. Relatively low levels of education encouraged the early entry of young people into the labor market and, apart from the above-mentioned cases, equally early family formation. Moreover, given the low level of female participation in the labor market, procreation was consequently relatively precocious and high.

6.2 The Second 'Great Transformation'

The changes, if not a complete and absolute break with the regime predominant in the middle of the last century, were quite sudden and in many ways unexpected. What is important to emphasize here, however, is that they affected the entire range of institutional infrastructure that had held the previous model together. The first signs came from demography. In the course of a few years, the rules that under the previous regime had governed family formation, reproductive plans, the stability of conjugal ties and the phases of the life course of the single members of the family were literally turned upside down:

> Marriages everywhere became rarer and took place later; de facto families or common-law cohabitation *more uxorio* increased; fewer and fewer children came into the world and the quota of illegitimate children grew; the number of divorces increased at a dizzying rate. ...
> In short, marriage became more and more fragile and unstable, and the conjugal family ... lost importance little by little, leaving room

for other types of family (Barbagli, 1990, pp. 10–11 [author's translation]).

It is not easy to explain why the first signs of the changes that turned out to be of such dramatic importance in the recent history of the advanced western societies should have originated in family custom and the affective and reproductive choices of individuals. It is equally difficult to understand why these changes took place at different rates in different countries, throwing the relative unanimity of the previous regime into disorder and, starting from the beginning of the 1970s, giving the green light to a variety of configurations that, to a certain extent, still continue. According to Lesthaeghe (1995, pp. 42–45) membership of a religion and religious belief (Catholicism and Protestantism *in primis*) and per capita gross national product levels are the two crucial factors that explain the different temporal rhythms of the second demographic transition in the different national contexts. Mayer (2001, p. 98) instead points to the economic situation and the different institutional configurations in the different countries:

> We might assume that in the good times of the postwar 'Golden Age,' differences between countries and between persons within a country in basic resources, institutional options and restrictions mattered less than in times of shortage and decline. ... We would, therefore, expect a growing divergence between countries as well as a growing heterogeneity and inequality within countries.

In these conditions, Mayer adds, 'national characteristics will have a greater impact on life course regimes than in the 1960s and early 1970s.'

Whatever the ultimate causes, since the 1960s behaviors and family structures have changed profoundly. The main elements of this transformation are well known, but are still worth recalling. Between 1965 and 1970 there was a decline in the number of marriages. This was very marked in Denmark and Sweden, slightly less so in Austria and France, and much less marked or hardly perceptible in Belgium, the Federal Republic of Germany, Finland, The Netherlands and the United Kingdom. In the countries of southern Europe, with the exception of Greece, there was actually an increase in the number of marriages, even though this would decline greatly from the 1980s onward (van de Kaa, 1987, p. 14). There was also a noticeable increase in divorce rates—once again with the exception of the Catholic countries, where divorce was introduced only after 1970. The decrease in the number of marriages was followed closely by a widespread decline in the total fertility rate which, from values near or above 2.4 children per woman in 1960 (apart from Ireland, The Netherlands, Portugal and Spain, which continued to have higher values), began to go down, at first slowly (around 2.0 to 2.2) and then faster during the next two decades (*Table 6.1*). In 1985, in all the European countries with the exception of Ireland, the fertility rate fell somewhat below the substitution level, with particularly important reductions in the four countries of southern Europe (van de Kaa, 1987, p. 19). The trend of births outside marriage went in the other direction. The frequency of births increased everywhere during this period but most particularly in Sweden (from 18.4 per 100 live births in 1970 to 46.4 in 1985), in Denmark (from 11 to 43) and in Norway (from 6.9 to 25.8), followed by France, Austria and the United Kingdom (Höhn, 1989, p. 202) (*Table 6.2*). In the countries of northern Europe a parallel trend to that of nonmarital births was the growing phenomenon of cohabitation (Trost, 1989, p. 367). All these changes, added together, obviously had repercussions on the typology of family forms which started, in fact, to ramify, once again with considerable variations from country to country. In southern Europe, right up until the end of the 1970s, the proportion of extended families that included other relatives or aggregated members, apart from the couple and their children, was still quite high (around 17 percent) while one-parent families and single-person households were much less common. The latter was quite an important part of the panorama of living arrangements in the countries of northern and central Europe: in 1971 single-person households amounted to 25 percent of households in Sweden, 26 percent in the Federal Republic of Germany and 22 percent in France, but were less than 13 percent of households in Italy (Roussel, 1988, p. 45; Saporiti, 1988).

6.3 From 'Golden Age' to 'Landslide'

The processes mentioned above were based on a profound transformation in the circumstances of women. Women had always worked either on family-owned land or as workers and employees in industry, but never before had so many women and mothers gone out to work, which in turn required a reorganization of their family and social life. Trends in women's participation in nonagricultural activities (as a percentage of the active population aged 15 years and over) were on the increase everywhere, starting from the 1960s. Around the 1970s, the participation of women in nonagricultural activities was between 35 and 44 percent; only in Belgium, Italy and The Netherlands were the values near or below 30 percent. Even including agricultural work and taking into account the activity rates of married women, these values remained much the same, while the differences were more marked as far as part-time work was concerned; in this case, with the exception of Finland, where this form of participation in the workforce was still uncommon (10.9 percent, similar to Italy with 10.6 percent), it was the Nordic countries that reigned supreme (Norway 44.9 percent, Sweden 46.2 percent) (Boh, 1989, p. 269).

Table 6.1. Total fertility rate: EU15, 1960–2000.

Country	1960	1970	1980	1990	2000
Denmark	2.54	1.95	1.55	1.67	1.76
Finland	2.72	1.82	1.63	1.78	1.73
Sweden	2.20	1.92	1.68	2.13	1.54
Belgium	2.56	2.25	1.68	1.62	1.65
Germany	2.37	2.03	1.56	1.45	1.34
France	2.73	2.47	1.95	1.78	1.89
Luxembourg	2.28	1.98	1.49	1.61	1.78
Netherlands	3.12	2.57	1.60	1.62	1.72
Austria	2.69	2.29	1.65	1.45	1.32
Greece	2.28	2.39	2.21	1.42	1.30
Spain	2.86	2.90	2.20	1.33	1.22
Portugal	3.10	2.83	2.18	1.57	1.54
Italy	2.41	2.42	1.64	1.30	1.25
Ireland	3.76	3.93	3.23	2.19	1.89
United Kingdom	2.72	2.43	1.90	1.84	1.64
EU15	2.59	2.38	1.82	1.57	1.53

Source: European Commission (2003a).

Table 6.2. Live births outside marriage per 100 live births: EU15, 1960–2000.

Country	1960	1970	1980	1990	2000
Denmark	7.8	11.0	33.2	46.4	44.9*
Finland	4.0	5.8	13.1	25.2	39.2
Sweden	11.3	18.6	39.7	47.0	55.3
Belgium	2.1	2.8	4.1	11.6	20.1*
Germany	7.6	7.2	11.9	15.3	20.3
France	6.1	6.9	11.4	13.1	40.7*
Luxembourg	3.2	4.0	6.0	12.8	21.9
Netherlands	1.4	2.1	4.1	11.4	25.1
Austria	13.0	12.8	17.8	23.6	31.3
Greece	1.2	1.1	1.5	2.2	4.0
Spain	2.3	1.4	3.9	9.6	14.1*
Portugal	9.5	7.3	9.2	14.7	22.2
Italy	2.4	2.2	4.3	6.5	9.2*
Ireland	1.6	2.7	5.0	14.6	31.8
United Kingdom	5.2	8.0	11.5	27.9	39.5
EU15	5.1	5.6	9.6	19.6	27.2*

Note: *Data refer to 1999.
Source: European Commission (1994), except 2000 figures from Eurostat (2005).

The nature of the transformation under way became clearer in the 1980s. At the beginning of that decade we can distinguish (i) a group including The Netherlands and the southern European countries, where a traditional model is predominant in both family behavior and the participation of women in the workforce and where over 60 percent of women are engaged in domestic activities and (ii) a group, to which France, the Federal Republic of Germany, Norway, Sweden and the United Kingdom belong, in which:

> It is typical that married women have a shorter or longer period of interruption from the job. The idea is that women are expected to stay at home when their children are small. Part-time jobs and other respective solutions, which help women to combine paid work and domestic responsibilities better than full-time work, are also typical of this pattern (Jallinoja, 1989, p. 108).

There is also a third model, made up of the countries of eastern Europe (German Democratic Republic, Hungary, Finland, Poland and the Soviet Union) where:

> Women's participation in the labor force is very high (over 70 percent) ... part-time work is atypical ... and most women do not interrupt their job careers longer than for the period of official maternity leave (Jallinoja, 1989, p. 109).

In configuring these patterns, a role was played both by material factors (i.e., the impact of industrialization and urbanization on the local nationality) and by factors belonging to the ideological or cultural milieu, where the norms and values of the family and women's behavior are expressed. Statistical relations obviously exist between them, although it is not always easy to identify them with the data available. What is certain is that from the 1970s to the 1980s onward, the life-course trajectories of the new generations, and in particular those of women, changed profoundly with respect to those of their fathers and mothers. Education became increasingly important in the initial phase of the life course. The pursuit of personal fulfillment through work was also superimposed on affective and familial choices for women and came into potential conflict with those choices. Procreation ever-more markedly connoted rationality and calculation and therefore tended to contract, while behaviors that were customarily disapproved of, such as cohabitation and divorce, not only became possible, thanks to the growing economic independence of women, but were considered legitimate options in an individualized and secularized conception of life.

From the point of view of the economy, the beginning of the transformation can be dated from December 1973, coinciding with the Yom Kippur War and the first oil shock: events that marked the passage from the 'golden age' to that of the 'landslide' in the western world (Hobsbawm, 1997). The consequences of the crisis were dramatic and marked the end of the expansive cycle. In the space of a few years, most of the conquests of the advanced industrial societies were challenged or changed direction; beginning with full employment—the challenge to which was the real *deus ex machina* of the social-democratic compromise of the postwar period.

The impact of those events on the political institutional plane was equally if not more important. The joint provisions of the demographic and family transformations and the economic recession eroded the foundations of the assumptions on which the Beveridgean–Keynesian welfare state rested: the demographic equilibrium between the active and inactive; family stability; the gender division of labor on the one hand and the growth of production and full employment on the other. Starting from the mid-1970s, a process of reduction in welfare policies began. Social expenditure was the most significant component of the total variation in public spending. In the countries of western Europe, the share of social spending in total general government expenditure rose from an average figure of 49.9 percent in 1960 to 57.4 percent in 1970 and to 60 percent and above in the 1970s, falling back to 58 percent in 1981 (Stolnitz, 1992, p. 387).

In part, the reactions of the governments represented a necessary choice, justified by the extent of the demographic shift in the different national contexts (decline in births and population aging); in part, too, they derived from the possibility of relying on the strength of ties and primary obligations in the different countries—or rather they were made possible by the different degree of 'family traditionalism.' Where aging was more pronounced, the measures taken by the governments to deal with the crisis favored the elderly component of the population. This effect was particularly noticeable in certain sectors of intervention. Between 1975 and 1981, for 11 western countries for which data are available, the growth rate of real expenditure on pensions was 5.7 percent a year, of which 3.2 percent was due to higher benefits, 1.8 percent to the demographic component and 0.6 percent to increasing coverage (i.e., extension to nonworkers and

dependents). However, considerable intercountry differences can be observed in both the growth of real expenditures and the relative importance of the demographic factor (Stolnitz, 1992, pp. 394–395). Where the decline in births was particularly rapid and intense and therefore the aging process more accentuated, as in Italy, the part of the growth rate of pension expenditures due to demographic variables was particularly high (close to one-third). In Ireland, which at the time had a high fertility level, the demographic component accounted for just one-sixth of the annual growth rates in real expenditure over this period; it was the same for France (less than one-eleventh). The position of Sweden was very close to that of Italy in terms of real expenditure growth (6.9 versus 7.7 percent per year), with the difference that while in Italy the process of demographic aging was strongly sup-ported by the generosity of the benefits dispensed (real benefits of +8.2 percent), in Sweden the growth due to this component was far lower (+2.3 percent).

Policies, as the comparison between Italy and Sweden shows, counted more than demography. The other component with an influence on the variability of the measures adopted was the strength of family ties. In the 1970s and 1980s, in spite of convergent trends, European families were still, overall, greatly diverse in character, with appreciable differences among countries in terms of the principal demographic and social parameters. From the second half of the 1980s, fertility increased regularly in countries where the decline had been more accentuated in previous years (Denmark, Norway and Sweden); there was a smaller recovery in fertility in Belgium, the Federal Republic of Germany, Luxembourg, The Nether-lands and the United Kingdom, but, from 1980 to 1990, fertility fell in Greece (from 2.21 to 1.42), Spain (from 2.20 to 1.33), Italy (from 1.64 to 1.30) and Por-tugal (from 2.18 to 1.54), where it had been higher at the beginning of the 1970s (European Commission, 1994, p. 13). At the beginning of the 1960s, the propor-tion of single-person households in Europe came within a relatively narrow band. Twenty years later, this band had widened considerably: from values around 10 to 18 percent in the Mediterranean member states of the European Union to values near or above 30 percent in Denmark, Germany and Sweden. There were also con-siderable changes in the proportion of households made up of two married people and at least one child. In 1981 this type of household had dropped to one-half of the total number of households in Denmark, while in Italy, Portugal and Spain it was still at quite high levels, between 63 and 68 percent (Eurostat, 1988, pp. 195–205). A similar trend also characterized the proportion of births outside marriage. From a not-too-dissimilar situation at the beginning of the 1960s, in the space of a few years a constant growth trend was recorded that at first concerned the countries of northern Europe (Denmark 33.2 percent in 1980), then in the following decade France and the United Kingdom as well (European Commission, 1994, p. 59).

The variability within the European Community also tended to increase with regard to the economically active population. In the 1981 census, economically ac-tive women made up 29.1 percent of the total female population (EU12), but with values that fluctuated from 46.1 percent in Denmark to 16.5 percent in Spain. The other countries ranged between these two extremes (Eurostat, 1988, pp. 82–83). Almost everywhere, younger women showed the highest rates of female economic activity, while these values tended to go down with family formation and the birth of children. The effect of family life on the presence of women in the labor market is not the same everywhere, however. As women grow older, the activity rate gen-erally tends to increase in the countries of northern Europe and to decrease some-times drastically, as in Italy, Portugal, Spain and the countries of southern Europe

(International Labor Organization, 1984, pp. 33–42). This is a clear sign that, in the Nordic countries, as women's family burdens increase, they are balanced by effective compensatory measures while, in the Mediterranean countries, women are left without adequate support in this respect and are obliged either to reduce their activity in the labor market or leave it altogether and dedicate themselves totally to their family and children.

This variability is based on numerous factors. However, it would be restrictive to explain the higher rates of female economic activity in the countries of northern Europe by a greater inclination on the part of women to enter the labor market or to win economic independence. This is certainly one of the reasons, another being that the rate of female education is higher in the Nordic countries than in southern Europe (UNESCO, 2004). What counts most, however, is that such behaviors are the product of a precise political choice, of a unique approach to 'equality' and worker protection, pursued with constancy and perseverance, year after year, by the governments of the Nordic countries through a bundle of policies expressly designed to change traditional gender roles both in the family and in working life. In Sweden as well as in the other Nordic countries, with different degrees of commitment and rhythms, the goal of gender equality has been coherently pursued through a battery of family-policy measures (Popenoe, 1988; Stanfors and Svensson, 1999). Across the entire spectrum of these policies, the choices made by the governments of northern Europe in the 1970s and 1980s differed to a great extent from those of the continental countries and most especially from those of the southern countries. The latter were always more inclined to protect family solidarity than to encourage women's entry to the labor market—something that, according to an ideology common to these countries, would weaken the cohesion of primary ties. The result, to some extent surprising and paradoxical, is that fertility, undoubtedly an important indicator of the functionality of the family, after a first phase of decline, recovered noticeably in the countries of northern Europe where the participation of women in the workforce has always been high, while it fell a good deal during the 1980s and 1990s in the countries of southern Europe where female employment has always remained much lower (Vogel, 2003, p. 138). These latter countries have thus paid a high price for choosing to defend the traditional family at all costs; they have paid the price of a fall in reproduction and also, as we will see, in terms of the formation of families by the new generations. Paradoxes apart, there is no doubt that the policies adopted by the Nordic countries also came at a high cost. As Esping-Andersen (1997, p. 67) writes:

> The costs of harmonizing women's family and work responsibilities with generous paid leave and child care provisions are very high. The gain, however, is stable and even rising fertility combined with mini-

mal risks of poverty entrapment and welfare dependence among vulnerable groups such as single mothers.

The continental and Mediterranean countries, to a greater or lesser extent, adopted a different strategy. Firmly anchored to the premise of full employment (male) that had in fact worked in the first 30 postwar years, these countries tried to protect wages and job security for the core workforce to the total disadvantage of the female component. According to Esping-Andersen (1997, p. 67), 'The concomitant discouragement of female labor supply ... both via the tax regime and via "familistic" social policy means' not only kept women's economic activity low but also resulted in an increase in the poverty levels of families with children that were unable to count on a double income. Moreover, there was a further aggravation of the situation when women decided to enter the labor market:

> ... since this occurs in a hostile environment in terms of youth unemployment, and from the point of view of harmonizing careers and family responsibilities, the result is delayed family formation and declining and even record-low fertility.

The decision to take different paths obviously did not emerge out of the blue. It was probably endogenous to material, cultural and ideal traditions and conditions rooted in the individual national contexts and, above all, to the strength of family relationships. The choices perceived as possible are conditioned by the existence of a certain type of family which, in turn, is influenced by them, although it is difficult to establish which is the cause and which the effect. In any case it is not difficult to show how in the countries of southern Europe the family retained, until the 1970s and 1980s and often beyond, certain fundamental characteristics of traditional societies:

1. From the structural point of view—a high proportion of extended households and a low percentage of single-person and single-parent households, unmarried couples cohabitating and children born outside wedlock.
2. From the point of view of legislation—inter alia, the tardy introduction of divorce; the respect for the principle of subsidiarity as an expression of the responsibilities that people have for each other's welfare; the constitutional codification of the family as a 'natural' institution; the weak or absent legal recognition of de facto families; the belated introduction of the principle of equal opportunities; the provision of care for dependent persons as a question of individual responsibility; the recognition of the child as a 'private good' instead of a 'public good.'
3. Finally, from the point of view of custom—a distinct separation in the gender division of labor; women with different responsibilities from men regarding the

care of dependent people and domestic duties; only a limited number of civil marriages; the extension of intergenerational—and also economic—obligations beyond the restricted circle of the nuclear family; and the individual's expectation of being able to count on the help of family and relatives in case of need.

All or almost all these characteristics had a high incidence in the countries of southern Europe and were as a rule weaker in the central and northern countries. More generally, the diffusion and intensity of these characteristics defined the duties, the role and the responsibilities of family obligations in the social division of welfare as well as the expectations of individuals toward the family and the other institutional spheres (market and state). The more obligations that are met by the family, the fewer 'residual' responsibilities there are for the market and, above all, for the state to assume. All things being equal, in these conditions there is a strong tendency on the part of the state to make a virtue of necessity: leaving the costs to fall where they are produced, not intervening, counting on the spontaneous (*natural*) strength of family ties, only shouldering the burden of those duties that families cannot fulfill or of the services that they are unable to purchase on the market—*tertium non datur*. According to this rule, social policy is based:

> ... on the premise that there are two natural (or socially given) channels through which an individual's needs are properly met: the private market and the family. Only when these break down should social welfare institutions come into play, and then only temporarily (Titmuss, 1974, pp. 30–31).

Where the rule has been rigidly applied, as in the countries of southern Europe, it has had paradoxical results. As the family is important as an essential social resource, it can face and resolve a large number of care and assistance problems, provide autonomously for the sharing of financial resources among the generations and even set to work to find a job for its members; as it is self-sufficient, it need *not* be helped to carry out these tasks but can be left to itself and abandoned to its fate. Ideology and the prevailing morality give an appearance of legitimacy to this state of affairs.

The solutions adopted in the member countries have led to the formation of distinct 'families of nations' based on a different equilibrium 'between the obligations of individuals to provide for themselves, families to provide for each other and governments to replace, supplement or enforce these provisions' (Millar and Warman, 1996, p. 7). Therein, changes in the role of women are of paramount importance. At the end of World War II, even in a country like Sweden which in many ways was a pioneer, childrearing and family were mainly a woman's concern (Stanfors and Svensson, 1999, p. 273). The differences become noticeable as female participation in the labor market grows; when, that is, the ticklish question of the conciliation of the dual role of the woman in the family and in the labor market becomes the focus of public attention. The European countries reacted in different ways to this problem—they initiated different policies. The Scandinavian countries and Denmark assisted women's entry to the labor market, introducing legislative reforms and support measures aimed at lightening family responsibilities. Apart from the development of ample employment opportunities in the public sector, especially in the public services, improved education for women, tax reforms and revisions of social and family policy all helped to produce and, in turn, were fueled by changes in attitudes that increased the motivation for mothers, even with small children, to be in the labor force. In Sweden:

> ... the tax system, and the ... increase in real wages since the end of the 1970s ... contributed a further economic incentive, as two paychecks increasingly have been needed to maintain family living standards (Hoem and Hoem, 1988, p. 408).

In the southern European countries the strategy was totally different. Being able to count on a greater stability and resiliency of family ties, and having at the same time to deal with greater economic difficulties, those countries chose to—or were obliged to (the question is controversial)—depend on the strength of those ties. Instead of supporting the activities of families and the double workload that women would inevitably have to shoulder as their participation in the labor market grew, they decided to go down the path of further 'capitalizing' on family obligations and thus on the energy and time of the female component—in effect, counting on the inexhaustibility of those resources. In other words, instead of enlarging the social pool of disposable resources and increasing existing human capital by encouraging the presence of women in the social life, those countries chose, to a greater or lesser degree, to gamble on the conservation of the social capital—via strong family and kinship ties with high intensity and frequency of contacts and a robust safety net of interfamilial assistance. The premise on which this choice was based was that families would continue, in spite of everything, to guarantee the same services as ever—that the significant fall in the birth rate that had already begun in the mid-1960s would sooner or later come to a halt; that the growth in female education and participation in the labor market would be compatible with the ever-greater economic and social needs that weighed on the family and the socialization of the new generations; and that the young would continue to marry and 'make' a family exactly as their parents had done. That choice proved to be rash. The birth rate continued to go down, while in the countries of northern and central Europe it had started to rise. Lacking sufficient services and without appreciable economic support, young couples found a way to reconcile costs and benefits in the only way open to them, that is, by reducing fertility or putting off the birth of children indefinitely. Marriages declined, but above all a phenomenon began that was in many ways unexpected, although easily explained given the state of affairs in those countries; that is, young people put off the transition to adulthood, continuing to live with their parents for longer and longer (Cordón, 1997; Iacovou and Berthoud, 2001; Sgritta, 2001).

6.4   Effects: Welfare Aging, Child Poverty and the Postponement Syndrome

The consequences of these many choices are quite well articulated. The transformations burst the boundaries of the family, affecting the working of the market and the policies of welfare. On the whole, however, these three institutions reacted coherently in the different national contexts, giving rise to relatively distinct patterns. In the first 30 years after World War II, the welfare systems had managed to guarantee adequate cover of the basic needs of families through contained fiscal pressure and a large number of programs in support of the new generations, family formation and families with children (Kamerman and Kahn, 1978). Thomson (1991, p. 8) defines this regime as a 'welfare state for youth,' comparing it to the years following the 1973 crisis (mentioned earlier) which had totally 'rewritten the rules of the exchanges between generations' and transformed itself into a 'welfare state for the aging.' From then on, in fact, the scenario changed. Previously, children and young people were the principal beneficiaries of welfare policies; now, more and more, it became the elderly. With the economic crisis and demographic aging as accomplices, this transformation affected, with the partial exception of the northern European countries, almost all the western world (Preston, 1984; Thomson, 1989; Chauvel, 1998; Sgritta, 1993). An analysis of trends in public spending in the ten most industrialized countries in the Organisation for Economic Co-operation and Development (OECD) concluded that, even in the most generous cases, aid to families with children was, in per capita terms, only a limited quota in comparison with the direct spending for the elderly. In the mid-1980s the incidence of the former to the latter was 21 percent in the United Kingdom and around 10 percent in France, The Netherlands and Sweden, and between 3 and 6 percent in the Federal Republic of Germany and Italy (Varley, 1986). At the beginning of the following decade, the ratio of transfers to the elderly to transfers to the nonelderly, already high in the continental countries and especially in the southern countries, increased even further, while decreasing in Nordic countries where the average values were around 0.7 against values of 3.5 in Italy, 2.2 in Austria, 1.7 in West Germany, 1.6 in France and 1.3 in Spain (Esping-Andersen, 1997, p. 65).

Social protection thus changed direction: it passed from the new generations to the older ones, and inevitably, the relative poverty rates of the two groups also changed. The poverty of the elderly, which had stayed at relatively high levels for the whole postwar period, gradually began to decline. On the other hand, the poverty of children grew almost everywhere in proportion to the reduction in the transfers directed to families with children. In this respect too, the policies of the governments of the northern European countries differed completely from those of the southern European countries. A study of eight countries of the OECD area in the 1979–1982 period shows the proportion of families with children left poor after tax and transfers to be much higher in Australia, Canada, the Federal Republic of Germany, the United Kingdom and the United States than in Norway and Sweden. In these last two countries, the overall poverty reduction rate, in 1979 and 1982 respectively, was equal to 47.1 and 57.7 percent against the 12.7 percent of the Federal Republic of Germany, the 39.7 percent of the United Kingdom and the 16.9 percent of the United States. The study shows, moreover, that the effectiveness of public transfers is systematically greater for elderly families than for families with children (Smeeding *et al.*, 1988, p. 113) and varies according to family typology, being greater for families with a single parent and lower for families with two parents.

The role of public intervention in modifying the initial situation is not the same everywhere. The rate of poverty reduction is less than 25 percent in Italy and the United States; just over 25 percent in Germany and Switzerland; near or over 50 percent in Ireland, The Netherlands, Norway and the United Kingdom; and reaches or is over 75 percent in Belgium, Denmark, Finland, France and Sweden. In the final analysis, 'low transfer societies ... produce less reduction in child poverty in any given year than do high transfer societies ...' (Rainwater and Smeeding, 1995, pp. 16–17). Other studies show that this relation is absolutely general: the lower the income-security spending on family income, the higher children's low income rates, and vice versa (Ross *et al.*, 1995, p. 92). Further confirmation of the differential role of public transfers in the standard of living of families with children comes from a comparative study carried out by the European Observatory on National Family Policies in 1995. The study looks at the composition of poor households (households having 50 percent of the average income after social security benefits and direct taxation) in nine selected European countries; it shows, with the exception of the Nordic countries, and to a lesser degree the United Kingdom, the poverty of the elderly (alone or as a couple) to be systematically less widespread than that of couples with children. In Italy and Spain the proportion of low-income families with children was 42.1 and 40.1 percent, respectively, as against 7.6 and 5.8 percent in Finland and Sweden (Ditch *et al.*, 1996, p. 55).

The different degree to which families and children receive economic aid and services probably tends to influence the future behavior of the generations. In fact, a further consequence of the changes that followed the crisis of the 1970s was the trend for young people to put off the stages that mark the entry to adult life. In this case too, the outcome of the process depends on the functional interdependence and division of responsibilities among the family, the state and the market. None of these spheres alone is able to determine the final result. If their actions were incoherent, if they did not operate in complete synchrony, like instruments of an orchestra playing the same score though at different tempos and rhythms, they would produce a confused and irregular plurality of formative processes rather than patterns or ideal types that 'shape the context in which this transition takes place' (Breen and Buchmann, 2002, p. 289). Thus the family counts; the education system counts; the labor market counts; finally, the welfare system counts, because upon its organization depend not only:

> ... the terms and conditions under which people engage in families, and the extent to which they can uphold an acceptable standard of living independently of the ... family

but also:

> ... the degree to which individuals, or families, can uphold a socially acceptable standard of living independently of market participation (Esping-Andersen, 1990, p. 37).

However, what counts most is the degree to which the working of each of these institutions proceeds with one accord, to which the action of the one prolongs and reinforces that of the other, without creating obstacles, adverse effects and contradictions.

6.5   The Coming Generations: Toward a Political Economy of the Transition to Adulthood in the EU

In every country, the fundamental channels that mark a young person's transition to adulthood are family, school and work. Each of these is capable of either promoting or postponing the conclusion of the journey; yet the result depends not only on the characteristics of those channels and how they operate but on how consistently and uniformly they function. For simplicity's sake, let us assume that, to reach adult status, it is necessary to pass through the following gates: the conclusion of formal education; entry to the labor market; exit from the parental home; marriage or at least the start of a relatively stable relationship as a couple; and reproductive choice. The rhythms and sequences determining how young people go through these gates can vary considerably from one context to another. Equally variable is the age at which these passages take place, and each phase of the transition may in its turn take on different forms and patterns (Cavalli 1993, p. 35). Education sometimes tends to be prolonged beyond the conclusion of the school curriculum. Access to work passes more and more often through a long experience of precarious activities, flexible work contracts and longer or shorter periods of inactivity or unemployment, possibly alternating with attendance at professional refresher courses or training. The same is true with regard to leaving the parental home which may be temporary, followed by frequent returns and periodic absences for study or work or for affective reasons. Marriage and the birth of children also fall into the same category. The variability of the journeys has thus increased, and today the pathways are in confusion everywhere. Nevertheless, the possibility of finding an order in the disorder (i.e., relatively widespread and recurrent patterns) is an interesting challenge in terms of analysing the formative processes of the young generations in the different institutional contexts.

Before beginning the analysis of the five fundamental 'gates' of the transition to adulthood, we must briefly illustrate the essential features of the principal institutional configurations. Although the experience of each country is, in certain regards, unique, it is possible to group the members of the EU15 into four models of welfare state regime.

The social-democratic model. In this model, which is typical of the Nordic countries, rights and prerogatives are the individual's due and guaranteed by the state through universalistic procedures. Basically, this regime tends to reduce the individual's dependence on both the family and the market. Thus, the target of social policies is not the family as such but rather its single components. Although the family's extraneousness from sociopolitical orientations is ideological in nature, this does not mean that the responsibilities connected with family life should not be given adequate consideration. As a rule, expenditure on social protection as a percentage of GDP is quite high in the Nordic countries, certainly well above the average of the countries of the European Union (*Table 6.3*). No less important is the fact that, as far as the expenditure classified under the heading 'family and children' is concerned, the distance between the Nordic countries and the rest increases rather than decreases. In 2000, although this expenditure absorbed 8.2 percent of the total average social benefits in Europe, it was three to five percentage points higher in the northern European countries: 13.1 percent in Denmark, 12.5 percent in Finland and 10.8 percent in Sweden (European Commission, 2003a, p. 186). Similar, if not greater, differences are likewise found under other expenditure headings, such as 'housing and social exclusion' or 'unemployment,' both of which

Table 6.3. Expenditures on social protection as a percentage of GDP: EU15, 2000.

EU15	B	DK	G	GR	SP	F	IRL	I	L	NL	A	P	FIN	S	UK
27.3	26.7	28.8	29.5	26.4	20.1	29.7	14.1	25.2	21.0	27.4	28.7	22.7	25.2	32.3	26.8

Note: B: Belgium; DK: Denmark; G: Germany; GR: Greece; SP: Spain; F: France; IRL: Ireland; I: Italy; L: Luxembourg; NL: Netherlands; A: Austria; P: Poland; FIN: Finland; S: Sweden; UK: United Kingdom.
Source: European Commission (2003a).

are directly or indirectly connected with the family or family formation. Esping-Andersen (2000, p. 110, p. 124) has calculated that, in relation to gross domestic product (GDP), public expenditure assigned to services for the family in the social-democratic regimes is five times higher than expenditure assigned to services for the family in the countries of continental Europe, about nine times higher than in the liberal regimes and 20 times higher than in the countries of the Mediterranean area. The same is also true of home care for the elderly.

The continental (or conservative) model. The second 'family of nations' covers many of the countries of the continental area, including France and Germany. On principle, the division of welfare in this regime is based on the complementary responsibilities of the family and the state although, as a rule, care and support obligations fall mainly on the nuclear family.

> Individuality is relatively little developed; benefit and taxes almost always recognize the reciprocal obligations between the husband and wife and between parents and children. As far as the services are concerned, they are mostly considered auxiliaries to the care given by the family (Millar, 1996, p. 6).

Accordingly, this model is consistent with a private, familial idea of child care. There are relatively few services for children and young people. The community, although it supports the family, does not replace it. Rather, it encourages the temporary absence of the parents, usually the mother, from the workplace during the crucial phase of the child's development. The main difference in comparison with the Nordic countries is that while the care of children is seen there as a collective public responsibility, in this model it is a private one assigned essentially to the family and centered on the maternal role; as such, it is worthy of protection and is indirectly supported by the state. In other words, in the social-democratic regime solidarity is universalistic and diffuse, while in the continental regime it is particularistic and restricted. The logic of subsidiarity and, within certain limits, the rule of *tertium non datur* predominate. Social expenditure in relation to GDP is higher

Table 6.4. Social benefits by group of functions (as percentage of total social benefits): EU15, 2000.

Country	Old age and survivors' benefits	Sickness, health care	Disability	Un-employ-ment	Family and children	Housing and social exclusion
Denmark	38.1	20.2	12.0	10.5	13.1	6.1
Finland	35.8	23.8	13.9	10.4	12.5	3.5
Sweden	39.1	27.1	12.0	6.5	10.8	4.5
Belgium	43.8	25.1	8.7	11.9	9.1	1.4
Germany	42.2	28.3	7.8	8.4	10.6	2.6
France	44.1	29.1	5.8	6.9	9.6	4.5
Luxembourg	40.0	25.2	13.7	3.3	16.6	1.2
Austria	48.3	26.0	8.2	4.7	10.6	2.1
Netherlands	42.4	29.3	11.8	5.1	4.6	6.8
Greece	49.4	26.6	5.1	6.2	7.4	5.4
Italy	63.4	25.0	13.7	1.7	3.8	0.2
Portugal	45.6	30.6	13.0	3.8	5.5	1.5
Spain	46.3	29.6	7.6	12.2	2.7	1.6
United Kingdom	47.7	25.9	9.5	3.2	7.1	6.8
Ireland	25.4	25.0	5.3	9.7	13.0	5.5
EU15	46.4	27.3	8.1	6.3	8.2	3.7

Source: European Commission (2003a).

than the European average but lower than in the Nordic countries. In comparison with the Nordic countries, the gap is also wider (on average, three to four percentage points) with regard to the quota of social expenditure on total social benefits assigned to the heading 'family and children' and narrower (on average, one to two percentage points) with respect to the expenditure grouped under the headings 'housing and social exclusion' and 'unemployment' (European Commission, 2003a, p. 186) (*Table 6.4*).

The southern model. This group of countries covers Italy, Greece, Portugal and Spain. The difference between the continental (or conservative) model and the regime predominant in the countries of southern Europe is one of emphasis. As both are based on the sharing of welfare responsibilities by the family and the state, some experts tend to put them on the same plane. In the southern version, however, the residual role of state intervention is further accentuated at the expense of family responsibilities and obligations that extend even beyond the limits of the nuclear family. Both the principle of subsidiarity and the rule of *tertium non datur* provide a copybook example in these countries. Social protection is based on the figure of the male breadwinner. The family is given the responsibility for the care and assistance of its members as a priority, and this obligation is decreed by law. The state intervenes only when the family shows itself to be irreparably incapable of fulfilling its obligations. In comparison with continental Europe, what is lacking or at least extremely inadequate in this model is a system of income maintenance, especially for young people—or at any rate for those who have not yet joined the labor market. A further aspect of this 'familistic' regime is its marked *particularism*, that is, the low degree of *stateness* that characterizes the way it functions in the field of both intervention and financing (Ferrera, 1995, p. 9). In terms of social expenditure this group of countries is, in fact, well below the values of the other European countries. The distance from the Nordic countries is on average five percentage points of GDP, with peaks that exceed 12 percent between Spain (20.1 percent) and Sweden (32.3 percent); but the difference is greater (on average eight percentage points) if one considers the proportion of social expenditure assigned to the family. Under the heading of expenditure relative to housing, Denmark (6.1 percent on total social benefits) spends over 30 times more than Italy (0.2 percent), while in terms of expenditure related to unemployment, there is a sixfold gap between the two (European Commission, 2003a, p. 186).

The liberal model. The last model is composed of countries where the social division of welfare is based on the individual–market duo. Among the EU15 this category covers Ireland and the United Kingdom. As it also embraces the United States and other Anglo-Saxon countries around the world, it has received a good deal of attention in the literature. In this model both the role of the state and the responsibilities given to the family are relatively marginal with respect to the previous three institutional regimes. In its ideal-typical form, this model is orientated so as to reduce the intervention of the state to the minimum and entrust the solution of social problems to the spontaneous and, as far as possible, unregulated action of the market. In this model therefore, as in the one predominant in the countries of southern Europe, public guarantees apply only where neither the market nor the family have been able to prevent the individual getting into difficulty (rule of *tertium non datur*); even in such cases, however, social protection does not automatically intervene through universalistic procedures extended to the majority of citizens but with selective measures based on a verification of the real existence of need. The main difference is that, in the *liberal* model, faith in the market always takes priority or is anyway predominant with respect to the obligations of the family. The reason that this model can be considered residual is that it finds its maximum expression on the other side of the ocean, in Australia, Canada and the United States. In Europe, among the English-speaking countries, only the United Kingdom comes near to approaching this regime, and then only to a certain extent. Ireland has distinct characteristics: closer to the southern European countries in demographic and family behavior; closer to the northern European countries with regard to social policies. As a proportion of GDP, expenditure on social protection in the United Kingdom is more or less at the same level as in the continental countries (26.8 percent versus 28.4 percent, Luxembourg excluded), while Ireland is at a much lower level (14.1 percent), actually ten or so percentage points below the average of the southern European countries. Expenditures grouped under the heading 'family and children' in the United Kingdom are quite close to those of some southern countries (Italy 7.4 percent and the United Kingdom 7.1 percent of total social benefits) but quite far from the levels of the Nordic countries to which Ireland, on the other hand, comes close. Ireland pursues strong policies in favor of the family (13 percent) in spite of high fertility rates (1.89 in 2000) and a high average number of persons per household (3.0). Family instability in the United Kingdom is just as high as in the Nordic countries, while the percentage of live births outside marriage is also similar to that of the northern European countries—something that is also very high in Ireland, however, unlike in the southern European countries. Housing policies in both these English-speaking countries are at the same levels as in Denmark, while expenditure levels in Ireland and the United Kingdom again differ with regard to unemployment benefit; this is very low in the United Kingdom—close to that of the southern area countries (3.2 percent) but much higher in Ireland (9.7 percent)—at Nordic country levels (European Commission, 2003a, pp. 179–81, p. 186).

6.6 'Gates' of Transition

The degree to which the risks are distributed among the principal institutions in each of the models of welfare-state regime should be reflected in the time it takes for young people to cover the distance that separates them from adulthood and achieving autonomy from the family. This time will be shorter where the responsibilities connected with bringing up the new generations are shared among different institutions and longer where they weigh exclusively or mainly on the shoulders of the family. Lacking alternatives, in fact, the young will tend to put off leaving home for the same reason that families will tend to hold on to them, even shouldering the costs of their maintenance until the age of the offspring is quite advanced—until, that is, the opportunities provided by the market or the state become a concrete and stable alternative to the economic support and services guaranteed by the family. The greater the intervention by the market or the state in support of or as a substitute for the family, the earlier the young achieve autonomy; vice versa, the wider and more indefinite the responsibilities delegated to the families, the more likely it is that the young will put off the moment of leaving home and thus of independence

Table 6.5. Young people aged 15 to 24 years still studying, by gender: European countries, 2002.

Country	Males and females	Males	Females
Denmark	72.0	71.1	73.0
Finland	71.4	69.2	73.6
Sweden	64.6	62.9	66.4
Norway*	24.0	23.8	24.2
Belgium	66.7	65.0	68.4
Germany	69.5	69.4	69.6
France	67.2	65.0	69.5
Luxembourg	69.3	69.7	68.9
Austria	60.3	59.7	60.9
Netherlands	71.7	72.9	70.5
Greece	60.2	59.4	61.0
Italy	59.6	57.2	62.2
Portugal	51.9	47.7	56.1
Spain	60.7	56.4	65.1
United Kingdom	61.6	61.0	62.3
Ireland	53.8	52.1	55.6
EU15	64.1	62.4	65.8

Notes: *Data for Norway refer only to education/training that would be important for the current or future job.
Source: European Commission (2003c).

from their parents. Having made this premise, we can now examine when and how the young Europeans pass through the different transition 'gates.'

Education. Education is still the first gate that the young pass through in their transition to adulthood. In some countries the beginning of higher education coincides with the exit from the family, but as a rule the definitive exit from the parental home takes place a few years after the completion of education. Almost everywhere, leaving home is followed by entry to the labor market and the formation of a family. However, the most important intercountry differences concern the age at which young people complete their education and the ways in which reaching the end of the educational path is combined with the other phases of the transition.

Prolonging education results in a postponement of the age at which the young succeed in becoming independent from the family (Galland, 2000, p. 21). Up to the age of 24 the majority of the young, male and female, are still studying (*Table 6.5*). Employment status, on the other hand, varies considerably. In northern Europe between 44 percent (Finland and Sweden) and 64 percent (Denmark) of the young aged between 15 and 24 are employed, while in the south, on average,

Table 6.6. Inactive population aged 15 to 24 and 25 to 54 (as a percentage of total population) and inactive in education (as a percentage of total inactive): European countries, 2002.

Country	Inactive (15–24)	Inactive (25–54)	Inactive in education
Denmark	31.2	18.0	13.7
Finland	37.7	19.5	9.1
Sweden	49.5	16.0	15.8
Belgium	66.2	29.1	0.7
Germany	50.0	24.3	12.5
France	63.1	23.3	18.4
Austria	44.3	25.0	13.2
Netherlands	26.1	23.0	6.5
Greece	63.7	30.7	14.7
Italy	64.7	33.9	14.3
Portugal	53.0	21.1	19.7
Spain	57.8	28.5	16.5
United Kingdom	37.5	21.8	8.7
Ireland	50.9	25.8	3.3

Source: European Commission (2003c).

only 31.9 percent are employed; moreover, in the liberal regimes (Ireland and the United Kingdom), on average more than 50 percent are employed. In all countries (Finland excepted), the percentage of those aged 15 to 24 declaring themselves unemployed is relatively low (between 4 and 9 percent, or just above); this means that the proportion of inactive youth (young people classed as neither employed nor unemployed) is particularly high in the south as compared with the north and the continental countries (United Kingdom included) (*Table 6.6*). In Greece and Italy 64 percent are in this position as against just over 30 percent in Denmark. Considering how many of the inactive are still studying, we find this proportion to be systematically higher in the southern countries than elsewhere (France and Sweden excepted): 16.3 percent on average against a range of values between the 0.7 percent of Belgium and the 13.7 percent of Denmark. An OECD study shows that in the 16–19 age group, Austria, Denmark, Germany, The Netherlands and the United Kingdom have the highest percentage of young people simultaneously working and studying, while in the south almost all the young people studying are not employed. In the 20–24 age group, southern European young people are higher up the country list in relative terms, but the percentage that have found a job is still low (OECD, 1999, p. 48). The first conclusion, therefore, is that one reason the young southerners continue their education is the lack of concrete job prospects. The southern countries, in fact, give far greater guarantees to the adult heads of households than to their children. In the south the gap between inactive young people (15 to 24) and adults (25 to 54) who find themselves in the same position is more than 30 percentage points, while in the other countries it is much less; in Denmark, for example, it is 13.2 percentage points, in Finland 18.2, and in the United Kingdom 15.7.

Although the gaps in education levels have tended to reduce, they are still significant in terms of the relationship between school and work: the countries of northern and central Europe try to encourage both school attendance and the participation of the young in the labor market; the countries of southern Europe, lacking adequate job opportunities for the young, tend instead to use school as a 'parking lot.' The effect is highly predictable. Italy, Greece and Spain share the unhappy record of having the highest rates of youth unemployment (more than 20 percent). In many cases this situation lasts over 12 months and is around ten percentage points higher for girls than for boys of the same age. On the other hand, in the social-democratic and liberal regimes, youth unemployment rates are at much lower levels (Finland excepted), the gap between males and females is small and, above all, unemployment tends not to last long. The pattern in the continental countries is the most difficult to interpret, but on average (France and Belgium excepted) youth unemployment, male and female, tends to be relatively lower (European Commission, 2003a, p. 184). Finally, there is another characteristic that distinguishes the southern countries from those of northern and central Europe; in the former, even young people with tertiary academic qualifications have difficulty finding a job. With the exception of Portugal, the employment rates of those aged 15 to 24 with a tertiary qualification are far lower than those of the other countries. The gap between Italy and Finland, for example, is over 40 percentage points, roughly the same as between Italy and the United Kingdom (European Commission, 2003b, pp. 82–83). The gaps are also wide in the next age group up. According to the OECD Education Database, in 1999 the unemployment rates for young adults aged 25 to 29 with a tertiary qualification were between 11.2 and 27.3 percent, respectively, in Portugal and Italy, and at much lower levels, on average around 6 percent, in the countries of northern and central Europe. At that time, only in France was unemployment of intellectuals in double figures (Bowers *et al.*, 1999).

Labor market.   Work is the principal means of achieving economic independence; in the absence of other possibilities, it is thus the basis for making choices, the first and foremost of which is living in a separate home and leading an autonomous life, independent of the family of origin. As a rule, countries with liberal and social-democratic regimes tend to encourage youth employment, even during the school career. The southern European countries, however, have particularly high levels of unemployment in terms of the younger age groups (in some Italian regions over 58 percent). OECD data relating to 1997 show clearly that in the whole of southern Europe, the percentage of young people who at the age of 22 combine education or training *and* employment is noticeably lower (just 1.9 percent in Greece and Italy, marginally higher in Portugal and Spain) than in other countries (Bowers *et al.*, 1999, p. 61).

Youth unemployment is systematically higher than adult unemployment in all the countries. The difference is that while in most of the continental and Nordic countries and in the United Kingdom the gap between the 15–24 age group and the next age group up (25 to 49) is generally a maximum of eight to ten percentage points, in the southern countries the gap increases to almost 20 points (European Commission, 2003b, pp. 184–185). The only exceptions are Finland (+21 percentage points) and Portugal (+6 percentage points). Another characteristic that distinguishes the southern countries from the others is that in the 15–24 age group the risk of unemployment grows or, at most, remains constant, as academic qualifications increase, whereas in most of the countries the opposite is true (European Commission, 2003b, pp. 186–187) (*Table 6.7*). Thus, while in the northern European and continental countries (United Kingdom included) studying is worthwhile because it increases the possibility of finding a job at a relatively early age, in the south this is not the case or seems much less so. While, in southern countries, the greater salary and career opportunities associated with a higher academic qualification will probably bear fruit later in the individual's working life, at a younger age they do not bring immediate advantages in the labor market. This anomaly brings the role of the family to the fore. The expression *work gerontocracy* sums up the character of this regime—a regime, in which the existence of:

> ... a strong system of occupational and wage guarantees in favor of employed workers—males, adults, with a family to support—which has actually reduced the competitive capacity of young people entering the labor market (Paci, 1995, p. 748 [author's translation]).

Coherently, because of the historically corporatist nature of this regime, the right to social protection ends up being linked to employment status. Accordingly, as

> ... there is no provision for income support for those who ... still represent the majority of the unemployed, that is, young men (and young women) looking for their first job ... the entire burden of the cost of maintaining the unemployed ... has been discharged on to the family (Pugliese, 1995, p. 470 [author's translation]).

In the family, resources (wages, transfers and pensions), costs and goods can be shared; thus, later exit (from the education system) and later entry (to the labor market) are the proper and logical coping strategy in such a situation.

Table 6.7.   Youth unemployment rate by gender aged 15 to 24 years: EU15, 2000.

Country	Males	Females
Denmark	7.0	7.5
Finland	21.1	21.6
Sweden	10.7	11.9
Belgium	15.1	20.8
Germany	9.8	8.2
France	6.1	22.3
Luxembourg	6.5	8.3
Austria	4.8	5.8
Netherlands	4.6	6.6
Greece	22.2	37.9
Italy	27.2	35.1
Portugal	6.8	11.6
Spain	20.6	33.2
United Kingdom	13.8	11.5
Ireland	6.1	7.0
EU15	14.9	17.6

Source: European Commission (2003a).

The negative aspect of family solidarity is that it reduces the need for state assistance. This is reflected in the lack of adequate programs or the weakness of programs aimed at supporting young people who have no work and who do not have an income above a hypothetical subsistence level or a minimum of resources. Greece and Italy have no programs of this kind; in Spain the minimum income is the so-called *renta minima*, but it is not a uniform measure and is controlled by the 17 regions (*comunidades autónomas*). In 1966 Portugal introduced a similar program, the *rendimento mínimo garantido*, but its effectiveness, as in the case of Spain, is somewhat limited. All the other European countries have noncontributory, nondiscretionary programs based on subjective rights that, in some cases, were already operative from the 1960s and 1970s (MISSOC, 1999, 458 ff.).

The generosity of these programs is anything but uniform. According to OECD estimates, adding up the maximum obtainable benefits available to an unemployed single person aged 20 years, living alone without family responsibilities and without an employment record, the most generous countries are Belgium, Denmark, Finland, Germany, The Netherlands and Sweden, which guarantee net replacement rates that are not far off the level of earnings of the average production worker; at the bottom of the list, with a much lower net replacement rate, are Portugal and Spain (Bowers *et al.*, 1999, p. 61). The effectiveness of these programs can be indirectly assessed in the light of the results of a 1997 Eurobarometer survey (*Table 6.8*). In the south a young person who neither studies nor works obtains most (between 60 and 70 percent) of his/her financial resources from the family and an absolutely negligible part through unemployment/social security benefits or training allowance/educational grants. In the north the package of resources comes in a quite different combination. Parents and family contribute just 10 to 20 percent of the total resources the young have at their disposal while the rest, between 60 and 80 percent of the total, comes from the public purse. The situation of the continental countries lies between the two extremes, with France closer to the southern countries and Austria, Belgium and Germany closer to the Nordic countries, while in The Netherlands young people can count on income from both casual work and state transfers. Ireland and the United Kingdom are quite close to the Scandinavian countries (Eurobarometer, 1997). In the south the family thus functions as a 'shock absorber.' The risk of youth unemployment weighs heavily on the family's shoulders, and this naturally reduces the stimulus for young people to look for a job and for the state to provide alternative resources. The proof is that the proportion of young people not in the labor force living in households where no other person is employed is much lower in the south than elsewhere (Bowers *et al.*, 1999, p. 66).

Family formation. All other things being equal, a prolonged education period and a depressed transition to employment push the age of family formation upward. In other words, late independence is invariably followed by late partnering. The mean age at first marriage has gone up all over Europe by about two years in the last decade (Eurostat, 2004). There have been slightly greater increases in the northern European countries where the average age at marriage was already relatively high at the beginning of the 1990s (Council of Europe, 2002, p. 54). This is not the point, however. What is most important is the variety of the paths that lead young people to marriage. A secondary analysis of the results of the European Community Household Panel shows that young people's living arrangements vary to an extraordinary extent in the four 'families of nations' (Iacovou, 2002, p. 55). In Finland and Denmark 34 and 44.2 percent, respectively, of women aged between 25 and 29 live with a partner. In Norway and Sweden the percentages are just as high (Vogel, 2003, p. 133). The countries of continental Europe have values that are a few percentage points lower: The Netherlands, 29.1 percent; France, 25.8 percent; Austria, 21.5 percent; Belgium, 16.9 percent and Germany, 15 percent. The United Kingdom is at more or less the same levels with 18.8 percent, while Catholic Ireland, with very low values (3.7 percent), heads the list of the southern European countries, which (Spain excluded) show even lower values. Considering the median age (i.e., the age by which 50 percent of young people are living with a partner), intercountry differences are clearly perceptible. In the Nordic countries

Table 6.8. Chief sources of money for young people aged 15 to 24 years: EU15, 1997.

Country	Parents or family	Partner	Regular job	Casual work	Work in the under- ground economy	Unempl./ social security benefits	Training allowance/ education grant
Denmark	18.7	1.7	64.8	3.5	4.2	8.5	28.2
Finland	40.5	2.7	24.7	19.5	0.8	15.2	25.3
Sweden	34.2	1.2	29.5	18.7	3.2	11.7	10.3
Belgium	48.0	5.8	33.0	9.2	2.7	10.3	2.3
Germany	37.8	4.9	51.2	15.8	2.4	7.8	5.8
France	47.8	8.3	40.2	14.7	7.0	5.7	5.3
Austria	41.0	3.2	45.5	8.2	1.7	4.7	13.5
Netherlands	32.5	4.7	33.8	22.8	3.8	5.7	24.7
Greece	50.8	5.3	40.5	5.3	0.3	1.7	–
Italy	67.5	2.3	26.2	15.5	3.5	0.2	1.3
Portugal	50.7	3.3	47.0	5.0	1.0	1.3	1.7
Spain	62.3	2.8	35.8	10.8	1.5	2.0	1.5
United Kingdom	17.4	6.1	56.8	6.3	0.5	18.3	2.8
Ireland	38.0	2.2	36.8	12.0	1.3	13.2	4.7
EU15	45.0	4.7	41.5	12.6	2.9	6.8	5.2

Source: Eurobarometer 47.2 (1997).

one-half of girls have already established a partnership by the age of 22.3 years. The same event occurs over a year later (23.7) in the continental countries and 3.4 years later, on average, in the Mediterranean countries. From this point of view the United Kingdom is very close to the average of the Nordic countries, while the young Irish do not behave differently from the young people of southern Europe. Apart from Ireland, the most significative anomalies in this panorama concern Italy and, to a lesser degree, Austria and Germany which, on average, show higher ages of entry to a partnership relationship than the other countries in their respective groups.

The precocity or otherwise of a partnership is closely linked to the age at which young people leave their families of origin. For both men and women, the earlier the exit from the family, the earlier the entry to a partnership relationship. Nevertheless, there are marked differences between one regime and another. In the northern European social democracies, an average of 3.65 years pass between a young man's exit from his family and his entry into a relationship with a partner; for a young woman the interval between the two events is shorter but still long (2.15 years) compared with other countries. In the continental countries (with the

Table 6.9. Median age of transition.

Country	Age by which 50% of people have left home		Age by which 50% of people are living with a partner	
	Males	Females	Males	Females
Denmark	21.4	20.3	25.4	22.2
Finland	21.9	20.0	25.2	22.4
Belgium	25.8	23.8	26.3	24.1
Germany	24.8	21.6	27.8	23.9
France	24.1	22.2	25.9	23.7
Austria	27.2	23.4	27.6	23.8
Netherlands	23.3	21.2	26.1	23.2
Greece	28.2	22.9	28.7	24.2
Italy	29.7	27.1	30.3	27.4
Portugal	28.0	25.2	28.2	24.9
Spain	28.4	26.6	29.0	26.5
United Kingdom	23.5	21.2	25.5	22.8
Ireland	26.3	25.2	28.3	26.7

Source: Iacovou (2002), based on European Community Household Panel Statistics, 1994.

exception of The Netherlands, which shows higher values), the interval between the two events goes down to 1.7 and 1.8 years, respectively, for males and females. Ireland and the United Kingdom come close to the continental countries—France, in particular—while in southern Europe just a few (0.5) months go by on average, between exit from the parental home and entry to an affective relationship. These results, together with the considerations mentioned previously, thus confirm the existence of different transition models with regard to the times of passing through the different gates and to the sequence in which the passage from one to the other is accomplished (see *Table 6.9*). In the social-democratic regime and to a certain extent in the liberal regime, at least one-half of the females have already left their parents' home by the age of 20 and have established a partnership relationship by 22. Elsewhere, both events are postponed: less so in the conservative regimes of the continent, where they occur on average about a year later than in the Nordic countries; much more so in the familistic southern European countries. However, the most significant fact is undoubtedly that, in the south, the beginning of an affective relationship with a partner and leaving the family of origin takes place practically without a break; in between, nothing or almost nothing occurs. Young people only free themselves from the family when they begin a new relationship, with few and sporadic experiences—affective and otherwise—in the course of the journey that takes them from their parents' home to one of their own.

Giovanni B. Sgritta

Table 6.10. Mean age of women at first childbearing: European countries, 1980–2000.

Country	1980	1985	1990	1995	1999	2000
Denmark	26.8	27.8	28.5	29.2	29.6	29.7
Finland	27.7	28.4	28.9	29.3	29.6	29.6
Sweden	27.6	28.4	28.6	29.2	29.8	29.9
Norway	26.9	27.5	28.1	28.9	29.3	29.3
Belgium	26.6	27.2	27.9	28.5	–	–
Germany	26.4	27.1	27.6	28.3	28.7	–
France	26.8	27.5	28.3	29.0	29.4	29.4
Austria	26.3	26.7	27.2	27.7	28.1	28.2
Netherlands	27.7	28.4	29.3	30.0	30.3	30.3
Greece	26.1	26.3	27.2	28.2	28.9	–
Italy	27.4	28.0	28.9	30.0	–	–
Portugal	27.2	27.2	27.3	28.1	28.6	28.7
Spain	28.2	28.5	28.9	30.0	30.7	–
United Kingdom	26.9	27.3	27.7	28.2	28.4	28.5
Ireland	29.7	29.8	29.9	30.2	30.5	30.6
EU15	27.1	27.6	28.2	28.9	29.3	–

Source: Eurostat (2002).

Childbearing. Like the age at marriage, the age at the birth of the first child has also gone up (see *Table 6.10*). This phenomenon dates back to at least the beginning of the 1980s and affects all the countries without any distinctions whatsoever (Eurostat, 2003, p. 89). The generations of women born after the 1960s have gradually postponed the decision to have a child by about two years compared with previous generations (Eurostat, 2003, p. 90). At the turn of the new millennium, the mean age of women at childbearing in the EU15 was 29.5 years. The intercountry differences are not significant, however. The countries with a mainly Catholic majority tend to have slightly higher values, but just as high average ages are found in France, The Netherlands and the Nordic countries; in the Nordic countries the mean age of the mother at childbearing is practically constant and exactly equal to the average of the southern countries. There are two fundamental reasons for this apparent anomaly. The first is that the young women of the Nordic and continental countries have more frequent and more precocious premarital relationships than the young women of the south. On the one hand, this to a certain extent makes them postpone the date of marriage—which, unlike in the southern countries, is not the only means of exit from the family—and, on the other hand, it increases the probability of bearing a child before marriage. The second reason is linked to the first. As has often been recalled, in fact, the proportion of births outside marriage is quite different in the northern and southern regimes. In the former, from 41 percent (Finland) to 55 percent (Sweden) of children are born before the couple is married. In the United Kingdom the values are only just below these (39.5 percent); Ireland, where the proportion of children born outside marriage fluctuates between 20 and 30 percent of total live births, is thus closer to the continental countries. With the exception of Portugal, these percentages are far lower in the south, from the 4 per-cent of Greece to the 14 percent of Spain (European Commission, 2003a, p. 181). The situation is also slowly changing in these countries. Ten or twenty years ago the percentage of live births outside marriage was very much lower. And yet, the golden rule is still valid today: while in the northern and, to a certain extent, the continental countries, young couples arrive at marriage having passed through pro-creation, in the south of Europe the exact opposite is true: the birth of children basically passes through the institutional gate of marriage.

Family exit. Exit from the family of origin is uneventful because it is sim-ply the sum of the debits or credits in terms of time, opportunities, resources and autonomy that the young have accumulated on the way. In certain cases, as in the north, it is not even an 'event' in the sense that it often happens before the end of education, even before finding a steady job and before being married and having a child. Although in recent years the age of exit from the parental home has also increased in the south, the gaps in the south are still huge (*Table 6.11*). Elaborations by Coomans (in a personal communication to the author) on the results of the 2002 Labor Force Survey show that at the age of 30 to 31 years, 50 percent of young men in Italy, Greece and Spain still lived with their parents. In Portugal the threshold is a little lower—about 29 years. This phenomenon has also become noticeable in the continental countries, but even there we are a long way—at least five to six years—from the record scores of the young southerners. The Labor Force Survey does not report the data of the Nordic countries, but it is probable that the age at leaving home is very much lower there than in the rest of Europe. According to the 2001 census, in Italy, which together with Greece stands at one extreme in this matter, 70.3 percent of those between the ages of 25 and 29 years still lived at home, as did 26.2 percent of those between 30 and 34 years and 10 percent in the 35–44 age group (that is to say, just under 900,000 'young people' in Italy alone). Surprisingly perhaps, these percentages do not vary much, whether one looks at the richer and more modern regions of the north or the less wealthy and more traditional regions of the south (Istat, 2004b).

Different elements and interests have an effect on the end result. As far as the young are concerned, the postponing of the time of entry into adulthood is not due exclusively to contingent *necessities* but also to *convenience*. According to Cook and Furstenberg (2002, p. 265), in Italy young people are trapped in the family,

Table 6.11. Age at which 50 per cent of young people leave parental home, by gender: European countries, 2002.

Country	Males	Females
Belgium	25.1	23.4
Germany	23.9	21.8
France	23.9	21.8
Austria	26.3	23.1
Netherlands	24.5	21.9
Greece	31.1	27.5
Italy	30.7	27.9
Portugal	28.7	26.2
Spain	30.0	28.0
United Kingdom	23.6	20.5
Ireland	26.4	22.9

Source: Coomans (personal communication to the author regarding the 2002 Labor Force Survey).

'but in a partly gilded cage. It is a cage that the young people have themselves codesigned.' Young adults enjoy a great deal of freedom, if not *outside* the family, then *within* it. Staying at home brings more advantages than disadvantages. They have a space of their own where they do as they like and from which their parents are often excluded. They plan what they do in complete freedom with few or no restrictions. They can associate with whomever they like without any interference from their parents. Interpersonal conflicts are reduced to a minimum. They are even given relative financial independence—a kind of 'subsistence income' that the parents, if they can afford it, never fail to provide and that guarantees the young adults an adequate degree of buying power (Sgritta, 2001, p. 77). On the other hand, parents do not put great pressure on their children to go their own way and to face the choices and responsibilities of life independently. Asked if having the children stay on at home was a problem, only 8 percent of the parents said yes. For 38 percent it is 'normal' and for 54 percent even a 'pleasure.' And to the question about the main reason why the son/daughter did *not want* to go and live on his/her own, a whopping 43 percent declared without mincing their words that 'they would have to give up the comforts of their home' and there were also those who admitted candidly that their son/daughter 'did not want to be independent' (17 percent), that he/she 'is not used to making sacrifices or giving things up' (7 percent) or 'to taking on responsibilities' (7 percent). All in all, more than one-half of the parents are likewise convinced that their children will miss life in the family when they leave (Bonifazi *et al.*, 1999, pp. 80–81). Is this 'family portrait' also valid for the other southern countries? Information is lacking in this respect, but apart from a few details the picture is unlikely to change much. In any case, the end result is the same.

6.7   Closing Remarks

What will Europe's coming generations be like? If, as is probable, the mortgage of the past and the present continues to weigh on future events, the next generations will continue to pass through the various life gates according to different timetables and in different ways: in a more rapid and blurred fashion in some families of nations, in a slower and more orderly fashion in others. However, a question still remains. As Cook and Furstenberg *et al.* (2002, p. 7) point out, western societies look remarkably similar for young people at age 15, when:

> ... virtually no one has left school, established an independent household, assumed a full-time job, formed a union, or begun childbearing. And they are almost as similar again at age 35, by which time a vast majority of adults in every nation have negotiated all of the transition.

Thus, however different the national pathways to adulthood, the end result still seems to be the same. So, do national differences in pathways through youth and early adulthood really matter (Cook and Furstenberg, 2002, p. 287)? The question is of considerable importance as the interval between the two extremes covers about one-quarter of a lifetime. It does not occur at an ordinary time in life but at one destined to have a profound, perhaps irreversible effect on character formation; it is a time when the foundations for future choices and projects are laid and the credentials are acquired with which young people will face their future journey in society, in the economy and in relationships—if not all, then almost all. Do national variations really matter then?

If the delay accumulated in the span of those crucial 20 years by the young people of southern Europe compared with their contemporaries in other countries is ultimately reabsorbed and has no repercussions on the following stages of the life course, then the answer to this question is no. On the other hand, if that delay produces long-term effects, the answer is yes. As usual, we cannot accurately predict future events. We can, however, make some conjectures on the basis of the present situation. As things stand, therefore, the evidence is that those delays do have tangible repercussions on the whole individual life course. As a study by Mayer (2001, pp. 100–101) demonstrates, 'institutional configurations and life course regimes co-vary in a systematic manner.' With regard to Italy in particular, an exacting longitudinal survey confirms that 'the greater freedom enjoyed by young adults ... is, so to speak, confined to the expressive sphere.' Compared with the countries of northern and central Europe:

... the more substantial family protections result, in the final analysis, in a greater and longer psychological and material dependence
which expresses itself, precisely, in longer and more difficult transitions toward adulthood (Schizzerotto, 2002, pp. 366–367 [author's
translation]).

The point is that these difficulties do not come to an end on the threshold of adult
life. As the most significant statistical aggregates demonstrate, they shape the general catalog of life-course outcomes. In an overall inventory of advantages and
disadvantages, the Mediterranean countries are probably at the bottom of the list.
At the education level, this is valid both with regard to the percentage of population
aged 25 to 64 years that has attained at least a high-school qualification and the percentage of adults involved in life-long learning. In the former case, Greece, Italy,
Portugal and Spain have percentages actually equal to one-half of the values of
Austria, Denmark, Germany, Sweden and the United Kingdom. In the latter group,
the gap is even greater: in Sweden 34.2 percent of adults participate in permanent
education courses against just 4 to 5 percent, on average, in the Mediterranean
countries (Istat, 2004a, p. 474). The percentage of young people aged 18 to 24 who
have left their studies and do not participate in any education or training program
is also higher in the southern European countries (Istat, 2004a, p. 476).

The relative disadvantage of the southern countries also remains when one considers employment. The employment rates of the population aged 15 to 64 are systematically lower in these countries than elsewhere; furthermore, the gap between
male and female employment rates is particularly high in Greece, Spain and Italy, in
that order. Equally negative records characterize these countries with regard to the
rate of youth unemployment and the quota of long-term unemployed, both many
percentage points above the EU15 average (Istat 2004a, p. 477) (see *Table 6.12*).
In terms of social cohesion, too, the picture of the southern European countries
is anything but comforting. An important indicator in this regard is the reduction
of poverty levels obtained through public transfers. Considering the percentage of
individuals who live in a family with an income equal to or lower than 60 percent
of the median income of their country, Eurostat estimates demonstrate that in the
whole area of southern Europe, plus Ireland, in spite of the transfers, the population
at risk of poverty is about 20 percent, that is, five percentage points more than the
EU15 average (Istat, 2004a, p. 476). Another indicator of social cohesion is the
gap in the levels of GDP within the same country. In this case too, Italy, Ireland
and Spain (with the addition of Germany as a result of the reunification process)
head the list. Italy registers the highest proportion of population living in regions
with per capita GDP below 75 percent of the national average. Almost the same
situation characterizes Spain, where in 2002 little more than one-fifth (21 percent)
of the population lived in disadvantaged regions (Istat, 2004a, p. 99).

Table 6.12. Labor market in the EU15, 2002.

| Country | Employment rate | | Part-time employ-ment (%) | Unem-ployment rate, 2003 | Youth unemploy-ment rate | Long-term unemplo-ment (%) |
	Males 15–64	Females 15–64				
Denmark	80.0	71.7	20.0	5.6	7.7	19.0
Finland	70.0	66.2	12.8	9.0	21.0	24.7
Sweden	74.9	72.2	21.5	5.6	11.8	19.9
Belgium	68.3	51.4	19.1	8.1	18.2	48.6
Germany	71.7	58.8	21.3	9.3	9.7	46.7
France	69.5	56.7	16.1	9.4	19.6	31.3
Austria	75.7	63.1	20.2	4.4	6.8	18.7
Netherlands	82.4	66.2	43.9	3.8	5.2	25.7
Luxembourg	75.6	51.6	10.6	3.7	8.3	27.4
Greece	71.4	42.5	4.5	9.3	26.4	51.2
Italy	69.1	42.0	8.6	8.7	27.2	59.1
Portugal	75.9	60.8	11.2	6.4	11.5	34.4
Spain	72.6	44.1	7.9	11.3	22.2	34.2
United Kingdom	78.0	65.3	24.9	5.0	12.1	21.9
Ireland	75.2	55.4	16.5	4.6	8.0	29.8
EU15	72.8	55.6	18.1	8.0	15.1	39.3

Source: Istat (2004a).

Gender distributive justice also contributes to social cohesion. Again, the situation in the southern countries is nothing to boast about. Take, for example, Italy, where the opportunity for a woman to have a job is drastically reduced when she has children. About four out of five women without children are employed, while less than one-half of mothers aged 25 to 44 work. The recent upsurge in part-time work has partially reduced the need for women to leave the labor market permanently when children are born, but the woman's path to work inclusion is still strewn with all kinds of obstacles: the meager amount of help in the home contributed by the partner, the low levels of pay and the chronic lack of services for children and the elderly. As in all the countries with familistic regimes, the woman is faced with the classic Gordian knot: either to form a family and have children or to devote herself to work and a career, in the latter case shouldering the burden of reconciling the needs of one with those of the other.

Nowhere else in the EU15 is the way out of this dilemma so problematic as in the southern European countries; in no other regime does it give rise to such an impressive sequence of delays and denials destined to accompany the individual life course: in union formation, in childbearing, in work stability and continuity and in the standard of living. We each have our own view on this situation, but to this author it seems that an enormous sacrifice of human resources is being laid on the altar of tradition and conservatism—a waste of human capital compared to which the delays accumulated in the course of the transition to adulthood are just warning signs, an announcement of a more widespread and worrying deferment of social citizenship. In the final analysis, this deferment of social citizenship is not so much the cause but rather the effect of a widespread situation of poverty and backwardness that some social categories are fated to experience—the young and women; the young of the lower classes and the women of the lower classes—a situation, moreover, that leads to 'half-citizenship' and, for the less fortunate, to no citizenship at all.

References

Barbagli, M. (1990) *Provando e riprovando. Matrimonio, famiglia e divorzio in Italia e in altri paesi occidentali*, Bologna, Italy: Il Mulino [in Italian].

Boh, K. (1989) 'European Family Life Patterns—A Reappraisal,' in Boh, K., Bak, M., Clason, C., Pankratova, M., Qvortrup, J., Sgritta, G.B. and Wareness, K. (eds) *Changing Patterns of European Family Life*, London: Routledge, pp. 265–298.

Bonifazi, C., Menniti, A., Misiti, M. and Palomba, R. (1999) *Giovani che non lasciano il nido. Atteggiamenti, speranze, condizioni all'uscita da casa. [Young People Who Do Not Leave the Family Nest: Attitudes, Hopes, and Conditions Relevant to Leaving Home.]* IRP Working Paper no 1/99(1), Rome, Italy [in Italian, with summary in English and French].

Bowers, N., Sonnet, A. and Bardone, L. (1999) *Giving Young People a Good Start: The Experience of OECD Countries*, See http://www.oecd.org/dataoecd/11/30/1953937.pdf/ accessed in December 2005.

Breen, R. and Buchmann, M. (2002) 'Institutional Variation and the Position of Young People: A Comparative Perspective,' in Furstenberg, F.F., Cook, T.D., Sampson, R. and Slap, G. (eds) *Early Adulthood in Cross-National Perspective*, The Annals of the American Academy of Political and Social Science, **580**: 288–305, special issue, March.

Cavalli, A. (1993) 'Senza nessuna fretta di crescere,' *Il Mulino*, **345**: 35 [in Italian].

Chauvel, L. (1998) *Le destin des générations. Structure sociale et cohortes en France au XX siècle*, Paris, France: Presses Universitaires de France [in French].

Cook, T.D. and Furstenberg, F.F. (2002) 'Explaining Aspects of the Transition to Adulthood in Italy, Sweden, Germany, and the United States: A Cross-Disciplinary, Case Synthesis Approach,' in Furstenberg, F.F., Cook, T.D., Sampson, R. and Slap, G. (eds) *Early Adulthood in Cross-National Perspective*, The Annals of the American Academy of Political and Social Science, **580**: 257–287, special issue, March.

Cordón, J.A.F. (1997) 'Youth Residential Independence and Autonomy. A Comparative Study,' *Journal of Family Issues*, **18**: 576–607.

Council of Europe (2002) *Evolution démographique récente en Europe*, Strasbourg, France: Council of Europe [in French].

Crouch, C. (2001) *Sociologia dell'Europa occidentale*, Bologna, Italy: Il Mulino [in Italian; translated from English].

Ditch, J., Barnes, H. and Bradshaw. J. (1996) *A Synthesis of National Family Policies in 1995*, York, UK: European Observatory on National Family Policies, Social Policy Research Unit, University of York.

Esping-Andersen, G. (1990) *The Three Worlds of Welfare Capitalism*, Cambridge, UK: Polity Press.

Esping-Andersen, G. (1997) 'Welfare States at the End of the Century. The Impact of Labor Market, Family and Demographic Change,' in *Family, Market, and Community: Equity and Efficiency in Social Policy*, Social Policy Studies, **21**, Paris, France: Organisation of Economic Co-operation and Development.

Esping-Andersen, G. (2000) *I fondamenti sociali delle economie industriali*, Bologna, Italy: Il Mulino [in Italian; translated from English].

Eurobarometer (1997) *Young Europeans, April–June 1997*, Eurobarometer 47.20VR.

European Commission (1994) *The Demographic Situation in the European Union*, Brussels, Belgium: Directorate-General V.

European Commission (2003a) *The Social Situation in the European Union, 2003*, Luxembourg: Office for Official Publications of the European Communities.

European Commission (2003b) *European Social Statistics. Labour Force Survey Result 2002*, Luxembourg: Office for Official Publications of the European Communities.

European Commission (2003c) *Labour Force Survey Results, 2002*, Luxembourg: Office for Official Publications of the European Communities.

Eurostat (1988) *Censuses of Population in the Community Countries 1981–1982*, Population and Social Conditions Series, Luxembourg: European Communities Statistical Office.

Eurostat (2002) *Demographic Statistics, 2001*, Luxembourg: European Communities Statistical Office.

Eurostat (2003) *Demographic Statistics, 2002*, Luxembourg: European Communities Statistical Office.

Eurostat (2004) See http://epp.eurostat.cec.eu.int/portal/page?_pageid=1996,39140985 &_dad=portal&_schema=PORTAL&screen=detailref&language=en&product=Year lies_new_population&root=Yearlies_new_population/C/C1/C13/cab11024/ accessed in January 2006.

Eurostat (2005) General and Regional Statistics, Datasets, See: http://epp. eurostat.cec.eu. int/portal/page?_pageid=0,1136162,0_45572082&_dad=portal&_schema=PORTAL/ accessed in January 2006.

Ferrera, M. (1995) 'Le quattro Europe sociali tra universalismo e selettività,' Università Bocconi, Milan, Italy: *Quaderni di ricerca*, **1** [in Italian].

Furstenberg, F.F., Cook. T.D., Sampson, R. and Slap, G. (2002), 'Preface' in Furstenberg, F.F., Cook. T.D., Sampson, R. and Slap, G. (eds) Early Adulthood in Cross-National

Perspective, The Annals of the American Academy of Political and Social Science, **580**: 6–15, Special issue, March.

Galland, O. (1986) 'Precarietà e modi di entrata nella vita adulta,' in Saraceno, C. (ed) *Età e corso della vita*, Bologna, Italy: Il Mulino, pp. 261–279 [in Italian].

Galland, O. (2000) 'Entrer dans la vie adulte: des étapes toujours plus tardives mais resserrées,' *Economie et Statistique*, **337–338**: 13–36 [in French].

Hobsbawm, E. J. (1997) *Il secolo breve. 1914–1991: L'era dei grandi cataclismi*, Milan, Italy: Rizzoli [in Italian, translated from English].

Hoem, B. and Hoem, J.M. (1988) 'The Swedish Family. Aspects of Contemporary Developments,' *Journal of Family Issues*, **9**(3): 397–424.

Höhn, C. (1989) 'Demographische Trends in Europa seit dem 2. Weltkrieg,' in Nave-Herz, R. and Markefka, M. (eds) *Handbuch der Familien- und Jugendforschung*, Band 1, Familienforschung, Neuwied, Frankfurt am Main, Germany: Luchterhand [in German].

Iacovou, M. (2002) 'Regional Differences in the Transition to Adulthood,' in, Furstenberg, F.F., Cook, T.D., Sampson, R. and Slap, G. (eds) *Early Adulthood in Cross-National Perspective*, The Annals of the American Academy of Political and Social Science, **580**: 40–69, special issue, March.

Iacovou, M. and Berthoud, R. (2001) *Young People's Lives: A Map of Europe*, Colchester, UK: Institute for Social and Economic Research, University of Essex.

International Labor Organization (1984) *Year Book of Labor Statistics, 44*, Geneva, Switzerland: International Labor Organization.

Istat (2004a) *Rapporto annuale. La situazione del paese nel 2003*, National Institute of Statistics, Rome, Italy [in Italian].

Istat (2004b) See http://dawinci.istat.it/ accessed January 2006 [in Italian].

Jallinoja, R. (1989) 'Women between the Family and Employment,' in Boh, K., Bak, M., Clason, C., Pankratova, M., Qvortrup, J., Sgritta, G.B. and Wareness, K. (eds) *Changing Patterns of European Family Life*, London, UK: Routledge, pp. 95–122.

Kamerman, S.B. and Kahn, A.J. (eds) (1978) *Family Policy. Government and Families in Fourteen Countries*, New York, USA: Columbia University Press.

Lesthaeghe, R. (1995) 'The Second Demographic Transition in Western Countries: An Interpretation,' in Mason, K.O. and Jensen, A.-M. (eds) *Gender and Family Change in Industrialized Countries*, Oxford, UK: Clarendon Press, pp. 17–62.

Mayer, K.U. (2001) 'The Paradox of Global Social Change and National Path Dependencies. Life Course Patterns in Advanced Societies,' in Woodward, A. and Kohli, M. (eds) *Inclusions and Exclusions in European Societies*, London, UK: Routledge, pp. 89–110.

Millar, J. (1996) *Family Obligations in Europe: Patterns and Policy Trends*, Paper prepared for the Seminar of the European Observatory on National Family Policies, Escorial, Madrid, 27–30 June.

Millar, J. and Warman, A. (1996) *Family Obligations in Europe*, London, UK: The Family Policy Studies Centre.

MISSOC (Mutual Information System on Social Protection in the European Member States and the European Economic Area) (1999) *Social Protection in the Member States of the European Union. Situation on 1 January 1998 and Evolution*, Luxembourg: European Communities.

OECD (1999) *Preparing Youth for the 21st Century. The Transition from Education to the Labor Market*, Paris, France: OECD.

O'Higgins, M. (1988) 'The Allocation of Public Resources to Children and the Elderly in OECD Countries,' in Palmer J.L., Smeeding, T. and Torrey, B.B. (eds) *The Vulnerable*, Washington, D.C., USA: The Urban Institute Press, pp. 201–228.

Paci, M. (1995) 'I mutamenti della stratificazione sociale', in *Storia dell'Italia repubblicana. La trasformazione dell'Italia: sviluppo e squilibri*, Turin, Italy: Einaudi [in Italian].

Parsons, T. (1954) 'Age and Sex in the Social Structure of the United States,' in Parsons, T. (ed) *Essays in Sociological Theory*, revised edition, New York, USA: The Free Press, pp. 89–103.

Popenoe, D. (1988) *Disturbing the Nest. Family Change and Decline in Modern Societies*, New York, USA: Aldine De Gruyter.

Preston, S.H. (1984) 'Children and the Elderly: Divergent Paths for America's Dependents,' *Demography*, **21**(4): 435–57.

Pugliese, E. (1995) 'Gli squilibri del mercato del lavoro,' in *Storia dell'Italia repubblicana. La trasformazione dell'Italia: sviluppo e squilibri*, Einaudi, Turin, Italy [in Italian].

Rainwater, L. and Smeeding, T.M. (1995) *Doing Poorly: The Real Income of American Children in a Comparative Perspective*, Maxwell School of Citizenship and Public Affairs, Working Paper no 127, Syracuse, NY, USA: Syracuse University Press.

Ross, D., Scott, K. and Kelly, M. (1995) 'Child Poverty: What Are the Consequences?' in Wintersberger, H. (ed) *Children on the Way from Marginality toward Citizenship. Childhood Policies: Conceptual and Practical Terms*, Eurosocial Report, 61, Vienna, Austria: European Center for Social Welfare, Policy and Research, pp. 67–100.

Roussel, L. (1988) 'Die soziologische Bedeutung der demographischen Erschütterung in den Industrieländern der letzten zwanzig Jahre,' in Lüscher, K., Schultheis, F. and Wehrspaun, M. (eds) *Die 'postmoderne' Familie. Familiale Strategien und Familienpolitik in einer Übergangszeit*, Konstanz, Germany: Universitätsverlag [in German].

Saporiti, A. (1988) 'Le strutture familiari,' in *Immagini della società italiana*, Rome, Italy: Istituto Nazionale di Statistica [in Italian].

Schizzerotto, A. (2002) *Vite ineguali. Diseguaglianze e corsi di vita nell'Italia contemporanea*, Bologna, Italy: Il Mulino [in Italian].

Sgritta, G.B. (1993) 'Il mutamento demografico: rivoluzione inavvertita,' *Il Mulino*, **345**: 15 [in Italian].

Sgritta, G.B. (1994) 'The Generational Division of Welfare: Equity and Conflict,' in Qvortrup, J., Bardy, M., Sgritta, G. and Wintersberger, H., (eds) *Childhood Matters. Social Theory, Practice and Politics*, Aldershot, UK, Avebury, pp. 335–362.

Sgritta, G.B. (2001) 'Family and Welfare Systems in the Transition to Adulthood: An Emblematic Case Study,' in Chisholm, L., de Lillo, A., Leccardi, C. and Richter, R. (eds) *Family Forms and the Young Generation in Europe*, Vienna, Austria: Österreichisches Institut für Familienforschung, Report of the Annual Seminar 2001 of the European Observatory on the Social Situation, Demography and Family, pp. 59–86.

Smeeding, T., Torrey, B.B. and Rein, M. (1988) 'Patterns of Income and Poverty: The Economic Status of Children and the Elderly in Eight Countries,' in Palmer, J.L. Smeeding, T. and Torrey, B.B. (eds) *The Vulnerable*, Washington, D.C., USA: The Urban Institute Press, pp. 89–119.

Stanfors, M. and Svensson, L. (1999) *Education, Career Opportunities, and the Changing Patterns of Fertility: A Study on 20th Century Sweden*, Paper presented at the Seminar on Women in the Labour Market in Changing Economies, Rome, Italy, 22–24 September.

Stolnitz, G. (ed) (1992) *Demographic Causes and Economic Consequences of Population Aging*, New York, USA: United Nations/Economic Commission for Europe, Economic Studies no. 3.

Thomson, D. (1989) 'The Welfare State and Generation Conflict: Winners and Losers,' in Johnson, P., Conrad, C. and Thomson, D. (eds) *Workers versus Pensioners: Intergenerational Justice in an Aging World*, Manchester, UK: Manchester University Press, pp. 33–56.

Thomson, D. (1991) *Selfish Generations? The Aging of New Zealand's Welfare State*, Wellington, New Zealand: Bridget Williams Books.

Titmuss, R. (1974) *Social Policy: An Introduction*, London, UK: Allen and Unwin.

Trost, J. (1989) 'Nichteheliche Lebensgemeinschaften,' in Nave-Hertz, R. and Markefka, M. (eds) *Handbuch der Familien- und Jugendforschung*, Band 1, Familienforschung, Neuwied, Frankfurt am Main, Germany: Luchterhand [in German].

UNESCO (2004) See http://stats.uis.unesco.org/TableViewer/tableView.aspx?ReportId=47/ accessed in January 2006.

van de Kaa, D. (1987) 'Europe's Second Demographic Transition,' *Population Bulletin*, **42**(1): 1–58.

Varley, R. (1986) *The Government Household Transfer Database, 1960–1984*, Working Paper no 36, Paris, France: Department of Economics and Statistics, OECD.

Vogel, J. (2003) 'European Welfare Regimes and the Transition to Adulthood: A Comparative and Longitudinal Perspective,' in Chisholm, L., de Lillo, A., Leccardi, C. and Richter, R. (eds) *Family Forms and the Young Generation in Europe*, Österreichisches Institut für Familienforschung, Vienna, Austria: Report of the Annual Seminar 2001 of the European Observatory on the Social Situation, Demography, and Family, Vienna, Austria, pp. 125–142.

Chapter 7

Youth Transitions and Family Support in a Transforming Social Context—Reflections from the New Member States

Siyka Kovacheva

Young people in the new member states of the European Union and the candidate countries of southeastern Europe share many common transitional experiences with their counterparts in the 'old' west. Among the most significant trends are a prolongation of studies, a delay in getting their first stable job, the postponement of marriage and parenthood, an earlier start to independent consumer behavior and attaching a greater importance to leisure and the quality of life (Wallace and Kovacheva, 1998; Roberts, 2003; Catan, 2004). Specific to the situation of youth in the eastern half of Europe is the simultaneous occurrence and overlapping of various transitions of post-Communist societies: the passage of young people from dependence to autonomy, the pluralization of family patterns and the societal transition from authoritarianism to democracy. These transformations are influencing each other—and not in a linear way. Each is composed of various processes, the interplay of which creates a complex picture of contradictions (*Figure 7.1*). Thus, at present, young people in the new member states have more education opportunities than 15 years ago but also face greater risks of unemployment after graduation. With labor

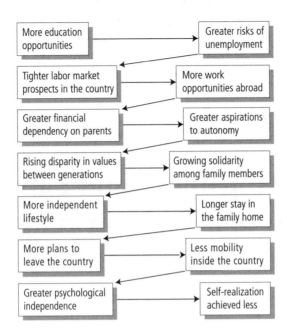

Figure 7.1. The paradoxes of youth transitions in central and eastern Europe.

market access tighter within their countries, the young are finding better work opportunities abroad. They are more dependent financially on their parents but more independent in their values and forms of behavior. There is a growing disparity in value systems between the generations in society but a strengthening of solidarity between them in the family.

To understand these paradoxes, we have to situate youth transitions in the framework of changing family relations and these, in turn, in the new relationships between the state and the market. Thus, young people's search for identity and autonomy is supported by parents who themselves are experiencing transitions in their socioeconomic position. While traditional parental support for the younger generation has been strong in the closely knit families in the region (Možný, 2003), in the new conditions this increasingly comes with unequal and diverging financial, educational, cultural and social resources. Eastern European societies also tend to diverge in many ways in terms of the structures of their economies and social protection systems. We can therefore expect different youth transition paths and varying patterns of family assistance.

This chapter focuses on two types of youth transition: from education to work and from parental home to independent housing and own family. In order to provide an in-depth assessment of youth transitions and family support, the chapter weaves together information from official statistical data on economic and welfare trends and research results on the values and experiences of young people and their parents from three comparative projects that cover central and eastern European countries (CEECs):

1. *Households, Work and Flexibility* (HWF), a representative survey of the working-age population on employment conditions and household strategies conducted in eight countries with national representative samples in 2001.[1]
2. *Families and Transitions in Europe* (FATE), a qualitative interdisciplinary study of young people's experiences and future plans one year after graduation from school and university and those of their parents, conducted in nine countries from 2001 to 2004.[2]
3. *Transitions: Gender, Parenthood and the Changing European Workplace*, a qualitative eight-country study, running from 2002 to 2005, currently in its second stage of data collection. *Transitions* consists of in-depth interviews and focus groups with young working parents in the changing European workplaces.[3]

As comparable information about the social situation in the new member states is extremely rare, this chapter mostly limits its analysis to five countries: the Czech Republic, Hungary and Slovenia, representing the new EU member states of eastern and central Europe, and Bulgaria and Romania, representing the candidate countries in southeastern Europe. Where possible, insights from other countries are also presented.

The chapter begins with a short description of the social context of youth transitions in the new member states and candidate countries, then presents the transforming patterns of those transitions and focuses on young people's entry into the labor market and family formation. The forms of family assistance are then examined, as is the lack of state support for which this family assistance frequently compensates. The chapter concludes with a discussion of some of the challenges facing overall European youth research and policy.

7.1   The Changing Context of European Youth Transitions—From a Bipolar to a Mosaic Pattern

Today's young people in central and eastern Europe are making their life transitions at a time when the societies they live in are also undergoing wide-ranging transition. For 15 years after the fall of the Berlin Wall these countries have experienced a liberalization of their economies, politics, culture and social relations. The complex and often contradictory character of the processes that comprise this transition have ended the artificial separation of the region from the rest of Europe and its broadly similar 'Communist' pattern of development. While the uniformity of these countries has never been as total as it seemed at the time of the Cold War and the east–west split of the continent, a major feature of the present transformation has been the growing diversity of objectives, trajectories, degrees and speeds of achieving the set goals. Indeed, the complexity of the post-Communist social transformation should not be underestimated (Illner, 1998).

Besides the regime transition from one-party rule to a political democracy and the economic shift from a centrally planned to a market economy, the societies in the region are experiencing other major forms of transition that strongly affect the situation of young people: integration into European structures, globalization, demographic transition and cultural change. While European integration is in itself a multifaceted process, for East European countries the paths to structural accession, even in its most obvious forms, have been diverse. While, for the central European countries, joining the North Atlantic Treaty Organization (NATO) preceded their acceptance into the European Union (EU), for the Baltic countries and Slovenia, both accessions largely coincided. Bulgaria and Romania, for their part, became members of NATO in April 2004, while their EU membership is expected in 2007. Globalization has brought about major economic restructuring, reducing the demand for unqualified labor, increasing flexible working and putting up unemployment (European Commission, 2004). In countries such as the Czech Republic, Hungary and Slovenia, the technological and communications changes have led to a considerable increase in service-sector employment, while in Bulgaria and, particularly, Romania, deindustrialization has been accompanied by a growth in agricultural employment. The societies in the region are also caught up in major demographic changes, resulting in a dramatic population decline in some countries (European Commission, 2003). Growing individualization and respect for individual liberties, personal initiative and human rights is the dominant trend in most countries (Ule and Rener, 1998; Machacek, 2004) but in others there are also signs of rising nationalism and traditionalism (Baranovic, 2002; Vrcan, 2002).

Studying the social transformation indicators, which represent the set of opportunities and constraints for youth development, we can no longer speak of a unified eastern European pattern (see *Table 7.1*). Instead, we see movements toward different models of society and welfare regimes of the kind discussed at length by Sgritta in Chapter 6. With some approximation we can identify a group of four eastern European countries—the Czech Republic, Hungary, Poland and Slovakia—that maintain a comparatively developed system of vocational education and training which, combined with relatively cheap housing rents, allows young people earlier independence from their family of origin. These countries are moving in the direction of a continental, employment-centered regime (Gallie and Paugam, 2000; Walther and Stauber, 2002).

Table 7.1. Selected social indicators in EU new member states/candidate countries.

	BG	CY	CZ	ES	HU	LV	LT	MT	PL	RO	SK	SL	IR
GDP per head (Index EU15 = 100, in PPS*)													
1995	33	83	62	34	46	25	37	53	34	28	46	63	27
2001	28	77	57	42	51	33	38		40	24	48	69	22
Population growth rates (per 1,000 population), 2000													
Total increase	-5.1	5.9	-1.1	-3.7	-3.8	-5.8	-1.6	6.8	-0.2	-1.1	0.7	1.2	14.8
Natural increase	-5.1	4.5	-1.8	-3.9	-3.8	-6.0	-1.3	3.3	0.3	-0.9	0.4	-0.2	14.8
Next migration	0.0	1.5	0.6	0.2	0.0	0.8	-0.3	3.5	-0.5	-0.2	0.3	1.4	0.0
Crude marriage rate (per 1,000 population)													
1960	8.8		7.7	10.0	8.9	11.0	10.1	5.9	8.3	10.7	8.1	8.9	
1970	8.6	8.6	9.2	9.1	9.3	10.2	9.5	7.4	8.6	7.2	7.9	8.3	
1980	7.9	7.9	7.6	8.8	7.5	9.8	9.2	8.6	8.6	8.2	7.9	6.5	8.2
1990	6.7	9.3	8.8	7.5	6.4	8.8	9.8	7.1	6.7	8.3	7.6	4.3	8.2
2000	4.2	12.3	5.4	4.0	4.8	3.9	4.6	6.2	5.5	6.1	4.8	3.7	7.7
Total fertility rate													
1960	2.31	3.51	2.11	2.16	2.02			3.62	2.96	2.33	3.07	2.18	6.18
1970	2.18	2.54	1.91	2.02	1.98	2.01	2.60	2.02	2.20	2.89	2.40	2.10	5.68
1980	2.05	2.46	2.10	2.05	1.91	1.90	2.00	1.99	2.28	2.45	2.37	2.11	4.36
1990	1.81	2.42	1.89		1.87	2.02	2.00	2.05	2.04	1.83	2.00	1.46	2.99
2000	1.25	1.83	1.14	1.39	1.33	1.24	1.33		1.34	1.30	1.20	1.25	2.50
Live births outside marriage (%)													
1960	8.0	0.2	4.9	14.1	5.5	11.9	7.3	0.7	4.5		4.7	9.1	
1970	9.3	0.2	5.4	18.3	5.4	11.4	6.4	1.5	5.0		6.2	8.5	
1980	10.9	0.6	5.6	27.1	7.1	12.5	6.3	1.1	4.7		5.7	13.1	
1990	12.4	0.7	8.6	27.1	13.1	16.9	7.0	1.8	6.2		7.6	24.5	2.9
2000	38.4	2.1	21.8	54.5	29.9	40.3	22.6	10.1	11.7	25.5	18.3	37.1	4.4

*Purchasing power standards.

Table 7.1. Continued.

	BG	CY	CZ	ES	HU	LV	LT	MT	PL	RO	SK	SL	IR
Crude divorce rate (per 1,000 population)													
1960			1.3	2.1	1.7	2.4	0.9		0.5	2.0	0.6	1.0	0.4
1970	1.2	0.3	2.2	3.2	2.2	4.6	2.2		1.1	0.4	0.8	1.1	0.3
1980	1.5	0.3	2.6	4.1	2.6	5.0	3.2		1.1	1.5	1.3	1.2	0.4
1990	1.3	0.6	3.1	3.7	2.4	4.0	3.4		1.1	1.4	1.7	0.9	0.5
2000	1.2	1.7	2.9	3.1	2.4	2.6	2.9		1.1	1.4	1.7	1.1	0.5
Population aged 18–24 by activity status (%), 2000													
In education and employment	4.0		6.0	4.0		6.0			2.0		10.0		
In education and not in employment	30.0		42.0	37.0		40.0			34.0		47.0		
Not in education and in employment	52.0		33.0	39.0		31.0			42.0		31.0		
Not in education and not in employment	14.0		18.0	19.0		23.0			23.0		13.0		
Females per 100 males in tertiary education													
1998/99	147	127	99	137	118	160	150	106	133	104	107	127	66
Youth unemployment rate (aged 15–24) by sex, 2001													
Total	39.5	9.6		24.6	10.9	22.6	31.3	16.7	42.0	17.0	38.5	16.9	
Males	36.1	6.7	17.4	24.7	13.7	21.1	27.6		34.3	19.3	40.0	14.8	
Females	29.6	14.2	16.4	22.4	10.4	21.3	27.4		37.2	15.9	33.3	18.5	
Youth long-term unemployment rate (aged 15–24, 6 months or more), second quarter of 2000													
Total	25.8	4.9	11.8	12.8	8.5	13.7	20.4		26.5	13.1	28.8	11.9	
Males	28.0	2.3	11.9	14.0	9.8	13.4	21.5		24.0	14.2	31.5	9.9	
Females	22.9	7.5	11.7	11.1	6.8	14.1	18.9		29.4	11.8	25.9	14.6	

Key: BG: Bulgaria; CY: Cyprus; CZ: Czech Republic; ES: Estonia; HU: Hungary; LV: Latvia; LT: Lithuania; MT: Malta; PL: Poland; RO: Romania; SK: Slovakia; SL: Slovenia; IR: Ireland.

Slovenia represents another developing pattern, being closer to a social-democratic, universalistic regime (Ule and Kuhar, 2003) with its well-developed youth policy that focuses on prevention of disadvantage and its comprehensive education system that addresses early school leaving and provides an additional focus on life-long learning. The southeast of the continent is a very diverse region. Bulgaria and Romania, although lagging behind the Baltic states in the process of EU accession, are far more stable than some of the war-torn former Yugoslav republics. Yet, because of their weaker economies, these two countries have been unable to sustain their previously universal and ample welfare states. They could be defined as a deinstitutionalizing model of social and youth policies (Wallace, 2002). What they offer youth are mostly marginal jobs and an undeveloped housing market. The countries that were former members of the Soviet Union also form several different groupings that follow diverging paths.

More research is needed so that the complexity of the developmental paths in central and eastern Europe can be grasped and a precise classification of youth transition regimes in the region can be created. It is important to note now that the divisions—because of these differences plus the north–south divide and other cleavages among the EU15—have given the European model a mosaic character rather than the bipolar opposition of the recent past (Chisholm and Kovacheva, 2002).

7.2 Transforming Patterns of Youth Transitions—From Past to Present

Youth transitions in the countries in the region have also gone through several big 'transformations.' Most of the central and eastern European societies were traditional agricultural societies under the great empires (Austro-Hungarian, Russian and Turkish), where youth was a very brief period, 'a sip of happiness' in the otherwise laborious life of the peasant (Khadzijski, 1974). Young peasants learned to labor inside the family; the formation of their own family and their transition to parenthood was arranged and sanctioned by the extended family. For craftsmen the transition was longer but no less strictly structured in terms of time and space. The child left the family to master a trade at the age of ten, and this was organized in two stages—four years as a junior apprentice and an additional four years as a senior apprentice. The training was always done outside the home—parents' love and care could not prepare the new generation for the 'work from dark till dark' philosophy (Khadzijski, 1974). The transition had a clear spatial dimension; it started at the 'crying stone' on the edge of the village where mother and child separated, continued at the master's home in the town and finished when the apprentice himself became a master, built his own shop and home and formed his own family.

Young women were socialized for different roles inside the household, but it was not considered that they ever really grew up and reached full autonomy.

Belated industrialization, particularly in the southern parts of eastern Europe, nevertheless caused a major transformation of the life cycle, creating the phase of adolescence which was facilitated by the advent of mass education, urbanization and the welfare state (Wallace and Kovacheva, 1998). A specific feature for most countries in the region was the simultaneous development of the nation state and the welfare state subsequent to the collapse of the big empires. The newly independent states established a predominantly Bismarckian model of social protection based on individual insurance of the employed. In addition to the state protection system, private schemes for social insurance and charitable organizations were set up. The major institutions of social policy in the region were the orphanages, the high demand for which was created by the many wars. The dominant model for both rural and working-class youth was for male and female to work for the whole of their lives, with child care being incorporated into parents' working arrangements in terms of time and often of place.

Communism once again restructured youth transitions, expanding educational opportunities for all and wiping out illiteracy, a significant development, particularly in southeastern and eastern Europe. For young people, there were clear-cut routes into work in the centrally planned economy: from compulsory education to low and unqualified jobs; from vocational secondary and upper secondary schools to qualified jobs, most often in industry; and from higher education to administrative and professional jobs. A career in the official youth organization led to the most privileged positions in the *nomenclatura* or the small elite in the state and party hierarchy. Work was not only a right but an obligation. There was no free labor market, and most young people made their transitions from school to work via the state allocation system of graduates to jobs. The role of state enterprises was also significant as they, under pressure because of the constant labor deficit (Kornai, 1979), provided grants to students in exchange for employment contracts lasting five or ten years. Youth transitions were linear and the one-party regime did not encourage transfers from one educational institution to another or from one enterprise to another. There was no official unemployment, and when some people dropped out of the planned system of employment, they were defined as being 'temporarily out of work.' This category, however, was not big and, for example, in Bulgaria for the whole of the Communist period it did not exceed 1 percent of the labor force. At the time, young people's dislike of the state allocation system was conceptualized as problems in self-realization caused by a mismatch between rising personal aspirations and the needs of the planned economy (Mitev, 1988).

Young people were among the main beneficiaries of the welfare policy of the one-party regime and were expected to play the main role in the construction of the classless Communist society. In exchange for their loyalty to the party, the young were provided with education grants in addition to a free education, subsidized leisure and privileged access to bank loans for housing. In the then Czechoslovakia, for example, the policies of state subsidies for young families, long, paid maternity leave and advantageous marriage loans were so successful in luring young people into early marriage that in the 1970s and 1980s the country experienced a drop in the average age at first marriage and at birth of first child, as well as a decline in the share of those living alone (Možný, 1994). Despite this, the young couple heavily relied on the multifaceted support of the family of origin for child care, social contacts, monetary gifts and accommodation. During Communism young people in the region's countries typically lived in their parents' homes into their twenties and even thirties. Usually they left home to study, join the army for compulsory military service or get married. They often stayed with their parents even after establishing their own family and having children of their own (about 80 percent of Czech couples started family life in the parental home). The age at marriage and birth of first child was low in comparison with that of young people in the west.

Gender inequalities in education were declining toward the end of the Communist regime, and in most countries the number of women in education reached the same number as men. The female employment rate was steadily growing, and in the 1980s it was well over 70 percent. Many specialist areas at school and in the employment sectors, however, were gender-biased, women being concentrated in low-paid and low-technology fields. Light industry, as well as education and medicine, were feminized, while governance, law and similar attracted mostly men. The woman's wage was about 79 percent that of the man (Corrin, 1992). Inequalities in terms of the urban–rural divide, class and ethnicity persisted. Vocational training, which was supposed to compensate for the underprivileged position of young working-class people under capitalism, soon began to act as a channel to provide easier access to higher education for children of the *nomenclatura*.

With market reforms and social restructuring under way, youth transitions have once again been shattered and changed. The previously clear-cut age limits of the youth phase (14 to 28) which coincided with the time span of membership of the official youth organizations in each country, have now become variously defined and range between seven years (Youth Work Act, Estonia) and 35 years (Law on Physical Education and Sport, Bulgaria). The new situation gives rise to numerous paradoxes, as the developing market system creates new opportunities as well as new risks for the young. We will explore these paradoxes by analysing the choices young people face in the two basic types of youth transitions: school to work and family/housing.

7.3 'Flexibilization' of Youth Transition from Education to Employment

In the transitional societies of central and eastern Europe, young people are experiencing a prolonged transit through the education system and a problematic entry into the labor market. The school-to-work transition of young people is not just extended but punctuated by frequent spells of unemployment, precarious jobs, attempts to start their own business and/or find work abroad, as well as additional studies and training, often in fields completely different from their initial orientation. Studies and work no longer follow each other but are often mixed in various combinations. The transformation can be described as a 'flexibilization' of the passage of youth from school to work, that is, a move toward destandardization and deregulation of youth transitions. Flexibility as a concept was first applied to explaining labor market changes, particularly in company management and workforce conduct (Atkinson and Meager, 1986; Felstead and Jewson, 1999). It encompasses various nonstandard forms of employment, for example, fixed-term, part-time jobs, with changing schedules, on a fee-only basis. Beck (1999) perceives flexible work as linked to individual development—a basis for devising a reflexive and self-created biography aimed at individual self-realization and the creative insecurity of freedom. However, choices that lead to self-realization and expand individual freedom need to be backed by sufficient resources, and these are in short supply for young people in the new member states and candidate countries.

The flexibility of youth transition from education to employment is characterized as becoming more risky and insecure, with less formal support from social agencies, which themselves are in the process of being restructured. Instead of the typical straightforward linear passage from school to work experienced by large numbers of young people in the past, the current paths are more irregular and winding, diversified and individualized. Flexible passages are essentially open and reversible, providing more choices and greater risks. Stressing the flexible character of the school-to-work transition does not mean a rejection of the structural links between origins, routes and destinations—a danger against which Roberts *et al.* (2003) warn. Rather, it denotes the pluralization of transition patterns in the transforming social context of post-Communist societies where modern, postmodern and premodern trends seem to clash, destroying the clear markers of the past and creating insecurity and changeability. Flexibility itself creates further structural inequalities among post-Communist youth, allowing some to profit from the new creative opportunities, while others remain caught in a downward spiral or stagnation.

7.3.1   Education transitions

Many of the paradoxes in youth transitions arise from the fluidity of young people's routes through the education system in central and eastern Europe. Educational reforms toward liberalization and pluralization have created more opportunities and greater insecurity in educational outcomes. The most significant trends causing a restructuring of youth transitions are a decline in vocational education and training and a rise in university enrollment. The first shift affects even countries where vocational education is a traditional feature, such as Poland and Romania (Slowinski, 1999). Not only is the state withdrawing from financing such expensive forms of studies but young people are becoming more interested in general studies, as these provide a better preparation for the university entrance examinations. This choice keeps opportunities open but is also very risky, as if they fail these exams, young people are left entering the labor market without qualifications. Young people aged 18 to 24 not in education and not in employment range from 13 percent in Slovenia to 23 percent in Romania and Lithuania (European Commission, 2003, p. 201).

A new choice for young people in post-Communist societies is to enroll in newly opened private schools teaching new skills such as information technology and foreign languages. All these schools charge fees that are high for the impoverished population. There is nothing unusual about getting parental help to pay school fees—this could be perceived as a continuation of the previous system of official and unofficial sponsorship. However, it was the post-Communist reforms that gave unprecedented impetus to private tuition and private lessons. The proportion of pupils in private primary and secondary schools is less than 4 percent in the countries of the region (European Commission, 2000) but taking private lessons in addition to state education has become a common practice for those preparing for entrance exams for colleges and universities. This is a flexible informal strategy on the part of young people, supported by their parents, to optimize their preparation in state schools.

A growing risk for young people in central and eastern Europe is to drop out of school before the end of compulsory education. Although there is a lack of reliable statistics, experts consider that while, during Communism, the trend had been toward a reduction in dropping out, this has been reversed under the new conditions of market reforms (Kovacheva, 2000). The European Training Foundation (2003) estimates that every year about 5 percent of young people in the region give up education at the age of 15. By the age of 18, over 40 percent of Bulgarians, Romanians and Slovaks have already left the education system (International Standard Classification of Education [ISCED] levels 1 to 6) (Dunne, 2003). Young girls are more likely to finish their compulsory schooling and show lower dropout rates from general and vocational educational programs. In most countries the process of dropping out primarily affects young people from ethnic minorities and those from families living in poverty. One reason is the limited opportunities for the children of ethnic minorities to be educated in their own language. Roma youth appears to be the most disadvantaged group in most central and eastern European countries—both educationally and in the labor market (UNDP, 2002).

Expanding higher education by increasing enrollment in state universities and establishing new private institutions has added new choices for youth in central and eastern Europe. The greater versatility of the education system has manifested itself in the opening of 'branches' in smaller cities and towns, in offering more part-time courses and types of distance education. There is a growing diversity and flexibility in curricula and in the contents and organization of lectures and seminars. Women have benefited the most from the expansion of higher education. In Bulgaria and Poland women have been in the majority in higher education since 1975. In Latvia and Lithuania there are at present 160 and 150 women, respectively, per 100 men enrolled in tertiary education. Only in the universities of the Czech Republic do men still slightly outnumber women (European Commission, 2003). The new multiplicity of educational forms has allowed greater flexibility for young people, and women in particular, to combine studying with other commitments, such as having a job or caring for children.

The opening up of new educational opportunities under post-Communism does not empower young people to accumulate more and more advanced academic qualifications. Often, their routes through the education system result in merely adding new diplomas to existing ones. Studying for a second degree is not uncommon; nor is following some vocational course (for example, catering or tailoring) after graduating from college in, for instance, public administration. The multiplication and diversification of institutions and types of study pose the problem of the quality of education and the legitimacy of the diplomas received, which makes studying an insecure process in itself.

For many young people, a flexible strategy for making the transition to employment is to combine education with paid work of some kind. This practice is becoming common and is caused by the economic pressures on households. It is parents and students who cover the rising costs of study. In many countries student loans are still only a formal possibility, as the conditions set by banks are very hard to fulfill. Students take part-time jobs or trade on their own account. Jobs during studies are valued for the income they bring in and also for the experience, skills and social contacts they provide for the young. However, official sources (European Commission, 2003, p. 201) report a low incidence of young people aged 18 to 24 combining education and employment: from 4 percent in Hungary to 10 percent in Slovenia. Experts estimate that the share is much higher in Russia and Latvia, where 15 to 20 percent and over one-third, respectively, of all students work (see Kovacheva, 2000). The difference between the figures is accounted for by most of this employment being in the grey economy, which is more flexible in responding to the irregularity of students' free time. These findings are in line with the conclusions of O'Higgins (2003) who argues that in transitional societies young people are disproportionately represented in the informal sector.

7.3.2 Flexibility of work

Flexible labor is obviously among the strongest factors that make youth school-to-work transitions flexible. The region's youth is the most flexible workforce in the developing market economies. The HWF survey studied the spread of flexible patterns in three western European and five central and eastern European countries. It found different types of flexibility among youth in different social contexts (Kovacheva and Tang, 2003). Young people in the west are more flexible in the time conditions of their jobs whereas young people in the transition countries and particularly in the southeastern countries are more flexible in the contractual conditions (see *Table 7.2*). In the new member states and candidate countries fewer young people undertake part-time work, preferring fixed-term jobs, usually for shorter periods than in the west. From this group, young people in the Czech Republic seem to be better protected in the labor market. In the two Balkan countries, Bulgaria and Romania, very few young people have modern flexible jobs such as agency work or telework, as is the case in Slovenia, but high proportions are self-employed or have no employment contract. These two least-regulated types of employment provide opportunities for both very high and very low incomes, but most of the work is only a strategy for survival in the face of high unemployment rates (Roberts *et al.*, 1999).

Education levels significantly influence the patterns of flexible labor among youth. The chance of getting a permanent contract rises in proportion to the level of education achieved by the young person. Nonstandard forms of employment are typical for only one-fifth of young workers who have completed their tertiary education, while almost half of those with primary education undertake such work (Kovacheva and Tang, 2003). Gender also affects the type of flexibility among youth, with young women concentrated in part-time work and young men in overtime work and with flexible schedules. Part-time work is more equally divided between the sexes in central and eastern Europe than in the west (European Commission, 2003). Analysing the occupational structure of flexible employment on the basis of HWF data, Stanculescu (2003) reveals a characteristic pattern. In the west, flexibility is concentrated among managers who enjoy greater control over their work conditions, whereas in the east, and particularly in Romania, flexibility mostly affects those at the bottom of the skills ladder and is correlated with informality and poverty.

Table 7.2. Patterns of flexibility of contractual conditions in youth employment (per cent).

Type of contract on the main job	Western Europe			East-central Europe			Southeast Europe	
	NL	S	UK	CZ	HU	SL	BG	RO
Young people (18–29)								
Permanent	68.1	75.3	62.9	66.8	66.2	43.7	51.2	66.0
Fixed term	21.9	16.2	2.4	12.8	10.8	24.0	28.4	3.7
Self-employed	1.3	2.4	2.9	8.0	4.1	3.6	9.8	13.0
No contract	–	1.4	18.2	5.4	13.5	9.6	9.3	14.4
Other flexible	8.7	4.7	13.6	7.0	5.4	19.1	1.3	2.9
Adults (30–59)								
Permanent	74.9	82.8	71.5	69.4	75.9	78.1	58.3	71.1
Fixed term	7.1	5.2	1.2	8.7	5.3	7.7	18.6	2.7
Self-employed	9.2	10.7	9.6	14.1	9.6	8.1	13.4	16.9
No contract	4.6	0.6	11.6	5.0	7.0	2.3	7.6	6.5
Other flexible	4.2	0.7	6.1	2.8	2.2	3.8	2.1	2.8
People near retirement (aged 60+)								
Permanent	76.4	82.7	63.1	67.5	59.1	64.9	62.9	36.6
Fixed term	3.6	3.0	–	8.6	8.8	5.2	15.2	2.1
Self-employed	7.6	13.2	12.1	12.4	16.4	14.3	8.4	51.0
No contract	7.3	0.4	18.4	8.6	14.6	6.5	10.7	8.3
Other flexible	5.1	0.7	6.4	2.9	1.1	9.1	2.8	2.0

Source: Unified international data collection from the HWF Survey, 2001.
Key: NL: Netherlands; S: Sweden; UK: United Kingdom; CZ: Czech Republic; HU: Hungary; SL: Slovenia; BG: Bulgaria; RO: Romania.

Not all young people experience flexible work in similar forms with similar consequences. Three groups of young people feature most prominently among flexible workers in the new member states and candidate countries. For the first group—young people still in education—flexible working schedules, flexible weekly hours and nonstandard contracts are most typical, which suggests that such flexible jobs are a transient work pattern providing an additional and temporary source of income as well as a way of accumulating skills and work experience. The second group—the lowest-qualified with only a primary education—experience flexibility in terms of work without a contract or temporary jobs. For them flexibility looks like a permanent rather than a transient pattern of employment. This is the group that bears the greatest risk of failure in the labor market and social exclusion. Young self-employed people, and among them farmers, are another highly flexible group in the region, experiencing traditional rather than modern patterns of nonstandard employment. To an even greater extent than for the other youth groups, their prospects for social integration depend on the social context of their work—the economic development, welfare policies and cultural norms of their own countries.

The HWF survey, in common with previous studies (Roberts *et al.*, 1999), suggests that young people accept this flexible type of work, preferring it both to unemployment and to low-paid and dead-end permanent jobs. Young people commonly look upon flexible work as a transitional stage in their career and hope for a better future when their country's economy improves and more demanding jobs are created with higher pay and requiring higher qualifications. It is difficult to say now whether this strategy is well grounded and beneficial in the long run, as in countries with liberal welfare regimes, such as Australia and the United States, part-time work is predominantly low-grade, semiskilled and unskilled. For casual employees in particular, it might act as a trap rather than as a bridge to more secure employment (Campbell, 2000).

7.3.3   Youth unemployment

Unemployment under post-Communism remains a predominantly youth phenomenon. In this, the countries of central and eastern Europe resemble those of the European Union where unemployment affects the younger population more frequently than other age groups. However, the youth (aged 15 to 24) unemployment rate in post-Communist societies turns out to be much higher than in the west. It varies from 11 percent in Hungary and 17 percent in Slovenia to 40 percent in Bulgaria and 42 percent in Poland (European Commission, 2003). Long-term unemployment affects more than one-quarter of young people in Bulgaria, Poland and Slovakia. Most of the young unemployed find themselves in this situation straight after school or after finishing their compulsory military service. They cannot accumulate work experience and skills, which makes them deprivileged in the labor market. The true unemployment rate may be much higher than the official rate if unregistered unemployment is taken into consideration. Most of the young unemployed in the comparative study of youth unemployment in east-central Europe have had periods of unregistered unemployment (Roberts *et al.*, 1999). Whether individuals registered themselves as unemployed depended on whether or not they were entitled to benefits; most of the young respondents did not believe that the labor offices would assist them in their search for the kinds of jobs they wanted. A study by the United Nations International Children's Emergency Fund (UNICEF) (2000) estimates that job vacancies reported to the offices represent only 30 percent of labor market openings.

The comparative survey measured the sociodemographic profile of the young unemployed in the region and found it significantly different from that of the young unemployed in the west (Roberts *et al.*, 1999). Some 90 percent of the young unemployed in post-Communist countries were from the national and religious majorities, came from families whose parents belonged to all the major occupational groups and had varied labor market experience. The young unemployed had varied educational backgrounds and were not concentrated only at the lowest educational level, nor were they only qualified in a limited range of fields. The most vulnerable group, pessimistic and detached from the labor market, were those who had never had a proper job, were younger, from a disadvantaged area, unqualified, unregistered and had received little support from family or friends and even less from state agencies. More recent studies, however, detect a process of concentration of disadvantage under way in the new member states and candidate countries, most prominently along the lines of ethnicity, particularly among the Roma, and disability (UNDP, 2002; Godfrey, 2003).

7.3.4   Flexibility in young people's perceptions of transitional experiences

Thus, to understand the school-to-work transition, it is important to know how young people are distributed among various forms of flexible work, unemployment and combinations of studying and working. Equally important is knowledge of young people's perceptions of flexibility in their transitional experiences. Valuable information about youth views on their labor market situation and future plans is provided by the FATE project which relied on in-depth interviews with young adults one year after graduation. The purposive sample was drawn from a sampling frame of respondents in a survey of students completing their education and stratified according to educational level (low, medium and high) and gender. Rich qualitative material was collected about 376 young adults and 219 of their parents, living in urban localities in nine European countries. The research portrays youth transitions in two post-Communist societies only—Bulgaria and East Germany (the former German Democratic Republic [GDR]). While the comparative analysis is still in its early stages, what emerges as common in young people's views and expectations in both countries is the acceptance of the prospect that their pathways in education and the labor market are becoming less linear, more varied and more fluid. Whereas the three most common situations of youth in both countries were 'back to education,' employment in precarious jobs and unemployment, the young commonly viewed their options as open and subject to individual agency.

FATE data clearly show that education is no longer perceived as an unquestioned, simple transition stage with a clear destination. Young respondents often spoke about their difficulties in choosing a school and a course and in judging their employment prospects. In Bulgaria the young voiced the additional fear as to whether their diplomas would be accepted as legitimate in the future European labor market. While at school, young people felt that they did not have enough control over their studies; they complained of having an insufficient choice of school subjects and about expensive school materials and textbooks. They viewed education as disappointing because of its poor employment prospects. Many respondents, who were unemployed one year after graduation, despite having diplomas for prestigious specialized subjects, were considering taking on another vocational course to get a job.

The labor market was looked upon with distrust by young people in both countries. A young German auto mechanic noted: 'I don't think you've got that many choices as a young person as they [in the labor office] tell you' (Menz and Kramolowsky, 2004, p. 12). In Bulgaria many young people were convinced that, 'education, skills, personal qualities have no value on our market' and that 'connections' were the best way of finding a job (Kovacheva and Mitev, 2004, p. 21). Most of the jobs available for the young were precarious, required low qualifications and were low-paid. The young accepted these casual jobs for the income they brought in and to avoid unemployment. This strategy had a double purpose: to find a money-earning job for the present while waiting for the better and demanding jobs they had been trained for in the future. This attitude represented a clear break with the inertia of the mid-1990s (Kovacheva, 1999) when young people adopted a passive strategy, waiting for the situation to improve (and relying upon the unconditional support of their parents). Another active strategy aiming to expand the career options of young people in the two former Soviet-bloc countries in the FATE sample was emigration.

Migration was present in young Germans' life plans most often as moving from East to West Germany. Migration was even more common among young people in Bulgaria who expressed varying degrees of readiness to leave their country. This finding is consistent with official statistics and representative surveys establishing the high emigration potential of youth in southeast and Baltic countries (European Commission, 2003; Mitev, 2003). Central European countries—the Czech Republic, Hungary, Poland and Slovakia—are themselves becoming a desired destination of young migrants in the region, which turns them into a buffer zone between eastern and western Europe (Wallace, 1998). For countries with grave economic difficulties, such as Bulgaria and Romania, as well as for regions with ethnic conflicts and wars, long-term emigration is the goal. FATE data show that youth emigration strategy takes the form of a wide variety of intentions and plans. For many young people, to leave their home country was the most important goal; the destination was not so important—'anywhere else will be better than here.' Youth plans for mobility were most often directed to the EU (France, Germany, Greece, Italy and the United Kingdom) but also as far away as Australia, Canada, South Africa and the United States. Ethnic links were also important for emigration plans, but large-scale surveys showed that 15 years after the mass exodus to neighboring Turkey, young Bulgarian Turks would now rather to emigrate to the EU than go to Turkey (Mitev, 2003).

7.4 Pluralization of the Patterns of Family/Housing Transitions

Young people's experiences of forming their own household and family in the new member states and candidate countries of central and eastern Europe are also underpinned by numerous paradoxes. The young have high aspirations for a family of their own but delay and often abandon its formation. In the same way, they place high value upon autonomy but prolong the period of living in the parental home. These contradictions may be understood by examining the diversification of partnership forms and the increase in the multiplicity of housing arrangements.

Official statistics (European Commission, 2003) testify to the speedy change in these patterns. In the 1990s the age of first marriage and the age at the birth of the first child grew by about two years in most countries, the marriage rate declined significantly (by more than double in Latvia and Lithuania) and the birth rate dropped below the population-replacement point. In 2000 the crude marriage rate (per thousand) was 3.7 in Slovenia and 3.9 in Latvia, whereas it was still quite high in Romania and Poland, with 6.5 and 5.5 respectively. Divorce rates had shown a more doubtful trend, with a tendency to rise, and were between 1.1 in Poland and Slovenia and 3.1 in Estonia. At present, population growth rates are negative in all new member states and candidate countries (with the exception of Slovakia and Slovenia) reaching –5.8 per thousand in Latvia and –5.1 per thousand in Bulgaria. The lowest total fertility rate in 2000 was 1.14 in the Czech Republic and the highest was 1.39 in Estonia (in Turkey, for example, it was 2.5). The number of children born outside marriage, a rare occurrence in Catholic and Orthodox countries before the start of reforms, has risen two or three times since 1990. In 2000 from onethird to one-half of children were born out of wedlock (Estonia being at the top with 54.5 percent of children born to unmarried parents and Poland at the other extreme with 11.7 percent—the latter nevertheless being an increase from 6.2 percent in 1990. Although comparative data on nonmarital forms of partnerships in the region are missing, experts (Ule and Rener, 1998; Wallace and Kovacheva, 1998; Ule and Kuhar, 2003) consider that a pluralization of relationships forms is under way, including a rise in living single, 'living apart together,' single parenthood and reorganized families.

One customary explanation for the destandardization of family transitions links this process to the economic difficulties inherent in the transition of countries and the declining purchasing power of households (see for an overview Cernigoj Sadar and Vladimirov [2002]; Matev and Kovacheva [2003]). Public discourse points at poverty as the main reason for the current situation, which is interpreted as no less than a 'population crisis of unprecedented proportions' (UNDP, 1999, p. 39).

The dominant view shared by the respondents in the *Transitions* study was similar. This project applied a case-study approach making use of qualitative interviews, self-completed questionnaires and document analysis in public- and private-sector organizations in 12 countries. Individual in-depth interviews with managers at various levels explored their perspectives on the workplace changes and the impact of these on organizational well-being. The employee perspective was generated by focus groups with employees aged between 25 and 39 expecting their first child or already having young children.

Delayed parenting and reducing the number of children, when discussed in focus groups and individual interviews, were most often attributed to the low standard of living of young families in the region: '... in this economic crisis young people can't afford to marry and have children' (Kovacheva *et al.*, 2004, p. 57). However, when young people spoke about their own experiences and plans, the explanations were not so financially centered, and other reasons for postponing parenthood came to the fore. It is true that growing poverty has been a feature of the region's development in the 1990s, affecting young people in particular (Caritas Europa, 2004), but this is not the best and certainly not the only explanation for declining fertility and other changes in the family transitions of young people. Studies of young adults in Russia and Ukraine have discovered that it is not the most economically pressed young people who are delaying marriage and parenthood (Roberts *et al.*, 2003). On the contrary, it is the poorer segments of the youth population who venture into earlier marriages.

Another widespread conviction explaining the paradoxes in family transitions in central and eastern Europe focuses on the difficult housing situation of young people and the low availability of housing. In the FATE study, only one in ten young people in Bulgaria were living independently of their parents. By contrast, in East Germany three out of four were doing so, having their own flats or renting or sharing a flat with a partner or friends. This contrast is no doubt a continuation of a tradition from the Communist past. While in the 1980s in the former GDR only about 20 percent of young families shared accommodation with their parents (Možný, 1994), in Communist Bulgaria it was the norm for young couples to start their family life in their parents' home (there is a lack of data on this important transition both before and after 1989).

While the link is acknowledged between the delay in forming a family or starting to cohabit with a partner and the delay in leaving the parental home by young people in many countries in the region, it does not mean that the unfavorable housing situation is the only reason for postponing family formation. Quite often, delaying family formation postponed the start of a young person's independent housing career. Parents with a flat or a storey in the family house for the young considered it an unnecessary expense for their offspring to establish independent households before forming independent families. Almost all parents in the FATE sample felt that it was their obligation to provide housing for their offspring and blamed themselves for their children's low income and their inability to pay rent or buy a new home. In Slovenia the young most often expected help from parents in solving their housing problem (Ule and Rener, 1998). In Bulgaria, where most (over 90 percent) of the housing stock was privately owned even before liberalization, young people's chances of an autonomous dwelling did not greatly decrease. Previously, flats were cheaper but more difficult to get, and families had to put their names on long lists to obtain permission to buy one. Though a housing market was developing, it was a very high-priced one. The young could realistically expect to get their own flat or house only through inheriting one or by buying one with their parents' money.

A third explanation for young people delaying family formation and parenthood lies in their leisure preferences. This was often pointed out by parents in the FATE study, especially when they compared their own transitions to those of their children. A 45-year-old research pathologist, father of a university graduate in English studies, remarked: 'At 24 I already had a wife and a child ... I had family responsibilities at his age, while now he is only enjoying himself' (Kovacheva and Mitev, 2004, p. 65).

Surveys in Slovenia and the former Soviet Union arrive at similar findings. For Roberts *et al.* (2003) it is the new importance of leisure and the attractions of single living in the new consumer societies that are responsible for the rising marriage age and declining birth rate. Ule and Kuhar (2003) offer a range of reasons, among which they stress the concerns for quality of life (independence, personal development and self-fulfillment). The growing individualization among youth under post-Communism has significantly changed their life plans and views on parenthood. At present, family formation is sensed as a loss (of freedom, of purchasing power) while previously it was an acquisition (freedom gained through marriage). Ule and Kuhar (2003) argue that young women in particular are not eager to take on 'the double burden' that their mothers accepted of a full-time job and child care.

In the FATE study young people linked their family and housing plans to achieving stability in their employment situation, thus offering a fourth explanation of post-Communist paradoxes. The young wanted to keep their options open, to have more time for making choices and not limit their opportunities in the employment transition by having family commitments. FATE respondents clearly stated that family responsibilities limited mobility and work choices. Many young Germans postponed marriage, considering that they might be forced to move to other cities in search of a job. Young Bulgarians contemplated emigration abroad before starting to plan a family.

In the *Transitions* study, in which Slovenia and Bulgaria represent the post-Communist countries, the demand for an improved system of reconciling work and wider life also came forward in young people's concerns when they were making their life transitions. In the focus groups comprising parents working in private and state organizations, respondents commonly criticized state withdrawal from family policies and the employers' neglect of their employees' difficulties in combining work and care. As one mother working as an accountant for a private bank put it:

> Previously it was all settled in one and the same way: you finished your studies, started work, had children, looked after them at home for the whole of the maternity leave, then went back to work and took all the sick leave that your child needed .... Now the social state is gone. The private owner looks after his own interest (Kovacheva *et al.*, 2004, p. 102).

Even though the policies of parental leave and sick leave for a child in Bulgaria and Slovenia are (still) generous in comparison with those in the western countries in the study, young parents complained that they could not afford to make use of them, fearing dismissal. The study established a significant gap between policies and implementation, even in the public sector. The new business ideology focusing primarily on cost-efficiency had already become dominant in the workplaces under transformation, and social concerns were seen as a thing of the past. The inflexibility of state legislation and the lack of family-friendly company policies were compensated for by a wide range of informal practices of mutual assistance among employees, often with the support of line managers. Another flexible strategy used by young parents was to involve grandparents and neighbors in child care—not as primary caregivers but in addition to the public institutional care provided by crèches and kindergartens.

The *Transitions* study revealed the continuing importance of work in the lives of young parents, and particularly mothers, in central and eastern Europe where dual-income households were the dominant model (see *Table 7.3*). The postponement of marriage and having children and the pluralization of transitional forms of relationships, most often cohabitation or 'living apart together,' were accompanied by a change in values that did not lead to a decline in the value placed on family or children, nor, for that matter, on paid work. Rather, young people attributed greater importance to a new quality of combining work, family and leisure. Understanding the problems of family transition lies at the intersection and harmonization of this transition with the school-to-work transition.

Table 7.3.   Frameworks for integrating jobs and family lives used by working parents.

Country	Employment patterns	Combining work and care
NORWAY SWEDEN Egalitarian model	Long part-time or full-time jobs. Short parental leave (one year)	Extensive use of public schemes supporting working parents (subsidized child-care arrangements, paid parental leave, flexible working hours...)
FRANCE Dual-earner model or 'working mother'	Long part-time or full-time jobs. Long parental leave (three years) for less-qualified or low-paid	Extensive use of public schemes supporting working parents (subsidized child-care arrangements, paid parental leave, flexible working hours...)
NETHERLANDS UNITED KINGDOM Modified male-breadwinner model	Short part-time jobs (as long as children are under school age)	Reduction in working time Kin/voluntary/market support for child care Family-friendly flexibility in the workplace
PORTUGAL Dual-earner model	Full-time jobs. Long working hours for both partners	Reduction in the number of children Kin/market support for child care
SLOVENIA Dual-earner model	Full-time jobs. Long working hours for both partners	Family or informal care for children under three Use of public schemes supporting working parents (subsidized child-care arrangements) Reduction in number of children
BULGARIA Dual-earner model	Full-time jobs. Long working hours for both partners	Long parental leave up to the first two to three years of the child's life Use of public schemes supporting working parents (subsidized child-care arrangements) Reduction in number of children

Source: Fagnani *et al.* (2004).

7.5   Transforming Patterns of Family Support

The exploration of family assistance for youth transitions in the new member states and candidate countries reveals another whirlpool of paradoxes. The young are becoming more dependent on their parents financially and socially, but they are also experiencing more freedom and autonomy in their attitudes and behavior. There is a considerable difference in the values held by the two generations but fewer conflicts within the family. Growing individualization is the dominant trend among the young, but the family, often composed of three generations and other relatives, stays closely knit in informal care networks.

Large-scale comparative surveys (Alber and Fahey, 2004) have documented the importance of intergenerational support and reliance on family in mitigating the consequences of financial hardship or unemployment for youth in the region. On the basis of national survey data, Slovenian researchers (Rener, 2002; Ule and Kuhar, 2003) claim that there has been an exceptional increase during the 1990s in the importance of parents at both the instrumental and emotional level and that, at present, the family is the institution most trusted by the young. Our qualitative studies (FATE and *Transitions*) have also shown that young people perceive family support as essential in their life transitions. Parents themselves consider that, with the reductions in the welfare state and the growing insecurity in the emerging market-oriented societies, parental support is becoming more important.

The strong dependence upon parents—for money, housing and social contacts—does not significantly inhibit young people's sense of autonomy and maturity. As far as the young are concerned, the explanation of this paradox lies in the fact that most young people trust their parents and rely on their unconditional support. They perceive this situation as normal and are not in a hurry to become fully independent. As far as parents are concerned, they are aware of the significant influence that they exercise over the young but also tend to grant them a great deal of freedom. The two generations have different values and lifestyles concerning work and leisure, friendships and sexual relationships, but parents do not impose their opinions, and both generations are tolerant of each other's differences. Parents understand how difficult the situation is for their children. They themselves have quite recently made transitions during their adulthood, forced by the restructuring of the state-planned economy. This makes them tolerant of their children's uncertainty about their life goals and their shifting strategies to achieve them.

The FATE study revealed the wide range of parental support for the young: financial, housing, educational (with lessons and contacts with teachers), emotional and practical (cooking, washing). Parents tried to ease young people's transitions with advice about education, jobs, friends and family, as well as with social contacts to help the young person get into a more prestigious school, find a job and do compulsory military service when and where the offspring wished. In some cases, parents have offered such opportunities, but the young have declined to take advantage of them and have chosen other options. Many parents feel that their useful contacts are being reduced in the same way as their financial resources accumulated during Communism. They complain that their friends and relatives are 'people like us' and cannot really help to speed the transition of their offspring. In this they recognize what sociologists term the 'degeneration of the second network' (Raychev, 2003, p. 5)—the slow but sure substitution of horizontal links among equal-status partners for vertical social relationships.

The extent of parental support in Bulgaria and Romania seemed higher than in the western countries being studied. While parents in Denmark encouraged early independence by stopping financial support when their children finished their studies, in Bulgaria parents supported their children financially even when the young had full-time jobs. Quite a few parents had advised their sons and daughters to leave their low-paid jobs in the belief that 'it is better for him to stay at home than tire himself for that money and be exploited by a fat-necked businessman,' as one mother working two jobs as a hairdresser explained (Kovacheva and Mitev, 2004, p. 76). The prevalent norm seemed to be life-long family support, or as a father, a retired teacher, put it: '. . . for as long as my eyes see and my legs move' (Kovacheva and Mitev, 2004, p. 73). Parents commonly considered that they themselves had not needed as much support when they were young as their offspring currently needed. Elisaveta Z. expressed a common belief:

> We did not need that much support from our parents at the time. It was easier for us. There were much fewer schools to choose from and many more factories to work at. Now the young and their parents are left to fend for themselves (Kovacheva and Mitev, 2004, p. 79).

When asked about the forms of state support their child had received in education or in the job search, many parents asked in turn: 'State support? What support?' A truck driver, father of an 18-year-old son, went even further, saying: 'State support? What state?' He was very bitter about the current reforms and considered that the state had totally turned its back on its responsibilities to the people (Kovacheva and Mitev, 2004, p. 79). While parents often blamed the state for its lack of support for young people's transitions, they blamed it more strongly for the slow economic development and the resulting high youth unemployment. They saw the state as responsible for severing the links between schools and enterprises. Moreover, the state did not provide enough information about the types of education on offer and what prospects these had of leading to employment.

There was a widespread conviction that the family had to come forward and fill the gap left by the state. The parents willingly limited their own consumption so that the young would have more freedom. When the children grew up, the parental bedroom was often turned into another room for an offspring and the parents moved into the kitchen or the living room. A similar limitation could be seen in parents' career aspirations. Many parents had limited their own career goals to enable their children to seek higher goals. At the same time young people did not blame their parents for the inadequacy of resources and did not rebel against their values and norms.

In view of the close emotional relations between parents and children, it was surprising that so many parents in the Bulgarian sample supported the emigration

Table 7.4. Parental support strategies.

Protective	Independent	Negotiating
'We parents know better. We have trodden the same paths, made the same mistakes.' 'The young should know their limits and respect them.'	'It's all up to the child. A parent should not interfere.' 'One has to learn from one's mistakes—to get burned—to know that this was a mistake.'	'We advise her but do not direct her. We discuss, and she takes decisions.' 'We discuss all important things in the family council, but the final decision is always his.'

plans of the young generation. Some invested money and social contacts to help their children leave the country; others viewed this as a final option but declared that they would not stop them, even though they were aware that 'happiness would leave the home together with the young' (Kovacheva and Mitev, 2004, p. 89). The high material standards of their children had become a very important aspiration for parents, even if they did not accept them as a value in their own personal lives. Parents were ready to sacrifice not only money but also their own emotional well-being for the economic success of their children.

The analysis of interview data from the FATE study reveals the existence of three major types of family support for youth transitions in the new member states and candidate countries: 'protective,' 'independent' and 'negotiating' (*Table 7.4*). The first is the post-Communist version of the patriarchal (premodern) family, where parents guide their children's transitions led by their own values and experiences, trying to cushion the negative effects of economic restructuring on their offspring. The second is the modern version of family support, where the young are encouraged to early independence by taking responsibility and learning from their own mistakes. The third model is that of the postmodern family with more equal relations between family members and a greater focus on the formation and transmission of social and identity capital.

FATE data suggest that family resources have influenced parental philosophies. While working class parents practiced all three styles, the most common was to encourage the child's autonomy. Often parents felt that this was an imposed decision and detested their own limitations in providing help. The protective style was most typical for the group with medium-sized resources. Middle-class parents in low-income jobs tried to compensate for their lack of resources by strongly interfering in their children's choices and at the same time imposing high expectations on them. The parents with the largest resources in our sample, those belonging to the developing upper-middle class, expressed preferences for a negotiating style, where issues were discussed openly in the family, the parents' role being to provide advice, information and contacts, while the decision was taken by the young person. Other factors influencing parental styles were gender and ethnicity. Fathers were expected to be more distant and reserved and to concentrate on providing for the young financially. Mothers were expected to offer emotional and practical support in solving everyday problems. They served as mediators within the family—between the young and the father and outside it—between the young and schoolteachers, employers and state officials (in the army and labor offices). Parents from ethnic minorities, Roma in particular, tended to have more gender-specific education strategies, wishing for traditional employment and domestic careers for their offspring. Their expectations for reciprocal support from their children were generally higher.

National differences also were detected among the FATE respondents. While the parental sample in Bulgaria was almost equally divided among the three styles of parental support, in East Germany the 'independent type' was visibly dominant. Menz and Kramolowsky (2004, p. 74) explain this pattern by East German parents having lived through an immense biographical shake-up and having the feeling that many of their life and work experiences had been devalued. In Denmark the general trend was toward a predominance of the negotiating strategy practiced by the 'network family' (Stolan and Morch, 2004), characterized by friendly relations among family members.

7.6 Conclusions

By exploring the paradoxes of youth transitions in the transitional societies of central and eastern Europe, we can learn a great deal about the social change beyond the region. With the accession to the EU of the new member states, the European landscape is changing and acquiring a mosaic pattern rather than remaining polarized. This poses new challenges to youth research and social policy.

Encompassing diversity is a key objective for youth and family research in Europe. Research has to become truly comparative and sensitive to the diversified context of youth transitions so as to reflect the fluid and destandardized course of youth passages to adulthood and autonomy. Comparative research also needs to overcome the lack of longitudinal studies if it is to become capable of explaining and assessing the choices and risks young people face in Europe today.

Across the continent, youth transitions are becoming prolonged, more insecure and more individualized than in the past, when growing up was more clearly benchmarked. The school-to-work transition is becoming more flexible—less standardized, more fragmented and often reversible. In some countries modern flexible jobs serve as stepping-stones for young people to social integration. In other countries, and for some disadvantaged groups of young people, precarious, often totally unprotected jobs act as a trap from which they cannot move on to socially recognized employment. At present, work flexibility is viewed positively by young people in central and eastern Europe as an intermediary solution during their life-stage transitions. Even insecure jobs operate as channels for social integration, providing experience, skills and social contacts for the young, backed by strong family support of a financial and emotional nature. Since the 1990s, just as in the west over the past few decades, unemployment has become a common experience for young people in the new member states, with the post-Communist specifics that it affects all educational groups. Nevertheless, those leaving education early without qualifications and coming from underprivileged, minority backgrounds tend to accumulate risks and obstacles that endanger their life transitions.

The transition to family formation is being consciously delayed by youth in the new member states and candidate countries. Though valuing family and children highly, the young regard them as a demanding project closely interwoven with building their employment careers and securing their desired leisure options. They react with a pluralization of transitional forms of relationships and housing situations. In central Europe, independent housing and cohabitation are more common than in the southeast of Europe where the young tend to stay longer in their parents' home. While young people in the Balkans and the Baltic states seem unwilling to be mobile inside their countries, they tend to actively embrace the opportunities to travel and work abroad. The young are staying in their family home longer but are looking far beyond it. Independent from their parents in terms of values and lifestyles, young people search for more and better transitional opportunities, often abroad; and parents are left to understand and support them as best as they can.

State withdrawal from an active youth policy, though to different degrees in different countries in the new member states and candidate countries, is compensated for by a growing support on the part of the family for youth transitions. Parents interfere actively to fill the gap caused by the reduction in the previously universal welfare state. While this practice seems accepted by both the young and their parents, it leads to a rise in social inequalities and a reproduction of disadvantage over generations. Parental material and educational resources come as a strong predictor of the success in young people's transitions. The most underprivileged families belonging to the low-skilled working class, often with minority status, have secured less assistance for the education of their children and even less for their transition into employment. A higher proportion of their children have low educational qualifications, are unemployed or in unskilled jobs. The most privileged families continue to invest in their children's education and do not push them toward employment. They have enough educational, financial and social capital to secure the prolonged transition of their children.

It can be expected that the exposure of the central and eastern European economies and societies to European integration and global influences and the increased mobility of people, particularly the young, will gradually undermine the strong family ties. At present, however, these tend to be much stronger than those in the west. The extended family ties still provide the young with a social safety net. The generations within the family stick together in the face of the growing insecurity. They feel that times are changing but cling to the traditions of lifelong parental support and choose compromise over conflict and cohesion over emancipation.

Under these conditions, a new type of youth and family policy is needed to preserve some of the achievements of the universalistic and comprehensive support of the past and enrich them with the key characteristics of the European social model. A priority for such a policy is for it to become less rigid and more adaptable itself so as to allow flexible combinations of youth transitions toward autonomy rather than to direct the young into limited linear trajectories. A second crucial point seems to be a holistic strategy building upon the interlinked experiences of the young with work, consumption, housing, partnership and parenthood. Social policy and youth work can help young people to make successful transitions, while at the same time recognizing their subjective motivation as they search for their desired work–life combinations.

Notes

1. See http://www.socsci-ulst.ac.uk/policy/fate/fate.html/ accessed in February 2006.
2. See http://www.worrkliferesearch.org/transitions/ accessed in February 2006.
3. See http://www.worrkliferesearch.org/transitions/ accessed in February 2006.

References

Alber, J. and Fahey, T. (2004) *Perceptions of Living Conditions in an Enlarged Europe*, Berlin, Germany: Social Science Research Centre (WZB) and Dublin, Ireland: Economic and Social Research Institute (ESRI).

Atkinson, J. and Meager N. (1986) *Changing Working Patterns: How Companies Achieve Flexibility to Meet New Needs*, London, UK: National Economic Development Office.

Baranovic, B. (2002) 'National Relation of Croatian Youth in the Period of Transition,' in Tivadar B. and Mrvar P. (eds) *Flying over or Falling through the Cracks? Young People in the Risk Society*, Ljubljana, Slovenia: Office for Youth of the Republic of Slovenia, pp. 47–52.

Beck, U. (1999) *World Risk Society*, Cambridge, UK: The Polity Press.

Campbell, I. (2000) 'The Spreading Net: Age and Gender in the Process of Casualisation in Australia,' *Journal of Australian Political Economy*, **45** (June): 68–99.

Caritas Europa (2004) *Poverty Has Faces in Europe. The Need for Family-Oriented Policies*, second report on poverty in Europe, See http://www.caritas-europa.org/module/ fileLib/PovertyhasfacesinEuropeweb.pdf accessed in January 2006.

Catan, L. (2004) *Becoming Adult: Changing Youth Transitions in the 21st Century*, Brighton, UK: Trust for the Study of Adolescence.

Cernigoj Sadar, N. and Vladimirov, P. (2002) *Work/Personal Life Arrangements within Organisations*, Paper presented at the Second International Conference of Human Resource Management in Europe: 'Trends and Challenges,' held on 17 October at Athens University of Economics and Business, Athens, Greece.

Chisholm, L. and Kovacheva, S. (2002) *Exploring the European Youth Mosaics. The Social Situation of Young People in Europe*, Strasbourg, France: Council of Europe.

Corrin, C. (ed) (1992) *Superwomen and the Double Burden*, London, UK: Scarlet Press.

Dunne, M. (2003) 'Education in Europe. Key Statistics 2000/2001,' *Eurostat: Statistics in Focus*, Theme 3, no 13, Luxembourg: Eurostat, pp. 1–7.

European Commission (2000) *Key Data on Education in Europe*, Luxembourg: Office for Official Publications of the European Communities.

European Commission (2003) *The Social Situation in the European Union 2003*, See http://europa.eu.int/comm/employment_social/publications/2003/keag03001-en.html/ accessed in January 2006.

European Commission (2004) *Employment in the Market Economy in the European Union. An Analysis Based on Structural Business Statistics*, Theme 4, Luxembourg: Eurostat.

European Training Foundation (2003) *Thirteen Years of Cooperation and Reforms in Vocational Education and Training in the Acceding and Candidate Countries*, See http://www.etf.eu.int/website.nsf/ accessed in January 2006.

Fagnani, J., Houriet-Segard, G. and Beduin, S. (2004) *Transitions: Context Mapping*, Manchester, UK: Manchester Metropolitan University.

Felstead, A. and Jewson, N. (eds) (1999) *Global Trends in Flexible Labor*, London, UK: Macmillan.

Gallie, D. and Paugam, S. (2000) *Welfare Regimes and the Experience of Unemployment in Europe*, Oxford, UK: Oxford University Press.

Godfrey, M. (2003) 'Youth Employment Policy in Developing and Transition Countries—Prevention as well as Cure,' *Social Protection Discussion Paper Series*, no 0320, Washington, D.C., USA: The World Bank.

Illner, M. (1998) 'Underestimation of Complexity: One Major Risk in the post-Communist Transformation,' in Genov, N. (ed) *Central and Eastern Europe Continuing Transformation*, Paris, France; Sofia, Bulgaria: UNESCO-MOST.

Khadzijski, I. (1974) *Optimistic Theory about Our People*, Sofia, Bulgaria: Bulgarian Writers' Press.

Kornai, J. (1979) 'Resource-Constrained versus Demand-Constrained System,' *Sociological Problems*, **1–2**: 37–57 [in Bulgarian].

Kovacheva, S. (1999) *Youth Unemployment in Bulgaria in Comparative Perspective—The Problem and Its Solutions*, Plovdiv, Bulgaria: Georgy Vanchev.

Kovacheva, S. (2000) *Sinking or Swimming in the Waves of Transformation? Young People and Social Protection in Central and Eastern Europe*, Brussels, Belgium: The European Youth Forum.

Kovacheva, S. and Tang N. (2003) 'Flexible Work and Young People's Labor Market Integration in the Process of Globalization,' in *HWF Survey Comparative Report*, vol II, Thematic reports, Vienna, Austria: HIS, pp. 169 ff.

Kovacheva, S. and Mitev, P.-E. (2004) *FATE Bulgarian National Report, Analysis of Qualitative Interviews*, Plovdiv, Bulgaria: University of Plovdiv.

Kovacheva, S., Matev, A. and Demireva, N. (2004) *Transitions. Bulgarian Case Study Report*, Manchester, UK: Manchester Metropolitan University.

Machacek, L. (2004) 'Orientations of Young Men and Women to Citizenship and European Identity,' Research briefing, *Slovak Sociological Review*, **3**. See also http://www.sociology.ed.ac.uk/youth/ accessed in December 2005.

Matev, A. and Kovacheva, S. (2003) *Transitions: Debates about the Reconciliation of Family and Employment in Bulgaria*, Plovdiv, Bulgaria: University of Plovdiv.

Menz, S. and Kramolowsky, U. (2004) *FATE Qualitative Survey*, 'Report on East Germany–Saxony,' Dresden, Germany: Technological University.

Mitev, P.-E. (1988) *Youth and Social Change*, Sofia, Bulgaria: People's Youth Press.

Mitev, P.-E. (2003) Youth 2002. Results from a National Representative Survey, Unpublished report, Bulgaria: Ministry of Youth and Sports.

Možný, I. (1994) 'The Czech Family in Transition: From Social to Economic Capital,' in Ringen, S. and Wallace C. (eds) *Social Reform in the Czech Republic*, Prague Papers on Social Responses to Transformation, vol II, Prague, Czech Republic: Prague Digital Arts, pp. 59–68.

Možný, I., (2003) *Why So Easy? Some Family Grounds for the Gentle Revolution*, Sofia, Bulgaria: East–West [in Bulgarian].

O'Higgins, N. (2003) 'Trends in the Youth Labor Market in Developing and Transition Countries,' *Social Protection Discussion Paper Series*, no 0321, Washington, D.C., USA: The World Bank.

Raychev, A. (2003) 'Genesis, Mutation and Degeneration of Second Networks,' *Sociologicheski problemi*, **1–2**: 5–13.

Rener, T. (2002) 'Mothers and Daughters,' in Tivadar, B. and Mrvar, P. (eds) *Flying Over or Falling through the Cracks? Young People in the Risk Society*, Ljubljana, Slovenia: Office for Youth of the Republic of Slovenia, pp. 217–224.

Roberts, K. (2003) 'Problems and Priorities for the Sociology of Youth,' in Bennett, A., Cieslik, M. and Miles, S. (eds) *Researching Youth*, Basingstoke, UK: Palgrave, pp. 13–28.

Roberts, K., Fagan, C., Foti, K., Jung, B., Kovacheva, S. and Machacek, L. (1999) 'Tackling Youth Unemployment in East-Central Europe,' *Journal for East European Management Studies*, **4**(3): 238–251.

Roberts, K., Osadchaya, G., Dsuzev, K., Gorodnichenko, V. and Tholen, J. (2003) 'Economic Conditions and the Family and Housing Transitions of Young Adults in Russia and Ukraine,' *Journal of Youth Studies*, **6**(1): 71–88.

Slowinski, J. (1999) 'Globalisation and Its Discontents: Impact of a Global System on Youth and Education in Central and Eastern Europe,' *Young*, **7**(3): 21–39.

Stanculescu, M. (2003) Socio-economic Status and Patterns of Work Flexibility, in *HWF Survey Comparative Report*, vol II, Thematic reports, Vienna, Austria: HIS.

Stolan, L., and Morch, S. (2004) *FATE National Report*, 'Denmark.'

Ule, M. and Rener T. (eds) (1998) *Youth in Slovenia. New Perspectives from the Nineties*, Ljubljana, Slovenia: Office for Youth of the Republic of Slovenia.

Ule, M. and Kuhar, M. (2003) *Young Adults and a New Orientation Toward Family Formation*, Paper presented at the ESA Conference, held in Murcia, Spain, September.

UNDP (1999) *Transition. Human Development Report for Central and Eastern Europe and the CIS*, New York, USA: United Nations Development Programme.

UNDP (2002) *Avoiding the Dependency Trap: The Roma in Central and Eastern Europe*, Bratislava, Slovakia: Regional Bureau for Europe and the Commonwealth of Independent States (RBEC) of the United Nations Development Programme.

UNICEF (2000) *Young People in Changing Societies*, Regional Monitoring Report no. 7, Florence, Italy: IRC.

Vrcan, S. (2002) 'Youth: Politics, Sub-politics and Anti-politics,' in Tivadar B. and Mrvar, P. (eds) *Flying over or Falling through the Cracks? Young People in the Risk Society*, Ljubljana, Slovenia: Office for Youth of the Republic of Slovenia, pp. 21–28.

Wallace, C. (1998) 'Crossing Borders: Mobility of Goods, Capital and People in the Central European Region,' in Brah, A., Hickman, M. and Mac an Ghaill, M. (eds) *Future Worlds: Migration, Environment, and Globalization*, London, UK: Macmillan, pp. 185–209.

Wallace, C. (2002) 'Overview: Households, Work and Flexibility,' in Wallace, C. (ed) *Critical Review of Literature and Discourses about Flexibility*, Vienna, Austria HIS, pp. 5–26.

Wallace, C. and Kovacheva, S. (1998) *Youth in Society. The Construction and Deconstruction of Youth in East and West Europe*, London, UK: Macmillan.

Walther, A. and Stauber, B. (eds) (2002) *Misleading Trajectories: Integration Policies for Young Adults in Europe?* Leverkusen, Germany: Verlag Leske & Budrich.

Chapter 8

Family Forms and the Young Generation in the New Europe: Future Trends

Claire Wallace

8.1   Introduction

Looking across the whole of the European Union (EU), we can see paradoxical trends toward both convergence and divergence with respect to young people. On the one hand, the tendency toward convergence is encouraged by, for example, the effects of globalized tendencies in education, the labor market and the harmonization of social and economic policies through the EU, the EU accession negotiations and benchmarking. The tendency toward divergence, on the other hand, is encouraged by the range of different welfare, family and gender regimes (Esping-Andersen, 1996; Gallie and Paugam, 1999), and is now further diversified by the inclusion of ten new member states (NMS) and two candidate countries (CCs), Romania and Bulgaria, which are themselves rather diversified, as well as having traditions of welfare, family and gender regimes that differ from those of the EU (Haas *et al.*, 2004). The contrasts among different populations across Europe, for example in terms of wealth and poverty, is now even wider than in the United States, despite Europeans generally priding themselves on their 'European social model.' Hence, we now have countries where many people live at subsistence level and others have a very high standard of living.

In Chapter 6 Sgritta follows the tradition of European comparison by identifying four families of nations within the 'old' Europe of 15 states in terms of welfare, family and gender regimes: the (social-democratic) Nordic countries, the (conservative) continental countries, the southern countries and the liberal countries (while noting that some countries do not fit easily within this typology). He looks at the situation of young people in terms of these clusters of countries but departs from the usual approach in arguing that the actions of young people actually drive these differences rather than being merely a product of them. Kovacheva (Chapter 7), in including the 'new' Europe of ten new member states and two candidate countries, argues that the previous east–west divide is replaced by a 'mosaic' of emerging patterns that nevertheless, to some extent, reflects the clusters found in the old Europe.

Despite this diversity, we can identify various common trends across eastern and western Europe—trends that have often taken an accelerated form in eastern and central Europe. The trends are ones that affect the population as a whole and young people in particular and may be driven by young people as they respond to the changing world around them. Here, I have identified four 'megatrends': changing family transitions, flexibilization of education and labor markets, the changing relationships among generations and new forms of mobility and association. Each of these contains a number of subtrends, and they interact with one another.

Based on these trends, I will sketch out two scenarios of change for future generations: flexibility and inclusion versus polarization and exclusion.

8.2   Trends

Trend 1: Changing family transitions

Much has been made of the decline in the birth rate and the aging of the population in terms of the 'second demographic transition.' These developments have been seen as little short of disastrous for economic prosperity and for maintaining the European social model. The postponement of family formation, although it takes place in different places for different reasons and in different ways, is a visible trend across the entire continent. Here, we have to identify various subtrends: exit from the natal family, setting up a new household, procreation and marriage. These are all more flexible, less standardized, less associated with one another and more reversible than in the past.

A common reason for the postponement of family formation is that it takes young people longer to train and qualify for positions in the labor market and to find secure employment. Another is that young women seek careers outside the home and, if they are not supported in this, the choice they face is between poverty and having a family and economic survival without one. As Sgritta has indicated in Chapter 6, this is the price that the southern and to some extent the continental European countries pay for maintaining the traditional model of the family. In southern European countries, there was also a tradition of later entry into marriage for men, if not for women. The process of 'individualization' means that young people seek out opportunities and are faced with risks that earlier postwar generations with more fixed family roles and more standardized transitions did not face (Wallace and Kovacheva, 1998).

However, in regions such as the Nordic countries, where there is support for diverse family forms, the young men and women are able to continue their roles inside and outside the labor market, as well as to develop a variety of personal relationships. Hence, in different parts of Europe, we find not so much that young people do not form families but rather that they have different ways of getting there: increasing cohabitation, births outside marriage, 'living apart together' and the formation of nonheterosexual and noncouple households (Roseneil and Budgeon, 2004). While such trends are clear in the Nordic countries, they can also be found in the more liberal regions, and this trend is also visible in the continental European countries, even if not in such an extreme form.

In the NMS and CCs there was previously also a more standardized set of transitions, along with relatively young entry into marriage and parenthood and rather high birth rates (Wallace and Kovacheva [1998]; see also, *World Social Situation Report* [2003]). However, these countries too have witnessed similar trends to those in western Europe, often in an accelerated form (for example, the trend toward nonmarital child rearing), although in some cases these tendencies even predated the collapse of Communism. Even within this group of countries, we find tremendous differences, with Cyprus and Malta perhaps not surprisingly following the more 'southern' tradition and the Czech Republic and Hungary starting to look more like liberal states. Other countries such as Poland appear to be more conservative, perhaps because of the strength of Roman Catholicism there. The extremely high rates of unemployment, as well as poverty among young people, make these tendencies toward postponed transitions even stronger.

The transitions into and out of the family reflect to some extent different welfare states and the role that young people occupy in the welfare system. The Nordic countries are notable for offering support for young people's independence based on policies that encourage autonomy, and they see young people as a resource for society (Bendit and Wallace, 2004). Hence, in these societies, diverse family forms are recognized and encouraged. This tends to reflect not only the Protestant tradition of individuality but also strong traditions of gender egalitarianism. The continental European countries, while having the longest-established tradition of youth policies, tend to see young people as people to be protected as well as promoted, and welfare provision tends to take place within the tradition of the Church and other nongovernmental organizations (NGOs) that reinforce a tendency toward the conservative family form. In the liberal countries, young people until recently were seen more as potential problems rather than as resources; hence, policies were targeted at these problem youth rather than at all young people (Bendit and Wallace, 2004). Finally, in the southern European group of countries, young people were seen until recently as the responsibility of the family and the Church, and the introduction of new youth policies to help young people become more autonomous has been relatively recent. The central role of the family in providing welfare tends to reinforce the conservative model of the family that is already strong in the Roman Catholic and Greek Orthodox traditions.

In the countries of central and eastern Europe, we can see increasingly divergent patterns in terms of the development of welfare regimes. Slovenia would seem most similar to the Nordic countries in terms of generous welfare support, while the Czech Republic, Hungary and Poland seem to be moving more in the direction of the continental welfare regimes, introducing social insurance systems and a conservative family model reinforced by state support. In these countries, young people's autonomy has been reinforced and, at least in Slovenia and Poland, birth rates remain high (although in other countries they have fallen dramatically). On the other hand, Romania and Bulgaria, facing a severe fiscal crisis, have been forced to cut back on welfare regimes, and this has led to subinstitutional coverage, with many people being forced back on their own resources, more like southern European countries. In these countries young people's autonomy has been undermined.

In terms of gender regimes, there has been a general liberalization and recognition of the desirability for equality between the sexes, especially among the younger generations (Inglehart and Norris, 2003). We find strong egalitarian traditions in the Nordic countries, something that forms a part of social policies as well as the domestic division of labor (Haas *et al.*, 2004). Hence, dual earners are common, with state support for children. Nevertheless, these countries are gender-divided in many ways in terms of labor-market and family roles. In the continental European countries, the conservative tradition of gender roles has been challenged by more liberal attitudes in the recent past, especially among young people. However, the conservative model of the family tends to prevail in welfare policies and labor market patterns, favoring the male-breadwinner model; this model is now being replaced by 'modified-breadwinner' families where women work part-time and men full-time. In the southern European countries, gender ideologies have traditionally been conservative, and the pattern of labor market participation has favored the male breadwinner; this, however, is also challenged by the younger generation, and in Portugal there has always been a strong tradition of female participation in the labor market. In the liberal group of countries, dual earners and modified-breadwinner families are also common but do not have the strong state support that we find in the Nordic countries. The countries of eastern and central Europe traditionally favored dual-earner households, and in these countries part-time work is very rare, certainly not a way of reconciling work and family for women. At the same time, the domestic division of labor was highly unequal and there was an anti-egalitarian, even 'masculinist' ideology (Mateeva and Wallace, 2004). In the transition period, we find that the traditional family ideology has been reintroduced through family policies that encourage women to stay at home in some countries (Czech Republic and Hungary) and the strong assertion of women's traditional caring role in others (Poland) (Regulska, 1998). Hence, we find more tendencies toward the male-breadwinner model. In Romania and Bulgaria where there is very high male unemployment, we find tendencies toward a female-breadwinner model, even though the cultural norm is two full-time earners. Ideologically, the division of labor remains traditional. Hence, young women in eastern and central Europe who wish to join a heterosexual partnership or have children are expected to shoulder a 'dual burden': to work full-time in the labor market and do most of the domestic work. Not surprisingly, many young women refuse to take up this burden.

Trend 2: The 'flexibilization' of education and labor markets

Delaying entry into the family is partly a product of delaying entry into work and the extension of education. In all countries, increasing opportunities in education and training, along with a diversification of opportunities, mean that young people spend longer periods in education and training, which in many countries is combined with part-time or casual work. In all countries, it is young people and women who are more likely to be found in the flexible areas of the labor market. As Kovacheva (Chapter 7) has indicated, this can be either a stepping-stone or a trap. Paradoxically, the more protection there is for workers, the more young people find themselves in this situation, as flexibility is displaced on to beginning workers rather than spread around the workforce (Sik and Wallace, 2003). Very high levels of youth unemployment in some countries exacerbate this situation.

In the NMS the older secure routes into the labor market with guaranteed work have been replaced by widespread unemployment, reaching 40 percent or more in Bulgaria and Poland but less than 5 percent in Austria and The Netherlands. In southern European countries, around one-quarter of young people may be unemployed (and this does not take into account that many young unemployed are not registered because they have not yet worked). Under these circumstances, young people resort to self-employment, working abroad and doing casual work to make ends meet.

However, trends in the labor market for young people reflect trends in education, with more young people staying on for education and training in an increasing variety of courses at a time when state support has declined. The private sector has become more predominant in offering education at either an individual or collective level, and the state has withdrawn from supporting young people through their educational transitions. This means that many of the young flexible workers are, in fact, young people supporting themselves through extended periods of education and training.

The promotion of the idea of 'lifelong learning' is a response to the fact that even if young people enter a regular job, they may not stay there for good. Rather, they may have to retrain, change careers or develop supplementary careers. There is evidence, for example, that young people do one job to earn a living while developing a supplementary career from which they cannot necessarily support themselves but that may be more important in terms of identity building (see Joanna Wynn's presentation of her longitudinal research on young adults in Australia [Dwyer *et al.*, 2003]). For example, someone working at a bank may, in fact, be pursuing a career as a musician or artist. The abolition of age limits, especially in the liberal regimes, helps this tendency by which people could theoretically slip in and out of work, training and education (sometimes doing all three simultaneously) throughout their lives. The reluctance to abandon traditional age-status traditions based upon the postwar 'golden age' of structured transitions in continental countries leads to serious rigidities in the labor market (for example, in restricting access to certain kinds of training or retirement because of age).

Trend 3: The changing relationship between generations

The changing relationship between generations takes place at two levels: the individual level and the aggregate level. On the first level, the postponement of other life transitions means that young people are more dependent on their parents for longer periods of time. This clearly happens in both eastern and western Europe and is a consequence of the trends described above, along with the fact that independent housing has become more expensive. It can mean either prolonged parental support through life transitions or actually living with parents for long periods. There are once again variations across Europe, with the Nordic countries sustaining young people's transitions out of the home through state support and young people in southern European countries staying at home for longer, although policies are being introduced to tackle this problem in some countries. In both the continental and southern European countries, the principle of subsidiarity means that families are the frontline support for young people. In eastern and central Europe we find that early independence is the norm in countries such as the Czech Republic or Slovenia; but this is much less so in countries such as Bulgaria and

Romania where multigenerational households are more common. It is paradoxical that this prolonged state support takes place simultaneously with the increased psychological and cultural independence of young people: parents support young people economically but have little control in other ways.

The relationship between the generations takes place at another level in terms of the aggregate populations. As there are more older people, they take a larger share of welfare resources and have more potential political power (Cote 2002; Adsett 2003). Sgritta (Chapter 6) has documented the increasing transfer of welfare resources to older generations, particularly in those countries where the birth rate has fallen, which can lead to a vicious circle, with the lack of support to children and young people producing further disincentives to have children. The aging of the population is a trend that we see in all the EU25 countries, although it takes place at a slightly different speed in different regions. This 'generational contract' has been a source of concern in welfare regimes.

Trend 4: Changing forms of mobility and association

The enlarged Europe leads to new possibilities for work and travel for which young people are better situated. The growing attraction of the 'gap year' is perhaps one aspect of this, meaning that a period of traveling around doing casual jobs is seen as part of a normal biography (Hartmann, 1995). Again, the extent of and the reasons for mobility vary, with young people in smaller countries at the center of Europe having more reasons to travel abroad than those in larger, more peripheral countries. Mobility and experience of other cultures and languages makes young Europeans more tolerant and also more receptive to supranational and European identities (Wallace *et al.*, 2004).

Mobility is facilitated by improved communication, both physical and virtual. Access to transport and the explosion in the means of transportation has affected young people, but they are even more affected by virtual networking that enables communication across borders and across homes (for example, texting, Internet chatting, sending photos). Mobility is also encouraged by European programs, sport and exchanges from which many thousands have benefited. However, while some mobility is driven by affluence, some is driven by poverty, as with the young people interviewed by Kovacheva (Chapter 7) in Bulgaria who saw no future for themselves at home and only wanted to go abroad.

Mobility is important for the growing psychological and cultural independence of young people as a way of escaping parental control. With this new form of communication, however, also come new forms of 'sociation.' The traditional forms of sociation are still important—joining youth and other organizations or being embedded in friendship groups. However, new forms of sociation are suggested by

the decline of traditional solidarities associated with spatial communities, working communities and trade unions (Pahl, 2000). The flexible entrance and exits
to living communities, work and education promotes looser networks of friends
and colleagues supported by subcultures. Internet chat rooms are much used by
young people as ways of communicating (Waechter, 2005), as is mobile texting.
Meanwhile, participation in society can take the form of lifestyle choices, such as
vegetarianism or the kind of loose but effective mobilization carried out through
Internet movements, as we saw with the antiglobalization demonstrations. Thus,
social capital can be sustained in the face of the decline of traditional organizations
and perhaps becomes more important as a way of sustaining young people through
life's uncertainties and risks.

8.3   Scenarios

It is clear that the 'golden age' of full employment for men, the traditional family
in which women were primarily carers and the welfare state that supported people
from cradle to grave through standardized transitions (education–work–marriage–
children–retirement) is a thing of the past. Of course, there are many people who
still make such standardized transitions within traditional careers, but alternative
destandardized transitions are becoming more common everywhere. The problem
is that welfare states were constructed around these standardized transitions and
patriarchal assumptions, and some politicians and social movements try to reassert
these traditional social relationships in the face of pervasive change (Abbott and
Wallace, 1992). According to Sgritta (Chapter 6), this is one of the reasons for the
fall in the birth rate. It is also a reason for the poverty and social exclusion of the
increasing number of young people who do not fit into these traditional categories.
The European social model must therefore adapt if it is to continue to provide social
protection for its populations.

Scenario 1: Flexibility and inclusion

In this scenario young people are able to choose a variety of options without any
end point: people can carry on trying out options all their lives; there is not necessarily any 'settling down.' They have increased opportunities for travel and for
working and studying abroad, as the European social model adapts to enable the
harmonization of welfare programs and supports young people in their striving for
independence. However, they are able to maintain links both with parents and
friends through a variety of communications media and sustain a wide variety of
different kinds of relationships. The opening of the borders between western and
eastern Europe has brought a variety of new opportunities for travel, scholarship

and association for the young people of eastern and central Europe. However, life has also become riskier in a number of senses: in terms of entry into the labor market, the trends are not as secure and jobs have become more precarious. Young people have to fashion and shape their own careers and opportunities without clear guidelines. They do this by putting together work and study, travel and personal relationships in a variety of configurations that also bring increased stress and un-certainty. Young people must prepare for more than one career and more than one significant relationship. They need to develop reflexive narratives of self in order to manage this. Starting a family is something that can be fitted in with work and with studying in a variety of different combinations, depending upon the kind of career they are pursuing. It may or may not be associated with getting married or finding a partner of a different sex. Increasing tolerance of alternative family forms means that young people are relatively open to a range of possibilities: life with a different sex partner (or a string of them), life with a same sex partner, living alone, living as a single parent, sharing a household with other young people, living apart together and so on.

In this scenario, working need not consist of a full-time job for life. It may involve working abroad or for an NGO for a period of time or undertaking 'civilian service' instead of military service.

In this scenario the European social model would be challenged to adapt to these biographies. Rights and benefits would thus be contingent on the individ-ual worker rather than the traditional patriarchal family. Contributions would be transferable between jobs and countries and could be banked in various ways to compensate for noncontributing periods. There would be no age restrictions on training, grants and education, which could be undertaken throughout life (even after the standard retirement age). Children would receive various kinds of social support, and women or men with children would enjoy various advantages to en-able them to balance work and family. Borders would be open to allow people to move where they wish.

Scenario 2: Polarization and exclusion

In this scenario the interests of the younger generation are sidelined in favor of the older generations who supply the majority of voters. Youth unemployment is high so that many young people are socially excluded, living out their days as family de-pendents without welfare support because they have never worked, never worked regularly or never worked outside the black economy. A small number of privi-leged young people manage to find secure careers that enable them to access wel-fare, income and 'normal' transitions out of the home. In a world where leisure and communication are increasingly commercialized, young people are also excluded from forms of communication and participation. The failure of the European social model to adapt to changing family forms and to mobility means that those who leave parental protection (or are expelled) face lives of insecurity and poverty. Living at home they face increasing family tension, parents being unable to understand why they do not find jobs as they did when they were young, and their growing cultural independence clashes with their economic dependence. Being alienated from politics, they no longer vote or register to vote and are thus increasingly politically excluded. It is increasingly difficult for them to contemplate starting a family because they are unable to establish separate households.

In this scenario European states have reacted against mobility, forcing many young people to become illegal migrants in their search for work or for better lives or subcitizens in an increasingly polarized world. Their exclusion from regular work and from regular citizenship makes young people more inclined to participate in illegal activities, so that crime increases and more money must be spent upon law and order.

Both these scenarios already exist, but for different groups of young people in different parts of Europe. Future cooperation and social policies will determine which one is likely to become dominant.

References

Abbott, P. and Wallace, C. (1992) *The Family and the New Right*, London, UK: Pluto Press.

Adsett, M. (2003) 'Change in Political Era and Demographic Weight as Explanations of Youth "Disenfranchisement" in Federal Elections in Canada, 1965–2000,' *Journal of Youth Studies*, **6**(3): 247–264.

Bendit, R. and Wallace C. (2004) *Youth Policies in Europe*, Paper, Vienna, Austria: Institute for Advanced Studies.

Cote, J. E. (2002) *Arrested Adulthood: The Changing Nature of Maturity and Identity*. New York, USA: New York University Press.

Dwyer, P., Smith, G., Tyler, D. and Wynn, J. (2003) *Life Pattern, Career Outcomes and Adult Choices: The Life-Patterns Study*, University of Melbourne, Australia: Australian Youth Research Centre, Faculty of Education.

Esping-Andersen, G. (1996) *Welfare States in Transition*, London, UK: Thousand Oaks.

Gallie, D. and Paugam, S. (eds) (1999) *Welfare Regimes and the Experience of Unemployment in Europe*, Oxford, UK: Oxford University Press.

Haas, B., Hartl, M. and Wallace, C. (2004) *Work inside the Home, Work outside the Home and Family Types across Europe*, Working Paper, Vienna, Austria: Institute for Advanced Studies.

Hartmann, J. (1995) 'The Significance of Youth Mobility and Travel: The Case of Sweden,' in Circle for Youth Cooperation in Europe (CYRCE) and Hübner-Funk S. (eds) *The Puzzle of Integration. European Yearbook on Youth Policy and Research*, vol 1, Berlin, Germany: Walter de Gruyter, pp. 63–74.

Inglehart, R. and Norris, P. (2003) *Rising Tide. Gender Equality and Cultural Change around the World*, Cambridge, UK: Cambridge University Press.

Mateeva, L. and Wallace, C. (2004) *Attitudes to Gender Equality in Enlargement Countries*, Working Paper, Vienna, Austria: Institute for Advanced Studies.

Pahl, R.E. (2000) *On Friendship*, Cambridge, UK: Polity Press.

Regulska, J. (1998) ' "The political" and its meaning for women: Transition politics in Poland' in Pickles, J. and Smith, A. (eds) *Theorising Transition: The Political Economy of Post-Communist Transformations*, London, UK: Routledge, pp. 309–329.

Roseneil, S. and Budgeon, S. (2004) 'Cultures of Intimacy and Care beyond "the Family": Personal Life and Social Change in the Early 21st Century,' *Current Sociology*, **52**:135–160.

Sik, E. and Wallace, C. (2003) 'How Much Flexibility is There? A Comparison of Eastern and Western Europe,' in Wallace, C. (ed) *HWF Survey Comparative Report Volume 2: Thematic Papers* (*HWF* Project), Vienna, Austria: Institute for Advanced Studies.

Waechter, N. (2005) 'Chat Rooms and Girls' Empowerment,' in Sherrod, L.R., Flannigan, C.A. and Kassimir, R. (eds) *Youth Activism. An International Encyclopedia*, vol 1, Westport, CT, USA: Greenwood Press, pp. 109–113.

Wallace, C. and Kovacheva, S. (1998) *Youth in Society. The Construction and Deconstruction of Youth in East and West Europe*, London, UK: Macmillan.

Wallace, C., Spannring, R. and Datler, G. (2004) 'Active Citizens? The Engagement of Young People in Europe,' Research Briefing 5, at the Final Project Meeting for *Orientations of Young Men and Women to Citizenship and European Identity*, Powerpoint presentation at the University of Edinburgh, UK, on 8 July, See http://www.sociology.ed.ac.uk/youth/Research_Briefings.html/ accessed in December 2005.

World Social Situation Report (2003) New York, USA: Division for Social Policy and Development, United Nations Department of Economic and Social Affairs.

Part IV
Migration Developments in an Enlarged European Union

Chapter 9

Migration, Migrants and Their Families in the EU15 Member States

Johannes Pflegerl

9.1 Introduction

In the last decade, migration-related issues have become increasingly important in the public and political debate within the European Union (EU). This has happened mainly because a rising inflow of migrants from different backgrounds, and for various reasons, have begun challenging the image that many European societies had hitherto had of themselves as—in many respects—nonimmigrant countries. The fact that, in the last 20 years, all member countries of the former EU15, as well as most of the new member states, have effectively become net immigrant countries has caused vigorous public debate on how to deal with and manage migration movements to the EU. Moreover, the issue of migration has also gained significant purchase at the political level of the EU with the coming into force of the Amsterdam Treaty in May 1999, when issues related to visas, asylum, immigration and external borders came under the jurisdiction of the European Community. The events of September 11, 2001 also mark a significant turning point, as they induced the EU governments to strengthen both their external and internal controls. As a result, there has been a growing tendency in European public and political debates to view migration as a security threat.

The topicality of migration-related issues encouraged the coordination team of the European Observatory on the Social Situation, Demography and Family (the Observatory) to adopt the topic of migration and to observe relevant developments in this field in the EU15 member states. To describe the situation in their respective countries the national experts dedicated one of their focused monitoring reports to migration. The annual seminar of the European Observatory in 2002, held in Helsinki, was also dedicated to immigration and family; it covered issues relevant not only to family migration but also to the demographic and socioeconomic aspects of migration in the EU and migration developments in relation to EU enlargement. A number of experts from the Observatory's network also made special contributions highlighting specific aspects of this issue.

In this chapter the main results of the Observatory's work on migration will be summarized and completed with new data and findings. This chapter is confined to the EU15 member states; developments in the new member states are analysed separately in the next chapter. After a brief examination of the various meanings of migration, there will be a short historical overview of the development of migration movements in the EU15. This will be followed by a description of the main demographic aspects of migration in the period of observation (1998–2004). The main trends covering the most important migration movements in this period to the EU15 will then be highlighted—labor migration, family-linked migration, asylum seekers and irregular migration. The chapter ends with a number of findings from Eurobarometer surveys of the last few years concerning the attitude of EU15 citizens toward foreigners and immigrants.

9.2   The Various Meanings of Migration

Definitions of migration have traditionally been associated with permanent settlement or long-term residence. In the social sciences, the permanent change of a place to stay is a decisive factor in defining migration and distinguishes it from other forms of mobility (Han, 2000, p. 9). In the last two decades, however, a growing diversification has been observed in migration movements.

As highlighted in the joint report on social inclusion by the Council of the European Union (2001, p. 7), migration movements lead 'to a growing trend toward ethnic, cultural and religious diversity' in the EU. This development also challenges theoretical endeavors and causes the classic approaches to migration theory, such as those that explain migration only as a result of push-and-pull factors, to be called critically into question. In an era of globalization, the existence of a worldwide migration system within which migratory movements occur must increasingly be taken into account. This global migration system is characterized by the emergence of migration networks and transnational spaces (Pries, 1997) as the context within which the life of many migrants takes place (Fernández de la Hoz, 2002, p. 30).

Migrants comprise different groups of people with different motives. It is often difficult to make clear distinctions between permanent and temporary forms of mobility. Permanent migrants, such as workers or ethnic migrants, have often changed their status from previously temporary to permanent residents.

As pointed out by Salt (2002, p. 4), temporary migrants also fall into rather diverse groups, including au pairs and domestic servants, agriculture, construction and manufacturing workers, and hotel, catering and cleaning staff. Many of these people are seasonal workers, others are frontier workers and others perhaps highly skilled corporate secondees. Also 'on the move' across borders are numerous other individuals whose residence status often cannot be clearly defined and blends into that of traditionally defined migrants. These comprise cross-border commuters, labor tourists and small traders, often engaged in forms of incomplete migration and most of whose livelihood is derived from frequent short-term visits to other countries. Other groups of migrants include asylum seekers, refugees, those in need of temporary protection, students and working tourists.

Consequently, some researchers suggest not thinking in terms of rigid categories nor placing 'migration at some defined point on the mobility continuum,' as Salt (2002, p. 4) puts it, arguing that:

> ... migration streams seen as mobility streams are dynamic and pliant, involve different types of people and motivations, have different roles and methods of insertion into host societies and are influenced and managed by different agencies and institutions.

As general developments on a macro level will be described in this chapter, it seems sensible to use a rather broad definition of migration so as to describe the wide spectrum of migratory movements and the reasons behind them

9.3 Migration in Europe: A Brief Historical Overview

Recent demographic figures indicate that immigration is having a significant impact on population change in Europe. Since the beginning of the 1990s net migration into the European Union has been higher than the natural population increase (*Figure 9.1*).

This development represents a remarkable reversal in European history. Looking back on two centuries of experience of European migration, one aspect stands out from all the others, namely, that until the 1960s, even though there had always been movement back and forth within the continent, migration in the context of

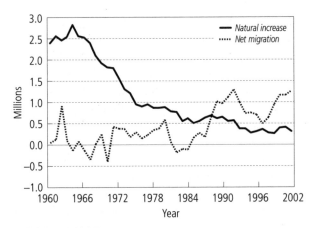

Source: Eurostat (2002 and 2004).

Figure 9.1. Population development in the EU15, 1960–2003.

the European continent was predominantly emigration. Between 1800 and 1960 more than 60 million people emigrated from Europe to another continent. About 40 million left for North America and another 20 million for South America, South Africa, Australia, New Zealand and Asian parts of Russia. Thereafter, however, migration patterns began to change greatly (Müller-Schneider, 2000). Between the late 1950s and the early 1970s, many western, northern and central European states started to recruit temporary migrant workers from southern Europe, and later from North Africa and Turkey, to meet their labor market demands in a period of booming economic growth. After World War II this development led to a first significant rise in immigrants to what are now European Union member states. With the 1973 oil crisis encouraging European states to impose restrictive immigration policies, the inflow of migrants in fact slowed down to continue on a lower level. Other grounds for migration, especially family reunification, began to partially replace the earlier type of labor migration. At the end of the 1980s and during the first half of the 1990s, the fall of the Iron Curtain, a deterioration in living conditions, ethnopolitical conflicts and civil and interstate wars created new refugee flows and other migratory movements, not only within the Balkans, eastern Europe, Turkey, Algeria and the Commonwealth of Independent States but also from these areas to the west. Thus, refugees, asylum seekers and illegal migrants entered the EU15. Migration movements to the EU15 therefore become more diversified. The population of foreign citizenship increased sharply and simultaneously in most European countries (Fassmann, 2002, p. 4).

9.4 Demographic Development of Migration, 1998 to 2004

The start of the observation period in 1998 falls at the beginning of a fresh rise in migration inflows that led to a new increase in net migration to the EU15. It followed a short period of decline in new immigration to the EU between 1993 and 1997 that was due, among other things, to legal measures imposed by several member states with the aim of restricting legal entry to their territory.

The observable rise in inflows and an increase in the foreign population stock in the EU15 from 1997 was accompanied by a further diversification of migration movements and an increase in the number of migrants' countries of origin.

Rising migration figures in this period in general were due to:

1. An increase in both permanent and, especially, temporary labor migration;
2. A continuation of family-linked migration;
3. An increase in refugees and asylum seekers;
4. A rising number of illegal migrants;
5. Continuing ethnic migration; and
6. Other forms of migratory movements, including migration of highly skilled people, students and pensioners.

9.4.1 Inflows and outflows of migrants in the EU15 member states

Table 9.1 clearly shows that between 1997 and 2001 most of the EU15 member states registered steady increases in the inflow of foreign nationals. The exceptions are Belgium, Denmark, Luxembourg, The Netherlands and Sweden which recorded some interim decreases. Nevertheless, on the whole, the increasing trend could also be observed in those countries. Some countries registered massive increases, such as Italy, where the inflow of foreigners more than doubled between 1998 and 1999, and Spain, where the inflow more than tripled between 1999 and 2000.

In contrast, the number of outflows between 1997 and 2002 was comparably smaller in most of the EU15 countries. Only in Germany in 1997 and 1998 did the number of foreign people leaving the country exceed the number moving to it. In the following years, however, inflows clearly exceeded outflows, showing that the EU15 had further consolidated its position as an immigration area.

The Organisation for Economic Co-operation and Development (OECD) has also observed a trend toward feminization of migration flows. In the last decade women have made up an increasing proportion of employment-related migration and refugee flows, whereas prior to that, female migration to the EU had merely taken place in the context of family reunification. Nevertheless, family reunification

Table 9.1. Inflow and outflow of foreign population to the EU15, 1997–2002.

	1997 thousands		1998 thousands		1999 thousands		2000 thousands		2001 thousands		2002 thousands	
	In	Out	In	Out	In	Out	In	Out	In	Out	In	Out
Austria	56.9*	49.8*	59.2	44.9*	72.4	47.3*	66.0	44.4*	74.8	51.0*	–	–
Belgium	49.2	34.6	50.7	36.3	68.5	36.4	68.6	35.6	66.0	24.5	–	–
Denmark	20.4	6.7	21.3	7.7	20.3	8.2	–	8.3	25.2	8.9	30.6*	17.7*
Finland	8.1	1.6	8.3	1.7	7.9	2.0	9.1	4.1	11.0	2.2	12.9*	3.4*
France	102.4	–	139.5	–	108.1	–	119.3	–	141.0	–	–	–
Germany	615.3	637.1	605.5	639.0	673.9	555.6	648.8	562.4	685.3	497.0	658.3*	505.6*
Greece	–	–	38.2	–	–	–	–	–	–	–	–	–
Ireland	23.5	29.0*	20.8	21.2*	21.6	29.0*	24.1	22.3*	28.0	19.9*	76.1*	–
Italy	–	–	111.0	7.9*	268.0	8.6*	271.5	12.4*	232.8	–	388.1*	–
Luxembourg	9.4	5.8	10.6	6.7	11.8	6.9	10.8	7.0	11.1	7.8	11.0*	–
Netherlands	76.7	21.9	81.7	21.3	78.4	20.7	91.4	20.7	94.5	20.4	86.6*	–
Portugal	3.3*	–	6.5*	–	10.5*	0.4*	15.9*	–	14.2*	–	17.0*	–
Spain	35.6*	–	57.2*	–	99.1*	–	330.9*	–	394.0*	–	443.1*	–
Sweden	33.4	15.3	35.7	14.1	34.6	13.6	33.8	12.6	44.1	12.7	47.6*	–
United Kingdom	236.9	148.7*	258.0	125.8*	276.9	139.2*	288.8	161.1*	373.3	159.2*	418.2	185.7*

Sources: OECD (2004, p. 305); *Salt (2003, pp. 56 and 57).

Table 9.2. Share of foreign population in the EU15.

EU15	Total Population	Foreigners	% of total population
1990	349,088	14,631	4.19
1995	353,640	17,706	5.01
2000	357,340	19,041	5.33

Source: Eurostat (2004).

still remains the main form of female immigration to most of the EU15 countries (OECD, 2001, p. 27).

9.4.2   Stock of foreign population in the EU15 member states

The rise in the inflows of foreigners and the lower rates of outflows has led to an increase in the foreign population in the EU15. Between 1990 and 2000 the share of foreigners in the EU15 increased from 4.19 to 5.33 percent of the total population (*Table 9.2*).

Increases could be observed in the foreign population stock in most of the EU15 member states between 1998 and 2001. Some countries such as Ireland, Portugal and Spain were affected by a remarkable expansion in the foreign population stock, especially between 1999 and 2001. In other countries like Belgium and Sweden, interim decreases, due mainly to comparatively high naturalization numbers, could be observed. Even though the number of inflows was rising, the total foreign population stock remained the same or decreased slightly.

Table 9.3 also clarifies the fact that there are large differences in the foreign population share within the EU15. Luxembourg has by far the highest rates (37.5 percent) followed by Germany (9.77 percent in 2002), Austria (9.4 percent in 2001) and Belgium (8.2 percent in 2001). Finland (1.9 percent in 2001), Portugal (2.35 percent in 2002) and Italy (2.4 percent in 2001) have the lowest percentages of foreigners.

In the EU15 member states about 30 percent of all foreigners are citizens of another EU member state. Two-thirds come from states outside the EU15. A closer look at the most important receiving countries in the EU15 member states shows that Turkish nationals, among them both ethnic Turks and Kurds, are the largest community. Around three million Turkish citizens are living in one of the EU15 member states. The second largest group are citizens of former Yugoslavia, mainly Croats, Serbs, Bosnian Muslims and ethnic Albanians. Ranked third and fourth are Moroccans and Algerians (Fassmann, 2002, p. 5).

Table 9.3. Stock of foreign population in the EU15 member states, 1998–2002.

in thousands	1998	1999	2000	2001	2002
Austria	737.3	748.2	757.9	764.3	
% of total population	9.1	9.2	9.3	9.4	
Belgium	892.0	897.1	861.7	846.7	
% of total population	8.7	8.8	8.4	8.2	
Denmark	256.3	259.4	258.6	266.7	265.0*
% of total population	4.8	4.9	4.8	5.0	5.2*
Finland	85.1	87.7	91.1	98.6	104.0*
% of total population	1.6	1.7	1.8	1.9	2.03*
France	–	3,263.2	–		
% of total population	–	5.6	–		
Germany	7,319.5	7,343.6	7,296.8	7,318.6	7,348.0*
% of total population	8.9	8.9	8.9	8.9	9.77*
Greece				762.2	
% of total population				7.0	
Ireland	111.0	117.8	126.5	151.4	
% of total population	3.0	3.2	3.3	3.9	
Italy	1,250.2	1,252.0	1,388.2	1,362.6	
% of total population	2.1	2.2	2.4	2.4	
Luxembourg	152.9	159.4	164.7	1,778.5	
% of total population	35.6	36.0	37.3	37.5	
Netherlands	662.4	651.5	667.8	690.4	700.0*
% of total population	4.2	4.1	4.2	4.3	4.52
Portugal	177.8	190.9	208.2	223.6	239.0*
% of total population	1.8	1.9	2.1	2.2	2.35*
Spain	719.6	801.3	895.7	1,109.1	
% of total population	1.8	2.0	2.2	2.7	
Sweden	499.9	487.2	477.3	476.0	474.0*
% of total population	5.6	5.5	5.4	5.3	5.6*
United Kingdom	2,207.0	2,208.0	2,342.0	2,587.0	
% of total population	3.8	3.8	4.0	4.4	

Note: *Data refer to 31 December of the respective year.
Sources: OECD (2004, p. 308); Eurostat (2004).

9.4.3   The impact of migration on population development in the EU15

Altogether, migration plays a significant role in population development in the EU15, having already made a critical contribution to population growth for several years now. The OECD (2004, p. 46) makes it clear that several EU15 countries would have seen their population fall had there not been an inflow of new immigrants, in particular, Germany since 1986, Italy since 1993 and Sweden since 1997.

Among the EU15 countries, France and Ireland stand out as exceptions, as their population growth rates are positive and have never fallen below 3 and 5, respectively. In France the contribution of births—rising steadily since 1993—to total population growth remains higher than the impact of migration. This can be explained by the fertility rate in France and Ireland being higher than the European average. In France the relatively high number of births to foreigners and births attributed to recently naturalized immigrants also contributes to this increase (OECD, 2004, p. 46).

In many EU member states, births to foreign and foreign-born nationals represent a sizable proportion of total births. In the late 1990s the share of foreign births in the total number of births was particularly high in Luxembourg (48 percent) and France, Germany and the United Kingdom (between 10 and 13 percent). As Bagavos (2004, p. 10) points out, these high birth rates are related to the total size and age structure of the foreign population as well as to the relatively high fertility of migrants. Foreign births can thus help to slow down some of the effects of population aging. Bagavos (2004, p. 11) also emphasizes that, to date, the impact of immigration by third-country nationals on the age structure of the EU15 population is rather weak. In fact, even if foreigners have a younger age structure and a higher fertility rate than EU nationals, their number is still too low to significantly influence population aging. Even though net migration has contributed to a further increase in the total population of the EU15, its impact on the age structure has been rather limited. Moreover, even though migration inflows were increasing, the share of people over the age of 65 in the total population of the EU15 also continued to increase (from 13.6 percent in 1985 to 16.2 percent in 2000). This increase was even higher than that which occurred in the period between 1970 and 1985 (when 12.2 percent of the population was older than 65), when the number of inflows was quite low.

This leads to the general question: to what extent does the immigration of young adults from outside the EU compensate for the aging structure of the EU, if at all? Lutz and Scherbov (2003) calculated a number of population scenarios for the European Observatory, combining different assumptions to develop fertility and immigration rates. They came to the conclusion that even extreme combinations of these assumptions affect the population aging process only quite slowly, as population size starts to grow significantly only in 2050 with a fertility rate of 1.8 combined with an annual net migration of 1,200,000 or more.

These scenarios are due to population age structure supposedly changing more rapidly and more profoundly than population size. Currently, the old age dependency ratio (defined as the proportion of the population above the age of 65 divided by the population aged 15 to 64) amounts to 0.24. Lutz and Scherbov (2003, pp. 7f f) point out that because of the inevitable changes preprogrammed into the

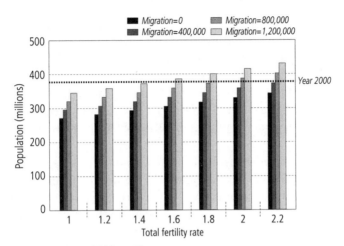

Source: Lutz and Scherbov (2003, p. 7).

Figure 9.2. Total population of the EU15 in 2050, according to alternative projections, assuming a wide range of fertility and annual net migration levels.

current age structure of the population, this ratio is bound to increase significantly under all scenarios. *Figure 9.2* shows that even annual net migration of around one million combined with higher fertility rates than today's level makes little difference to the old age dependency ratio in 2050 (*Figure 9.3*). They conclude that while immigration can contribute to filling certain specific gaps in the European labor market, it can in no way stop or reverse the process of significant population aging in Europe.

9.5   Main Trends in Labor Migration

9.5.1   Inflows and stock of labor migrants in the EU15 member states

During the observation period most of the EU15 member states were affected by a continuous increase in the number of labor migrants, which also led to migrants having a higher share in the total labor force in most countries (*Table 9.4*; *Table 9.5*). Big increases for this time period were especially noted in Portugal (a fivefold increase of foreign workers within seven years), Spain (a fourfold increase of foreign workers between 1995 and 2002) and Finland (number of foreign workers more than doubling between 1995 and 2002). In other countries the number remained relatively constant or the share of foreign workers in the total labor force even decreased slightly, as in France, Germany and The Netherlands, although these countries did receive a significant number of foreign workers. The inflow of

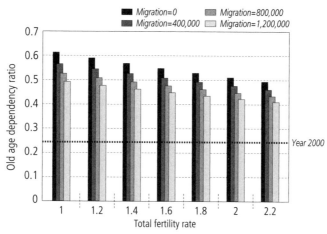

Source: Lutz and Scherbov (2003, p. 8).

Figure 9.3. Old age dependency ratio for the EU15 in 2050, according to alternative projections assuming a wide range of fertility and annual net migration levels.

foreign workers was also balanced in these countries by foreign outflows, naturalizations and, in the case of France, by a sustained demographic growth by nationals (OECD, 2003, p. 51).

The increase in foreign workers was due to a rising number of permanent as well as temporary labor migrants to the EU. Many countries introduced specific measures to facilitate the recruitment of skilled foreign workers as well as special programs to enable temporary labor migration; these measures allowed seasonal workers to be employed, mainly in agriculture, construction and the service sector (especially tourism and—a recent development—household services). The OECD (2003, p. 57) points especially to the general increase in female employment rates, changes in family structures and an aging population, leading to a growing need to provide public and private services to care for young children and the elderly— activities with high female participation rates. Within this framework the need for household services is expected to increase. In southern Europe, especially in Greece, Italy and Spain, over 10 percent of foreign workers are employed in household services.

Nevertheless, the figures also reveal that labor migrants are unevenly distributed within the EU15. Luxembourg has by far the highest rate of foreign labor migrants—more than 43 percent of the total labor force, the overwhelming majority of which (90 percent) come from other EU15 countries. It is followed by Austria (9.9 percent of the total labor force), Greece (9.5 percent) and Germany (8.9 percent). Compared with those countries, Finland has the lowest rate (1.4 percent of

Table 9.4. Stock of foreign labor force in the EU15.

	1995 (in thousands)	% in total labor force*	2002 (in thousands)	% in total labor force*	Source
Austria	366	9.7	387	9.9	LFS
Belgium	327	7.9	357	8.2	LFS
Denmark	84	3.0	104	3.7	R
Finland	18	0.8	38	1.4	LFS
France	1,566	6.3	1,612	6.2	LFS
Germany	3,505	9.1	3,511	8.9	LFS
Greece*	****		413	9.5	C
Ireland	42	3.0	101	5.6	LFS
Italy**	332	1.6	801	3.3	WP
Luxembourg***	65	39.1	83	43.2	LFS
Netherlands	281	3.9	295*	3.6	LFS
Portugal	21	0.5	125	2.5	LFS
Spain	121	0.8	490	2.7	LFS
Sweden	186	4.2	205	4.6	LFS
United Kingdom	1,011	3.6	1,406	4.8	LFS

Note: *Foreigners who entered Greece for employment purposes; **Foreigners employed and percentage of foreigners in workforce; ***Resident workers (excluding cross-border workers); ****No data available.
LFS: Labor Force Survey; R: Population Register or register of foreigners; C: Census; WP: Work permits.
Source: OECD (2004, p. 50).

the total labor force), followed by Portugal (2.5 percent) and Spain (2.7 percent). The latter two countries, however, have faced high increases in labor migration in the last few years.

9.5.2 Participation in the labor market and unemployment of labor migrants in the EU15

Non-EU nationals are likely to have a lower participation rate in the labor market, except in Greece where there is a higher participation rate for non-EU females. In Austria, Luxembourg and Spain, the participation rate of male foreign workers exceeds that of nationals. In some countries such as Belgium, Denmark, France, Germany and The Netherlands, the difference amounts to ten or more percentage points.

According to *Table 9.6* non-EU labor migrants are generally more under the threat of unemployment than nationals. In most of the EU15 member states, the unemployment rates for both male and female non-EU nationals are much higher than for nationals, except in Greece and except for males in Italy. A rather high

Table 9.5. Participation rates of nationals and nonnationals aged 15 to 64 in the EU15 member states.

	Men		Women	
	Nationals (%)	Non-EU nationals (%)	Nationals (%)	Non-EU nationals (%)
Austria	75.3	76.6	61.4	58.0
Belgium	68.9	44.7	52.5	18.1
Denmark	80.8	57.9	73.5	42.7
Finland**	79.4	83.1	74.6	60.2
France	70.2	57.0	57.7	29.1
Germany	72.4	62.3	60.3	39.8
Greece	71.1	84.5	42.4	50.7
Ireland	74.8	67.1	55.3	47.5
Italy**	73.6	87.7	46.6	50.7
Luxembourg	72.9	73.0	47.9	44.5
Netherlands	83.7	57.8	66.7	40.2
Portugal**	79.0	81.5	64.0	65.3
Spain	72.6	78.5	57.5	56.8
Sweden*	80.5	71.0	76.9	60.4
United Kingdom*	82.7	76.4	68.7	56.3

Note: *OECD (2004, p. 51) data refer not only to non-EU nationals but to all foreigners; **OECD (2003, p. 60) data refer not only to non-EU nationals but to all foreigners.
Source: Eurostat Labor Force Survey (2002).

difference (at least double) between male unemployment of nationals and of non-EU nationals can be observed in Belgium, Denmark, Finland, France, The Netherlands, Portugal and Sweden. Moreover, female third-country nationals tend to have higher unemployment rates than males, except in Austria, Germany, Sweden and the United Kingdom, where men are at higher risk of unemployment. The difference between foreign males and females is rather high in Belgium (11.3 percentage points), Greece (8.8) and Italy (13.9).

9.5.3 Impact of labor migration on the labor markets in the EU15 member states

Foreign workers are overrepresented in certain sectors such as construction, hospitality, catering and household services (OECD, 2004, p. 56). The proportion of such workers in these sectors is higher than their share in total employment. Immigrants are therefore still overrepresented in low-skilled and unskilled occupations, often working in blue-collar jobs in undesirable working conditions.

During the 2002 annual seminar of the European Observatory on the Social Situation, Demography and Family, Muus (2002, p. 16) affirmed that the unfavorable labor market position of immigrants and ethnic minorities can be explained not

Table 9.6. Unemployment rate of nationals and nonnationals aged 15 to 64 in the EU15 member states.

	Men		Women	
	Nationals (%)	Non-EU nationals (%)	Nationals (%)	Non-EU nationals (%)
Austria	4.6	10.5	4.2	9.2
Belgium	5.4	28.7	7.0	42.0
Denmark	4.1	13.2	4.2	–
Finland**	10.0	24.2	11.2	29.9
France	7.1	22.9	9.3	28.6
Germany	8.2	17.1	8.0	14.6
Greece	6.4	6.2	14.9	15.0
Ireland	4.3	4.9	3.7	–
Italy**	8.0	7.4	13.9	21.3
Luxembourg*	1.3	2.4	1.9	4.2
Netherlands*	2.2	5.1	2.6	5.0
Poland**	3.1	8.4	5.1	9.6
Spain	7.6	12.9	16.3	18.7
Sweden*	4.9	12.1	4.3	9.3
United Kingdom*	5.3	8.4	4.1	7.5

Note: *OECD (2004, p. 51) data refer to 2000–2001 average, not only to non-EU nationals but to all foreigners; **OECD (2003, p. 60) data refer to 2001–2002 average, not only to non-EU nationals but to all foreigners.
Source: Eurostat Labor Force Survey (2002).

only by supply and demand factors but also by the developments of the past few decades, for example, the restructuring of the European economies, which made many of the labor migrants recruited in the past redundant; moreover, only a small part of migration is directly linked to formal labor market needs, a part that may increase in the future if the changing demographic composition of European countries necessitates some kind of 'replacement migration.'

The OECD (2004, p. 56) observed a gradual dispersal of foreign employment toward the tertiary sector. Foreign jobs have increased in the education sector and to a greater extent in the health sector because of labor shortages in those fields. According to the OECD, the dispersal of foreign workers toward the service sector reflects the trend observed among nationals for the past few decades; in other words, foreign workers are gradually adjusting to changes in labor market demand in the receiving countries—a trend that is partly due to the arrival of new foreign workers. Foreign workers who have migrated in the past five years are generally underrepresented in mining, manufacturing and energy and construction. Concurrently, newly arrived foreign migrants are overrepresented in services, particularly unskilled labor, such as cleaning or catering (OECD, 2004, pp. 56ff).

In general, the employment of migrants undergoes greater fluctuations as they become more exposed to overall economic trends and various forms of discrimination. According to Bagavos (2004, p. 15), the presence of immigrants in the labor market of the host countries seems to confirm the theory of labor market segmentation for the very reason that migrant workers are willing to take on the unattractive jobs that the indigenous workers refuse to do.

9.6   Family and Migration in the EU15 Member States

9.6.1   Development of family-linked migration movements

In the last two decades, family-linked migration developed into the most important form of legal migration within the European Union. Family-linked migration ranges from the classic family reunification of pioneer migrants, marriage migration of second and subsequent generations who bring in partners from their homeland, international marriages by citizens and noncitizens arising from tourism, business, education and professional activities, to—finally—the movement of entire families (Kofman, 2003, p. 4).

The rise in family-linked migration to the European Union is a consequence of former labor migration movements. The economic crisis at the beginning of the 1970s led to a moratorium on labor migrants. Those workers who were still needed often obtained long-term permission to stay and, as family reunification was embodied in many bilateral recruitment treaties, were entitled to bring over their families.

This, however, is not a sufficient explanation for the increase in family reunification. From the viewpoint of national economies, during times of recession and growing unemployment any increase in migration can only be seen as undesirable and a principle that the state is unable to support. Nevertheless, some striking reasons prompted European governments to back family reunification. According to Müller-Schneider (2000, p. 255) European governments were willing to do this for humanitarian reasons based on the protection of family life as enacted by law. Family reunification is not an inevitable result of labor migration but the logical consequence of the humanitarian commitment espoused by European states to protect families.[1]

This development changed the pattern of labor migration decisively in many European countries. In practice, migrants stayed increasingly longer after bringing in their relatives, even though the majority still kept to their plan of returning home. This was mainly because family reunification entailed an unexpected hike in the cost of living: what it cost for the family to live together ended up exceeding the combined earnings of those family members who were earning an income. Thus, the intention of returning often turned out to be an illusion. The real status of foreign workers changed from temporary labor migrants to long-term residents—immigrants, in fact (Pflegerl *et al.*, 2003, p. 75).

9.6.2   The meaning of the family in the process of migration

Various researchers agree that the family plays a decisive role during the process of migration, as changing countries is a critical event entailing both risks and opportunities (Dietzel-Papakyriakou, 1993; Camilleri and Vinsonneau, 1996; Pumares, 1996; Tribalat *et al.*, 1996 ; Nauck, 1999; Fernández de la Hoz, 2002).

During the annual seminar of the European Observatory on Immigration and Family, Bracalenti (2002, p. 5) pointed out that the family—reunited or separated, nuclear or extended—represents the mediatory factor between the host country and the country of origin. The family constitutes the base from which it is possible to begin restructuring new forms of collective expression, intergenerational relationships and exchange networks between the past and the present.

Bracalenti (2002, p. 8) also states that the migratory process involves a certain amount of psychological distress both for individuals and families. Immigrant families must make a huge effort to adjust, negotiate and revise relationships. The immigrant family thus has a greater ambivalence than it would be expected to have in a monocultural environment. On the one hand, migration can result in individual and collective identity shifts, and even changes, in gender roles that can undermine traditional family structures. On the other hand, there is an implicit assumption that the well-being of the individual depends on having positive family (or other emotional ties).

Therefore, the family may be seen in two ways: family cohesion helps to a crucial extent to overcome problems in the host country; however, the emotional, symbolic and material importance of the family may frequently cause conflicts and contradictions when family members respond differently to their new social environment and develop different interests (Fernández de la Hoz, 2002, pp. 31ff.). Moreover, family ties do not only provide emotional support but also contribute to the emergence of social networks, which are a source of social capital. Family members already residing in the host country help newly arriving relatives to find jobs, housing or other assistance they need. This process of chain migration further strengthens familial networks.

Intergenerational relations play an important role in this context. For the same reason that many immigrant families in EU member states have migrated from countries without extensive systems of social security, migration projects and related goals can be legitimized and met only in intergenerational relationships. Intergenerational relationships are also crucial for transmitting the culture of the society of origin. Nauck (2002, p. 32) contradicts the assertion that intergenerational differences will result in increasingly endangered relationships between generations at the individual level.

Based on in-depth studies of Turkish migrant families, Nauck (2002, pp. 31ff) also points out that intergenerational transmission is an essential and integral part of the socialization of second-generation immigrants. He argues that, despite all the differences between the generations in assimilation behavior and reactions to the receiving society, the dense interactive structure of migrant families undoubtedly results in a high degree of concordance between generations regarding basic value orientation and preferences for a certain type of behavior. He also proves that the intergenerational transmission of norms leads not only to a higher concordance of attitudes in migrant families when compared to nonmigrant families but also produces a high level of coorientation regarding the attitudes and values of family members. Therefore, Nauck's (2002) findings may be taken to indicate that intergenerational relationships become even stronger after migration.

Fernández de la Hoz (2002, p. 32) concludes that family life appears to be a critical interface between the public and private spheres—a place where objective and subjective experiences, structural conditions and personal projects, interests, experience and options will converge. Strategies to cope with the challenges to the life of migrants and the way of using opportunities will strongly depend on the balance between a migrant's own resources and his/her environment. Family ties are thus a vital factor in determining how migrants and their children will integrate into their host society. Appropriate legal, social and economic arrangements to enable chances and perspectives for migrants in the receiving country are also just as important for successful integration processes. The lack of such opportunities may otherwise weaken the capacity of families to integrate.

9.7 Asylum Seekers in the European Union, 1997 to 2004

9.7.1 Asylum applications and recognition rates in the EU15 member states

Between 1997 and 1999 the number of asylum applications to the European Union increased by about 26 percent after a short period of significant decline from 1992—the immediate consequence of legal measures implemented by several European governments to limit potential asylum applications (*Table 9.7*).

Nevertheless, not all countries were affected to the same extent by this development. Whereas in Austria, Belgium, Denmark, Finland, France Italy, Ireland and the United Kingdom a sharp increase in numbers could be observed, other countries, namely, Greece, Luxembourg, The Netherlands, Portugal and Sweden were

Table 9.7. Asylum applications submitted in the EU15, 1998–2003.

	1998	Change 97–98 (%)	1999	Change 98–99 (%)	2000	Change 99–00 (%)	2001	Change 00–01 (%)	2002	Change 01–02 (%)	2003	Change 02–03 (%)
Austria	13,810	105.5	20,100	45.5	18,280	–9.1	30,140	64.9	39,350	30.6	32,340	–17.8
Belgium	21,970	86.3	35,780	62.9	42,690	19.3	24,550	–42.5	18,810	–23.4	16,940	–9.9
Denmark	9,370	84.1	12,330	31.6	12,200	–1.1	12,510	2.5	6,070	–51.5	4,560	–24.9
Finland	1,270	30.9	3,110	144.9	3,170	1.9	1,650	–47.9	3,440	108.5	3,080	–10.5
France	22,380	4.5	30,910	38.1	38,750	25.4	47,290	22.0	51,090	8.0	51,400	0.6
Germany	98,640	–5.5	95,110	–3.6	78,560	–17.4	88,290	12.4	71,130	–19.4	50,450	–29.1
Greece	2,950	–32.6	1,530	–48.1	3,080	101.3	5,500	78.6	5,660	2.9	8,180	44.5
Ireland	4,630	19.3	7,720	66.7	11,100	43.8	10,330	–6.9	11,630	12.6	7,900	–32.1
Italy	11,120	497.8	33,360	200.0	15,560	–53.4	9,620	–38.2	7,280	–24.3	–	–
Luxembourg	1,710	297.7	2,920	70.8	620	–78.8	690	11.3	1,040	50.7	1,550	49.0
Netherlands	45,220	31.3	42,730	–5.5	43,900	2.7	32,580	–25.8	18,670	–42.7	13,400	–28.2
Poland	370	23.3	310	–16.2	220	–29.0	230	4.5	250	8.7	110	–56.0
Spain	6,650	33.5	8,410	26.5	7,930	–5.7	9,490	19.7	6,310	–33.5	5,770	–8.6
Sweden	12,840	32.9	11,230	–12.5	16,300	45.1	23,520	44.3	33,020	40.4	31,360	–5.0
United Kingdom	58,500	41.0	91,200	55.9	98,900	8.4	91,600	–7.4	103,080	12.5	61,050	–40.8
EU15	311,430	23.7	396,750	27.4	391,260	–1.4	387,990	–0.8	376,830	–2.9	288,090	–22
EU14	300,310	20.2	363,390	21.0	375,700	3.4	378,370	0.7	369,550	–2.3		

Sources: UNHCR (2003); UNHCR (2004).

confronted with varying developments, and Germany continuously faced falls in the number of asylum applications.

This new development was partly due to the Kosovo crisis which caused mass refugee movements, especially in 1999. On the other hand, asylum applicants from a growing number of countries outside Europe, involved in either civil war struggles or other military conflicts with neighboring countries, also tried to find refuge in the member states of the EU15. In addition to people from Kosovo, most applications between 1997 and 1999 were made by people from Iraq (91,171 applications), Turkey, mainly Kurds (68,892) and Afghanistan (46,410), with other applications being made by people from the Democratic Republic of the Congo, Iran, Somalia and Sri Lanka.

Between 2000 and 2002 a slight decline in the number of new asylum applications could be observed. In 2000 the United Kingdom for the first time received more asylum applications than Germany, which had previously had the highest number of asylum seekers. Whereas the number of applications from Serbia and Montenegro, most of them from Kosovo, decreased continuously from 38,050 in 2000 to 26,132 applications in 2002, the number of asylum seekers from Iraq, which became the most important sending country, increased from 38,404 in 2000 to 42,197 in 2002.

In 2003 the number of new applications declined sharply by about 22 percent, reaching the lowest level since 1997. Especially in the United Kingdom, still the most important receiving country, the number of asylum applications fell by about 40 percent. The only major increases in the number of asylum applications in 2003 were recorded in Luxembourg and Greece. As in 2002, the most important sending country of asylum seekers was Iraq, but in line with the general trend, applications from Iraqis dropped by 50 percent to 20,903[2] applications.

First-instance recognition rates of asylum seekers in the European Union, however, are rather low (*Table 9.8*). In 2000 the number of refugees recognized in the EU15 according to the Geneva Convention was 11.2 percent rising to 12.6 percent in 2001 and declining to 8.4 percent in 2000, then increasing slightly to 8.98 percent in 2003. There are differences in the EU member countries regarding the recognition of refugees. Whereas, from 2000 to 2003, in Austria the recognition rate ranged between 17 and 29.6 percent and in Belgium between 23 and 27 percent, comparable figures in Sweden merely varied between 1 and 2 percent of all applications. In some countries, strong declines in recognition rates could be observed between 2000 and 2003. In The Netherlands they fell from 12 percent in 2000 to 1 percent in 2001, slightly increasing to 2 percent in 2003. In Greece they also fell from 11 percent in 2000 to 0.1 percent in 2003.

Table 9.8. Refugee recognition rate (RRR) by first instance (FI), 2000–2003.

Country	2000 (%)	2001 (%)	2002 (%)	2003 (%)
Austria	17	23	20	29.6
Belgium	23	27	25	23.1
Denmark	17	21	13	14.5
Finland	1	0	1	0.5
France	12	12	13	9.8
Germany*	15	24	7	4.3
Greece	11	11	0.4	0.1
Ireland	4	9	13	5.9
Italy	7	16	not known	11.3
Luxembourg	1	5	not known	6.9
Netherlands	12	1	1	2
Portugal	17	15	9	9.1
Spain	15	12	10	8.6
Sweden	2	1	1	1.7
United Kingdom	14	12	13	7.3
EU15	11.2	12.6	8.4	8.98

Note: Recognized divided by the total of recognized, humanitarian and rejected (as a percentage).
*New applications (no FI application).
Sources: UNHCR (2003); UNHCR (2004).

9.7.2 Political reactions in the EU15 member states

As a response to the crisis in Kosovo, especially after the air strikes in early 1999, most European states were at first convinced that protection for refugees from Kosovo should be provided within the region for as long as possible to avoid big refugee movements to western Europe. However, the fragile political situation in Macedonia, where many people had first moved, led to the decision to evacuate thousands of refugees from camps located in this region. Several member states, among them Austria, Belgium, Germany and Italy, granted the refugees a temporary protection status or similar forms of protection to the French *asile territoriale*. This form of protection is granted to refugees not recognized under the Geneva Convention but provides assurance against return to the place where the threat exists—the so-called *nonrefoulement* guarantee. Temporary protection status outside the normal asylum procedures was introduced for the first time in some countries of Europe during the Bosnian crisis of the early 1990s. It grants immediate protection for the persons concerned and legal permission to stay for a certain period of time.

In reaction to the increasing number of asylum seekers, many EU15 member states tried to further tighten up their laws and accelerate the processing of applications and appeals so as to limit the stay of asylum seekers in their territory. In the processing of applications new principles were also adopted, providing for the refusal of manifestly unfounded applications. Some countries also restricted access of asylum seekers to the labor market and canceled social benefits, especially accommodation, subsistence and financial aid for those whose applications were deemed unlikely to be approved by the relevant authorities.

Generally, the United Nations High Commissioner for Refugees (UNHCR) has been monitoring developments regarding asylum in the EU15 member states since 1998 on the basis of the growing tendency on the part of governments to act on this issue from an immigration control perspective rather than from an approach based on international law and refugee rights. According to UNHCR, monitoring is due to rising concerns over irregular migration, abuse of asylum procedures, the rising costs of refugee support, difficulties in dealing with rejected asylum seekers and, last but not least, declining public support (UNHCR, 2000, p. 358). With rising concern, UNHCR observes that asylum seekers are increasingly intermingled with other people on the move in the search for better opportunities in western Europe.

Nevertheless, several researchers point to the fact that, because of a global change in migration development, it has indeed become increasingly difficult to distinguish clearly between refugees seeking asylum and other international migrants. Thus, not only persons seeking asylum under the Geneva Convention, but others too, have no other choice but to migrate in response to a complex set of threats and hardships (Butterwege, 2000; Raper, 2001; Wihtol de Wenden, 2002; Crisp, 2003). Raper (2001, pp. 64ff) points out that, more than ever, refugees are part of a complex migratory phenomenon in which ethnic, economic, environmental and human rights factors combine and lead to population movements. This development will pose further challenges to the EU member states, as the public climate toward people seeking asylum from persecution has become increasingly more hostile. According to UNHCR, these trends foil efforts by western European countries to find the right balance between the control of migration and the protection of refugees (UNHCR, 2001, p. 421).

9.8 Irregular Migration

9.8.1 Recent developments in the EU15 member states

Recurring incidents, such as, for example, the arrival of overloaded ships with people from Albania or Turkey in Italy, people from northern Africa abandoned by smugglers and drowning near the Spanish coast, the detection of illegal prostitutes from poor third-world countries trafficked to the EU or other secret forms of entry to the EU15 have increasingly alerted public and political attention to the multifaceted phenomenon of irregular migration. For that reason this issue has become one of the priorities of the European Union migration debate and why measures to combat illegal migration have received priority on the EU political agenda in the last few years.

In general, as irregularity affects entry status, residence and employment, several different forms of irregularity may be distinguished,[3] the most important of which include:

1. Persons legally entering the European Union such as tourists, seasonal workers, business travelers, asylum seekers or refugees who are working illegally either because the job is not declared or because their residence permit does not allow them to work.
2. Persons legally entering the country, living there illegally because their work permits are either invalid or have expired and staying and working longer than officially approved.
3. Persons illegally entering or crossing the border with forged documents or without documents, then staying in the country often illegally and working there without being registered. This form of irregularity also includes persons who are illegally smuggled to the EU by transnational organizations specializing in this trade and that often abuse the total dependency of the migrants and force them to live and work under terrible conditions.
4. Persons who have entered the country secretly, have a residence permit (through regularization or because of a change in their status through marriage) and work illegally (Bade, 2003, p. 20).

Forms of irregular migration also have a time dimension. From the viewpoint of immigrants, an illegal status may represent either a temporary phase in the migration cycle or a permanent state.

Various researchers agree that the restriction of legal opportunities to migrate to the EU has a direct impact on various forms of irregular migration, making them become more widespread and differentiated (Bade, 2003, p. 20). Ishai (2000, p. 253) points out that although undocumented migration has existed for many years, its socioeconomic context has changed in many countries in the face of the recent global economic recession. Widespread poverty and income inequality now exist in the context of a global communication revolution that forces—but also enables—undocumented migrants to move over longer distances.

It is, however, rather difficult to estimate both the exact number of migrants entering countries illegally and the stock of migrants irregularly residing or working in the EU. Estimates of the scale of trafficking and smuggling are even more difficult to make. Despite serious efforts to harmonize methods of achieving reliable figures for irregular migrants, the credibility of such figures is still rather doubtful.

Usually, attempts to calculate the levels of illegal migration are estimates based on the views of officials or on the proportion of migrants illegally crossing the border who have been apprehended. It is, however, unclear if the number of border apprehensions reflects the real flow of migrants entering the EU countries illegally or if rises and falls in these numbers are due to changing detection methods. While most EU member states provide some statistics on illegal border crossings, there is as yet only little information on trafficking and smuggling. Most statistical data on trafficked persons are based on crude estimates. The only official data come from apprehensions, court records and deportations. As these are partial and refer to migrants who were picked up, they reflect neither the whole number trafficked nor the number of traffickers themselves (Salt, 2000, pp. 37–39; Tapinos, 2000, pp. 231).

9.8.2   Political reactions in the EU15 member states

EU15 member states have tried to take a number of measures to combat the rise in illegal migration. Measures to tighten border controls play an essential role in this context. The EU15 member states have also introduced and increased the severity of criminal and administrative sanctions against illegal employers.

The terrorist attack of September 11, 2001, in particular, led to an even further tightening of border controls in all EU15 member states and more intense cross-national border-control measures. For example, information exchange among police and other intelligence services has become more formalized and more regular in the fight against irregular migration and human trafficking. This security motivation has increased still further with the subsequent bombings in Madrid and London.

Remarkably, it is not only those countries with a long history of immigration, such as France and the United Kingdom, that have been affected by irregular migration movements but, in particular, countries in the south of Europe with rather more recent immigration experience such as Greece, Italy, Portugal and Spain. For a long time some national authorities were convinced that their countries were merely transit countries, but when other traditional immigration countries started to close their borders they had to accept that they themselves had become settlement countries with a significant number of irregular migrants. As many migrants decided to stay, governments had no option but to start regularization programs to deal appropriately with the social consequences of increased irregular immigration.

In 1998 several member states, among them France and Greece, launched programs to regularize undocumented foreigners—aimed, in most cases, at those who already lived in the country and had family ties and jobs. In France about 143,000 regularization applications were received during the 1998 program and almost 80,000 residence permits were granted (OECD, 1999, p. 75).

The regularization program in Greece was implemented at the beginning of 1998. It was originally due to end in July 1998, but the deadline was extended to April 1999, as a large number of applications were received and applicants had insufficient time to obtain the information requested. The program comprised two phases. In the first phase, workers without papers had the opportunity to submit an application for regularization and to obtain a temporary residence permit, the white card, if their application was eligible. During the second phase, extended until April 1999, a green card was issued to workers holding a temporary permit who could prove that they had worked for at least 40 days between January and July 1998. By April 1999, 374,000 people had received the white card, of whom 220,000 had submitted the necessary documents to apply for a green card. By September 2000 the green card had been issued to over 147,700 people. In a new regularization initiative in 2001, some 351,000 applications were registered.

Italy, which launched regularization programs in 1986, 1990 and 1996, decided to implement a new program in 1998 and early 1999, and this was extended until 2000. Initially, it was planned to accept not more than 38,000 people; because of the large number of applications, however, the quota was increased to 300,000. Migrants from Albania, Morocco, Romania and Tunisia were the first to benefit from this regularization program. In 1998 a total of more than 217,000 permits were granted.

In 2000 Spain also began a regularization operation. It was applied to all foreigners residing in Spain in June 1999 who had held either a work permit or a residence permit between February 1997 and February 2000, had requested such a permit before the end of March 2000 or had lodged an asylum application before 1 February 2000, as well as to family members of third-country nationals. One-third of the applications were made by people from Morocco. By the end of October 2000, 124,000 applications had been accepted.

In Belgium a regularization program implemented in January 2000 examined over 50,000 applications submitted by people from the Democratic Republic of Congo. More than 12 percent of all applications came from people from Morocco (OECD, 2001, p. 81).

According to the OECD, the qualitative and quantitative impact of these regularizations on the number and characteristics of new arrivals is not yet well known. Furthermore, it is not really possible to foresee how these programs will increase future family-related migration in terms of new migrants coming to join regularized relatives. There is also little knowledge about the employment situation of regularized persons (OECD, 2003, p. 70). Tapinos (2000, p. 34) points out that no regularization program in Europe, particularly since 1973–1974, has ever put an end to irregular migration in the sense of affecting the decisive factors and mechanisms underlying illegal migration. Nevertheless, that does not mean that regularizations

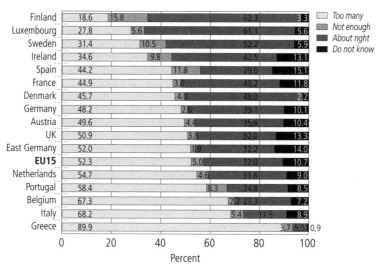

Source: Eurobarometer (2001), own calculations.

Figure 9.4. Response to question: In relation to the number of foreigners in your country, which of the following statements best describes your own view?

should be ruled out, but it is important to realize their real impact: that of effacing the past without having any impact on future developments. Tapinos (2000, p. 34) concludes that recent experiences in Europe show that it is not an option to decide whether or not to have an amnesty; the choice is rather between repeated amnesties and discreet amnesties performed on a case-by-case basis.

9.9 Public Opinion toward Migrants in the EU15 Member States

A 2001 Eurobarometer survey in which European citizens were asked about their attitude toward the presence of foreigners in their country seems at a first glance to reflect a restrictive attitude on the part of citizens of the EU15 member states. More than 52 percent are convinced that there are too many foreigners in their country; 32 percent think that the number of foreigners is about right; 5 percent are convinced that there are not enough; 11 percent do not know how to answer the question.

Nevertheless, *Figure 9.4* illustrates that there are rather heterogeneous opinions among the different member states of the EU15. To some extent this may be because of differences in the way foreigners are perceived among European member state countries as well as differences in the way EU15 member countries have been affected by recent migration developments. Whereas nearly 90 percent of Greek

citizens are convinced that there are too many foreigners in their country, this opinion is shared by only 18.6 percent of Finnish citizens. More than 62 percent of the
Finnish population and only 5.5 percent of the Greek population are also convinced
that the number of foreigners is about right.

Following at some distance behind the negative opinion of Greek citizens, 68
percent of Italian, 67 percent of Belgian, 58 percent of Portuguese and 55 percent
of Dutch nationals are also convinced that there are too many foreigners in their
country. At the other end of the scale, this opinion is shared by 28 percent of Luxembourg, 31 percent of Swedish, 35 percent of Irish, 44 percent of Spanish and 45
percent of French nationals. In Sweden more than 50 percent and in Luxembourg
more than 60 percent of citizens are convinced that the number of foreigners is
about right.

Further analysis, however, reveals that European citizens make clear distinctions between legally established foreigners and illegal migrants. In a Eurobarometer survey, 2,000 people were asked questions, some in depth, about their attitude
toward migrants and asylum seekers. Whereas nearly 59 percent of European citizens are convinced that all illegal immigrants should be sent back to their country
of origin without exception (*Figure 9.5*), nearly two-thirds also express the belief
that legally established migrants from countries outside the European Union should
have the same social rights as national citizens (*Figure 9.6*). It is also remarkable
that in all member countries of the EU15, more than 50 percent of the population
express this opinion. Most convinced are people from Spain (over 82 percent),
Italy (80 percent), Denmark (over 74 percent), The Netherlands and Sweden (70
percent), Portugal (nearly 69 percent), Greece (67 percent) and France (almost 65
percent). At the other end of the scale is Belgium with 51 percent.

There are also large differences among EU15 member states concerning how to
deal with illegal migrants. Altogether, the opinions of European citizens concerning illegal migrants are divided into two groups. Whereas more than 76 percent
of Greek, 69 percent of German, 66 percent of Italian, 64 percent of Finnish and
63 percent of Dutch nationals are convinced that all illegal migrants should be sent
back, only 34 percent of Spanish, 37 percent of Irish, 42 percent of Swedish and 43
percent of Portuguese nationals agree.

9.10   Conclusion

In the period of observation (1998 to 2004) there were increasing inflows of migrants into most of the EU15 member states, and this led to an increase in the
foreign population of the EU15. These inflows were accompanied by a further diversification of migration movements and an increase in the number of migrants'
origin countries.

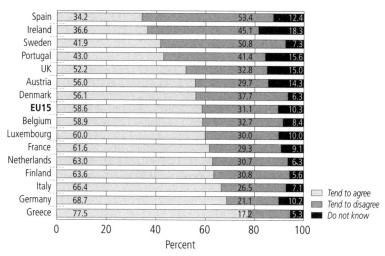

Source: Eurobarometer (2000), own calculations.

Figure 9.5. Response to statement: All illegal immigrants should be sent back to their country of origin without exception.

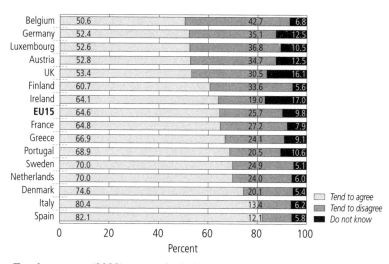

Source: Eurobarometer (2000), own calculations.

Figure 9.6. Response to statement: Legally established migrants from countries outside the European Union should have the same social rights as (national) citizens.

In contrast to Australia, Canada and the United States, none of the EU15 member states regards itself as an immigrant society. During the European Observatory's annual seminar in 2002, Fassmann (2002, p. 10) pointed out that despite Europe's multifaceted experience most Europeans still consider mass migration as the historical exception and that lifelong residence in one place is still considered normal. At first glance, this general attitude also seems to be reflected in recent Eurobarometer surveys that reveal the conviction of more than 50 percent of European citizens that there are too many foreigners living in their country.

Nevertheless, there are some contrary indicators that point to a readiness on the part of European citizens to accept certain groups of migrants. Nearly two-thirds of European citizens state that legally established foreigners should receive the same social rights as European citizens. Other results reveal that it is mainly the illegal migrants who are being repudiated by the European population. The high acceptance rate of legally established migrants may be seen as a hopeful sign that it is possible to bring to fruition policies promoting social inclusion of migrants. Public opinion will be more accepting of migrants than is often assumed.

Furthermore, the acceptance of immigrants is important as, according to Fassmann (2002, p. 11), European societies need immigration to balance the uneven age structure and to fill gaps in the labor market, especially after 2010 when the baby boomers reach retirement age. These results should be taken as a mandate by European policy makers to develop further measures to integrate legal immigrants, to develop their human capital and to use their talent as Fassmann (2002, p. 11) suggested during the annual seminar of the European Observatory in 2002. This will be a necessary contribution to securing future human capital formation for the whole of the European Union.

Notes

1.   This argument proves appropriate when describing the situation in the oil-producing countries of the Middle East that have also recruited a great number of foreign workers. Migrants in these countries are not given any real opportunity to bring in their relatives, even if they are legally entitled to do so. Contrary to the European countries, some Middle Eastern countries were even prepared to expel migrants no longer needed in the workforce. At the beginning of the 1990s during the Gulf War, 800,000 Yemenis were expelled (Müller-Schneider, 2000).

2.   Excluding Italy, as there were no data available.

3.   In this context Gächter *et al.* (2000, p. 9) point out that the terms *illegal* or *irregular* apply not to persons but to status (e.g., migration, entry, residence or employment). Migrants may only be called *undocumented*. With regard to certain regulations concerning, for example, work permits, permission and allowances, this may differ among EU countries. Thus, becoming an undocumented migrant strongly depends on the legal framework of the country in question.

References

Bade, K.J. (2003) *Legal and Illegal Immigration into Europe: Experiences and Challenges*, Wassenaar, The Netherlands: Netherlands Institute for Advanced Study in the Humanities and Social Sciences.

Bagavos, C. (2004) *Quantitative Aspects of Migration Trends in Europe with Emphasis on the EU15 Countries*, Vienna, Austria: European Observatory on the Social Situation, Demography and Family, See http://www.oif.ac.at/sdf/sdfpuzzle02-04Bagavos_final.pdf/ accessed in January 2006.

Bracalenti, R. (2002) *The Role of the Family in the Process of Integration of Migrants*, Paper presented at the Annual Seminar of the European Observatory on the Social Situation, Demography and Family, held in Helsinki, Finland, June.

Butterwege, C. (2000) 'Zuwanderung und Wohlfahrtsstaat im Zeichen der Globalisierung. Antagonistischer Widerspruch oder nützliche Wechselbeziehung,' in Butterwege, C. and Hentges, G. (eds) *Zuwanderung im Zeichen der Globalisierung. Migrations-, Integrations- und Minderheitenpolitik*, Leverkusen, Germany: Verlag Leske & Budrich, pp. 258–286 [in German].

Camilleri, C. and Vinsonneau, G. (1996) *Psychologie et culture. Concepts et methods.* Paris, France: Armand Colin [in French].

Council of the European Union (2001) *Draft Joint Report on Social Inclusion—Part I*, Brussels, Belgium: The European Union, See http://europa.eu.int/comm/employment_social/news/2001/oct/socincl_report_en.pdf/ accessed in January 2006.

Crisp, J. (2003) 'A New Asylum Paradigm? Globalization, Migration and the Uncertain Future of the International Refugee Regime,' in Crisp, J. (ed) *New Issues in Refugee Research Working Papers: 100*, Geneva, Switzerland: The United Nations High Commissioner for Refugees (UNHCR), available from UNHCR web site.

Dietzel-Papakyriakou, M. (1993) *Altern in der Migration. Die Arbeitsmigranten vor dem Dilemma: zurückkehren oder bleiben*, Stuttgart, Germany: Enke Verlag [in German].

Eurobarometer (2000) Eurobarometer No. 53, Data Set.

Eurobarometer (2001) Eurobarometer No. 54.2, Data Set.

Eurostat (2002) *European Social Statistics 2002*, Luxembourg: Eurostat.

Eurostat (2004) *Population Statistics 2004*, Luxembourg: Eurostat.

Fassmann, H. (2002) *Immigration into the European Union: Causes—Patterns—Future Trends*, Paper presented at the Annual Seminar of the European Observatory on the Social Situation, Demography and Family held in Helsinki, Finland, June.

Fernández de la Hoz, P. (2002) *Migrantenfamilien und Integration in den EU-Mitgliedsstaaten*, Report of the European Centre for Social Welfare Policy and Research, Vienna, Austria [in German].

Gächter, A, Waldrauch, H. and Çinar, D. (2000) 'Introduction: Approaches to Migrants in an Irregular Situation,' in Çinar, D. Gächter, A. and Waldrauch, H. (eds), *Irregular Migration: Dynamics, Impact, Policy Options*, Vienna, Austria: European Centre for Social Welfare Policy and Research, pp. 9–28.

Han, P. (2000) *Soziologie der Migration*, Stuttgart, Germany: Lucius and Lucius [in German].

Ishai, M. (2000) 'Irregular Migration: Dynamics, Impact, Policy Options,' in Çinar, D. Gächter, A. and Waldrauch, H. (eds) *Irregular Migration: Dynamics, Impact, Policy Options*, Vienna, Austria: European Centre for Social Welfare Policy and Research, pp. 253–271.

Kofman, E. (2003) *Women Migrants and Refugees in the European Union*, Paper presented at the conference, 'The Economic and Social Aspects of Migration,' organized by the European Commission and the Organisation for Economic Co-operation and Development in Brussels, Belgium, 21–22 January.

Lutz, W. and Scherbov, S. (2003) *Can Immigration Compensate for Europe's Low Fertility?* Interim Report IR-02-052, Laxenburg, Austria: International Institute for Applied Systems Analysis.

Müller-Schneider, T. (2000) *Zuwanderung in westliche Gesellschaften*, Leverkusen, Germany: Verlag Leske & Budrich [in German].

Muus, P. (2002) *Migration, Immigrants and Labor Markets in EU Countries*, Paper presented at the Annual Seminar of the European Observatory on the Social Situation, Demography and Family, held in Helsinki, Finland, June.

Nauck, B. (1999) 'Sozialer und intergenerativer Wandel in Migrantenfamilien in Deutschland,' in Buchegger, R. (ed) *Migranten und Flüchtlinge. Eine familienwissenschaftliche Annäherung*, Vienna, Austria: Austrian Institute for Family Studies, pp. 13–69 [in German].

Nauck, B. (2002) *Intergenerational Relations in Turkish Families in Germany*, Paper presented at the Annual Seminar of the European Observatory on the Social Situation, Demography and Family, held in Helsinki, Finland.

OECD (1999) *Trends in International Migration*, Paris, France: Organisation for Economic Co-operation and Development.

OECD (2001) *Trends in International Migration*, Paris, France: Organisation for Economic Co-operation and Development.

OECD (2003) *Trends in International Migration*, Paris, France: Organisation for Economic Co-operation and Development.

OECD (2004) *Trends in International Migration*, Paris, France: Organisation for Economic Co-operation and Development.

Pflegerl, J., Khoo, S.E., Yeoh, B.S.A. and Koh, V. (eds) (2003) *Researching Migration and the Family*, Singapore: Asian MetaCentre for Population and Sustainable Development.

Pries, L. (1997) *Transnational Migration*, Baden-Baden, Germany: Nomos.

Pumares, P. (1996) *La integración de los immigrantes marroquíes. Familias marriquíes en la comunidad de Madrid*, Barcelona, Spain: Fundación 'La Caixa' [in Spanish].

Raper, M. (2001) 'Forced Migration. An Overview of Refugees and Forcibly Displaced People Today,' in D'Souza, S. (ed) *Population and Poverty Issues at the Dawn of the 21st Century*, New Delhi, India: Indian Social Institute, pp. 64–78.

Salt, J. (2000) 'Trafficking and Human Smuggling: A European Perspective,' *International Migration*, **38**(3): 31–56.

Salt, J. (2003) *Current Trends in International Migration in Europe*, Strasbourg, France: Council of Europe.

Tapinos, G. (2000) 'Irregular Migration: Economic and Political Issues,' in OECD (ed) *Combating the Illegal Employment of Foreign Workers*, Paris, France: Organisation for Economic Co-operation and Development, pp. 13–44.

Tribalat, M., Simon, P., and Riandey, B. (1996) *De l'immigration à l'assimilation. Enquête sur les populations d'origine étrangère en France*, Paris, France: Editions La Découverte/INED [in French].

UNHCR (2000) *UNHCR Global Report 1999*, Geneva, Switzerland: United Nations High Commissioner for Refugees.

UNHCR (2001) *UNHCR Global Report 2000*, Geneva, Switzerland: United Nations High Commissioner for Refugees.

UNHCR (2003) *Asylum Applications Lodged in Industrialized Countries: Levels and Trends 2000-2002*, Geneva, Switzerland: United Nations High Commissioner for Refugees.

UNHCR (2004) *Asylum Trends Levels and Trends: Europe and non European Industrialized Countries*, Geneva, Switzerland: United Nations High Commissioner for Refugees.

Wihtol de Wenden, C. (2002) *Motivations et attentes de migrants*, Projet 272, December [in French].

Chapter 10

International Migration Patterns in the New EU Member States

Dušan Drbohlav

10.1 Introduction

From the end of the 1980s onward, the central and eastern European countries (CEECs) saw their discredited former systems go through a process of transition and transformation. The ultimate aim of these countries was to build developed, democratic and pluralistic societies based on parliamentary democracy and a free market economy. That process was cemented by the inclusion of CEECs in various western political, economic and military structures, in particular—from 1 May 2004—the European Union (EU). The transformation processes were, and are, typical of the dramatic changes that have affected all spheres of society in these countries. Obviously, one of the phenomena associated with the new political and economic structures is international migration together with its complex impacts, such as how immigrants adapt to the new societies and their activities within them.

The aim of this chapter is to describe and partly explain migration patterns in eight new member states (NMS) of the EU—the Czech Republic, Estonia, Hungary, Latvia, Lithuania, Poland, Slovakia and Slovenia.[1] The chapter is divided into sections, as follows: a brief historical overview; a survey of types of migration and overall migration scales; an assessment of the factors contributing to migrant movements; an evaluation of the impact of migration on societies; and a study of

migration policies and practices. A final section, dealing with conclusions and recommendations, includes several remarks on the probable future development of the
migration movements in the NMS. The contribution, to some extent, draws on two
sources: first, the results of the European Commission project,[2] 'Sharing Experience: Migration Trends in Selected Applicant Countries and Lessons Learned from
New Countries of Immigration in the EU and Austria' (see below, Divinský [2004];
Drbohlav [2004]; Korys [2004]; Zavratnik-Zimic [2004]); and second, the study by
Salt (2003) that maps current international migration trends in Europe. Other important sources were also used (see, e.g., Wallace and Stola [2001]; Kielyte [2002];
Niessen and Schibel [2003]; Nyíri [2003]; Zsoter [2003]; Krieger [2004]; European
Commission [2004a]). Information/statistical sources and related analytical materials on the migration situation differ both quantitatively and qualitatively according
to the country concerned.[3] In contrast with other NMS, there is not very much
information available on the Baltic states. For that reason and also because, comparatively speaking, international migration flows are still rather low there, more
attention is paid to the other NMS. Limited space here prevents a focus on theoretical issues. This, however, is a subject worth tackling in terms of both the Baltic
states and the NMS as a whole.

10.2   Migratory History

Historically speaking, throughout the nineteenth century and until World War I, European nations contributed significantly to the mass migrations across the Atlantic
to the New World (Nuget, 1995). Those living in the NMS (largely citizens of the
Austro-Hungarian Empire) were no exceptions to the overall European trend. The
interwar period brought about mixed migratory patterns in the NMS—mainly labor
migration from some of those countries toward western Europe (e.g., from Poland
or Slovakia), with emigration prevailing over immigration and some resettlements
also occurring.

The aftermath of World War II (with its peace treaties, voluntary and forced
resettlements and evictions) significantly modified the ethnic map of Europe, especially in the CEECs and resulted in the overall homogenization of countries'
ethnic structures. According to one of the estimates, such war-related adjustments
represented movements of some 30 million people, of whom 12 million were ethnic Germans (Fassmann and Münz, 1995). Within the NMS it was mainly the
populations of Czechoslovakia, Hungary, Poland, Yugoslavia and the Baltic states
that were intensively involved in these rather complicated spatial transfers and exchanges. Moreover, new ethnic geographies created in that period (concentrations
of particular ethnic groups in foreign countries between circa 1850 and 1950) are

among the important explanatory variables in any analysis of contemporary migratory patterns.[4]

Since the end of the 1940s, the migratory history of the NMS has had one common and crucial aspect: all these countries became Socialist/Communist Soviet-bloc countries with undemocratic political regimes and centrally planned and weak economies that resulted in rather low standards of living for their populations. Accordingly, 'normal' international migration movements did not exist at all, as Communist governments heavily suppressed the free movement of their inhabitants by means, for example, of strictly guarded borders and stringent visa requirements. Korys' (2004, p. 9) explanation of a situation in Poland fits that in many other NMS:

> As in other communist countries, the Polish authorities controlled the right to leave the country ... (until the late 1980s the keeping of passports at home was not allowed ...). The difficulties encountered while applying for the permit to leave, as well as possible repression on return in the case of a 'lawless stay' (i.e., a stay prolonged beyond the date of return ordered by an internal security office), all transformed the possibility of leaving the borders of communist rule behind into a symbolic 'getaway from the cage'. Thus the main aim was to settle down abroad and possibly to bring in other family members.

A specific form of this east–west migration was the ethnically based movement of mainly Jews and ethnic Germans. To sum up, the reasons for emigrating were mostly political and economic, although these motives were often closely interwoven.[5]

As to how many migrants there were, countries' official data were greatly biased (underestimated), as illegal emigration flows were totally omitted from them. On the other hand, Fassmann and Münz (1995) estimate that, between them, the CEECs lost more than 14 million people to the western developed world between 1950 and 1992/1993 via different types of migration movements. This includes emigration from the former German Democratic Republic, which amounted to around 8.9 million. Salt (1992, pp. 62–63) states that 'from the beginning of the 1970s to the mid-1980s, emigration from the Warsaw Pact countries was about 100,000 per year, half of whom were of German stock.'[6]

After migration there was very often almost no way back—emigration was considered as a criminal offence, property was confiscated, relatives were sometimes persecuted. Though people were constantly escaping from the Soviet-bloc countries (many of these emigrations were illegal, but some were legal as they were tied to family reunion/creation), huge emigration waves occurred in the wake of political upheavals—namely, in Hungary in 1956, Czechoslovakia in 1948 and 1968 and Poland in 1980/1982.

Being isolated from the west, the CEECs also experienced an internal exchange of (labor) migrants within the Communist-bloc countries, namely, workers/students 'exported' from the periphery (usually Angola, Cuba, Mongolia and North Korea) to the core European Communist countries. These immigrants gained skills and work experience and, at the same time, temporarily filled gaps in the local labor market (e.g., in various branches of industry and in agriculture). The system of recruiting students, apprentices and workers functioned mostly via intergovernmental agreements. The number of these workers was not negligible;[7] however, in terms of a classic immigration scheme established by a host country, such stays may be considered as very specific. It would be more accurate to term the immigrants 'purpose-selected ethnic groups'—separated and segregated enclaves of people whose presence was limited to particular plants or localities.

When classifying the NMS in terms of how liberal (or rather how restrictive) their migration policy was, one should probably assign the countries to one of three categories ranging from the more liberal to the extremely restrictive. First, Slovenia (former Yugoslavia)[8] and Hungary[9]; second, Poland and Czechoslovakia; and third, the Baltic states (in which the already pro-Soviet system was strengthened through direct colonization/immigration by hard-core Russian Communists). To put it simply, throughout history the following migratory links have been established and developed in the NMS:[10]

1. The Baltic states: Russia, Finland, Germany;
2. The Czech Republic: Slovakia, Germany, United States;
3. Hungary: Romania, former Yugoslavia, Slovakia;
4. Poland: former Soviet Union, Germany, France, United States;
5. Slovakia: the Czech Republic, United States, Hungary;
6. Slovenia: former Yugoslavia, Germany, Austria, Italy.

What can be learned from this history? First, the NMS with their heritage of separation and emigration have very little recent experience of normal international migration issues in general and immigration in particular—the way these influence institutions, the managerial and supportive roles of the state and the population itself. There has not yet been enough time to bring everyone up to date on everything to do with international migration, and in such an environment, fears of migration/migrants and even xenophobia or racism can flourish. Second, based on past migration flows, relationships—sometimes weak but at other times quite close—have been established between the country of origin and certain destination countries. Obviously, settled diasporas or pseudo-diasporas can, do and will function as one of the motors of further migrant flows, making migration and adaptation to a host society easier for their own compatriots (in moral, psychological, economic and social terms). Third, geographically speaking, migration links generally depend on the distances involved, although Germany is clearly a very important migratory magnet for most of the NMS, regardless of the distance factor.

10.3 Migratory Types and Overall Migration Scales

Since the hectic revolutionary era that began the 1990s, CEECs in general and the NMS in particular have significantly changed their migratory character. CEECs (including the NMS, of course) have jumped from controlled emigration and very limited immigration into 'a highly complex migration field that is characterized by an enormous variety of both long- and short-term movements from, to, and within the region' (Council of Europe, 2002, p. 5), and this development is difficult to encapsulate (Salt, 2003). Even without differentiating among the NMS,[11] there is a huge diversity of migratory types/forms and new migration dynamics to be found in the region, with, of course, specific examples within individual countries or groups of countries. For more details, see Frejka *et al.* (1998); Okolski (1998); Juhász (2003); Divinský (2004); Drbohlav (2004); Korys (2004); Zavratnik-Zimic (2004). Thus, as well as the classic permanent migrants, one can also find circular (temporary) labor—generally taking low-skilled and low-paid jobs (many of them seasonal workers) in both the regular labor market and the black market. Small traders and labor tourists stay for an even shorter time, while cross-border commuters near border zones commute regularly back and forth. There are also many transit migrants (often connected with smuggling and trafficking in human beings) who usually try to get through a country as quickly as possible. As indicated, many of these migratory forms are illegal/irregular in character. Moreover, new ethnically based migrations (that take a number of forms) are a visible consequence of past nationalism and minorities (Council of Europe, 2002). Romas on the move are a specific group with no homeland to return to (Krištof, 2003). Here, one must also mention asylum seekers and other applicants accepted by countries on various humanitarian grounds. There are also the quasi-asylum seekers—'masked' economic migrants or/and transit migrants who make use of the asylum channel to legalize their stay for a time.

Western immigrants, while nowhere nearly as numerous as the above-mentioned groups, fit very different immigrant categories—they are mostly better-off, highly skilled and qualified and able to take on prestigious jobs in both the state sector (advisors, teachers) and the private sector (managers, business people). Mutual migration exchange among the NMS, despite creating the core of a newly established migratory system (except for the distant Baltic states), has not, to date, been very intensive. *Table 10.1* gives a very rough estimate of overall migration mobility in the NMS, confirming the position of the Czech Republic, Hungary and

Table 10.1. International migration patterns in the NMS: Estimate—beginning of the 2000s.

Country	Into	Out[1]	Through
Czech Republic	++++	++	+++
Estonia	+	+	+
Hungary	++++	++	+++
Latvia	+	++	+
Lithuania	+	++	+
Poland	++++	++++	++
Slovakia	++	++	+++
Slovenia	++	+	++

Notes: + denotes very weak flow; ++++ denotes very strong flow.
[1] This concerns the country's own 'domestic-majority' population—a very subjective assessment; estimates of illegal/irregular migrants are included; the population is 'measured' in absolute terms; the length of stay is not taken into account, for example, circular (temporary) versus permanent/settlement migration movements.

Source: Based on Drbohlav and Kunze (2003), modified.

Poland as the most mobile countries. In contrast, the Baltic states fall significantly behind.

What role does international migration play in the context of total population change? Population growth comprises two elements—natural increase and net migration. The annual rate of population growth—a combination of the natural growth rate (or the difference between births and deaths per 1,000 population) and net migration (or the difference between arrivals and departures per 1,000 population) (Salt, 2003)—was negative in all the NMS except Slovakia and Slovenia for the 2000–2002 period (see *Table 10.2*). The latter two countries had positive, albeit very low, values. There was a negative natural increase in all the NMS except Poland and Slovakia (again very low positive numbers). As for net migration,[12] the NMS are divided into two groups—those with negative net migration: the Czech Republic, Latvia, Lithuania and Poland; and those with positive net migration: Estonia, Hungary, Slovakia and Slovenia. Only in Slovenia, however, has migration been sufficient to compensate for negative natural increase (Salt, 2003; Council of Europe, 2003). All in all, overall demographic development in all the NMS has been affected by very low fertility rates (in 2002 the TFR ranged between 1.17 in the Czech Republic and 1.37 in Estonia [Council of Europe, 2003]). As in many other EU countries, this situation, along with increasing life expectancy, will lead to the phenomenon of an aging population (see, for example, the case of the Czech Republic in Burcin and Kučera [2003]). There is no doubt that international migration, as in most western European countries and within the NMS, is becoming important and will become even more important, in other words, a truly major component of population change (Salt, 2003).

Table 10.2. Population, area and components of population change in the NMS.

Country	Population,[1] thousands	Area, km^2	Natural increase,[2] annual average 2000–2002 (%)	Net migration,[3] annual average 2000–2002 (%)	Growth rate,[4] annual average 2000–2002 (%)
Czech Republic	10,203.3	78,865	–0.17	–0.08	–0.25
Estonia	1,356.0	45,100	–0.40	0.01	–0.39
Hungary	10,142.4	93,031	–0.36	0.10	–0.26
Latvia	2,331.5	64,500	–0.53	–0.18	–0.71
Lithuania	3,462.6	65,200	–0.24	–0.24	–0.48
Poland	38,218.5	312,683	0.01	–0.04	–0.03
Slovakia	5,379.2	49,035	0.01	0.02	0.02
Slovenia	1,995.0	20,251	–0.04	0.17	0.12

Source: [1] See Council of Europe (2003), [2,3,4] cited in Salt (2003).

As for migration itself, *Table 10.3* provides a selection of important migratory parameters. The foreign population stock is (in absolute terms) by far the largest in the Czech Republic, Estonia and Latvia. In Estonia and Latvia, however, this has very little to do with current immigration—the majority of the two countries' huge mass of foreigners are Russians or representatives of other former Soviet Union countries who moved in rather a long time ago.[13] In contrast, almost one-quarter of a million foreigners currently in the Czech Republic are (postrevolutionary) immigrants, while about two-thirds came primarily for economic reasons (new foreign labor force). Hungary's foreign population stock is one-half that of the Czech Republic, with more than 100,000 migrants. Slovenia is next with more than 40,000, while stocks in the other countries fluctuate at around 30,000. Leaving aside the specific Estonian and Latvian cases and measuring reality in relative terms, Slovenia is of equal importance to the Czech Republic, while Hungary shifts downward. The stock of foreign population in Poland is apparently relatively minimal. Regarding the development of the foreign population stock over time, the numbers in Estonia and Hungary seems to have been declining during the five years from 1998 to 2002. On the other hand, the stock in Latvia has been growing (Salt, 2003), while in other countries it has more or less stabilized or is hard to analyse because of a lack of data (Salt, 2003). To sum up, even in the Czech Republic and Slovenia where the proportion of foreigners is the largest, the NMS have so far differed from the 'old' EU member states, where the foreign population share has now reached 5 percent (Poulain and Herm, 2003). With the exception of the Baltic states where the respective numbers are very small, a glance at the stock of foreign (immigrant) labor only confirms the picture sketched above, with the Czech Republic dominating

Dušan Drbohlav

Table 10.3. Selected migratory parameters. Stocks in NMS, 2002.

Country	Stock of foreign population[1]	Stock of foreign population per 1,000 inhabitants	Stock of foreign population as a share of total population (%)[6]	Stock of foreign labor
Czech Republic	231,000[2]	22.6	2.3	161,711[10]
Estonia	269,500	198.7	19.7	
Hungary	115,900	11.4	1.1	49,800[11]
Latvia	439,500[3]	184.8	18.5[7]	
Lithuania	32,700	9.5	1.0[8]	
Poland	34,100[4]	0.9	0.09[9]	24,643[12]
Slovakia	29,500	5.5	0.6	9,117[13]
Slovenia	44,700[5]	22.4	2.2	36,000[14]

Notes:

[1] Data for Latvia are from 2000, Slovenia from 2001 and Lithuania from 2003.

[2] Data include those holding a permanent residence permit and visa for a period exceeding 90 days.

[3] Stock of foreign-born population (2000 population census).

[4] Data include residents staying temporarily in Poland for over two months. Some 66 per cent of registered incomers are long-term immigrants, staying in Poland for 12 months or longer and 33 per cent are short-term migrants, staying in Poland for a period of 2–12 months (Korys, 2004).

[5] Number of residence permits.

[6] Data for Latvia and Slovenia are from 2001; for Lithuania, from 2003.

[7] Stock of foreign-born population as a share of total population—based on 2000 population census.

[8] Includes immigrants who stay on both permanent and temporary basis (Development and Trends, 2003).

[9] See Korys (2004).

[10] Foreigners—holders of work permits, job licenses; and Slovaks registered by job centers. See Drbholav (2004).

[11] Individual work permits issued to foreign citizens (Zsoter, 2003).

[12] Number of work permits granted to foreigners in Poland, both to individual applicants and those subcontracting foreign companies for different time periods—only exceptionally for more than 12 months (Kepinska, 2003).

[13] Foreigners—holders of job licenses and work permits and registered citizens of the Czech Republic (Divinský, 2004).

[14] Number of valid work permits. See Zavratnik-Zimic (2004).

Source: Based on Salt (2003), enlarged, and to some extent modified.

in absolute terms, Slovenia catching up in relative terms and Slovakia and Poland falling significantly behind.

Juxtaposing the different migratory-flow data to improve the comparability of the figures is problematic (see *Table 10.4*). By doing this, one can achieve only a basic orientation, as characteristics used for comparison frequently do not correspond

Table 10.4. Selected migratory parameters. Flows in NMS, 2001–2002.

Country	Inflow of foreign population, average for 2001–2002[1]	Inflow of foreign population, average for 2001–2002, per 1,000 inhabitants	Outflow of population, average for 2000–2002[6]	Outflow of population, average for 2001–2002 per 1,000 inhabitants
Czech Republic	28,800[2]	2.8	27,000[7]	2.6
Estonia	1,400[3]	1.0	900[8]	0.7
Hungary	19,500[4]	1.9	1,900[9]	0.2
Latvia	1,200[3]	0.5	4,600[10]	2.0
Lithuania	4,900[3]	1.4	7,200	2.1
Poland	6,600[5]	0.2	24,000[11]	0.6
Slovakia	2,300	0.4	1,200	0.2
Slovenia	7,300	3.7	4,200	2.1

Notes:

[1] Data for Estonia are for 2000 and for Hungary for 2001.

[2] Registered immigration to the country; since 2001 persons in receipt of a visa issued for a period exceeding 90 days who stayed in the country for more than a year were included in the same category as immigrants with permanent residence permits.

[3] Recorded as 'external' migration flows referring to non-Baltic countries. See Salt (2003). According to the web site, http://www.csb.lv, data for Latvia are slightly different—the average outflow is 4,900.

[4] Data refer to foreigners with long-term residence permits or immigration permits, excluding foreigners with work permits (Salt, 2003).

[5] Immigrants are persons granted a permanent residence permit. Numbers may be underestimated, as not all children accompanying immigrants are registered.

[6] Data for Estonia and Hungary are for 2001.

[7] Data are underestimated as they include only those emigrants who reported their departure (Salt, 2003; Drbohlav, 2004).

[8] Clearly, in the Baltic states too, numbers are underestimated as not all immigrants report their movements to the authorities.

[9] Data refer to foreigners with long-term residence or immigration permits, excluding foreigners with work permits (Salt, 2003).

[10] According to the web site, http://www.csb.lv, data for Latvia are slightly different.

[11] Only persons who register their intention to establish a permanent residence abroad with the authorities are included in the statistics (Salt, 2003).

Source: Based on Salt (2003), enlarged, and to some extent modified.

internally to each other in a precise way (see notes in *Table 10.4*).[14] In absolute terms, inflows of foreigners to the Czech Republic and then Hungary are currently the most numerous as compared with Slovakia, Estonia and Latvia which have the smallest numbers. In proportional terms, Slovenia, followed by the Czech Republic, traditionally dominates the whole group. When pinpointing some of the more

Table 10.5.   Number of asylum applications submitted in the NMS, 1998–2003 (in thousands).

Country	1998	1999	2000	2001	2002	2003
Czech Republic	4.1	7.3	8.8	18.1	8.5	8.1
Estonia	0	0	0	0	0	–
Hungary	7.1	11.5	7.8	9.6	6.4	1.9
Latvia	0.1	0	0	0	0	–
Lithuania	0.2	0.1	0.3	0.4	0.5	0.6
Poland	3.4	3.0	4.6	4.5	5.2	5.1
Slovakia	0.5	1.3	1.6	8.2	9.7	6.2
Slovenia	0.5	0.9	9.2	1.5	0.7	0.8

Note: – Data not available. In fact, the number of asylum applications in Latvia between 1999 and 2002 were 22, 5, 14 and 32, respectively. Nevertheless, vis-à-vis the national statistical offices, UNHCR Data Summary Sheets and UNHCR (2003) give slightly different figures for the Baltic states. Similarly, the number of asylum applications in Estonia between 1999 and 2002 were 30, 3, 12 and 9, respectively.

Data for Estonia and Latvia in 2003 are available but unreliable, as they were only provisional and subject to change (UNHCR, 2003).

Source: Salt (2003); http://www.migracija.lt; http://www.ocma.gov.lv; UNHCR (2003).

significant trends over time (1998 to 2002) (Salt, 2003), it seems that, importantly, the inflows to the Czech Republic, Lithuania and Slovenia are growing (although, in the Czech Republic, growth has also been due to significant statistical changes and the recategorization of the country). A different picture appears when the outflows are analysed. In absolute terms the most intensive outflows affect the Czech Republic and Poland while, relatively speaking, Latvia and Lithuania join the Czech Republic and Slovenia at the top of the group. (Significantly, Estonian outflow was diminishing between 1998 and 2001 [Salt, 2003]; moreover, importantly, Latvian negative net migration has fallen, as compared with the mid-1990s, because of decreasing outflows). The current net migrations may indicate significant population losses in Latvia, Lithuania and Poland due to migration.

The number of asylum applications submitted in the NMS between 1998 and 2003 are presented in *Table 10.5*. The figures reflect a rather wide and complicated set of 'pulls' that attract asylum and quasi-asylum seekers to individual countries. The Czech Republic, followed by Slovakia and Poland, dominate in terms of the numbers of asylum seekers (in absolute terms) in 2003, while the recent attractiveness of the Baltic states and Slovenia in this regard is rather marginal. In terms of how the situation has developed over time, no coherent trends have appeared, although a decrease in or stabilization of the numbers rather than an increase is evident. Recognition rates remain low in the NMS.[15] Asylum procedures are often discontinued because quasi-asylum seekers disappear from asylum

Table 10.6. Basic macroeconomic characteristics of NMS, 1995–2003.

Country	GDP growth, annual average % change, 1995–2001	GDP/head (PPS[1]) average 1999–2001, EU15=100	Unemployment rate, total, 2000	Annual inflation; inflation—annual average rate of change, 2003/2002
Czech Republic	1.5	59.8	7.3	–0.1
Estonia	5.2	37.1	10.3	1.4
Hungary	4.0	49.5	5.9	4.7
Latvia	5.7	31.8	12.1	2.9
Lithuania	5.1	35.6	13.7	–1.1
Poland	6.3	41.1	19.9	0.7
Slovakia	3.9	43.9	18.7	8.8
Slovenia	5.1	67.1	6.3	5.7

[1] Purchasing power standard.
Source: A New 2004; see http://europa.eu.int/comm/eurostat/ accessed in January 2006.

centers before having completed the asylum formalities and try, often illegally, to cross state borders,[16] which reduces the recognition rates (Kunze, 2004).

10.4 Factors Contributing to Migration Movements

There are several important 'pull' factors attracting immigrants and migrants to and through the NMS. The most dominant examples are the economic situation and the socioeconomic climate, including the labor market situation and the strong and never-ending desire of employers for a cheap and flexible labor force. This is especially true in the more prosperous NMS—Slovenia and the Czech Republic (see *Table 10.6*). In the other NMS there are still relatively favorable economic environments and consequently a reasonable standard of living in comparison with other countries in transition or other typical representatives of the 'far-distant' developing world.[17] Among other 'pulls,' democratic regimes and relative political stability, geographical position (bordering on the classic, more prosperous western societies) and to some extent relatively liberal legislation and tolerance toward immigrants,[18] seem to be crucial in explaining mobility into the NMS. As well as the factors already mentioned, cultural closeness, social (mainly family) networks and informal links also play a role. As a corollary of the 'pulls' mentioned, the following types of migrants have been entering the NMS: economic immigrants, sometimes bolstered by identical ethnicity or affinities of ethnicity, language and culture (to all the NMS[19]); asylum and quasi-asylum seekers (to the Czech Republic, Hungary, Poland and Slovakia); and transit migrants[20] (to the Czech Republic, Hungary, Poland, Slovakia and Slovenia). Moreover, short-term circular migrants commute across borders into border-zone areas (Czech Republic, Hungary, Poland Slovakia and Slovenia), 'pushed' by economic motives—to improve their 'not-all-that-bad' living standards. Further details on how particular factors are linked with individual migratory inflows/flows are beyond the scope of this chapter. Perhaps, except for Poland (with its huge and vulnerable agricultural sector), there are no strong 'push' factors that would propel a mass migration of NMS citizens out of their mother countries. Regarding Poland, Korys (2004, p. 29) states:

> The crucial push factor that contributes to a permanent substantial out-flow for short and long-term migration[21] stems from the current shape of the Polish economy. The most visible aspects are the high unem-ployment rate and a limited supply of attractive job offers, especially in peripheral and underdeveloped regions and relatively low income in comparison with EU member states.

Hence, uniquely in the NMS, Poland typifies the 'double-step' shift of significant (really massive) workforces from the east to the west (from Poland to western Eu-rope, as mentioned) and at the same time from the former Soviet Union to Poland.[22]

A rather specific 'push/pull' factor within the NMS is the perception by the majority of the population of would-be or existing immigrant groups. This factor, influenced by many different circumstances (e.g., historical patterns, the socioeco-nomic situation, a number of particular new immigrants and compatriots) must be taken into account, especially when assessing the Roma situation. Generally, Ro-mas, in contrast with many other ethnic immigrant groups, are the object of persis-tent prejudice in the NMS (for the Czech Republic and Slovakia, see Krištof [2003] and Drbohlav [2004]). Nyíri's (2003) study reaches important conclusions. First, the level of xenophobia varies among the NMS, and the level has been changing over time. According to Nyíri (2003, p. 21):

> Hungary's level of xenophobia is, by all accounts, high and rising, Slovenia's is low and falling. The Czech Republic, Slovakia and Poland are somewhere between but have a falling level of xenophobia.

Second, based on comparisons among the CEECs, Nyíri (2003, p. 1) also found:

> ... xenophobia levels do not seem to be correlated to living standards, cultural–historical experience, education, civic society patterns or even the number of immigrants.

In contrast, he considers the role of political communication, public discourse and the level of discretionary power given to officials as crucial for explaining the level of xenophobia in given countries.

10.5   Impact of Migration Movements on Societies

Assessing the impact of immigrants on host societies in the NMS is a great challenge and presents many different problems. The complexity of the issue springs from the different effects that immigrants have over time and across space, the geographical scale of the problem and the limited amount of data to work with. Nevertheless, it is possible to make several observations. It is economically driven immigration that particularly helps to power the motor of transformation processes; this occurs mainly in the most important urban poles of development (capital cities), and it is probably the most important impact that immigrants have on the NMS and their societies[23] (e.g., in the Czech Republic and Slovenia, and also in Hungary). A similar effect is also evident at the local level, when circular labor migrants engage in transborder commuting to improve their living standards and at the same time improve the local/regional milieu (Czech Republic, Hungary, Poland, Slovakia, Slovenia). There is no doubt that foreign immigrants (companies) coming to the NMS (especially to their capitals and sometimes also to border regions) have transferred, albeit to a limited extent, know-how and new technologies from the west. Immigrants, often highly skilled, have also facilitated:

> ... diffusion of cultural patterns (such as new management techniques or the capitalist work ethos) that were necessary for the introduction of the capitalist economy and democratic institutions (Korys, 2004, p. 41).

In fact, as in other developed immigration countries, the presence of economic immigrants brings with it both pros and cons for the country and for the immigrants themselves. Let us pinpoint in this context frequent illegal/irregular economic activities[24] (mainly employment) that cause a waste of brain power (deskilling) (see Divinský [2004]); Drbohlav (2004) very often represents the exploitation of immigrants (in terms of, for example, their income, working conditions and career development). Obviously, illegal/irregular migration, especially transit migration, destabilizes the principle of the rule of law on which democratic societies are based. Consequently, in the eyes of the majority of the populations, it casts a long shadow over all foreigners living in a country.

As far as immigration vis-à-vis cultural contributions, demographic changes and changes in the social and geographical structures are concerned, immigrants in the NMS have not, to date, had a nationwide influence on these issues—only a partial influence at the local level and usually a long way off the levels known in western Europe, not to mention the traditional highly developed immigration countries. Thus, in NMS capitals, though westernization due to western immigrant communities does exist, the reality is that ethnic minorities have not, to date, created very significant areas of concentration within cities or regions and 'not many important ethnic social or political structures have evolved which would unite, unify and organize new immigrants' (see Drbohlav [2004, p. 62], whose comments for the Czech Republic are valid for most other NMS). This is completely typical of an immature stage of the whole migration/adaptation issue and the way it is managed.

10.6   Migration Policies and Practices

Before their accession to the EU, the NMS were supposed to fulfill the remaining accession requirements by harmonizing their legislation with the EU *acquis*.[25] The law and practice relating to migration was developed or revised to meet international standards (UNHCR, 2004). Logically, within the mandatory aligning of domestic legislation with EU norms, the NMS have followed broader EU approaches toward migration, such as reinforcing border controls, tightening visa regimes and applying strict asylum schemes (UNHCR, 2004). Accordingly, a policy that is more restrictive than more tolerant has generally prevailed and still does prevail in the NMS. One of the biggest challenges was, of course, the expansion of the EU's external borders. With accession, the NMS have had to face multiple responsibilities, both within the EU and along their borders. In the asylum sphere, the most important responsibilities are those under the Dublin II Convention and EURODAC[26] that are automatically applicable to new member states[27] (UNHCR, 2004). Besides their other commitments, the NMS are also responsible for managing secondary movements and checking irregular migration.

Though the NMS did start tackling the issues of migration/immigrant adaptation, coherent and mutually complementary policies (including corresponding practices) in that field are still, to a large extent, missing. Divinský's (2004, p. 88) words regarding the situation in Slovakia have broader validity:

> State migration policy should more cover a set of responsible subjects
> operating in synergy along with conceptual intentions, a legislative
> plan, information systems, public relations, and the like.

Although it is very difficult to assess, it seems that the Czech Republic, followed by Poland and Slovenia, did rather more than other NMS in forming their migration adaptation policies and practices (Niessen and Schibel, 2003; Nyíri, 2003; Divinský, 2004; Zavratnik-Zimic, 2004). As Vildziuniene (1998) points out, the migration policies of the Baltic states focus mainly on softening the negative consequences of past migratory movements.

'State integration activities' (often mediated through various nongovernmental organizations [NGOs]) depend on the given migratory type with which they are linked and generally range from asylum seekers via recognized refugees[28] to ethnically based immigrants. The best integration measures are tied to ethnic immigrants of the state's main national group in the course of resettlement programs (e.g., Poles or Czechs from Kazakhstan or Volhynian Czechs from Ukraine at the beginning of the 1990s fall into this category). A preferential status for compatriots living abroad is embodied in the legislation of some of the countries (e.g., Hungary and Slovakia). In Hungary especially, which has a large pool of ethnic Hungarians outside the mother country (see above), the issue is highly controversial (see Kováts *et al.* [2003]); opinions and approaches often verging on 'nationalism' cause an emotional atmosphere and are perceived rather negatively abroad (Juhász, 2003; Nyíri, 2003; Danielová, 2004).[29]

Labor migration in the NMS has, to date, been a mostly accepted but not highly regulated phenomenon.[30] While there are some relatively successful integration programs (or subprograms) that aim to ease the integration of refugees into many different spheres of society (e.g., in the Czech Republic—Drbohlav [2004]; Poland—Korys [2004]; Slovenia—Zavratnik-Zimic [2004]), the integration of immigrants into legal domestic labor markets as a whole has posed problems everywhere. Nevertheless, there is at least one good example of a proactive and progressive policy dealing with filling gaps in the domestic labor market. A new state program (a pilot initiative) targeted at attracting a skilled/qualified foreign labor force to the Czech Republic was launched in summer 2003, making it easier and quicker for selected immigrants from Bulgaria, Croatia and Kazakhstan[31] to obtain permanent residence status (based on a points system; see more in Drbohlav [2004]).

10.7 Conclusions and Some Recommendations

Accession to the EU on 1 May 2004 crowned the efforts of the NMS to normalize their regimes and to convert them reasonably and effectively into more prosperous and democratic societies integrated with other developed western European democracies. Changes in migration patterns now fall into this newly drawn path. The accession to the EU (with all its preparatory legislative and practical steps) brought the NMS closer to the old member states. Nevertheless, even before the accession, the 'normalization of reality' in the NMS often brought about new migratory patterns similar to, rather than different from, what was occurring in the EU. Thus, more intensive mobility, more immigration and a greater number of transit movements have been seen, while emigration from the NMS has generally been stabilizing or decreasing. As noted, in terms of migratory patterns, the NMS do not form a homogeneous group. Whereas especially the Czech Republic, Hungary and Slovenia, followed by Poland and Slovakia, resemble, to a greater or lesser extent, the old member states, the migration patterns in the Baltic states are, for many reasons, at a more immature stage. Regarding the former group, whereas quantitative resemblance to the western world is still rather weak (the only exception, perhaps, being the Czech Republic), the conditionality of migration, the qualitative aspects of the migratory process and the nature and whole development of migration policies and practices are closely related and are already very similar to those in western Europe.

Regarding the future development of migration patterns, one can only agree with Salt's (2003, p. 39) words:

> Past experience and several studies of the prospective enlargement have failed to indicate that further large scale movements from the new to the existing member states will occur, although there is bound to be some redistribution of population as the economies of the EU become more integrated.

The European Commission (2004b, p. 2) presents the results of Krieger's (2004) study as follows:

> There will be no flood of migrant workers. Migration flows from the accession countries into EU15 states are likely to be small: just 1 percent of those aged 15 and over declares a firm intention to migrate.[32]

In absolute terms, this would mean about 600,000 persons on the move westward in the next five years under the conditions of free circulation. In the context of a total population in the EU15 of 375 million, this is not too great a number.[33] This somewhat low intention to migrate is supported by socioeconomic, social and sociocultural perceptions (namely, relative income, poverty, social exclusion and family values). Research on these issues shows that such perceptions in the NMS are often not too different from those in the old EU member states[34] (European Commission, 2004b). What can also be expected in addition to the continuing, albeit modest and often only short-term migration movements westward, are further partly increased inflows from the old EU member states into the NMS. An increase in movements among the individual NMS within the already established migration system will also be supported.[35]

As for the future and the management of migration and related processes, we are at the dawn of a new era. Very low fertility along with low mortality and growing life expectancy in Europe are leading to declining and markedly aging populations. This, together with the growing globalization of some labor market segments, gaps in the labor market (competition particularly for 'brains' but also for other qualified and unqualified foreign labor), immigrant adaptation problems and the indirect lowering of pressure on illegal/irregular movements (Baršová, 2004), means that active recruitment policies are likely to be needed—to attract both settlement migrants (see, e.g., programs in the Czech Republic and United Kingdom) and temporary migrants[36] (Germany, United Kingdom) (Baršová, 2004). How can the NMS cope with all these challenges? Based on the current reality, some broad general policy recommendations are given below on how to improve the management of the whole international migration process, strengthen its positive features and mitigate the negative ones:

1. Develop a migration policy that is as transparent, systematic, comprehensive and coherent, but also as flexible, anticipatory and farsighted as possible. Such a policy should be supported by mutually complementary subpolicies.
2. Formulate a general strategic vision and make specific decisions regarding the economic, demographic, cultural and social aspects of diversity.
3. Ensure migration practices are fully in harmony with the relevant legislation.
4. Design an active migration policy, especially in those spheres where individual states—not the EU—play the most important role, namely, economic immigration and immigrant integration (e.g., new special recruitment programs and cooperation agreements on commuting in border-zone areas).
5. Initiate broad discussion on migration issues and ensure that objective information on migration issues is provided to the public.
6. Improve cooperation among and within state bodies, NGOs and international organizations responsible for migration issues.
7. Ensure some decentralization of migration responsibilities. Local and regional administration and governments should be more involved in handling this issue.
8. Work intensively on better monitoring, on more sophisticated, reliable and detailed international migration statistics (collecting, processing, tabulation, dissemination and harmonization of data).
9. Launch more integration programs and pay more attention to intercultural learning and communication. Devote special and really comprehensive attention to the Roma population.
10. Combat all forms of illegal/irregular migration, from smuggling and trafficking in human beings to illegal employment activities: the more restrictive the measures, the more effective the fight.

Finally, the last comment touches a geopolitical issue in its character. All NMS should make use of their historical ties and continue to cooperate with other CEECs in managing migration movements in the broad sense of the word—namely, with Belarus, Bulgaria, Moldova, Romania, Russia, Ukraine and countries of the former Yugoslavia. Erecting new barriers between those who are 'in' and those who are 'out' and between the 'rich world' and the 'poor world' would only serve to exacerbate problems.

Notes

1.   Other new member states (Cyprus and Malta) were omitted as they did not experience a common 'Communist history,' and their socioeconomic, geographical and, indeed, migratory patterns also differ (see, e.g., European Commission [2004a,b]).

2.   Coordinated by the International Organization for Migration (IOM) in Vienna, Austria.

3.   In this context the author expresses his gratitude to the UNHCR office, Prague, for providing relevant data sources, to Ilmars Mezs from the IOM Office in Riga, Latvia and Juris Krumins, from the University of Latvia, Riga, for valuable comments on the situation in the Baltic states.

4.   For example, 'in the interwar period 2.1 million people left Poland, heading for France, Belgium, Germany and both Americas' (Frejka *et al.* [1998], cited in Korys [2004, p. 8]). Mostly as a result of geopolitical, political and socioeconomic realities, almost three million Hungarians lived outside their mother country, often in nearby European countries.

5.   In fact, there were many factors in the decision-making process that resulted in emigration, including housing, working, traveling and environmental; in other words, there was total disillusionment with the political climate (Drbohlav, 1993).

6.   Frejka (1996) and Okolski (1998) according to Salt (2003, p. 17) put the number much higher.

7.   For example, in the Czech Republic during the 1980s, as many as 60,000 foreign workers (converted to the 'one migrant per day unit') were resident altogether in the country. For more details, see Boušková (1998).

8.   See also Drbohlav and Kunze (2003). Temporary economic migration was allowed and was at its most intensive in the second half of the 1960s and at the beginning of the 1970s (Zavratnik-Zimic, 2004); for example, shopping tourism can be traced back to the late 1970s and early 1980s; inter alia, 'along the Slovene–Austrian and Slovene–Italian border local inhabitants could cross the border very easily on the basis of special documents' (Zavratnik-Zimic, 2004, p. 9).

9.   Hungary has allowed its citizens to travel to the west since the late 1970s (Szoke, 1992).

10.   As well as the selected countries, see, for example, Kielyte (2002); Juhász (2003); Divinský (2004); Drbohlav (2004); Korys (2004); Zavratnik-Zimic (2004) for others.

11.   Doing so is beyond the scope of this chapter. Nevertheless, we would again pinpoint a specificity of the Baltic states, where the magnitude/scale and intensity of migratory processes is, vis-à-vis other NMS, quite marginal.

12.   Because of unreliable statistics (i.e., underestimation of emigration), some changes in migratory categories used in the statistics (e.g., in the Czech Republic) and often-problematic mutual comparisons (different subcategories being compared to each other), the picture is distorted.

13. 'Immigration has strained Estonian society considerably as almost 1.4 million of mostly Soviet citizens have passed through the country in the last 45 years' (Kielyte, 2002, p. 4; see also Katus *et al.* [2002]).

14. In fact, the stock data above suffer from the same problems.

15. When positive decisions between 1998 and 2002 and applications during the same period are juxtaposed, the recognition rate for the Czech Republic is 1 percent, for Poland 3.5 percent, for Slovakia 0.6 percent, for Slovenia 0 percent (Kunze, 2004), for Lithuania 6.2 percent (but 0.7 percent in 2001 and 0.2 percent in 2002 [see http://www.migracija.lt/ accessed in January 2006]). In Latvia only eight people were granted asylum between 1998 and May 2003 (see http://www.ocma.gov.lv/ accessed in January 2006); in Hungary the rate was 3.8 percent between March 1998 and August 2000 (Juhász, 2003).

16. For example, such proportions have reached recently 75 percent in Hungary (Juhász, 2003). In 2002 the Czech Republic had 8,480 asylum applications and in the same year 7,797 asylum seekers 'disappeared' from a refugee centre and 2,067 asylum seekers were caught trying to illegally cross the state border (Drbohlav, 2004).

17. Of course, salary levels and living standards there are far below that of 'old' member states (see *Table 10.6*).

18. Rather liberal legislation enabling foreigners to do business (e.g., in the Czech Republic and Poland; see Drbohlav [2004]; Korys [2004]) or infrequent, inadequate and inefficient controls of legal employment (e.g., in the Czech Republic and Slovakia [Drbohlav, 2004, Divinský, 2004]).

19. In this regard, important and intensive relations, due especially to specific historical ties, do exist between the Czech Republic and Slovakia, Poland and the former Soviet Union, Hungary and Romania, Slovenia and the former Yugoslavia, Estonia and Latvia and the former Soviet Union.

20. One can imagine how huge this often illegal flow is: (e.g., 178,000 persons were caught between 1997 and 2002 illegally trying to cross Czech Republic borders [Drbohlav, 2004]). The same figure for Poland is 22,560 (Korys, 2004), for Slovenia 103,000 (Zavratnik-Zimic, 2004), and for Slovakia 56,000 (Divinský, 2004). Juhász (2003, p. 4) states that 'since 1990, the border guards recorded 152,000 cases of foreigners attempting to enter illegally and 80,000 efforts to leave Hungary illegally.'

21. Whereas official contracts for Poles doing seasonal work in Germany were 268,000 in 2002, estimates are as high as 350,000 (Korys, 2004).

22. Between 100,000 and 300,000 migrants from the former Soviet Union are employed in Poland's secondary labor market (Korys, 2004).

23. Filling gaps in given labor markets (e.g., substituting for a nonexistent domestic labor force in construction, agriculture, some industrial branches and some services is part of the deal).

24. Estimated numbers are high: as many as 200,000 irregular migrants may stay longer and for the most part be economically active in the Czech Republic; in Hungary illegal, employed foreign nationals are estimated at between 70,000 and 140,000 (Juhász, 2003), while between 100,000 and 300,000 migrants (regular and irregular workers) from the former Soviet Union are employed in Poland's secondary labor market (Korys, 2004). For immigrants' economic activities, see also Wallace and Stola (2001).

25. Regarding individual countries, some exceptions were made and more flexible deadlines were allowed so that countries had the chance to fully harmonize specific migratory areas. Also involved are such important issues as joining the Schengen Agreement.

26. Community-wide system for the comparison of the fingerprints of asylum applicants.

27. 'This means that a large number of asylum-seekers could be returned for the determination of their asylum claims to the new border States' (UNHCR, 2004, p. 441).

28. Generally, support structures are available for these categories including health care and education, legal and social counseling and, for recognized refugees, some language courses as well as help with arranging 'safer' jobs and housing. While there is a lack of experience in such matters and a lack of financial resources, the quality of the care is often comparable to what is offered in 'old' EU member states (e.g., in the Czech Republic and Poland) (Drbohlav, 2004; Korys, 2004).

29. There is positive discrimination toward immigrants—ethnic Hungarians. On the other hand, open discrimination, xenophobia and sometimes racism are often applied to other eastern immigrants and the domestic Roma population (Danielová, 2004).

30. On the other hand, an asylum seeker's right to work is usually withheld or is very limited/restricted in the NMS.

31. Since recently, Byelorussians and Moldovans have also been allowed to enter the program.

32. For Poland it was 1 percent; for Slovenia (data provided along with Cyprus and Malta) 0.7 percent; for the Czech Republic, Hungary and Slovakia 0.6 percent; and for the Baltic states 0.8 percent (see more in Krieger [2004]).

33. The current migratory reality also indicates that a provisional ban on free movement that many old member states started applying to delay the inflow of workers from the NMS to their territories was unnecessary.

34. There is one, however, rather unpredictable factor: Romas, who were underrepresented in surveys (Krieger, 2004). The Roma population is numerous (their proportion in the total population in the Czech Republic represents about 2.7 percent, in Hungary 5.6 percent and in Slovakia 9.5 percent [Barany, 1998]). Romas with their 'culture of poverty' (Krištof, 2003, p. 35), entrenched, nomadic way of life, their position at the very bottom of social hierarchy and their existing strong social networks in many countries find it easy to be on the move.

35. The core of such a system has been created by Austria, Byelorussia, the Czech Republic, Germany, Hungary, Moldova, Poland, Slovakia and Ukraine. Besides representatives of these countries, the main people also entering 'the system' have been other west Europeans, Americans, Russians, Romanians, Bulgarians, Vietnamese and Chinese and (in terms of asylum seekers and transit migrants) other post-Soviets and other Asian migrants.

36. Obviously, the aging and the population loss in many developed countries cannot be offset by international migration—and the NMS are no exception. This hypothesis follows from the concept of 'replacement migration' which, despite omitting/not including much of importance, seems, on this point, to be quite realistic.

References

Barany, Z. (1998) 'Ethnic Mobilization and the State: The Roma in Eastern Europe,' *Ethnic and Racial Studies*, **21**(2): 308–327.

Baršová, A. (2004) *Pracovní migrace v EU: Nové politiky členských zemí týkající se imigrace občanů třetích zemí za účelem práce jako zdroj inspirace pro Českou republiku*, Paper presented at the workshop 'Economic Immigration to the Czech Republic,' held at the Senate of the Czech Republic, Prague, 30 June [in Czech].

Boušková, P. (1998) 'Pracovní migrace Cizinců v ČR v 70. až 90. letech,' in *Národní diskuse u kulatého stolu na téma vztahů mezi komunitami*, Ministerstvo vnitra ČR, Prague, Czech Republic, pp. 34–45 [in Czech].

Burcin, B. and Kučera, T. (2003) *Perspektivy populačního vývoje České republiky na období 2003–2065*,' DemoArt pro Přírodovědeckou fakultu UK v Praze, Prague, Czech Republic [in Czech].

Council of Europe (2002) *Toward a Migration Management Strategy*, European Committee on Migration, Strasbourg, France: Council of Europe Publishing.

Council of Europe (2003) *Recent Demographic Developments in Europe*, Strasbourg, France: Council of Europe Publishing.

Danielová, K. (2004) *Rasismus a xenofobie v Ma'arsku*, See http://www.migraceonline.cz/ accessed in January 2006.

Development and Trends of Migration Processes in the Republic of Lithuania in 2003, See http://www.migracija.lt/MDEN/LRV-pranes-anglu-htm /accessed in January 2006.

Divinský, B. (2004) *Slovak Republic (Volume V), An Acceleration of Challenges for Society*, European Commission Project, Vienna, Austria: International Organization for Migration (IOM).

Drbohlav, D. (2003) *The Past, the Present, and the Probable Future of International Migration in Poland, the Czech Republic, Slovakia, and Hungary (with Special Respect to the Czech Republic and Slovakia)*, Background study for research project, 'East-Central Europe, 2000,' Prague, Czech Republic: The Institute of Sociology, Academy of Sciences of the Czech Republic.

Drbohlav, D. (2004) *Czech Republic (Volume II). The Times They Are A-Changing*. European Commission Project, Vienna, Austria: International Organization for Migration (IOM).

Drbohlav, D. and Kunze, M. (2003) *Migration Trends Linked to EU Enlargement*, Unpublished presentation made at the Metropolis Conference, Vienna, Austria, 17 September.

European Commission (2004a) *A New Partnership for Cohesion: Convergence Competitiveness, Cooperation*, Luxembourg: European Commission.

European Commission (2004b) *Perceptions of Living Conditions in an Enlarged Europe*, Brussels, Belgium: European Commission.

Fassmann, H. and Münz, R. (1995) 'European East–West Migration, 1945–1992,' in Coehn, R. (ed) *The Cambridge Survey of World Migration*, Cambridge, UK: Cambridge University Press, pp. 470–480.

Frejka, T. (ed) (1996) *International Migration in Central and Eastern Europe and the Commonwealth of Independent States*, Geneva and New York: United Nations.

Frejka, T., Okolski, M. and Sword, K. (eds) (1998) *In-Depth Studies on Migration in Central and Eastern Europe: The Case of Poland*, New York: United Nations.

Juhász, J. (2003) *Hungary: Transit Country between East and West*, See http://www. migrationinformation.org/Profiles/display.cfm?ID=181/ accessed in January 2006.

Katus, K., Puur, A. and Sakkeus, L. (2002) 'Immigrant Population in Estonia,' in Haug, W., Compton, P. and Courbage, Y. (eds) *The Demographic Characteristics of Immigrant Populations*, Strasbourg, France: Council of Europe, pp. 131–192.

Kepinska, E. (2003) 'Recent Trends in International Migration, Poland 2003,' Working paper no 52, *Seria: Práce Migracyjne*, Warsaw, Poland: Institute for Social Studies of Warsaw University.

Kielyte, J. (2002) *Migration Movements in the Baltic States: Determinants and Consequences*, Paper presented at the WIDER Conference on Poverty, International Migration and Asylum held in Helsinki, Finland, 27–28 September, See http://www.wider.unu.edu/conference/conference-2002-3/conference%20papers/ kielyte.pdf/ accessed in January 2006.

Korys, I. (2004) *Poland (Volume III), Dilemmas of a Sending and Receiving Country*, European Commission Project, Vienna, Austria: International Organization for Migration (IOM).

Kováts, A., Nyíri, P. and Tóth, J. (2003) 'Hungary,' in Niessen, J. and Schibel, J. (eds) *EU and U.S. Approaches to the Management of Immigration: Comparative Perspectives*, Brussels, Belgium: Migration Policy Group (MPG), pp. 49–276.

Krieger, H. (2004) *Migration Trends in an Enlarged Europe*, Dublin, Ireland: European Foundation for the Improvement of Living and Working Conditions.

Krištof, R. (2003) *Závěrečná zpráva k projektu Analýza soudobé migrace a usazování příslušníků romských komunit ze Slovenské republiky na území České republiky*, (OAMP-948/2003), Prague, Czech Republic: International Organization for Migration (IOM) [in Czech].

Kunze, M. (2004) (Scientific Coordinator) *Migration Trends in Selected EU Applicant Countries*, in six volumes, Vienna, Austria: International Organization for Migration.

Niessen, J. and Schibel J. (eds) (2003) *EU and U.S. Approaches to the Management of Immigration, Comparative Perspectives*, Brussels, Belgium: Migration Policy Group (MPG).

Nuget, W. (1995) 'Migration from the German and Austro-Hungarian Empires to North America,' in Cohen, R. (ed) *The Cambridge Survey of World Migration*, Cambridge, UK: Cambridge University Press, pp. 103–108.

Nyíri, P. (2003) *Xenophobia in Hungary: A Regional Comparison*, See http://www.ceu.hu/ papers.php/ accessed in February 2006.

Okolski, M. (1998) 'Regional Dimensions of International Migration in Central and Eastern Europe,' *Genus*, **54**: 1–26.

Poulain, M. and Herm, A. (2003) *An Overview and Comparison of the State of Migration in EU Countries. What the Data Reveal* (Working Papers E 16/2003), Paper presented at the Second Workshop on Demographic and Cultural Specificity and Integration of Migrants, organized by the Population Research Institute (PRI) and Network for Integrated Population Studies (NIEPS), 21–23 March, Helsinki, Finland, pp. 7–58.

Salt, J. (1992) 'Current and Future International Migration Trends Affecting Europe,' in *People on the Move: New Migration Flows in Europe*, Strasbourg, France: Council of Europe Publishing, pp. 41–81.

Salt, J. (2003) *Current Trends in International Migration in Europe*, CDMG (European Committee on Migration), Strasbourg, France: Council of Europe Publishing.

Szoke, L. (1992) 'Hungarian Perspectives on Emigration and Immigration in the New European Architecture,' *International Migration Review*, **26**(22): 305–323.

UNHCR (2003) *Asylum Applications Lodged in Industrialized Countries: Levels and Trends, 2000–2002*, Geneva, Switzerland: United Nations High Commissioner for Refugees.

UNHCR (2004) 'Central Europe and the Baltic States,' in *UNHCR Global Report*, Geneva, Switzerland: United Nations High Commissioner for Refugees, pp. 440–445.

Vildziuniene, A.(1998) *Outlines of Migration Policy in Lithuania, Latvia, and Estonia*, See http://www.sociumas.lt/Eng/Nr9/migrac.asp/ accessed in January 2006.

Wallace, C. and Stola, D. (2001) *Patterns of Migration in Central Europe*, New York, USA: Palgrave.

Zavratnik-Zimic, S. (2004) *Migration Trends—Slovenia—Volume VI—The Perspective of a Country on the Schengen Periphery*, European Commission Project, Vienna, Austria: International Organization for Migration (IOM).

Zsoter, L. (2003) *Report for Hungary* (draft version) of SOPEMI (*Système d'Observation Permanente sur les Migrations*).

Chapter 11

The Future European Union Facing Migration

Catherine Wihtol de Wenden

International migration poses some fundamental challenges to all European societies. Western and eastern Europe, departure points for the Americas, Africa and Asia for several centuries, have, over the past 20 years, become immigration destinations themselves (*Box 11.1*). Europeans have only recently become aware that the situation has changed; having long considered immigration as a provisional response to temporary labor bottlenecks or political crises, they are reluctant to accept it as part of their national or European identity.

The globalization of migration flows currently being experienced by Europe—flows that are about to turn the continent into one of the world's leading immigrant reception regions—has happened for a variety of reasons:

1. In the countries of southern Europe (Greece, Italy, Portugal, Spain) and eastern Europe (Hungary, Poland, Russia), the transition from emigration to immigration country has been so extensive that it is hard to distinguish between the two, with some countries simultaneously acting as receiving (or transit) and sending countries. This is particularly true of a number of eastern European countries.
2. In the past 20 years passports have become more generally available. Only a few countries (e.g., China, Cuba, North Korea) still issue them parsimoniously; even otherwise-mostly authoritarian regimes allow their nationals to

---

Box 11.1. Immigration in Europe.

1. In 2000 nonnationals accounted for 5.1 per cent and non-EU nationals for 3.5 per cent of the total EU population. In the same year positive net migration (annual inflows and annual outflows) totaled 700,000 migrants (i.e., 0.2 per cent of the EU population, three-quarters of whom came from third countries).
2. Turkish nationals are by far the most common foreign nationality in the EU, with 2.7 million people, followed by nationals of the former Yugoslavia. The Maghreb, more specifically Morocco, is another major region of origin, with 2.3 million migrants from the region living in Europe, while sub-Saharan Africa is represented by one million and Asia by 2.2 million migrants.
3. Some 1.5 per cent of Europeans live in another member state of the EU, and 47 per cent of Europeans claim to know only their own mother tongue.
4. Asylum seekers represent 400,000 annual entries.
5. European enlargement in 2004 added ten more countries and another 75 million inhabitants to the European Union. The gross national product (GNP) per head of the new entrants amounts to a mere 40 per cent of that of the current member states, but only 335,000 migrants are expected (i.e., 0.1 per cent of the current EU population).

Source: European Commission (2002).

---

travel. This has resulted in a generalization of the right to leave (i.e., an expression of the right to mobility as enshrined in the human rights agenda) at a time when rich countries are stepping up measures to restrict entry (visas).

3. Applications for asylum are being filed on a global scale, are no longer restricted to a few hotspots and have assumed hitherto inconceivable proportions (the Balkans, the Caribbean, Great Lakes Africa, Near and Middle East, Southeast Asia).
4. Transnational networks based on chain migration (for example, from the Balkans, China, Romania, West Africa) are being activated. These frequently illegal migration flows circumvent state borders that are a source of national income.
5. Shuttle-type 'round-trip' migration flows have developed where people no longer depart for good but merely for short periods of time with the aim of improving their living standard back home. In Europe this has been occurring not only from east to west (after the fall of the Berlin Wall) but also from south to north.
6. Countries are getting closer, not least because of the general drop in the cost of transportation (especially air fares); moreover, potential migrants have an

image of Europe that is defined by foreign television and radio broadcasts, by local markets that brim with western goods and by the money transfers made by migrants. All this gives people aspirations toward Europe even in the remotest places of our world.

Frequently under pressure from a discontented public, European governments continue to have reservations about migration, often making it difficult to meet the dual challenge of an aging population and sectoral skills bottlenecks—two realities already stressed by a United Nations report in March 2000 (United Nations, 2000).

All European policy responses aimed at tackling this phenomenon have been based on assumptions and scenarios that have turned out to be wrong. Twenty years ago most European countries shared the view that the era of mass migration had come to an end, ushering in a new period in which: (i) foreign labor would be replaced by national labor (partly because of rising unemployment); (ii) a new international division of labor would emerge (with non-Europeans returning to and being reinserted into their countries of origin); (iii) more Europeans would move freely within a European Union (EU) free of internal borders (only 1.5 percent currently do so); and (iv) codevelopment would be a viable alternative to migration. Reality has belied most of these grand designs, and European and national policies have focused on border controls to implement security blueprints that are based on reducing the likelihood of migration and fueled by an obsession with the challenges of 'integration.'

The dichotomy between migration pressures and European and national responses to such pressures could risk the benefits of a positive immigration policy based on prospective data being overlooked.

11.1 Europe: A Continent of Immigration against Its Will

11.1.1 Slow but continuing immigration despite closed borders

While closing the borders to new foreign workers for almost 30 years accelerated family reunification and prompted families eventually to settle in their host countries, it did not prevent other migration flows into Europe, either officially under international protection or clandestinely (families, refugees, illicit migrants, experts, students). In contrast with former migrants who were mainly laborers, those currently wishing to seek their fortunes are attracted (pull factor) to other countries rather than driven out (push factor) of their countries of origin. Moreover, today's migrants, unlike their predecessors during the years of mass migration in the 1960s, come less from illiterate rural origins than from an educated, middle-class, urban background.

On 1 May 2004, prior to the entry of the ten new member states into the European Union, the EU's 380 million people included 20 million foreign nationals, five million of whom were from other EU countries. The non-EU nationals were distributed unevenly across Europe. Despite globalization, each country has its own foreigners, be it for reasons of colonial heritage, privileged bilateral relations or geographical proximity, and this has resulted in the creation of 'migration couples' made up of foreign nationals and their host country (France/Maghreb, Germany/Turkey, United Kingdom/Commonwealth).

Some 60 percent of the foreign nationals living in Europe have been there for over ten years, and in most European countries those 60 percent come from just four or five sending countries. This holds true even if we break the figures down by country of emigration and type of migrant and even if we bear in mind that roughly ten European countries host almost all these migrants.

Apart from family-driven migration (which makes up the majority of the influx) and strictly regulated migration driven by manpower requirements, the category of migrants that has increased most in recent years is that of asylum seekers.

Intra-European mobility is most pronounced in Luxembourg, followed by Switzerland, Ireland, Belgium, Portugal, Sweden, Spain and Greece. The share of third-country nationals has increased in the past 20 years, with some nationalities having become increasingly important (such as migrants from central and eastern European countries (CEECs) in Germany, Moroccans and Senegalese in France and citizens of the former Yugoslavia in the Netherlands). Today, new nationalities are dotting the migration landscape: Chinese, Iranians, Pakistanis, Sri Lankans and Vietnamese.

In Eastern Europe the fall of the Berlin Wall caused certain ethnic groups to return to their homelands (e.g., *Aussiedler* to Germany). The collapse of the eastern-bloc regimes did not, however, result in the migration waves anticipated but rather in migration to neighboring countries (Czechs to Slovakia, Romanians to Hungary, Ukrainians to Poland) and, even more so, in round-trip or incomplete migration (Poles to Germany and back, Romanians to France or Italy and back), meaning that people settled down into mobility as a way of life, shedding the constraints of short-term visas. The largest group of migrants are Poles, followed by Ukrainians and Romanians. The agreements on free access to the EU labor market provide for a maximum transition period of seven years.

In the south we find a similar phenomenon of chain migration, the Maghreb being both a sending and receiving (or transit) area for sub-Saharan migration. In fact, Africa is constantly being crossed by migration flows: from North Africa to Europe, as well as to Canada, the Gulf States and the United States. The Maghreb has also become a place of immigration or transit for sub-Saharan migrants tempted by the transit possibilities of the Straits of Gibraltar or the Sicilian islands.

11.1.2 New factors of international mobility: Migration fallacies and transnational networks

Throughout the world, mobility is regulated by transnational networks of familial, economic, commercial and criminal origins. These are only superficially affected by the border-control policies adopted by receiving countries because migrants' determination is often much stronger than dissuasion strategies.

These networks, which violate state borders and produce nonstate players, are based on migration fallacies that fuel the desire to depart. The existence of diasporas or quasi-diasporas abroad (some 50 million Chinese worldwide, several million Turks and Moroccans in Europe), as well as travel agencies and racketeering organizations that promise transport to distant lands, help to create potential migrants who believe they have no hope for improving their lot at home and are looking not only for better economic but also cultural, political or even sexual conditions. On the southern shores of the Mediterranean, for instance, 50 percent of the population is under 25 and living under regimes and in economic conditions that offer few career or other prospects. The fascination with our western El Dorado is great—hence, their aspirations toward Europe. The rural exodus from poor regions (the Balkans, third-world countries) is targeted on the major cities of departure which are stopovers with a prosperous economy linked to borders and overcoming them (i.e., trafficking of workers, humans, drugs, contraband). Huge markets are emerging in these zones of friction and encounter between two worlds—between departure and arrival: Ceuta and Melilla (the Spanish enclaves in Morocco), Berlin and Vienna right after the fall of the Berlin Wall and the Black Sea cities between Turkey and the former Soviet Union. Local exchange markets—migration hubs—are frequently close to national borders: the Kaliningrad enclave, Vlores (Albania), Bucharest and Istanbul, to mention a not-too-distant few. Sometimes the entry ticket to the European dream is marriage, the traditional or mixed marriage rather than the marriage of convenience (*mariage blanc*); sometimes it is a religious network (Christian and Muslim)—for borders are open only to the most privileged (merchants and business people, experts, students, university graduates).

Among these new types of migrants, we find various groups: young men with university degrees from urban middle-class backgrounds who harbor vague thoughts of western modernity; educated single women who aspire to economic and individual independence and sometimes also to freedom of political expression (but who, especially the younger women, may end up being exploited); minors whose motives are hard to fathom; highly qualified elites in search of professional careers in keeping with their skills and talents; low-skilled workers ready to do manual labor to improve their standard of living; whole groups on the move such as the Mali peasants in the Kayes region, the Chinese of Wenzhou, the Romanians of the Oas area, the Tamils and finally refugees whose departure points vary depending on the world's major conflict zones. Except for refugees and marriage-based immigrants, many of these new migrants tend to prefer mobility to definite settlement. They frequently consider their stay as a stopover on the way to other, more coveted destinations (Canada, United States) or as part of a round trip between 'here' (i.e., away from home) and 'there' (i.e., back home). These trends are likely to continue, given the persistent imbalance in today's world—the dichotomy between a desire for individualism and the existence of collective migration networks in the countries of departure: a situation that is exacerbated by the reluctance of admitting countries to take into account these new types of mobility.

Driven by economic, demographic, cultural and political imbalances, the migratory pressures on Europe persist outside its external borders in the east and more particularly in the south where the Mediterranean Sea is increasingly assuming a role similar to that played by the Rio Grande between Mexico and the United States. Stricter border controls coincide not only with the liberalization of trade and the development of transnational networks but also with the lack of any real alternative to migration: neither international free trade, nor progress in the countries of origin, nor dissuasive migration policing offer any short-term solution to potential migrants. Europe's immigration countries want to stop the influx of migrants who intend to settle in their territories for good. But they also hope—often without admitting it—for the arrival of temporary migrants to meet labor market demands, thereby ignoring such migrants' longer-term needs. EU rules have become less stringent for several eastern countries, with the nationals of the so-called Visegrad countries (Czech Republic, Estonia, Hungary, Poland and Slovenia) no longer requiring short-term visas and the CEECs being removed from the negative Schengen visa list (the last to be removed being Bulgaria, as of 31 December 2000 and Romania, as of 31 December 2001). However, stricter controls for southern countries highlight the existing divide and frustrate any attempt to create a regional integration zone around the Mediterranean. The dependence of European states on immigration is likely to increase given the demographic structure of most industrial societies (declining birth rates and a growing number of older people).

11.2   The European Response and National Immigration Policies: Europeanization in Reverse

While the effectiveness of policies designed to control migration flows will depend on there being greater confidence in the European instruments available, each country is paradoxically trying to remain in charge of migration policies, especially policies that need to be 'explained' to the general public.

11.2.1 The Europeanization of migration policies

The European migration area was established in several phases. The complexity of the European system means that the focus has shifted on to control mechanisms (improved cooperation at the European level, adoption of the *acquis communautaire*[1] by the accession countries), while the project of harmonizing European policies has enjoyed little progress because of the veto option available to member states (*Box 11.2*). Superimpose the several normative levels of reference (Council of Europe, European Parliament, European Court of Human Rights, European Court of Justice) and the existence of subsystems that are partially integrated into the EU (the Nordic labor market that includes Norway, which is not a EU member; the fact that Denmark, although in the Schengen area, does not participate in the Community's border-control system, while Iceland and Norway, although outside the EU, are part of the Schengen system), and one can understand just how difficult decision making is at EU level.

Nevertheless, and without admitting it to the public, European states have progressed toward the achievement of common migration policies, as evidenced in:

1. States' trust in each others' border controls and their solidarity regarding the treatment of illegal migrants, asylum seekers and 'rejectees';
2. The gradual alignment of alien to nonalien legislation based on residence and the right to live with one's family rather than where one works; and
3. The obligation of new member states to adopt the EU *acquis*, which generally represents the lowest common denominator of national laws: visa regimes; European labor taking priority over foreign labor; criteria for obtaining long-term residence; efforts against illegal immigration and illegal labor.

There does, however, appears to be a tendency toward opt-in/opt-out deals, toward creating a Europe à la carte.[2]

There is an EU-wide framework for asylum and immigration in existence, but each member state is in charge of the application of that framework (efforts against illegal immigration and illicit labor). The European states remain reluctant to relinquish sovereignty for the sake of European border controls.

Although the events of 9/11 did not have a major impact on European migration policies, they did result in the upgrading of security measures and in immigration being viewed in the context of crime and Islamic terrorism. This tendency is not new and dates back to the late 1990s when the member states' home affairs ministers tried to wrest control over the migration issue from other ministries. The real challenges, however, lie elsewhere: free movement of persons and workers, long-term demographic developments, integration, a choice between half-opening or closing the borders and respect for human rights.

Box 11.2. Toward harmonized Community migration policies.

Signed by the EU15 member states on 2 October 1997, the Treaty of Amsterdam aims to strengthen harmonization under the 'third pillar' (justice and home affairs). Adoption of a common European migration policy, however, would mean transfer of this question to the 'first pillar' (Community-wide harmonization of this area of sovereignty).

Asylum and immigration are currently subject to common and mandatory applicability rules that must be transposed by the individual member states into their national laws. Unanimity is still required on any Community decision, however, for at least the next five years. Only later will the qualified-majority system apply, under which the European Council of Ministers would take decisions that are binding on member states (i.e., the latter would lose their sovereignty). But for this to happen, all member states had to agree unanimously on the adoption of such a European codecision model, which they did on the eve of 1 May 2004.

Does this radical change in the decision-making process mean an end to the exercise of sovereignty in this area and to democratic debate and national legislation on entry and residence? How effective is a law decided by one authority and applied by another, if member states, which have the local expertise that Brussels lacks, have to implement it against their will?

More generally, is this the end of national immigration policies? This development may have one major advantage, in the sense that if Brussels makes a decision this may take the heat out of an excessively politicized debate. One must look at the problem in its entirety to understand that an effective response is no longer possible on a simply national basis and that insisting on sovereign national solutions out of fear of public opinion is likely to produce an undesirable outcome.

11.2.2   State-centered policies

The migration flows of the 1980s, their slowdown around 1992–1993 and their resurgence almost everywhere in Europe from 1997 to 1998 prompted European states to make frequent changes to their relevant laws, specifically in the late 1990s, when new regulations were introduced on entry, residence and nationality— regulations that effectively gave more weight to the concept of the *droit du sol* (citizenship based on place of birth and residence) that was sometimes used to regularize the position of undocumented immigrants.

European countries have something else in common: the right of residence, today linked more to the duration of previous stays than to employment, which was certainly not the case in the 1960s and 1970s. Moreover, the 'opposability of employment' regime applies automatically to all non-Europeans seeking jobs in the EU labor market. Since 1992 there has been an acute asylum crisis in Europe as a result of the restrictions introduced on obtaining refugee status and the uneven distribution of asylum applicants among European states.

While the procedures applicable at the point of entry are now harmonized (the CEECs had to adopt the whole body of EU entry-control regulations, along with asylum and human rights commitments before accession), actual residence provisions remain within states' sovereign preserve because of the principle of subsidiarity.[3] These provisions, which lie at the root of the major disparities between receiving countries, include: variable length of residence permits (one, three, five, ten years...); access to the labor market immediately on entry or after a specific length of stay; varying provisions governing access to social security; differing interpretations of the Geneva Convention relating to asylum; different criteria for addressing the social situation of asylum seekers whose applications are currently being processed (in some countries they are permitted to work, in others not); asylum types that differ from one country to the next; a wide range of definitions of family reunification (i.e., who is eligible) and of nationality laws that cover the granting of citizenship of a receiving country. All these elements contribute to a situation in each receiving country that varies in terms of its attractiveness and selectivity—labor market, wages, welfare systems, sectoral employment niches and preexisting or new family networks.

The road to Europeanization is obstructed by the concern of individual countries about public opinion, which makes them pursue specific immigration policies defined by specific national laws governing everything not covered at entry (residence, conditions of asylum and admission, nationality and citizenship, integration).

Moreover, European states also have to reckon with greater mobility on the part of migrants, some of whom who no longer aspire to settle, for example, migrants such as those from the east or from transnational Asian migration networks that offer their compatriots admission structures, which are not always integrationist (i.e., employment niches based on ethnic or regional origins). The differentiation between resident and nonresident is increasingly being replaced by a differentiation between European and non-European which, itself, has superseded the 'national versus foreign national' approach. Despite these gradually converging residence rights, the harmonization of residence policies still lags behind. This is partly because of receiving states' reluctance to lose control in an area so emblematic of their identity as nationality rights—even though the balance between nationality rights based on place of birth and residence (*droit du sol*) and those based on kinship (*droit du sang*) is being reached only slowly. It is also partly because of the importance of local politics in the day-to-day implementation of integration and the principle of subsidiarity.

There are two major models of integration:

1. The postcolonial model (France, The Netherlands, the United Kingdom and, to a lesser degree, Portugal and Spain); and
2. The functional model of 'guest workers' (Germany, Luxembourg, Switzerland), now also espoused by Greece and Italy.

Today, these two models have converged to some extent and coexist with the various migration profiles superimposed by new migrants. Three factors underpin the integration policies:

1. The more or less 'all-encompassing' right of nationality, under which admission countries attach greater or lesser importance to the *droit du sol* and to the length of stay in granting nationality and at the same time give foreigners and migrant populations access to political representation;
2. The labor market situation—the key to integration and socialization through common experience; and
3. Equal opportunities policies: community policies (school, housing and access to employment, social support and cultural events), policies against racial discrimination, promotion of citizen involvement via the development of associations and the right to participate in local elections.

One might add here the place given to Islam. Western Europe is home to 12 million Muslims, four million of whom live in France. The countries most affected try to facilitate a kind of 'citizenization of Islam' by recognizing the Muslim organizations that represent the various Islamic tendencies in Europe.

11.3   Outlook: Codevelopment, Quotas, Right to Mobility

With the recent EU enlargement, one of the concerns of the countries of the EU is its capacity to control migration flows along the new external borders: the emergence of transit-type migrations produces irregular immigration flows and illegal workforces, especially from Russia and the Balkans which, not being part of the group of Visegrad countries, are affected by restrictions on movement. This new border, which applied to the new member states from the moment they entered the EU in 2004, may give rise to new barriers that frustrate regional ties between once closely linked neighbors.

In the west, the progressive Europeanization of entry control (the 1985 Schengen Agreement and the 1990 Dublin Convention) has led to enhancements in the remote control of borders and has made gatekeepers of the countries bordering on 'Fortress Europe'—a job they do for Europe in exchange for cooperation and codevelopment agreements. But this 'area of freedom, security, and justice,' as defined by the 1997 Treaty of Amsterdam, is very porous. 'Gray zones' are developing in the former sending countries of southern Europe that have, in the meantime, become receiving countries.

On the opposite shores of the Mediterranean, the attempts to replace the movement of persons by the movement of goods (1995 Barcelona Agreement on a European–Mediterranean partnership) modeled on the North American Free Trade Agreement (NAFTA) have so far proved futile, as the movement of goods frequently also involves the movement of people—putting the casualties of progress and competition with Europe out on the street, forcing people en masse out of the countryside and into the large cities and ultimately to emigrate. Migration policy is an inherently short-term concept, and the migration–codevelopment equation is flawed for the simple reason that the migration time frame does not coincide with that of the various development strategies (transfer of funds, improvements in living standards): the more development, the more changes in the socioeconomic balance, the more migration. For the would-be migrants harboring false hopes, thoughts of any long-term development prospects for their region are often secondary to the temptations of migration, no matter how perilous or even deadly it may be. Further south, globalization has made the poor aware of the riches of the north. The poor know that if these riches will not come to them, they must get up and go to them. In fact, it is not the poor who depart but rather the migration networks that send them. More specifically, closed borders foster illegal entry and settlement, whereas open borders generate a free flow of migrants.

Dramatic events involving the death of illegal migrants (Dover in June 2000; Straits of Gibraltar in July 2002) highlight the hypocrisy of closed borders which— because of their impenetrability by legal means—encourage the establishment of mafia networks and create a modern version of slave labor: illegal migrants, having been smuggled in and provided with false papers, have to work for their 'benefactors' for years to come.

The European response to labor bottlenecks and aging populations (United Nations, 2000) is twofold: proactive (i.e., readmission of migration flows, opening of borders in the long term) and defensive (i.e., closing of borders for fear of the consequences of 'integration').

In the face of such disparity among European mechanisms of migration control and the apparent realities of the situation, there is an ever-growing number of adverse effects, and no clear-cut solutions are being offered by admission countries. Will the Europeanization of decision making provide a tool that is more efficient than the state-centered approach to dealing with this matter? Are we heading toward a deadlock in European negotiations, a relinquishing of (or return to) state sovereignty, to privatization of public policies through a growing reliance on private operators or to a delocalization of decision making? What short-term solutions have been adopted to respond to labor demands or asylum applications? What national regulations or quotas have been announced? Has the burden of asylum seekers been shared out more fairly? Have more diversified visa policies and a 'preaccession perspective' led to the readmission of migrants by the various business sectors?

The challenge for Europe is to find a compromise between the reticence of public opinion, the satisfaction of labor demand, demographic perspectives and compliance with international commitments (such as human rights, respect of the right to asylum and of the right to live with one's family, dialog and codevelopment with departure countries and the prevention of a brain drain). At the same time, there are the newly emerging rights, such as the right to mobility and the democratization of borders. The idea that European countries cannot stand in the way of human mobility for an indefinite period of time is slowly gaining ground, and albeit timid claims are being made for a right to migrate, even though the right to leave a country, including one's own—as asserted by the 1948 Universal Declaration of Human Rights—is hardly respected by a world that is adopting increasingly stringent criteria for entering a country. Those who are denied entry through the main entrance, however, often try to use the back door.

At the start of the new century, we must ask ourselves whether closing our borders is a valid option in view of the adverse effects this has had and the discrepancy that exists between closed borders and Europe's economic or demographic needs and between closed borders and the aspirations of those who try to reach European soil at any cost.

Immigration as such contributes to the definition of European citizenship and identity, both concepts that are currently in search of new contents: immigration will introduce new values such as multiculturalism, multiple citizenship based on residence, multiple allegiances and new rights, such as the dissociation of citizenship from nationality, especially at local levels, the fight against discrimination, the safeguarding of minority rights and taking into account the rights of those who have none, as well as the reinvention of secularism and the image of the 'other' in the face of Islam. In the final analysis, immigration plays a role in the establishment of a collective European 'we,' a cultural and symbolic 'we' which, far from being a finished product, is constantly and permanently being reinvented.

Notes

1.   The *acquis communautaire* is the entire body of European laws specifically established by the Schengen and Dublin agreements. It includes the signing and application of

the Schengen Agreement, the treaties of Maastricht and Amsterdam concerning the control of the EU's external borders, free movement of Europeans inside the EU and readmission agreements.

2.   Although the United Kingdom has signed the Dublin Convention governing the examination of applications for asylum, it does not participate in the EU's joint immigration and asylum policy. Denmark, also a Schengen country, has opted out of the Title IV measures on immigration and asylum of the Amsterdam Treaty, although it does participate in common visa policies. Iceland and Norway, on the other hand, both members of the Nordic free trade area as well as applicant states, have been obliged to adopt the entire Schengen *acquis* and to cooperate in justice and home affairs matters.

3.   By virtue of this principle, inspired by the federal system of Germany, the European Union can act in areas where it does not have exclusive power only if the member states are unable to achieve the objective stated. As anything that concerns the lives of citizens or that relates to local and national identities is placed in the hands of local communities and national administrations so as to remain responsive to citizens and their needs, the subsidiarity mechanism applies to the integration of immigrants.

References

European Commission (2002) *The Social Situation in the European Union 2002*, See http://europa.eu.int/comm/employment_social/news/2002/jun/soc_situation_en.html/ accessed in January 2006.

United Nations (2000) *Replacement Migration: Is it a Solution to Declining and Ageing Populations?* ST/ESA/SER.A/206, New York, USA: United Nations Population Division.

Part V
Family and Health in an Enlarged European Union

Chapter 12

Family and Health: A Model and European Facts

Hans-Joachim Schulze

Despite the family having an obvious, central, day-to-day role in our lives, it has been studied relatively little as a determinant of health trends. Comparative studies are especially thin on the ground. This chapter aims to show how unfortunate this neglect has been, for the family is a key element in understanding health. The European Observatory on the Social Situation, Demography and Family has provided an important comparative perspective on this issue, and the Observatory's annual seminar in 2003 took as its theme 'The Family in the Health System.'

This chapter begins with a first section describing a family and health model. The next three sections show in part how the model can be applied. The second section deals with family, health care and mortality in the different phases of the life course, with factual information and explanations covering childhood, youth, adulthood and old age. The third section focuses on some of the features of the national health-care systems and the development of health care in the European Union (EU). The fourth section deals with four aspects of the interaction and changing relations between different systems of the model presented in the first section.

12.1   Family and Health: A Model

No matter what definition is selected, the term *family* refers to a group of people who are of unique and high mutual relevance. In formal and official definitions, at least one adult and one child are needed to form a family, and the age of the child often determines how long this definition will apply during an adult's life course. From a social science perspective one can say that family, in the sense mentioned, includes parenthood. However, the majority of families we observe in the European Union consist of a combination of partnership (marriage or cohabitation) and parenthood (Tyrell and Schulze, 2000; European Commission, 2003). Moreover, the development of a family frequently begins with a love-based partnership and is completed by parenthood. Family members often share much of their everyday life and through their interactions develop a common memory of the past, establish rules and customs and collect and exchange knowledge and beliefs. However, the way (and extent to which) individual family members and the family group as a whole communicate with each other and with the outside world obviously varies from family to family.

Family members generally see each other as people who can be called upon for support (Branje *et al.*, 2002). Support among family members has three different aspects: general task sharing (e.g., preparing a meal), care and health care. General task sharing will not be dealt with here. If a person requires care, this is usually related to a lack of competence, which typically decreases in the course of childhood and youth. Roughly speaking, competence increases as people grow up and declines as they grow old. The lack of competence of children, the elderly and the infirm creates a need for care. Illness frequently means the temporary loss of a physical and/or mental faculty. Thus, care in this context means taking steps to remedy the illness and restore the lost faculty; if care is successful we can speak of a cure (Cresson, 2003/A[1]). Care and health care overlap, for example, in the case of chronic disease where a given illness cannot be cured and a person needs permanent support by at least one person (and perhaps also by a professional carer). Care and health care also overlap in that the way children are cared for teaches them how to care for themselves and for others who may need support. Receiving care as a child when growing up and when sick are very important elements of an individual's personal and health development. Moreover, both types of care are relevant to the development and maintenance of the social capital of a given population—the potential demand for professional health care on the one hand and its potential impact on the other (Kritsotakis and Gamarnikow, 2004).

Most family members 'know' whether they have a healthy or unhealthy life style and whether they are resilient or vulnerable to illness—health is a common item in surveys. The external perspective regarding differences in families' susceptibility to illness and their health-related behavior is provided by the professional observation system. Both the internal and external perspectives of the family must be looked at independently. Many diseases are left untreated because people do not take care of themselves and either do not notice symptoms of sickness or fail to respond to them. Illness may also be treated and cured within the family.

12.1.1   Health within the family

A model will now be presented in which family and health are related but which does not take the family environment into account. (This will be dealt with later.) This model (and the model following, which includes the environment of the family) is inspired by the 'family health and illness cycle' (Doherty and Campbell, 1990, cited in Doherty, 1993), the reformulation of social information-processing mechanisms (Crick and Dodge, 1994) and 'the ecology of developmental processes' (Bronfenbrenner and Morris, 1998).

To develop the model, we start from the situation of a family that does not have health problems. One day a family member notices that another member of the family has a symptom, for example, a parent detects that his/her child has a fever (1). This symptom is interpreted in the light of the standards and knowledge of one or both parents (Kankkunen *et al.*, 2003); it is eventually discussed between the parents and different responses are selected (2). A response decision is taken, for example, to apply a wet compress to reduce the fever (3). One of the parents accordingly applies the compress and informs the child what is happening to secure the child's cooperation (4). The next step is to assess the action taken and make a decision to stop, continue or change the treatment (5). To conclude our example, if the child no longer has a fever and feels well, the parent(s) can decide to take no further action. Thus, the health status quo of all family members is considered as restored. If the first or another symptom of illness is observed, the cycle from steps one through five can be resumed (*Scheme 12.1*). The resources needed by the family to deal with health matters can thus be summed up as (i) affective, (ii) cognitive and (iii) practical (Cresson, 2003/A).

We should not forget that family and health are particularly related in the situation where *no* family member is suffering from bad health, as the strongest contribution of family to health is presumed to be the family's ability to lead a successful and healthy life (Taskinen, 2003/A/B[2]). This may entail the possession of tangible goods and status, but it especially means that the members are able to live together in a manner that every member feels comfortable with. This feeling may be connected with being open and mutually supportive; it may also be connected with such adapted life-style habits as eating and drinking, and the rhythm of work, free time and rest.

Scheme 12.1. How the family deals with illness without using professional health care. A five-step model.

Family	
A group with members related by parenthood and often partnership of high mutual relevance, shared memory, interaction patterns, knowledge and beliefs. Affective, cognitive and practical resources are used to maintain health, to cure or to care.	(1) Detection and selection of symptom. (2) Interpretation of symptom. (3) Selection of a response. (4) Enactment of the response. (5) Assessment of the situation (and possibly starting again with the first step).

12.1.2 Health and family in a broad context

Having dealt with family as a health-related system exclusive of its environment, we now include in the model the external systems that are also relevant to our theme. One of the most significant aspects of the environment of a family are relatives, especially if they live nearby. They can either give support or ask for it if they are ill and need care. The same holds true for friends and sometimes also for neighbors. Systems characterized by participants being expected to deliver normed contributions (schools, paid work) are an arena for both positive and negative experiences and are thus indirectly relevant to family members' health and well-being. Also of high relevance to good health or risk of illness is the market for goods and services, for example, food and water supply and the availability of health-supporting or health-care professionals on a local, regional, national or even international level. The media must be mentioned here, as, although they are often unrelated to the local level, they act as a bridge between the family's everyday life and a global world that is not directly experienced (and thus mediated).

This bridge points to further contexts that are central to our theme. From the view of the family we can say that there is a health-care and cure system 'out there' that is fashioned according to abstract rules and regulations (Cresson, 2003/A). These rules and regulations are subject to binding decisions of the political system, be it on the national or supranational level; formal rules are implemented and controlled by law and the legal system. Of indirect relevance to health care is the economy whose fundamentals affect every family, the state budget and, within it, the health-care system. Last but not least, we must mention science as a societal system that defines knowledge about health and treatment dynamics as well as the expectations of family members with respect to what is feasible in terms of health care. Independent of the complex systems of health-care policy, the legal system, the economy and science, we must take into account beliefs that can be labeled *culture* and that may penetrate societal systems, the family environment and the

Scheme 12.2. Family and health in a broad context.

Family and its own health resources:	Environment		Culture
	Close	Distant	
– affective – cognitive – practical	– Relatives – Friends – Schools, firms	Indirectly health-related political system – Legal system – Economy – Science	Health as a very strong value
	Media		
	– Goods and services, including, for example, medical professionals and the pharmacy	Directly health-related: – Health care and cure system (professions, organizations)	

everyday life of families in different ways. Health is one of the most pervasive values (*Scheme 12.2*).

12.1.3   Relations between family and environment

The implication of *Schemes 12.1* and *12.2* is that we can, in principle, combine the five-step model of family and health with the model of the relationship between environment and health. Without going into detail, a symptom of illness perceived within the family can obviously be interpreted as a 'serious' problem needing professional medical help. If the relevant medical professional is overburdened by patient demand, this could be because the state has decided not to expand the medical services so that it can reduce the costs of medical care. Thus, the perceived health problem may be left untreated and may worsen. This shows that everyday demand can be linked to local conditions that are based on decisions made at a higher level. In the field of family and health, the micro level of the family is in indirect contact with the distant macro level of the health-care system through decisions implemented in the close environment.

This exchange between family or family members and professional health-care representatives is not necessarily successful. This is partly because at the local and more distant level the health-care system is very complex and in a state of flux and partly because the family has changed considerably within the last decades with respect to social structure (e.g., the composition of households) and cultural beliefs (e.g., as a result of international migration). In this context there are three general conditions that enhance the chance of success (cure of a given health problem or care being received in a given case). These are i) communication, ii) cooperation and iii) responsiveness (Schulze and Wirth, 1996).

Scheme 12.3. Relations between family and environment on the field of health.

Family	Close environment	Distant environment	Culture
Making use of the opportunities for health	Offering opportunities	Defining characteristics of opportunities	Values and beliefs
communication=> *cooperation=>*	*<=communication* *<=cooperation* *<=responsiveness*	Important for the responsiveness of opportunities for health care are:	Health as a strong value
		<=comprehensiveness *<=specificity* *<=accessibility*	

Here, communication means that a person presents information in such a way that the listener can understand it. Communication cannot be taken for granted, all the more so if those communicating are from different fields (for example, professional health care on the one hand and patients on the other).

Unlike the distribution of material goods, health to a large extent involves at least some kind of service. This implies that production and consumption take place simultaneously. It is this characteristic of social service delivery that requires the personal participation of clients and professionals. Moreover, the effects of health service must be regarded as coproduced. Coproduction presupposes a shared definition of the situation, complementary actions and mutual adjustment. The aspects mentioned suggest that cooperation between professionals and patients is not guaranteed.

Responsiveness is alert behavior on the part of parents to their children and, in addition, the capacity of an actor or organization to satisfy the needs of those who are dependent upon its services within a given set of rules. With respect to the health system we can mention three aspects that are related to its level of responsiveness. These are i) comprehensiveness, ii) accessibility and iii) need specificity (*Scheme 12.3*).

The relationship between the family and the professional health-care field is full of traps with poor communication, far from optimal cooperation and a low level of responsiveness. If we assume that the relationship between the family and health and between the family and the health-care (cure) system is fraught with problems, then we become less optimistic about the results of any interaction between them being positive. To put it another way, we can say that successful cooperation between lay persons or family members and health-care (cure) professionals (and the communication they have with each other) cannot be taken for granted. Moreover, lay persons and specialists in the field of health have to take into account one specific feature of health: we can do our best to live a healthy life according to well-proven standards and yet we have no guarantee of being/staying healthy or of experiencing well-being and longevity.

12.1.4 Conclusion

Our health-care model has three parts. The first places health matters exclusively within the frame of the family unit. The second presents the family within its environment and focuses on health matters at the interface of family and health-care provision. The third part deals with the exchange between family and environment.

The decision to base a health and family model on the family is supported by the assumption that it is here—and nowhere else— that the key to the further development and maintenance of health for the majority of the population lies. For economic and social reasons, the highly elaborate system of professional health care cannot be the general basis for health and health care. That is why concepts of health and family that place health matters solely in the hands of professionals are merely unrealistic ideas about the convenience of a seemingly 'all-conquering' medical profession with the potential to override the family and its health-promoting and health-care potential (Cresson, 2003/A). The closer one looks at health questions, the more the conviction grows that the relationship between the professional health-care system and the family has to be reversed.

12.2 Family and Health at Different Stages of the Life Course

The multifaceted theme of health and family can be broken down by making use of different stages of the life course and themes that are, so to speak, parallel to the life course (i.e., gender, status and social class). We will present those stages now and combine them with the other themes where possible. Where health risks, morbidity and mortality are presented quantitatively, we must realize that these data result from many interacting factors (i.e., genetic, biological, psychological, social, economic, scientific, political, technical, cultural and, last but not least, administrative and statistical (Dumon, 2003/B; Kaizeler, 2003/A; Richter, 2003/B). As there is an almost endless amount of information, the presentation must be restricted to the space available, which, of course, may make it seem somewhat arbitrary.

12.2.1 Childhood and parenthood

The symbiotic mother–child relationship during pregnancy implies that the mother's or family's role is greatest when it comes to children's health (Taskinen,

2003/A/B). From the first day of pregnancy onward, and even before that, many psychological and social factors within the family and the kin network will have an impact on the child. Traditions, attitudes, habits and subcultural beliefs of the mother-to-be and father-to-be affect the pregnancy, birth, growth and development of the child. Moreover, different types of health information contribute to shaping the emotional and cognitive atmosphere into which the child is born. The social and psychological situation of the mother is of high relevance to giving the baby a good start in life. Does the mother want to have the baby and is the baby expected with joy or indifference—or is despair, shame or hate involved? Are both sexes equally welcome, or is one sex wanted more than the other?

Frequently, an expectant mother will go through a period of ambivalence regarding her future relationship with her baby. Usually, even if the baby is not wanted initially, the feelings of the mother may mature during the pregnancy and she may come to accept the birth. Sometimes, however, her reluctance is too great. Evidence from follow-up research in Hungary in the 1980s shows that children of mothers who had applied twice for abortion but had their requests turned down on average had a lower life expectancy than their peers 20 years later. Even if the child is genuinely wanted but for the wrong reasons, for example, to save the marriage, the prognosis for a healthy life is also poor. As attachment research shows, parents are often their child's first recourse in the event of a frightening experience such as sickness. Thus, parents or those in charge of the child are of crucial importance in terms of detecting and evaluating symptoms and taking the decision to seek treatment for the child. As the cognitive, emotional and practical resources of parents are not always adequate with respect to the disease the child may be suffering from, parents can unintentionally worsen the health of the child by not consulting a doctor soon enough. If, when they were children themselves, parents did not experience sensitive and responsive care, they are at a higher risk of not responding adequately to their own child's needs. Thus, a child that, biologically, is able to have a healthy life can have a life that is fraught with physical and/or mental health problems based on parental behavior patterns that are aggravated by the developing response patterns of the child. A problematic parent–child relationship with ensuing health problems may start the other way round. If the parents experience their child as very difficult, they may often see themselves as inadequate and helpless. If this helplessness cannot be overcome with the support of experienced family members, friends or professionals, and the parents feel isolated, there is a greater risk of physical abuse or neglect of the child. Either way, the child experiences negative developmental conditions which can be the basis for fragile health. The chance of children growing up healthy is not attributable only to the parents but also to the ongoing interaction between the child and its parents.

Today, we associate the start of a human life with longevity. That a life can end long before the average age of death cannot, however, be overlooked. At a time when fertility is low, it is extremely important to protect every single child to enhance the chances of its longevity. Although many precautions are taken to make children safe, many children and young adolescents have an enhanced risk of dying.

Globally, boys have a higher risk of dying at birth and during the first year of life (Danielsson, 2003/A). In countries where infant mortality is very low, death occurs most often shortly following birth and during the neonatal period. Differences between the sexes at these early stages can hardly reflect disparities in living conditions. Instead, it must be assumed that there is a biological explanation. One such explanation is that boys are born more immature than girls even after the same length of gestation period.

Gender differences in child mortality (1 to 14 years) are primarily due to injuries. Child mortality from injuries varies a great deal between the European countries, but a male predominance is seen everywhere (*Figure 12.1*).

According to an analysis of the effects of parental leave schemes in 16 countries, Ruhm (2000) comes to the conclusion that the length of parental leave (maternity or paternity leave) affects child mortality. Prolonging the duration of parental leave by ten weeks has been shown to reduce child mortality by between 2.5 percent and 3.4 percent. The degree of mortality reduction is, however, dependent on specifics. If parental leave is *unpaid*, the length of leave shows no effect on the reduction of mortality.

12.2.2   Adolescence and young adulthood

Adolescents belong to an age group that very often live at home and are financially dependent on their parents while enjoying the increasing freedom of running their lives in their own peer-group style. As far as health is concerned, parental influence will probably prevail when the young person takes responsibility for his/her own behavior rather than being influenced by peers.

That the period from adolescence to adulthood is marked by growing mobility and the growing use of motor vehicles implies an age- and sex-specific risk for health (Danielsson [2003/A]; see also for Germany, Bien [2003/B]). *Figure 12.2* illustrates the causes of death for adolescent and young adult men. Boys and young men aged 15 to 24 had nearly three times the mortality rate of girls and women of the same age, mainly because of men's higher risk of death from traffic accidents, other accidents and suicides. Numbers in parenthesis indicate excess male risk for each cause—a '4,' for example indicates a fourfold higher mortality rate in men than women.

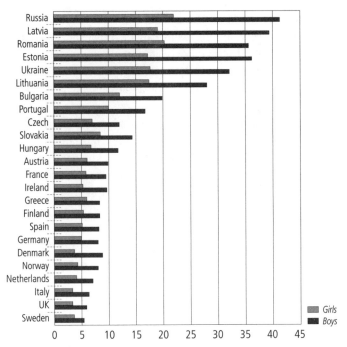

Source: Danielsson (2003/A).

Figure 12.1. Deaths caused by injury in girls and boys from 1995 to 1999 in the 1–14 age group per 100,000 children in the age group, sorted for total child mortality in this group. Several countries were omitted because of insufficient or unreliable data (Health for All [HFA], 2003).

Apart from death from accidents, physical or mental problems in many cases clearly seem to cause death in this age group. Morbidity risks can be attributed to nutritional habits, consumption of alcohol and drugs and sexual behavior. Information from the United Kingdom stresses this last aspect. Recently, the first systematic prevalence study of genital *chlamydia trachomatis* in men in the United Kingdom revealed a high incidence, particularly in the younger age groups. There has also been a rise in the rates of other sexually transmitted diseases, notably gonorrhea, while a survey of 1,077 of young people in the 11–15 age group across the United Kingdom found that the majority knew very little about how to prevent the spread of these diseases (one in ten thought that HIV/AIDS could be transmitted by kissing). Issues related to sexual health were, however, top of their list of concerns (with 66 percent worried about HIV/AIDS, 64 percent about other sexually transmitted diseases [STDs] and 61 percent about pregnancy). The Family Planning Association (FPA), which launched a Contraception Awareness Week in the United Kingdom

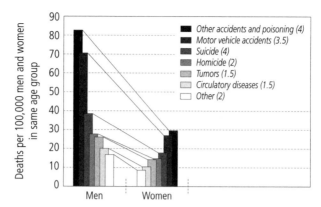

Source: Danielsson (2003/A), Processing of European 'Health for All' database, World Health Organization, Regional Office for Europe.

Figure 12.2. Gender differences in mortality from different causes among 15–24 age group in the EU, 1999.

in 2002, has used this information to argue that government-backed, single-issue, health-promotion campaigns have clearly failed and that many parents still do not discuss sex with their children. As a result, the FPA believes that a public health strategy aimed at young people is needed which would take a more holistic approach to sexual health rather than simply focusing on tackling infections (Roberts, 2003/B).

12.2.3 Adulthood: Gender differences in morbidity of adults

We now turn to adults belonging to the age groups that, to a high degree, participate in paid work. In almost all (80–90 percent) of European countries, more women than men perceive their health as bad. This is true for the 15–24, 25–44 and 45–64 age groups for which comparative data exist. As the same methodology is used for both sexes in each country, valid comparisons can be made among them.

Why is there a difference in perceived health between the sexes? Perceived illness is essentially subjective; it is impossible to measure objectively how ill someone is. Nevertheless, it could be interesting to relate these differences to what we know about gender differences in terms of different diseases and the extent to which they can be explained by differences in measurable morbidity.

In previous studies, three major areas of significance were found for gender-specific morbidity in a public health perspective that differed substantially between women and men (Danielsson and Lindberg, 2001). These studies could also be of relevance for other European countries, as gender differences exist in most European countries, even though their level may vary.

The first area is that of *musculoskeletal* ailments, which are very common. As well as reporting more back, neck and joint pain, women are also more likely to be hospitalized for such problems, take more painkillers and receive disability retirement for musculoskeletal illnesses. All these indicators are, of course, highly imperfect measures of gender differences in disease, as they could all be affected by other gender-differentiating circumstances such as type of work, propensity for reporting symptoms and so on. However, studies of functional ability among old persons using simple tests such as picking up an object from the floor have revealed a greater impairment among women. Old women also report more disability than men of the same age. It seems altogether likely that there are important and real gender differences in morbidity in this area.

Research in occupational medicine in Sweden has demonstrated that gender differences in working conditions and occupation are of major significance for explaining these differences. Women, to a higher degree than men, tend to remain stuck in relatively monotonous jobs that involve substantial physical work. There are also important gender differences when it comes to psychosocial conditions at work. In general, women have less opportunity compared with men to determine their work pace; they receive less help and support from their superior(s), more often perceive their work as stressful and have little influence on how it is structured. When comparing men and women with equal working conditions with regard to stress control and physical load, the most typical finding is that there are practically no gender differences in musculoskeletal complaints. Women's subordinate position in paid work and the fact that the majority do the lion's share of housework is thus a likely cause of women's higher morbidity in this area (see also, Schulze [2003/A/B]).

The second area is psychological disorders and psychiatric diseases. From school age to old age, far more women than men in Europe state that they suffer from psychological complaints, such as anxiety, fatigue, headaches and disturbed sleep, and in general, there are more women than men suffering from varying degrees of depression, which seems to be a consistent finding in different parts of the world. In all European countries, more men than women commit suicide, which seems to be the case globally, except for rural China. Worldwide, more men than women are imprisoned, and many prisoners suffer from psychological and psychiatric disorders. It is difficult to say who suffers more from psychological disorders—men or women. It depends on what is considered a psychological disorder and whether these observations truly reflect gender differences in psychological distress levels. Nevertheless, men and women exhibit consistently different patterns—patterns that are also linked to gender differences in physical health.

The third area that contributes to gender differences in health are problems connected with women's reproductive functions. Globally, illnesses connected to childbearing and giving birth, as well as abortion, are of immense importance in terms of female morbidity and a major cause of premature mortality. This is also the case with sexually transmitted diseases, not least HIV/AIDS, which are now impacting more women than men in heavily affected countries. Excluding hospitalizations from complications of pregnancy and delivery, research in Stockholm County, Sweden, revealed that only about 10 percent more women than men between 25 and 44 years of age were hospitalized. If all treatment for gynecological problems is excluded from the comparison, we find that 6 percent more men were hospitalized in this age group for injuries and alcohol-related illnesses.

As well as these three areas that can, to some extent, be captured in routine medical statistics, there is another important cause and outcome of gender disparities in perceived health and morbidity—male violence against women. Although gender violence is a significant cause of female morbidity and mortality, it is almost never seen as a public health issue. World Bank estimates of the global burden of disease indicate that in established market economies, gender-based victimization is responsible for one in every five working days lost to women of reproductive age (Heise *et al.*, 1994).

If we conclude that women are indeed more likely to be sick, is it then a paradox that they live longer than men? The greater longevity of women despite higher rates of illness is undoubtedly related to different illness patterns. For example, women's higher rates of ailments associated with the musculoskeletal system are only weakly related to increased mortality.

12.2.4 Adulthood: Marriage, divorce, widowhood and health

Married people have lower rates of mortality, morbidity and mental disorders than the unmarried; this has been attributed to either marriage selection or the protective effects of marriage (Gore, 1973). The former explanation involves healthier people being selected into marriage; the health-protective effects of marriage supposedly work through one or more pathways, including regulation of health-risk behaviors, social integration and greater economic resources. While earlier research tended to favor the health-protective hypothesis, more recent research finds evidence for the operation of both processes—selection and protection (Beckett and Elliot, 2002); however, most of this literature is from the United States, and selection may be less significant in Europe. The relative strength of these processes at different ages is unclear, but a number of studies have concluded that marriage is more significantly related to the physical and mental health of men than women (Anderson, 2003/A).

One study in the United Kingdom looked at the health status of the whole population aged 15 or over, based upon census data for a 20-year period and using bed occupancy in health and social care facilities as a proxy for ill health (Prior and Hayes, 2001). The study concluded that married men and women are healthier than unmarried people and that the strength of this relationship had increased from the 1970s. It also reported that, within the unmarried population, the widowed are most at risk among women and the single are most at risk among men. In a prospective two-year study of a national population of middle-aged adults in the United States (Beckett and Elliot, 2002), the beneficial effects of marriage were again confirmed but were very largely explained by initial health and socioeconomic differences. Finally, a nationally representative study of adults in England aged 65 to 84 also emphasized that socioeconomic indicators were most consistently related to health (Roberts, 2003/B), while marital status was not clearly associated with health status—perhaps reflecting the exclusion of (the relatively smaller number) in institutional care (Grundy and Slogett, 2003).

The causes of the relative benefits of marriage for men and women are complex. Among the complicating factors it may be that selection into marriage is not only in favor of healthier men. In one study tracking 4,000 men over a 22-year period (Lillard and Paris, 1996), there was evidence that healthier men tended to marry later and to postpone remarriage while relatively unhealthy men tended to pursue marriage more actively and to be more likely to remarry following a divorce or the death of a spouse. The authors argue that this supports the idea that the health status of men affects their marital decisions.

There appears to be more consistent support for the hypothesis that a stable marital relationship protects the mental health of men and women. However, men and women respond to marital transitions with different types of emotional problems (Simon, 2002). Likewise, a study of older adults in the Health Survey for England (Grundy and Slogett, 2003) reports that social resources (marital status and social support) had the greatest impact on the assessment of psychological health and also contributed significantly to variations in overall self-rated health.

The ending of marital relationships, specifically widowhood, appears to be a key risk factor for poor health and death. The Finnish study of Martikainen and Valkonen (1996) reports that, on average, men have a 21 percent higher risk of dying after the death of their spouse than do married men of the same age, while for women the mortality risk is 9 percent higher after the death of their husband.

One must, however, go beyond analyses of marital status to consider household composition or living arrangements, which better reflect the domestic context influencing health. A longitudinal Danish study (Lund et al., 2002) suggests that cohabitation status accounts for more of the variation in mortality than marital status. An analysis of data from the first two waves of the United States Health and Retirement Study (Hughes and Waite, 2002) finds prospective links between household structure, mobility limitations and depressive symptoms—perhaps not surprisingly, married couples living alone or with their children are the most advantaged, while single women living with children appear disadvantaged on all health outcomes (Bernhardt, 2003/B).

The relevance of interaction patterns within marriage for the respective health of the spouses becomes clear when we see that positive social relations have discernible consequences for physiological processes (Uchino *et al.*, 1996). It can be shown that negative behavior during marital conflict is associated with immunological down-regulation (Kiecolt-Glaser *et al.*, 2003). In other words, we have biological evidence that the quality of social relations has an impact on health, that is independent of personal perceptions.

12.2.5 Mortality of middle-aged adults

Men between 35 and 44 have double the mortality rate of women. Excessive male mortality in accidents and suicides are of the same magnitude as in the younger age group, but other causes of death become more important killers. In this relatively young age group, diseases of the circulatory system (heart disease and stroke) begin to be an important killer of men, but tumors cause more deaths among women than men. Tumors are, in fact, the only major public health diseases in Europe that cause more premature deaths among women than men, but this holds only up to the age of 50. The excess mortality is due to breast and uterine cancers.

Between 55 and 64 years of age, men still have double the mortality rate of women, mainly because of tumors and circulatory diseases. Women's elevated risk is due to breast and uterine cancer, while men's higher risk of dying of tumors is due to lung cancer (Danielsson, 2003/A; see also Bonke, 2003/B).

12.2.6 Old age and kin relations

Assuming the costs of care are shouldered by the family, care within the family of older people can be viewed as a cost-reducing factor by governments. Care can be costly for families in practical, economic, social and emotional terms, but it can also be financially costly for a government to support the family (Phillips, 2003/A; see also Martin, 2003/A/B). To provide an insight into private and organized care and the relationship between them, some general results regarding the support of older people by family members are now presented from the project 'Old Age and Autonomy: The Role of Service Systems and Intergenerational Solidarity' (OASIS), which took place in five countries (England, Israel, Germany, Norway and Spain) and represented a diverse range of welfare regimes and different family cultures:

1. The OASIS study confirms that the family is the bedrock of care provision. Even in countries such as Norway where there is wide-ranging service provision by the state, the family still has an important role to play.
2. The second significant factor of change in the family context is heterogeneity in family structure and living arrangements (Kaufmann *et al.*, 2002). Complexity and diversity are the key contexts in which care is negotiated. All these factors will have an impact on the well-being and health of older people and their carers.
3. The quality of intergenerational relationships, one of the most important elements influencing subjective well-being, will affect the health of the family and the quality of life of older people. There was little evidence in the survey of conflict in intergenerational relationships, although in face-to-face interviews this did emerge as a 'hidden' dimension.
4. Ambivalent feelings between parents and children emerged more in the face-to-face interviews, with older people experiencing such feelings during periods of chronic illness and disability when roles were renegotiated (Lowenstein and Ogg, 2003).

The OASIS study also aimed to explore the extent to which solidarity, conflict and ambivalence were experienced in parent–child relationships, particularly during periods when such decisions and renegotiations about care arrangements took place. Different styles of parent–child relationships were examined, and four styles were identified:

1. *Harmonious* relationships (24 percent), characterized by parents feeling extremely close to their child.
2. *Steady* family relationships, the largest category, representing 32 percent of parents. These parent–child relationships were more emotionally distant than the first group but still close.
3. *Ambivalent* family relationships, the second largest group, representing 27 percent of parents. These parents tended to feel neither emotionally close to nor distant from their children. Occasionally, the relationships in this group could have unpleasant moments, but there were attempts to keep the family harmonious.
4. In the *distant* group (17 percent), relationships showed signs of emotional distancing, and there was more likely to be conflict, mixed feelings and a difference of viewpoint.

There were clear age, country and gender differences relating to the dimensions of quality of life. Health, income and education were universally important for people's subjective quality of life, regardless of age. Intergenerational relationships were positively related to two quality-of-life dimensions: physical health and psychological well-being. This effect seems to be especially strong when elderly parents have one or two children compared to none. Family networks had limited relevance for quality of life. Help from families and services were negatively related to quality of life, probably because these were not sufficient to compensate for needs and dependencies. The authors conclude that strengthening the individual resources of older people is crucial in terms of supporting their autonomy and quality of life.

12.2.7   Mortality of people older than 65 years

More and more people are living longer (e.g., Bagavos, 2003/B), and there are some typical findings about the last phase of our life.

In all age groups above 65, men have a greater risk of dying than women of the same age, in other words, more men die each year than women. The actual number of men who die keeps decreasing compared to women, as the male population is shrinking faster than the female population. Cancer and circulatory diseases are the main causes of death for both sexes. Men's shorter life span results largely from accidents, violence, alcohol abuse, smoking and suicide and is closely associated with risky behaviors. Cancer is the only significant cause of death in Europe that afflicts more women than men (to the age of 50). Breast and uterine cancers are linked to physical rather than behavioral disparities between the sexes.

12.3   Features of the Health-Care Systems in the EU

The organized national health-care systems are quite different. Two aspects will be used to illustrate this: the funding source and one of the input factors of the primary care system, namely, the number of physicians and consultations.

There are two types of health-care systems in the EU. One type is tax-based (Denmark, Finland, Ireland, Italy, Portugal, Sweden, United Kingdom) and the other type is insurance-based (France, Germany, Luxembourg, The Netherlands) (see *Scheme 12.4*). Some national systems are clearly a mix of both systems (Austria, Belgium, Greece; for these clusters see Graph 49 in European Commission [2003, p. 73]). Moreover, on average, all people in all countries spend some private money on additional health care (in Luxembourg and the United Kingdom, private spending is low; in Italy and Portugal, private spending is relatively high). This leads us to assume that level of health and the socioeconomic situation of the family are negatively associated (Sgritta, 2003/B).

Scheme 12.4. Tax-financed and social health-insurance systems: Basic features.

	Taxation	Social Health Insurance
Entitlement based on:	Citizenship	Contributions
Levied on:	All income/transactions	Wages
Benefits are:	Comprehensive in theory (implicit rationing)	Defined (explicit rationing)
Choice:	Usually no choice of insurer Some choice of provider	Some choice of insurer possible Some choice of provider
Controlled by:	State/government	Independent funds, including representatives of trade unions and employers

Source: Mossialos (2003/A).

During the last decade one of the outstanding themes in all national debates was that health system costs could no longer be covered. The intention to contain or reduce costs showed different pathways.

In tax-based systems this has meant the establishment of internal-market-type mechanisms, thereby forcing a split between purchasers and providers. In mandatory social insurance systems, it has meant allowing individual insurance funds to compete for patients and patients to freely choose insurance funds, while universal access is maintained. The process of ongoing reforms and its effects are under-researched.

There are considerable differences in the primary care systems of different EU nations in terms of one of the input factors—the number of physicians per 100,000 inhabitants. While Italy has about 600 physicians, Ireland and the United Kingdom have close to 200 physicians for the same reference population. That the highest provision is about three times the lowest underlines the big variations in this field. The number of times general practitioners and medical specialists are consulted shows the same tendency and is obviously associated with access regulations. While in some countries, patients must be referred to a medical specialist by a general practitioner ('the gatekeeper principle'), in other countries both can be approached independently by a patient. Thus, frequency of consultancy differs greatly (European Commission, 2003, p. 74).

More research about the effectiveness of different national health systems is needed urgently. To date, research has been scarce, and we do not know which system produces more health at a given price. If health budgets are high and rising, then more evidence-based knowledge on this subject is clearly required.

12.4 Relationship between Family, the Organized Health-Care System and EU Policy

12.4.1 Three examples of the relations between the distant environment and family health

In our model, the interaction between the formal health-care (cure) system and the family is indicated in general terms. Three aspects are presented, and the section finishes with former and actual perspectives of the EU with respect to health matters.

The reorganization of a health system has an impact at the macro and micro level. As qualitative research from Portugal shows, it is not easy to navigate the world of the organized and differentiated health-care system, but if this system is under reconstruction, then the knowledge base of the network members deteriorates and finding a timely remedy becomes increasingly difficult (Carapinheiro, 2003/B). This should be a warning against introducing reforms without adequately taking into account the perspective of the users, as not to do so is detrimental to the objective of improving the state of health of a given population. Moreover, from the perspective of the family that requires professional health care, it also contravenes the criteria of communication, cooperation and responsiveness (see *Scheme 12.3* above) (Borsenberger, 2003/B).

Our next example, which justifies the model of health and family, is of the relationship between tax income at the national level, funding for elderly-care programs and the allocation of care responsibilities (Bernhardt, 2003/B). In the 1960s and 1970s, the Swedish state took over a substantial part of what families had done in terms of care for the elderly; there was a 'substitution' effect wherever family care was replaced by different forms of official care. In the last two decades, and in particular in the 1990s, there has been a reversal of the previous trend of substituting public care for family care, a *resubstitution* process where both home help and institutional care have been cut back substantially. Nationally representative surveys of care for elderly people living in the community (i.e., not institutionalized) demonstrate that reduced public services have been matched by increased input from families, hence the reversed substitution effect (Sundström *et al.*, 2003). Surveys show that today, home help users tend to be very old, frail and living alone, but with relatively small social-class differences (National Board of Health and Welfare, 2000).

Every system puts up boundaries and excludes those who have no right to access; thus, the formally organized health system is designed to be inclusive and exclusive (Fernández de la Hoz, 2003/A; see Richardson [2003/B]). But, for example, what are the criteria for being accepted in so-called universal systems? Typically, migrants or nonnationals have no access or not the same access to the health-care system as regular citizens. If a health-care system is based on insurance, then those who do not pay insurance (or have no rights derived from the membership of a relative) are excluded from the services and products that these offer. As we know, health-care systems are under pressure and costs have to be reduced. This encourages not only the reduction of membership but actual exclusion. Denial of membership can be based, for example, on nationality, income, employment and handicap (Bagavos, 2003/B); or it can mean reduction in services or a combination of both strategies. The resultant inequalities may have consequences for the health status of socioeconomically divergent groups (Sgritta, 2003/B).

12.4.2   Health and EU policy

The political system (see *Scheme 12.2*) itself is differentiated, containing a local, very often a regional and always a national level—and now, with the EU, another political level has been added. Since the 1993 signing of the Treaty of Maastricht, we can speak of an EU public-health policy. This first step was continued, and in May 2000 the Commission proposed a new and integrated European Community health strategy (COM, 2000, 285 final of 16.5.2000), in which health matters are seen as a part of social protection, and the latter is defined as a means of ensuring efficient and dynamic modern economies.

The guidelines for health care and long-term care for the elderly can be summarized in three points: access for all, regardless of income or wealth; a high level quality of care; and financial sustainability of care systems.

As these aims imply, financial challenges can no longer be the only basis for assessing the health system. 'To be effective, reform must also ensure that policies continues to be imbedded in solidarity and basic values of society' (Fotakis, 2003/A, p. 18). The guidelines make it clear that the EU has far-reaching and noble aims. Sharing those goals, however, does not mean ignoring obstacles on the way to achieving them. Some of those obstacles will be mentioned here.

The EU perspectives are universal and the national political systems and health-care systems are divergent; the problem arises as to whether universal measures can be translated into equivalent national, regional and local steps of implementation. Moreover, it was the success of the health-care system in the past—better health and longevity—that brought about, inter alia, the financial difficulties being faced everywhere. We may assume that the very success of the organized health system is one of its greatest challenges. If treatment improvement is positively rewarded by success, people will expect more and more from the health system and, moreover, their expectations will be raised by the scientific success stories disseminated by the media. Thus, the internalization of health care and long-term care for the elderly:

> ... may also increase the risk that the perspective of individual clients becomes lost, unless client-related standards of responsiveness are included in the operational guidelines of European programs, and unless social service research provides systematic and comparative information on service needs, offers and impacts with regard to the improvement of the actual living conditions of social service users and their families (Schulze and Wirth, 1996, p. 13).

There are several stimuli that keep the formal health system in a state of flux, and to date, a sustainable equilibrium has not been reached.

This brings us back to family with its fundamental partnership and parenthood values. We must support family not only as a health and prevention 'system' but also as an institution that applies values and rules to health provision, ensuring that it is fair and thus benefits all members of a community during their life course.

Notes

1.   All references marked /A refer to papers presented at the symposium, 'The Family in the Health System—A Cost-Raising or Cost-Reducing Factor?' held in Tutzing, Germany in June 2003.

2.   All references marked /B refer to Focus Monitoring Reports written by or on behalf of members of the European Observatory for The Social Situation, Demography and Family.

References

Beckett, M.K. and Elliot, M.N. (2002) *Does the Association between Marital Status and Health Vary by Sex, Race and Ethnicity?* Santa Monica, CA, USA: RAND Corporation.

Branje, S.J.T., Van Aken, M.A.G. and Van Lieshout, C.F.M. (2002) 'Relational Support in Families with Adolescents,' *Journal of Family Psychology*, **16**(3):351–362.

Bronfenbrenner, U. and Morris, P. (1998) 'The Ecology of Developmental Processes,' in Damon, W. and Lerner, R.M. (eds) *Handbook of Child Psychology, Volume 1: Theoretical Models of Human Development*, New York, USA: John Wiley and Sons, pp. 993–1028.

Crick, N.R. and Dodge, K.A. (1994) 'A Review and Reformulation of Social Imformation-Processing Mechanisms in Children's Social Adjustment,' *Psychological Bulletin* **115**: 74–101.

Danielsson, M. and Lindberg, G. (2001) 'Differences between Men's and Women's Health: The Old and the New Gender Paradox,' in Östlin, P., Danielsson, M., Diderichsen, F., Härenstam, A. and Lindberg, G., *Gender Inequalities in Health. A Swedish Perspective*, Boston, MA, USA: Harvard University Press.

Doherty, W. (1993) 'I'm O.K., You're O.K., but What about the Kids?' *The Family Therapy Networker*, **17**: 46–53.

Doherty, W. and Campell, T.L. (1990) *Families and Health*, Newbury Park, CA, USA: Sage Publications.

European Commission (2003) *The Social Situation in the European Union 2003*, Luxembourg: Office for Official Publications of the European Communities.

Gore, W.R. (1973) 'Sex, Marital Status and Mortality,' *American Journal of Sociology*, **79**(1):45–67.

Grundy, E. and Slogett, A. (2003) 'Health Inequalities in the Older Population: The Role of Personal Capital, Social Resources and Socio-economic Circumstances,' *Social Science and Medicine*, **56**(5):935–947.

Heise, L., Pitanguy, J. and Germain, A. (1994) 'Violence Against Women: The Hidden Health Burden,' *World Bank Discussion Papers, 255*, Washington, D.C., USA: The World Bank.

HFA (2003) European 'Health for All' database, 2002, World Health Organization, Regional Office for Europe, See http://www.euro-who-int/hfadb/ accessed in February 2006.

Hughes, M.E. and Waite, L.J. (2002) 'Health in Household Context: Living Arrangements and Health in Late Middle Age,' *Journal of Health and Social Behavior*, **43**(1): 1–21.

Kaufmann, F.-X., Kuijsten, A., Schulze, H.-J. and Strohmeier, K.P. (eds) (2002) *Family Life and Family Policies in Europe. Problems and Issues in Comparative Perspective*, vol 2, Oxford, UK: Clarendon Press.

Kankkunen, P.M., Vehviläinen-Julkunen, K.M., Pietilä, A.-M.K. and Halonen, P.M. (2003) 'Parents' perceptions of their 1–6-year-old children's pain,' *European Journal of Pain*, **7**(3):203-211.

Kiecolt-Glaser, J.K., Bane, C., Glaser, R. and Malarkey, W.B. (2003) 'Love, Marriage, and Divorce: Newlyweds' Stress Hormones Foreshadow Relationship Changes,' *Journal of Consulting and Clinical Psychology*, **71**(1): 176–188.

Kritsotakis, G. and Gamarnikow, E. (2004) 'What Is Social Capital and How Does It Relate to Health?' *International Journal of Nursing Studies*, **41**: 43–50.

Lillard, L. E. and Paris, C.W.A. (1996) 'Marital Status and Mortality: The Role of Health,' *Demography*, **33**(3): 313–327.

Lowenstein, A. and Ogg, J. (eds) (2003) *Old Age and Autonomy: The Role of Service Systems and Intergenerational Family Solidarity*, University of Haifa, Israel: OASIS Final Report.

Lund, R., Due, P. and Madvig, J. (2002) 'Cohabitation and Marital Status as Predictors of Mortality—An Eight Year Follow-up Study,' *Social Science and Medicine*, **55**(4): 673–679.

Martikainen, P. and Valkonen, T. (1996) 'Mortality after Death of Spouse by Cause of Death,' *American Journal of Public Health*, **86**: 1087–1093.

National Board of Health and Welfare (2000) 'Bo hemma pääldre dar' ['Living at Home in Old Age'], *Äldreuppdraget*, 2000:11, Stockholm, Sweden: The National Board of Health and Welfare (Socialstyrelsen) [in Swedish].

Prior, P.M. and Hayes, B.C. (2001) 'Marital Status and Bed Occupancy in Health and Social Care Facilities in the United Kingdom,' *Public Health*, **115**(6): 401–406.

Ruhm, C. J. (2000) 'Parental Leave and Child Health,' *Journal of Health Economics*, **19**(6): 931–960.

Schulze, H.-J. and Wirth, W. (1996) 'Social Services and Their Users: The Role of Communication, Co-operation and Responsiveness,' in Schulze, H.-J. and Wirth, W. (eds) *Who cares? Social Service Organizations and Their Users*, London, UK: Cassell, pp. 3–14.

Simon, R. W. (2002) 'Revisiting the Relationships among Gender, Marital Status and Mental Health,' *American Journal of Sociology*, **107**: 1065–1096.

Sundström, G., Lennarth J. and Hassing, L. (2003) 'State Provision Down, Off-spring's Up: The Reverse Substitution of Old-age Care in Sweden,' *Ageing and Society*, **23**(3): 269–280.

Tyrell, H. and Schulze, H.-J. (2000) 'Stability of Parenthood and Instability of Partnership,' in Schulze, H.-J. (ed) *Stability and Complexity: Perspectives for a Child-Oriented Family Policy*, Amsterdam, The Netherlands; Oxford, UK; Boston, MA, USA: VU University Press pp. 201–219.

Uchino, B.N., Cacioppo, J.T. and Kiecolt-Glaser, J.K. (1996) 'The Relationship between Social Support and Physiological Processes: A Review with Emphasis on Underlying Mechanisms and Implications for Health,' *Psychological Bulletin*, **119**: 488–531.

Zimmet, P., Alberti, K.G. and Shaw, J. (2001) 'Global and Societal Implications of the Diabetes Epidemic,' *Nature*, **414**: 782–787.

/A

Papers presented at the symposium, 'The Family in the Health System—A Cost-Raising or Cost-Reducing Factor?' held in Tutzing, Germany in June 2003, cited in the text:

Anderson, R. 'Health Risks and Resources in the Life Course and in Different Living Arrangements.'

Cresson, G. 'Families and Health Care.'

Danielsson, M. 'A Gender Perspective on Health in Europe.'

Fernández de la Hoz, P. 'Familienleben: Gesundheitsressourcen und -risiken aus der Perspektive der sozialen Inklusion.'

Fotakis, C. 'Recent Developments On European Policies in the Area Of Health.'

Kaizeler, I. 'Health in the EU: Looking Beyond Healthcare—Social Situation Report 2003.'

Martin, C. 'Family: A Problem or a Solution for the Well-Being of People? Comment on the Two Preceding Papers.'

Mossialos, E. 'Health Care Reforms in the EU (PowerPoint presentation).'

Phillips, J. 'The Role of Formal and Family Support in the Care of Older People.'

Schulze, H.-J. 'Comment on the Three Preceding Papers.'

Taskinen, S. 'The Family as Health-Care Agent: A Psychological Perspective.'

/B

Focus Monitoring Reports written by or on behalf of members of the European Observatory for The Social Situation, Demography and Family. The author and the country reported on are presented in alphabetical order:

Bagavos, C. (Greece); Bernhardt, E. (Sweden); Bien, W. (Germany); Bonke, J. (Denmark); Borsenberger, M. (Luxembourg); Carapinheiro, G. (Portugal); Dumon, W. (Belgium); Martin, C. (France); Richardson, V. (Ireland); Richter, R. (Austria); Roberts, C. (United Kingdom); Schulze, H.J. (The Netherlands); Sgritta, G. (Italy); Taskinen, S. (Finland).

Chapter 13

The Polish Health System in Europe: Situation, Reforms and Challenges

Christoph Sowada

13.1 Introduction

On 1 May 2004 the European Union (EU) grew by a further ten countries. For the eight countries that were part of the former eastern bloc, accession constituted another step toward economic and social transformation. That transformation, however, though it has meant a return to democracy and a market economy, has also caused social tensions, difficulties and problems that are particularly evident in the health-care system. In common with the 'old' EU15 member states, the newly acceded states have repeatedly been forced to reform their health systems. For these new members, however, reform is all the more difficult. In spite of enjoying relatively strong economic growth, they have considerably fewer resources available to cope with such challenges than the EU15 has. Compounding the difficulties are the numerous problems left over from the Communist era, as well as country-specific organizational, financial and social challenges.

This chapter discusses the state of the health system in the largest of the new member states, Poland. The Polish system appears to be a particularly complex one, with two health-care reforms, in 1999 and 2003, having been perceived as

Table 13.1. Financing of health-care systems in the CEE accession states in 2000.

Country	GDP share	Share of public spending	Share of private spending	Per capita expenditure in US$ (PPP*)
Czech Republic	7.2	91.4	8.6	942
Estonia	6.1	76.7	23.3	426
Hungary	6.8	75.7	24.3	640
Latvia	5.9	60.0	40.0	239
Lithuania	6.0	72.4	27.6	304
Poland	6.0	69.7	30.3	403
Slovakia	5.9	89.6	10.4	618
Slovenia	8.6	78.9	21.1	1,154

Note: *PPP = purchasing power parity.
Source: World Health Organization (2002).

failures by the population. Health facilities are deteriorating rapidly in Poland; patients are facing long waiting periods and, frequently, poor service. Among politicians, a feeling of helplessness and hopelessness prevails. The situation was further
aggravated when the Polish constitutional court held the Insurance Act, the most
important law governing the health sector, to be unconstitutional.

This chapter has five sections: an introduction and short comparative survey
of health systems in the central and eastern European (CEE) accession states; a
concise overview of the Polish health system; a review of the current problems and
the latest discussions on reform; a consideration of the challenges arising from EU
enlargement for the whole EU and for the EU15 specifically; and a short summary
and conclusions. There are two Annexes. *Annex 1* provides health-care statistics
for Poland in tabular form. *Annex 2* gives a list of the country's major health-care-
related legal instruments.

13.2   Health Systems in the CEE Accession States

Fifteen years after the beginning of the transformation of the central and eastern
European states, the CEE health systems have lost all resemblance to the socialist Siemaszko model. All new members of the EU from the CEE have introduced
health-insurance systems modeled along Bismarckian lines, although there are obvious differences among the individual systems, especially in structural terms. With
regard to health-care financing, a key role is assumed by public funding, but in some
states the percentage of private funding is markedly higher than the EU average. As,
with the exception of Slovenia, private health-insurance schemes are a negligible
factor, the share of informal contributions to health-care financing is relatively high
(see *Table 13.1*) (Murthy and Mossialos, 2003).

In none of the CEEs is there is any formal limitation of note on the scope of guaranteed benefits. The right to benefits typically follows the obtaining of insured status; in the Czech Republic and Slovakia, insured status is based on permanent residence, and in Slovenia on citizenship. In actual day-to-day practice, however, this inherent generosity comes up against serious budgetary restrictions that, combined with the structural weaknesses of the system and widespread corruption, are responsible for implicit rationing and unequal access to health benefits. Moreover, affluent citizens can expect better and more rapid services by paying for them out of their own pockets (Alber and Köhler, 2004).

13.3   The Polish Health System: Structure and Financing

In recent years the Polish health system has undergone two thorough reforms. The General Health Insurance Act, which entered into force on 1 January 1999, provided for 17 independent health-insurance bodies to manage the financing of health care. In April 2003 financing was recentralized by the National Health Fund Insurance Act, but this Act was declared unconstitutional in January 2004 and amendments were required by the end of 2004. The new Law on Health-Care Services Financed from Public Funds was passed by parliament in August 2004. This law is now the key legal foundation of the Polish health-care system, together with the Health-Care Facilities Act (1991).

Numerous reforms, full of gaping holes, are responsible for the current system being a rather chaotic mix of decentralized and centralized, bureaucratic and market-oriented and legal, semilegal and totally unofficial solutions. Hence the organizational complexity of the sector as a whole (see *Figure 13.1*).

13.3.1   Health-care providers

Polish patients have a choice of public and private health-care facilities, and these have had equal standing since 1991. Basic outpatient care is usually provided by so-called first-contact physicians, comparable to the family doctor in other countries, many of whom run private surgeries. Basic medical services are also offered at public facilities, especially in urban areas.

The reform of 1999 assigned a 'gatekeeper' function to the first-contact physicians—with access to specialists and hospitals (with very few exceptions) requiring referral by a first-contact physician or other general practitioner [GP]). Subsequently, there was a policy reversal, and the list of specialists who can be consulted directly (i.e., without referral by a GP) has once again been substantially extended.

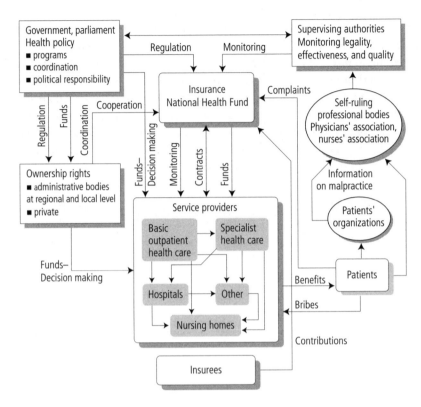

Figure 13.1. Structure of the Polish health system.

Insurees are free to choose their own GP and change him/her every six months without paying a fee. Specialists can similarly be chosen at the patient's own discretion, although the patient does need to be referred by a physician contracted to the National Health Fund. Specialist care is provided by private and public facilities, with private surgeries dominating in some fields (such as dentistry). In general, Poland can boast of an adequate number of well-educated specialists, with only a few fields (anesthetics, physiotherapy, gerontology) and the regions suffering from shortages (see *Table 13.2*).

Only about 60 out of a total of 730 Polish general hospitals[1] are privately run. Most public hospitals are managed by regional and local government authorities.[2] Added to these are university hospitals, scientific institutes, practical institutes and specialist hospitals that usually report directly to the health ministry. In theory, patients can choose from among all the hospitals that are contracted to the National Health Fund. In practice, however, they tend to choose the nearest hospital to where they live.

Table 13.2. Resources of the Polish health system, 1990–2003.

	1990	1995	2003
Physicians per 10,000 inhabitants	21.4	23.2	23.0
Dentists per 10,000 inhabitants	4.8	4.6	3.6
Pharmacists per 10,000 inhabitants	4.0	5.0	6.3
Nurses per 10,000 inhabitants	54.7	54.8	48.1
Midwives per 10,000 inhabitants	6.3	6.3	5.6
General hospitals	677	705	732
—of which public		696	660
Hospital beds per 10,000 inhabitants	57.2	55.4	48.7

Source: GUS (2004a).

The first-contact physicians are paid on a pro rata basis by the number of patients registered with them and have to cover their costs from these payments. For a time, the National Health Fund required its physicians to spend at least 10 percent of their fees on basic patient diagnostic examinations. Outpatient specialists are usually paid in terms of services rendered or number of patients treated. The National Health Fund limits the scope of services/examinations provided, especially those of the expensive kind. Hospital services are also limited. Initially (until 1999), hospitals received lump-sum daily fees; they were then paid, as a rule, according to the number of patients referred to them, with payment rates based on the treatment duration and type of hospital department. When hospitals exceeded their patient quotas, the cost of treating 'excess patients' was refunded only in part or not at all. From 2004 payments were made on the basis of treatment type. This made for a complex mixture of fees for service and diagnosis-related groups that required an inordinate amount of administrative backup.

13.3.2   State institutions and regional administrative bodies

According to the Polish constitution, the state is responsible for health-care provision. In 1999, however, the government backed out of its responsibility by introducing a social health-insurance scheme, under which the country was divided into 16 'health districts' (UNUZ, 2001). Between 1999 and 2002 there was no sign of any state health policy in Poland nor of any coordination and control of the activities of the health-insurance schemes (Sowada, 2000 and 2003). In 2003 the schemes were dissolved and the system was centralized under the 'manual' control of the health minister, which further destabilized the situation.

Nor has the government been much better at fulfilling its financial duties. Some special benefits, such as transfers and restructuring programs, are financed from the state budget, but funds are inadequate and there is enormous wastage of those funds that are available.

There is also failure at the regional and local government levels, with the stakeholders—the local, district and voivodship[3] bodies— being unwilling to fulfill their obligations. Their lack of interest in facilities whose cost they are unable to cover, a shortage of financial and human resources, a lack of political will to privatize the facilities and disastrous legal loopholes are plunging public-health facilities into chaos and debt.

13.3.3 Health insurance

Until April 2003 the social health-insurance system consisted of one sectoral and 16 regional health-insurance schemes; it currently consists of a central health fund with 16 regional subsidiaries. General health insurance is mandatory and applies to almost 100 percent of the Polish population. Obligatory insurees are divided into 35 professional and social groups, and family members (children, spouses, parents and grandparents) are coinsured for as long as they themselves are not subject to mandatory insurance and live in the same household as the main insuree. Anyone living off investment income, the sale of assets, inheritance or other 'profits' is exempt from the mandatory insurance scheme. Persons not covered by mandatory schemes may make voluntary insurance contributions. For the last several years, however, there has been a rise in the number of persons without an official income who are uninsured (e.g., workers in the shadow economy and the homeless).

Insurance funds are derived mainly from earnings-based contributions made by mandatory insurees. In 2006 contributions were 8.75 percent, with rates due to increase annually by a quarter of a percentage point until 2007. Contributions of up to 7.75 percent of the income that is subject to contribution can be offset against tax. There is no upper limit to the contribution level in the Polish health-insurance system, with the exception of farmers' contributions, which are not income-linked.

13.3.4 Benefits

Legal titles

Article 68 of the Polish constitution stipulates:

> All persons are entitled to health protection. Regardless of the individual's material situation, the state shall guarantee each citizen equal access to the health services financed by public funds.

According to the National Health Fund Insurance Act and the Law on Health-Care Services Financed from Public Funds, insurees have a legal title to medical examinations and consultations, high-tech diagnostic examinations, outpatient and inpatient treatment, emergency assistance, prenatal, neonatal and nursing care, access to rehabilitative and preventive medicine and supply of medication and therapeutic appliances. The catalogue of services is not, however, defined in detail, with the exception of a few dental and medical treatments and some benefits excluded from insurance. These are issue of certificates of driving competency, regimens not directly connected to treatment for the main illness, treatment abroad unless international covenants decree otherwise, costs of treatment and accommodation at a nursing home, inoculations not prescribed by law, dental treatment beyond a basic and restrictively defined standard, plastic surgery beyond what is necessary to correct injuries, disease or congenital defects, sex reversal and acupuncture that does not serve to treat pain.

The vague nature of the entitlements and their limited availability to insurees only were found to be unconstitutional. According to the constitutional court, equality was not guaranteed, as stipulated under the law, simply by making everybody, including the noninsured, eligible for basic benefits in the event of accident, poisoning, childbirth or imminent life-threatening disease. Nor was it enough for all citizens undergoing treatment for tuberculosis, contagious diseases, sexually transmitted diseases, psychological disorders and addictions to have standard benefits. The same also applied to medical services for newborns to the age of three months. Finally, constitutionality was not achieved by giving all citizens equal claim to special state-funded benefits. The law currently in force only partly specifies the list of nonguaranteed services. The preparation of a full list was deferred.

Copayments

Polish law provides for some services to be paid for by the patients themselves. For medication, copayments range from a small fee for basic medication to a 30–50 percent payment for supplementary medication and 100 percent payment for all other medicines. Some of the drugs and other adjuvants for treating severe and chronic disease (such as cancer, Alzheimer's, Parkinson's and diabetes) are free of charge. Some groups (especially war veterans) do not pay anything; this, inter alia, causes the insurance system to spend, on average, six times more on medication for war veterans than for other insurees.

A health ordinance regulates the conditions insurees must meet to obtain free orthopedic prostheses and simple wheelchairs. It stipulates a three-to-five-year waiting period and a 30 percent contribution for spectacles and other visual aids. While hearing aids for children and the young are normally free, adults are charged 30 percent of the total price for the simplest device, all subject to time restrictions. With regard to dentistry, the insurance system only provides contributions toward some basic benefits.

Implicit rationing of benefits

Much more important than the explicit limitations mentioned above is the implicit rationing of benefits. Polish law does not provide for any income-related threshold on patient contributions, which often discourages people on a low income from having their prescriptions filled. Moreover, the insurance system's restrictive financing policy and the fact that the benefits defined in the insurance contracts are lower than actually required often give rise to waiting periods of several months or even years for life-saving treatments such as radiation therapy for cancer.

13.3.5   Financing and health expenditure

Health-care spending currently makes up some 6.6 percent of gross domestic product (GDP) in Poland, significantly lower than the EU-member-state average. Altogether, some PLN 51 billion (approximately €12.0 billion in 2003 values) are spent on health care (Ministry of Health, 2004). This is financed from four sources:

1. Insurance contributions (approximately PLN 29 billion [€6.8 billion] in 2003—around 55 percent of total spending);
2. State budget (approximately PLN 3.1 billion [€0.72 billion]—around 6 percent of total spending);
3. Budgets of the regional governments (almost PLN 1.0 billion [€0.25 billion]—mostly financial support for hospitals and for combating alcoholism); and
4. Private means (more than 35 percent—approximately PLN 18.3 billion [€4.3 billion] in 2003); two-thirds is in the form of insuree contributions and official direct payments (e.g., private purchase of medication). Unofficial payments are estimated to be between PLN 0.5 and PLN3 billion (€0.2 to €0.8 billion).

Figure 13.2 shows the structure of expenditure broken down by categories. It differs substantially from that of the health-insurance system, where the biggest spending blocks in 2003 were for intramural hospital treatment (41.83 percent), supply of pharmaceuticals (21.76 percent), basic outpatient treatment (11.51 percent), specialist outpatient treatment (6.37 percent), dental benefits (3.19 percent) and the emergency/ambulance system (3.25 percent) (GUS, 2004a).

13.4   Problems and Challenges

The Polish health system is in a very precarious state. Hospitals, debt-free prior to the introduction of the health-insurance scheme, now have a debt level of PLN 8–10 billion (€2 billion). Health staff are among the worst-paid workers. Decapitalization of assets has long since passed the 50 percent average threshold (Ministry

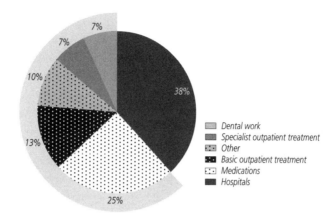

Source: Own calculations based on data from the insurance system and the statistics office; private spending based on estimates obtained in a panel study carried out by the author.

Figure 13.2. Structure of expenditure broken down by categories, 2001.

of Health, 2004). Restructuring of the hospital sector proceeds at a very sluggish pace, if at all; privatization has been limited to outpatient facilities.

Dissatisfaction on the part of the population is very high. Experts agree that both the Solidarność government of 2001 and the socialist government of prime minister Miller in 2004 foundered because of their failure to provide a proper health policy. Consequently, the Polish health system today is faced with the same enormous challenges and problems that confronted it in 1990 and 1999.

13.4.1 The main challenges

The decline in the birth rate, apparent since 1989, has meant that many pediatric and maternity wards are used, on average, at half capacity and should long since have been closed, whereas there is an increasing shortage of elderly-care facilities. So far, however, hardly anything has been done to prepare the system for an aging population.

The Polish health system is suffering from the consequences of capital-intensive technological progress. Labor is still quite cheap in Poland, but many technologies and pharmaceuticals need to be imported at global market prices, which has pushed spending up considerably. Unless the prices of imports are submitted to strict state control and the prescribing of low-cost generic drugs is systematically promoted, the Polish system could suffer a financial collapse in the near future. Yet, at present, the country does not even have any clear criteria as to which drugs are cofinanced by the insurance system.

As insurance contributions are earnings-related, financing of the health system depends on economic growth. Poland has for years been suffering a high rate of unemployment (20 percent in winter 2003–2004, 17 percent now, with almost 80 percent of the jobless not eligible for unemployment benefit), which also affects insurance revenues. The government, by raising the contributions, forestalled a drastic drop in revenue, but if the current financing model is maintained, the problems of the Polish health sector will prove insoluble unless the economic situation improves substantially.

Certainly, a major task is to restore the population's confidence in health-care coverage. Most people are convinced, not entirely without reason, that they will not get adequate medical treatment unless they can use private contacts or bribery. If the money spent on bribes could be made to flow into the state system, this would critically improve the financial situation of the health sector. So far, however, there are hardly any institutions (such as private insurance schemes) in Poland that would be able to attempt this feat. People have been used to paying bribes for decades and appear unwilling to change their way of doing things.

The Polish population must be made to understand that the state cannot guarantee every possible benefit to each citizen. But a majority refuses to accept any reduction of coverage, so that politicians as a rule are not willing to consider the need for explicit rationing.

In addition to rationing, even stricter streamlining of expenditure must be implemented. As the public funds made available for health care are unlikely to be increased, maximization of the use of available resources is paramount. Much has already been done with this in mind over the past four years. In many areas, costs could be cut without noticeably reducing the benefit levels and service quality. Yet, enormous amounts still go to waste, especially in hospitals. Politicians are not without blame, as they keep promising to wipe out hospital debt. The providers' efficiency is also affected by the ownership issue which has yet to be solved. As noted above, districts and voivodships are unable to perform their ownership obligations, yet are still formally responsible for any debts run up by their facilities, albeit only after the facilities have been shut down. As it is rather difficult to close a hospital, this has not yet happened, and owners are therefore not particularly bothered about ensuring that their facilities are efficient. Another challenge is to set up functioning information systems. Incredibly, reforms to date have been instituted without first determining the actual needs of the Polish population, not least because Polish physicians have for years successfully sabotaged the development of databases for patients and services.

Economic troubles and increasing poverty in large social groups have fostered the reemergence of diseases (such as tuberculosis) that were thought to have been eradicated. Charities warn that millions of Poles suffer from inadequate nutrition and are thus more prone to illness. The situation appears particularly alarming in the east and north of Poland. On the other hand, it has been impossible to date to change the unhealthy lifestyle of the Polish. Among other factors, their high tobacco and alcohol consumption is responsible for the greater prevalence of lung cancer and cardiovascular diseases in Poland compared to western Europe. But there is no money for preventive health care or positive health promotion.

Attention also needs to be given to the challenges that derive directly from the country's accession to the EU. New EU member states are obliged to ensure the right to protection of health (European Social Charter, Article 11), to observe basic democratic rights (the right of choice) and patients' rights, to guarantee equal access to basic medical services, to stabilize health-system financing in the long term and to optimize health systems to prepare them for the upcoming demographic challenge. In all these fields, there is still much left for Poland to do. Experts also warn about the implications of European jurisdiction, chiefly in connection with the Smits–Peerbooms ruling[4] that treatment abroad must be approved when a similar treatment is not offered at home or when the waiting period is overlong. Considering that the entitlements of Polish citizens have not been concretized, and in view of the long waiting periods for much treatment, this ruling is bound to pose financial risks to the Polish system.

13.4.2   Reform discussion in 2004

The ruling of the constitutional court has rekindled the discussion about reform in Poland. Previous experience of reforms shows that a policy of 'marginal solutions' (initial total demolition of the system, followed by centralization and 'manual' control from 2003) is the worst possible alternative, so that most experts are now proposing to proceed warily toward reform.

Of the proliferation of reform concepts, two have met with particular media attention. The first concept was submitted by the Commission for System Solutions in the Health Sector. Appointed by the health minister, the Commission devoted itself to developing a low-cost system where patients know what is due to them and what they can expect if they decide to cofinance treatment. Under this concept it was proposed that all health services be categorized into guaranteed services, recommended services and nonstandard services.

A financing guarantee by the National Health Fund would be given only for services guaranteed to all citizens (these would be only necessary services of proven efficacy with a high cost–benefit ratio). Under this model, guaranteed services are, as a rule, provided free of charge for the patient, with patient contribution used solely to control demand, especially to limit the *moral hazard*.[5]

The category of 'recommended services' includes treatments of proven efficacy where the cost–benefit ratio is not excessively high and where financial restrictions render full financing by the public health insurance scheme impossible. To facilitate access to services such as these, cofinancing is not entirely excluded. The third category includes all other services which, while effective, are less important for direct health care.

The Commission advocates maintaining the monopoly enjoyed by the Health Fund and the solidarity principle for guaranteed services. It recommends that the competences of the regional funds be expanded both with regard to contracting and distributing resources. It proposes instructing an independent professional agency to identify the content of these 'baskets of services,' calculate their cost–benefit ratios, and, to the extent necessary, specify rules for waiting periods and contribution levels. The Commission also calls for more flexibility regarding the issue of contracts to health-care providers. By offering global budgets, health-care providers would be given greater freedom without weakening financial discipline.

The second reform concept was developed by a panel of 36 experts headed by Professor Zbigniew Religa and presented in spring 2004. The panel proposed a decentralized system of four to six regional and independent schemes, each covering eight to ten million people. According to this model, insurance schemes initially enjoy a regional monopoly, offering a broad spectrum of services that range from basic health care to complex special services. The model also provides for private insurance to be taken out by the wealthy, which, while weakening the solidarity principle, still rejects contributions and contributions to food costs by patients while they are hospitalized. The Religa expert group also called for funds to be shifted from old-age insurance (i.e., sickness benefits and invalidity pensions costing approximately PLN 25 billion or €8 billion) to the health-insurance system. The group expect such a shift to reduce the number of sick days and of invalidity pensions; they also advocated the introduction of a general nursing-care insurance scheme.

13.4.3   The law proposed by the Polish government

In mid-June 2004 the Polish government presented its concept for the reform of the health system. In spite of the strong criticism voiced by many health and law experts, the draft law on services financed from public funds was submitted to parliament because there was simply no time to develop a better proposal. Had parliament failed to pass a law by October 2004, the Polish health system would have lost its legitimacy at the start of 2005. It would have been possible to levy contributions (these sections of the National Health Fund Insurance Act do conform to the constitution) but the contributions could not have been passed on to the providers of medical services.

In its Law on Health-Care Services Financed from Public Finds, the government attempted to consider the stipulations of the constitutional court and to define citizens' entitlements in more detail. Services are split into guaranteed services, alternative services and others. Guaranteed services are thus entirely financed from public funds; alternative services get partly public and partly private financing and other services are totally financed from private means. In a first step, the 'other services' are to be identified in 'negative lists.' The second step will comprise a comprehensive 'positive list' for guaranteed and alternative services. The important thing is that, under this law, guaranteed services are due not just to insurees but to all citizens. Services for the uninsured are financed by local government. No provision has been made to introduce obligatory insurance for all Polish citizens.

Many health experts complain that this law once again guarantees services only on paper. The planned extension of the negative list is too insubstantial to ensure financing of the 'guaranteed services,' especially as the government submitted to the pressure of populist politicians and, at the last moment, dispensed with contributions for guaranteed services. In doing so, however, it ignored one of the key stipulations of the constitutional court which had requested realistic rather than just programmatic guarantees.

The government advocates continuing the monopoly of the National Health-Insurance Fund while simultaneously decentralizing the system by diverting competences to regional funds. To strengthen the Fund's position in contract negotiations, a ban on associations among service providers has been introduced to prevent revolts such as that at general-practitioner level in January 2004. Such a ban, however, is highly likely to be unconstitutional.

13.5 Enlargement Challenges for the EU

The process of enlarging the EU also poses enormous challenges for the EU15 and the European institutions. Although the EU enjoys only selected competences in health affairs, these are quite substantial when it comes to matters of public health. In their own interest, the EU15 need to help the new members fight contagious diseases. And we must not forget that with its new eastern borders, the EU now adjoins countries that have an extremely high incidence of HIV/AIDS.

The expensive western health systems are confronted with problems of patient migration. In this respect, the European Court of Justice has already caused some disquiet among national health systems by deciding on important rules for the cross-border supply of medical services. Price gaps may and will entice many patients to go to eastern Europe, especially to places that guarantee an appropriate service quality and where patients contribute a large amount to the costs. Even statutory insurance systems (such as German health insurance) attempt to buy more services for their insurees from Poland, the Czech Republic and Hungary. Of course, patient migration may also occur in the other direction, but in that case it will cause financial problems for the poorer countries in the east (McKee *et al.*, 2004).

The chief goals of the EU include efforts to harmonize living conditions, including health care, within its member states. Thus, financial help is expected both for projects in the field of health infrastructure and for programs to promote health and prevent disease. Similarly, support in building databases is of great importance because the lack of these makes it impossible to implement the new European health policy based on the new open coordination method.

13.6   Summary and Conclusions

Fifteen years after launching their transformation, all the new EU member states from central and eastern Europe have health-insurance systems based on the Bismarckian model. The systemic change has been associated with great difficulties, as can clearly be observed in Poland. In the eyes of the Polish population, the two health-care reforms (in 1999 and 2003) were failures. Health-care facilities are deteriorating and users are running out of patience. Added to the woes is the failure of politicians who have not even been able to adopt laws that conform to the constitution.

The Polish system is currently a rather chaotic mix of decentralized and centralist, bureaucratic and market-oriented, legal, semilegal and completely unofficial solutions. Although the health-insurance law provides broad benefit guarantees, these cannot be utilized because of inadequate funding, faulty structures and large-scale waste; meanwhile corruption, a key reason for income-based discrimination against patients, is flourishing. Centralization of the insurance system in 2003 not only failed to eliminate regional inequalities but also caused further destabilization. High patient contributions to the cost of drugs frequently cause poorer patients to forego filling their prescriptions. Benefit restrictions cause long queues even for such 'basic' treatments as cancer radiotherapy. Consequently, the health sector in Poland is faced with enormous challenges if it is to emulate the highly developed systems in the EU15 member states. Among the most urgent needs are the restructuring of health facilities and preparing the system for demographic and technological changes. System financing needs to become more detached from economic development. The Polish state must strive to regain its population's confidence in the public health-care system. This cannot be achieved as long as benefit guarantees are not worth the paper they are written on. It will be necessary to talk explicitly about rationing, even though the majority of Poles and their politicians have so far refused to listen. Not only is rationing advisable, but expenditure also needs to be submitted to stricter streamlining. Added to this are key responsibilities in combating diseases and changing the very unhealthy lifestyles of Polish citizens, as well as the need for efforts to raise the legal system to European standards.

In ruling the National Health Insurance Act unconstitutional, the Polish constitutional court once again stirred up a discussion on reform in Poland. Most experts propose cautious reforms, with the wishes of the population being defined and subsequently implemented. Concepts vary considerably with regard to the role of patient contributions and how the system will be organized (monopoly versus competitive health-insurance schemes). In its latest Law on Health-Care Services Financed from Public Funds, the Polish government proposed a single monopolist fund, extending benefit guarantees to all citizens, no patient contributions for guaranteed benefits, and defining benefit claims by way of positive lists and disclosure of waiting lists. The Act has come in for severe criticism, however, being accused of wishful thinking by health-care and legal experts alike.

Notes

1.   This total includes hospitals of all types (general hospitals, military hospitals, police hospitals, etc.).

2.   These authorities operate at local, district and regional (voivodship) levels. Even though Poland is not a federal state, such administrations enjoy several competences within the scope of the health system.

3.   A voivodship is an administrative region, of which there are 16 in Poland.

4.   Ruling of the European Count of Justice in July 2001 in the case of Smits–Peerbooms that mentions undue delay as justification for cross-border care within the EU.

5.   Behavioral changes caused by a health service financed by an insurance scheme or through taxes that act as incentives and that could increase both the probability of falling ill (e.g., by inferior care or an unhealthy lifestyle) and the cost of treatment (demand for the most expensive service, unnecessary duplication of examinations, consulting a doctor for minor complaints).

Annex 1: Health-Care Statistics for Poland

Table 13.1A. Infant mortality.

Year	Rate	Year	Rate
1990	19.3	1996	12.2
1991	18.2	1997	10.2
1992	17.3	1998	9.5
1993	16.1	1999	8.9
1994	15.1	2000	8.1
1995	13.6	2001	7.6

Source: GUS (2004b, p. 122).

Table 13.2A. Life expectancy.

Males aged	1990	1995	1999	2002
0	66.5	67.6	68.8	70.42
15	53.1	53.9	54.8	56.23
30	39.1	39.8	40.6	42.01
45	26.0	26.7	27.3	28.48
60	15.3	15.8	16.3	17.19
Females aged	1990	1995	1999	2002
0	75.5	76.4	77.5	78.78
15	61.8	62.6	63.8	64.51
30	47.2	47.9	48.6	49.77
45	33.0	33.6	34.3	35.35
60	20.0	20.5	21.1	22.15

Source: GUS (2003b, p. 107).

Table 13.3A. Cause of death (per 100,000 inhabitants).

Cause	1996	2001 Total	Men	Women	Urban	Rural
Total	998.2	940.0	1,027.6	857.3	907.4	992.1
Cardiovascular disease	503.2	449.8	440.6	458.5	417.0	502.2
Cancer	203.7	223.7	262.3	187.2	232.8	209.1
External causes	70.5	64.8	99.1	32.4	61.2	70.6
Contagious diseases	5.9	6.0	7.9	4.2	6.2	5.7
Pneumo-respiratory disease	37.0	40.8	49.5	32.6	37.3	46.4
Gastro-intestinal disease	32.4	37.7	43.6	32.1	41.2	32.0

Source: GUS (2004b, p. 121).

Table 13.4A. Number of health-care staff, 1990–2003.

	1990	1995	1999	2003
Physicians	81,641	89,421	87,524	89,317
Dentists	18,205	17,805	13,260	14,017
Pharmacists	15,110	19,447	21,587	25,217
Nurses	207,767	211,603	197,153	184,169
Midwives	24,016	24,440	22,683	21,692

Source: GUS (2004a, p. 217).

Table 13.5A. Physicians by specialization, at 31 December each year.

	Total			Second-degree specialization		
	1995	1999	2002	1995	1999	2002
Total	70,572	72,162	74,390	36,660	42,980	48,038
As % of all physicians	78.9	82.4	84.5	41.0	49.1	54.5
Anesthetists and intensive-care physicians	3,507	4,069	3,873	1,656	2,191	2,617
Surgeons	9,239	9,599	9,743	5,555	6,120	6,648
Pulmonologists	1,647	1,694	1,699	1,308	1,395	1,460
Internists	14,885	13,385	12,120	5,781	6,109	6,365
Dermatologists	1,717	1,649	1,683	732	853	939
Cardiologists	495	766	942	476	766	942
Medical practitioners	231	2,507	3,665	231	2,507	3,665
Neurologists	2,616	2,775	2,899	1,367	1,643	1,877
Ophthalmologists	2,865	2,803	2,858	1,357	1,429	1,638
Oncologists	94	109	95	77	99	82
Otolaryngologists	2,507	2,373	2,405	1,267	1,284	1,410
Pediatricians	10,566	8,717	8,252	3,799	3,649	3,802
Gynecologists	6,179	5,962	6,217	3,806	3,920	4,271
Psychiatrists	2,170	2,497	2,616	1,218	1,416	1,659
Radiodiagnosticians	2,172	2,684	2,762	1,134	1,442	1,550
Dentists		7,734				2,484
As % of all dentists		71.8				23.1

Source: GUS (2004b, pp. 285–286).

Table 13.6A. Hospital beds (per 10,000 inhabitants).

1990	1995	1999	2003
57.2	55.4	51.4	48.7

Source: GUS (2004a, p. 18 and 2004b, p. 293).

Table 13.7A. Public health expenditure.

	1999	2002
State budget in thousand PLN	138,401,200	182,064,364
%	100.0	100.0
of which for health in thousand PLN	6,312,645	3,420,668
%	4.56	1.88
Regional and local government in thousand PLN	65,115,441	83,181,772
%	100.0	100.0
of which for health in thousand PLN	2,043,305	1,974,427
%	3.14	2.37
Health insurance	23,538,386	29,942,145
Total public health expenditure,		
of which for health in thousand PLN	28,589,383	34,118,346
% of GDP	4.65	4.42

Source: GUS (2001, p. 53 and 2003a, p. 56).

Annex 2: Major Health-Care-Related Legal Instruments

Ustawa z 17 maja 1989 r. o izbach lekarskich, Dz. U. z 1989 r. nr 30, poz. 158, z póź. zm.; Law of 17 May 1989 on Physicians' Chambers, Journal of Laws No 30, clause 158, with later amendments.

Ustawa z 19 kwietnia 1991 r. o izbach aptekarskich, Dz. U. z 1991 roku Nr 41, poz. 179; Law of 19 April 1991 on Pharmacists' Chambers, Journal of Laws No 41, clause 179, with later amendments.

Ustawa z 19 kwietnia 1991 r. o samorzadzie pielegniarek i położnych, Dz. U. 1991 r. Nr 41, poz. 178; Law of 19 April 1991 on Nurses' and Midwives' Chambers, Journal of Laws No 41, clause 178, with later amendments.

Ustawa z 5 lipca 1996 r. o zawodach pielegniarki i położnej, Dz. U. 1996 r. Nr 91, poz. 410; Law of 5 July 1996 on the profession of nurse and midwife, Journal of Laws No 91, clause 410, with later amendments.

Ustawa z 5 grudnia 1996 r. o zawodzie lekarza, Dz. U. 1997 r. Nr 28, poz. 152; Law of 5 December 1996 on the profession of physician, Journal of Laws 1997 No 29, clause 152, with later amendments.

Ustawa z 8 marca 1990 r. o samorzadzie terytorialnym, Dz. U. Nr 16, poz. 95, z pozn. zm.; Law of 8 March 1990 on local governments, Journal of Laws No 16, clause 95, with later amendments.

Ustawa z 22 marca 1990 o terenowych organach rzadowej administracji ogólnej, Dz. U. Nr 21, poz. 123; Law 22 March 1990 on local agencies of governmental administration, Journal of Laws No 21, clause 123.

Ustawa z 17 maja 1990 r. o podziale zadań i kompetencji określonych w ustawach szczegółowych pomiedzy organy gminy a organy administracji rzadowej oraz o zmianie niektórych ustaw, Dz.U. Nr 34. poz. 198, z późn. zm.; Law of 17 May 1990 on the division of obligations and competencies, regulated in detail by respective acts, between gmina's agencies and governmental administration agencies, and on the change of some acts, Journal of Laws No 34, clause 198, with later amendments.

Ustawa z 27 czerwca 1997 r. o służbie medycyny pracy, Dz. U. 1997 r. Nr 96, poz. 593; Law of 27 June 1997 on occupational health (medical) service, Journal of Laws No 96, clause 593, with later amendments.

Ustawa z 19 sierpnia 1994 r. o ochronie zdrowia psychicznego, Dz. U. 1994 r. Nr 111, poz. 535; Law of 19 August 1994 on mental health, Journal of Laws No 111, clause 535, with later amendments.

Ustawa z 22 sierpnia 1997 r. o publicznej służbie krwi, Dz. U. 1997 r. Nr 106, poz. 681; Law of August 1997 on public blood service, Journal of Laws No 106, clause 681, with later amendments.

Ustawa z 26 października 1995 r. o pobieraniu i przeszczepianiu komórek, tkanek i narzadów, Dz. U. 1995 r. Nr 138, poz. 682; Law of 26 October 1995 on collecting and transplanting cells, tissues and organs, Journal of Laws No 138, clause 682, with later amendments.

Ustawa z 30 sierpnia 1991 r. o zakładach opieki zdrowotnej, Dz. U. z 1991, Nr 91, poz. 408, z późn. zm. Law of 30 September 1991 on health care institutions, Journal of Laws No 91, clause 408, with later amendments.

Ustawa z 6 lutego 1997 r. o powszechnym ubezpieczeniu zdrowotnym, Dz. U. 1997 r. Nr 28, poz. 153 ze zmianami; Law of 6 February 1997 on universal health insurance, Journal of Laws No 28, clause 153, with many later amendments.

Ustawa z 23 stycznia 2003 r. o powszechnym ubezpieczeniu w Narodowym Funduszu Zdrowia, Dz. U. 2003 r. Nr 45, poz. 153 ze zmianami; Law of 23 January 2003 on universal health insurance in the National Health Fund, Journal of Laws No 45, clause 391, with later amendments.

Ustawa z 27 sierpnia 2004 r. o świadczeniach opieki zdrowotnej finansowanych ze środków publicznych, Dz. U. 2004 r. Nr 210, poz. 2135; Law of 27 August 2004 on Health-Care Services Financed from Public Funds, Journal of Laws No 210, clause 2135.

References

Alber J. and Köhler U. (2004) *Health and Care in an Enlarged Europe*, Report to the European Foundation for the Improvement of Living and Working Conditions, Dublin, Ireland.

GUS (2001) *Podstawowe dane z zakresu ochrony zdrowia w 2000 r.* (Basic Data on Health Care in 2000), Warsaw, Poland: Główny Urzad Statystyczny [in Polish].

GUS (2003a) *Podstawowe dane z zakresu ochrony zdrowia w 2002 r.* (Basic Data on Health Care in 2002), Warsaw, Poland: Główny Urzad Statystyczny [in Polish].

GUS (2003b) *Rocznik Statystyczny Województw 2003*, Warsaw, Poland: Główny Urzad Statystyczny [in Polish].

GUS (2004a) *Podstawowe dane z zakresu ochrony zdrowia w 2003 r.* (Basic Data on Health Care in 2003), Warsaw, Poland: Główny Urzad Statystyczny [in Polish].

GUS (2004b) *Rocznik Statystyczny 2003*, Warsaw, Poland: Główny Urzad Statystyczny (wersja elektroniczna) [in Polish].

McKee M., MacLehose L. and Nolte E. (2004) *Health Policy and European Enlargement*, Berkshire, England: Open University Press.

Ministry of Health (2004) *Raport Finansowanie ochrony zdrowia w Polsce – Zielona Ksiega* (Report of the Financing of Health Care in Poland—Green Book), Warsaw, Poland: Ministry of Health [in Polish].

Murthy A. and Mossialos E. (2003) 'Informal Payments in EU Accession Countries,' *Euro Observer*, **5**(2): 1–3.

OECD (2004) *Health Data 2004*, Paris, France: Organisation for Economic Co-operation and Development in Europe.

Sowada C. (2000) *Grundversorgung mit Gesundheitsleistungen in einer Krankenversicherung. Normative Prinzipien und die Umsetzung in der allgemeinen Krankenversicherung in Polen*, Bayreuth, Germany: Verlag P.C.O. [in German].

Sowada C. (2003) 'Health Care—Country Study Poland,' in Gesellschaft für Versicherungswissenschaft und -gestaltung (ed) *Social Protection in the Candidate Countries*, in four volumes, Berlin, Germany: Akademische Verlagsgesellschaft Aka GmbH, pp. 98–144.

UNUZ (2001) *Powszechne Ubezpieczenie Zdrowotne w latach 1999–2001. Analiza funkcjonalna w świetle doświadczeń*, Warsaw, Poland: Urzad Nadzoru Ubezpieczeń Zdrowotnych (UNUZ) [in Polish].

World Health Organization (2002) *Reducing Risks, Promoting Healthy Life*, Geneva, Switzerland: World Health Organization.

Chapter 14

Issues for the Future of Health Care in an Enlarged EU

Robert Anderson

14.1   Introduction

The value of good health and the protection of health are incorporated into the fundamental goals of the European Union (EU). While the organization and delivery of health care is a matter for the individual member states, the European Commission promotes exchange of information on health status and performance of health systems. This monitoring and information role must include the perspectives of citizens and service users. Some of their views and experiences, in the older EU member states (EU15), the ten new member states (NMS) and the three candidate countries (CC3) (Bulgaria, Romania and Turkey) are presented in this chapter.

Enlargement underlines the diversity in the EU and the challenges this poses. The health situation in the post-Communist accession countries deteriorated during and after their economic transition. During the 1990s death rates began to fall and life expectancy increased, but there were large differences among countries in the pace of improvement. Today, many of the main causes of death remain more prevalent in the NMS than in the EU15 (World Health Organization and European Commission, 2002).

Social inequalities in health, associated with gender, income, education and employment, are found in all EU15 member states (European Commission, 2003) and are emerging as an important feature of the health situation in the NMS and candidate countries (Alber and Köhler, 2004). Clearly, health policies and systems alone cannot address these inequalities, but the health and social services have an important role to play.

The promotion of equity in and accessibility to health and care systems has become a key element in the debate on social protection in Europe. European Commission policy documents increasingly stress measures to improve the quality of care and cooperation in the field of health care and long-term care as a contribution to the sustainable modernization of the European social model and greater social cohesion. A key issue here is the care of older people, where the central contribution of families is increasingly recognized (European Parliament, 2004).

These policy concerns constitute the basis for the main themes explored in this chapter. The analysis begins with an overview of health status and its distribution among and within countries. While it is recognized that this is only one of many studies that have considered inequalities in health, there is a need to examine experiences across the 28 countries that, together, comprise the EU15, the new member states and the candidate countries. On the other hand, there is rather little information on the views and experiences of service users in these 28 countries. The chapter looks at, but does not examine in depth, some aspects of both access to and the quality of services, as well as the future of care, specifically for older people.

14.2   Data Sources

This chapter draws upon data from two recent surveys carried out in all 28 countries of the enlarged European Union and the three candidate countries. In spring 2002 a Eurobarometer survey on quality of life was carried out in the 13 accession and candidate countries, and this provides information that is comparable with data from a series of previous Eurobarometer surveys in the EU15. An integrated data set was prepared, and the main results have been published (Alber and Fahey, 2004; Alber and Köhler, 2004).

Most of the chapter is based upon the European Quality of Life (EQLS) survey carried out from May to August 2003. Around 1,000 people aged 18 and over were interviewed face-to-face in each country, except in the smaller countries—Cyprus, Estonia, Luxembourg, Malta and Slovenia—where around 600 interviews were conducted. The sample sizes enable an accurate picture of the social situation to be drawn but are too small to allow detailed analysis of subgroups like immigrants or single-parent families. Furthermore, the questionnaire covered a broad range of topics, so that none of the individual topics can be covered in great depth. The main descriptive report of the survey is published as 'Quality of Life in Europe' (European Foundation, 2004). Both surveys cover aspects of health status as well as access to and quality of/satisfaction with health care.

Table 14.1. Long-standing illness or disability in relation to age.

	Proportion reporting long-standing illness or disability (%)					
	Age					
	18–24	25–34	35–49	50–64	65+	Total
EU15	8	9	14	28	37	20
NMS	12	13	23	48	66	32
CC3	7	13	22	34	54	23
EU25	8	10	16	31	42	22

Source: EQLS (2003).

14.3 Health Status

Self-rating of health has proved to be a relatively good measure of health status (Robine *et al.* 2003), and many studies (e.g., the European Community Household Panel Survey) have used the questions applied in the EQLS to measure health and the prevalence of disability or chronic illness.

Altogether, 35 percent of people in the EQLS reported that, in general, their health was 'excellent' or 'very good.' However, this proportion varied markedly in the different countries, in the EU15 ranging from 61 percent in Denmark and Ireland down to only 18 percent in Portugal, and in the NMS from 68 percent of people in Cyprus to only 9 percent of respondents in Latvia. The proportions of people in different countries who regarded themselves as in 'poor' health are shown in *Figure 14.1*.

In general, perceived health is more likely to be rated 'poor' in the NMS (16 percent of respondents) than in the EU15 (6 percent). This pattern reflects generally higher morbidity rates, particularly in the accession countries of central and eastern Europe. Not surprisingly, reporting of both poor health and long-standing illness or disability increases with age. This is shown in *Table 14.1* for the question:

> Do you have any long-standing illness or disability that limits your activities in any way? By long-standing I mean anything that has troubled you over a period of time or that is likely to affect you for a period of time.

The overall figures for the country groupings are similar to results from previous Eurobarometer surveys (Alber and Köhler, 2004).

The extent of long-term illness or disability reported by people aged 65 and over is striking; in the EU15 this figure exceeds 50 percent only in the United Kingdom (52 percent) and Finland (61 percent), but this proportion is over 50 percent in all the NMS and CC3, except Cyprus and Malta. Although many of those reporting such disability do not have a severe problem (Grammenos, 2003),

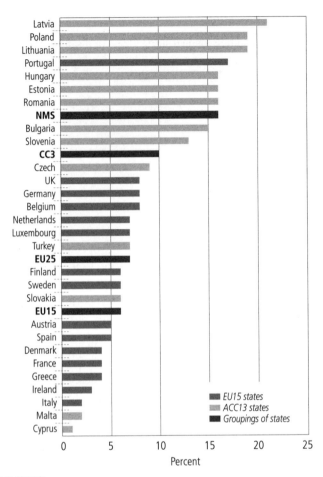

Source: EQLS (2003).

Figure 14.1. Country differences in self-reported health as 'poor' in response to EQLS question 43: In general, would you say your health is excellent, very good, good, fair or poor?

the numbers indicate a major challenge for health-care systems as the population ages—notwithstanding potential improvements in the health of the next generations.

Educational attainment is an important factor influencing lifestyle, opportunities and awareness of risks: people with more education have been found to rate their health more positively (European Commission, 2003). Altogether in the EQLS only 8 percent of people rated their health as poor, but this figure rose to 38 percent among those in the NMS who had completed their full-time education at

Table 14.2. Health differences between income groups.

	Household income quartiles[1]		
	Lowest quartile	Middle quartiles	Highest quartile
Proportion reporting long-standing illness or disability (%)			
EU15	25	21	15
NMS	37	38	24
CC3	27	24	17
Total	27	24	16
Proportion reporting poor health (per cent)			
EU15	9	6	3
NMS	19	20	10
CC3	18	10	4
Total	12	9	4

Note: [1]Income quartiles refer to the household equivalence income (new scale of Organization for Economic Co-operation and Development).
Source: EQLS (2003).

15 years or younger; the proportion was 40 percent or higher in Bulgaria, Latvia, Lithuania and Poland.

The literature on income and health (e.g., Berkman and Kawachi, 2000) shows that within countries poorer health is associated with lower income, although it appears that the improvement in health from a fixed increase in income is smaller at higher income levels. Data on income generally suffer from a relatively high nonresponse, and these data capture the situation only at a single point in time. Nevertheless, looking at quartiles of household income there is a relationship between health status and income, both overall and in most countries. This picture is more consistent in the EU15 countries, although the relationship is not apparent in Austria, France and Luxembourg. In the NMS and CC3, the highest-income quartile reports better health in all countries, but there is no consistent difference between the lowest quartile and the two middle quartiles; the figures are in *Table 14.2*. Again, this is similar to results in the 2002 Eurobarometer survey (Alber and Köhler, 2004). On the whole, these relationships are weaker than reported elsewhere (European Commission, 2003) and need to be explored further, particularly in the new central and eastern European member states.

The highest rates of long-standing illness or disability (more than 40 percent) are reported in the lowest-income quartiles in Finland, Hungary, Latvia, Lithuania and the United Kingdom and among the middle-income quartiles in Poland. The highest proportions rating their health as poor (more than 25 percent) were in Hungary, Latvia, Lithuania and Portugal, among the lowest income quartile, and again in Poland, among people in the medium quartiles. These figures illustrate that poorer health is not only found in some country groups; there are many over-

Table 14.3. Difficulties in access to medical care.

Proportion reporting (%):	Very difficult	A little difficult	No difficulty
Distance to doctor's office/hospital	8	18	74
Delay in getting appointment	14	25	61
Waiting time to see doctor on day of appointment	14	29	57
Cost of seeing the doctor	13	19	69

Note: Response to EQLS question 43: On the last occasion you needed to see a doctor or medical specialist, to what extent did each of the following factors make it difficult for you to do so: distance to doctor's office/hospital/medical centre; delay in getting appointment; waiting time to see doctor on day of appointment; cost of seeing the doctor?
Source: EQLS (2003).

laps between the reports from the EU15 and the NMS—but in general people with the lowest incomes are those in greatest need of health and care services.

14.4   Access to Health Services

A number of questions in the EQLS were designed to assess aspects of access to and quality of health services. Although considerable information is available on the structure and organization of care in the NMS and CC3 as well as the EU15 (World Health Organization and European Commission, 2002), there is much less systematic and comparable data on the views and experiences of service users. Clearly, such information is essential for the monitoring, planning and evaluation of service provision and for policy development.

Several aspects of access to a doctor were examined, relating to the last occasion when the respondent needed to see a doctor or medical specialist. Access was not, on the whole, a major problem for large numbers of people (*Table 14.3*). These issues of access have become key subjects of debate around social protection on the EU agenda. From a public health perspective, there are concerns about access and quality of services in relation to country, urban–rural area, income, gender and age (European Parliament, 2004).

Across the four dimensions of access—distance, delay, waiting and cost—the most consistent reporting of difficulties appears in the Mediterranean countries of the EU15 and in the CC3. Altogether, there was no significant difference between the experience of service users in the EU15 and the NMS, but if the Mediterranean countries are excluded then the proportion finding it 'very difficult' to access services is twice as high in the NMS and CC3 as in the rest of the EU15; the figures are in *Table 14.4*.

Of course, reporting of difficulty reflects not only experience but also cultural differences in expectations and inclination to complain. Nevertheless, it seems

Table 14.4. Country differences in access to services.

	Proportion reporting 'very difficult' (%)						
	Greece	Italy	Portugal	Spain	Rest of EU15	NMS	CC3
Distance	11	9	9	5	2	6	26
Delay	16	24	24	13	7	14	27
Waiting	16	23	27	13	7	15	29
Cost	21	26	17	4	4	15	32

Source: EQLS (2003).

clear that many citizens of Greece, Italy and Portugal, and especially Bulgaria and Turkey, identify important problems in accessing their medical services.

In general, country of residence was the clearest factor influencing views on access to services. Within countries, urban–rural differences are not generally important. This may partly be because the questions address access to a doctor in either a hospital or clinic or in general practice. Alber and Köhler (2004) report that severe problems in time in getting to a doctor are not very widespread, although rural populations in the candidate countries of Bulgaria and Romania had greater difficulty in accessing hospital care. Likewise, in the EQLS, significant disadvantages for people in rural areas were most marked in the CC3: 40 percent of people in rural areas of Turkey reported that distance to a doctor was 'very difficult' compared with 24 percent in urban areas; corresponding figures for Romania are 22 percent and 8 percent. The only other countries with urban–rural differences of 5 percent or more were Portugal (10 percent compared with 5 percent); Slovenia (11 percent compared with 3 percent) and Latvia (15 percent compared with 5 percent). There were no consistent differences between urban and rural areas in relation to the other dimensions of access.

It is striking that income inequalities show a pattern of advantage for people in the highest income quartile in access to services across all four dimensions. This pattern is evident in all country groupings, although to the least extent in the EU15 and most markedly in the candidate countries, largely reflecting experience in Turkey (income was not at all a factor in Bulgaria). The figures are shown in *Table 14.5*.

As *Table 14.5* illustrates, differences by income are most clear in relation to the proportion of people reporting that the cost of seeing the doctor made their last visit 'very difficult.' Again, three of the Mediterranean countries reveal serious problems with 'cost,' as well as marked differences in the experience of the lowest- and highest-income quartiles: Greece (30 percent compared with 13 percent); Portugal (22 percent compared with 8 percent); Italy (31 percent compared with 18 percent). Thus, money as a barrier to use of services has not been overcome in several of the EU15 countries. In the new member states, the greater disadvantage of those in the

Table 14.5. Access to medical services and income.

	Difference in the proportion reporting 'very difficult' between the lowest and highest income quartile (%)			
	EU15	NMS	CC3	Total
Distance	3	5	24	6
Delay	4	4	17	10
Waiting	3	5	20	7
Cost	6	12	27	11

Source: EQLS (2003).

lowest income quartile was 10 percent or more in all countries except Cyprus and the Czech Republic.

Concern about socioeconomic inequalities in access to services is widespread; and at European level, in particular, there is concern regarding the needs associated with an aging population (European Parliament, 2004). This reflects both the greater health-care needs of older people and concerns about disadvantage or discrimination experienced by this age group. There was no consistent evidence that older people found it more or less easy to get an appointment nor that age was related to waiting times on the day of an appointment. However, people aged 65 and over had more difficulty in relation to distance to the doctor's surgery: this was especially the case in the new member states where 13 percent of people aged 65 and over reported that distance made the most recent visit 'very difficult' compared with 5 percent of younger people.

Difficulties associated with the 'cost of seeing the doctor' were not related to older age in general; however, it appeared to be an issue for people aged 50 and over in some of the new member states— Latvia, Lithuania and Slovakia, in each of which around 30 percent of people aged 50 and over found the cost 'very difficult.'

Altogether, the survey offers substantial evidence of social inequalities in access to medical services, particularly for people on lower incomes and for older people. These are important and urgent issues to be addressed as part of the challenges to improve health services in the new EU and in the candidate countries (European Commission, 2004).

14.5 Quality in Health Services

One set of questions in the EQLS asked respondents to rate the general quality of a number of public services in their country. The mean scores for health services in each country are presented in *Figure 14.2*.

On the whole, as *Figure 14.2* shows, assessments of the quality of health services fall into two groups, with the EU15 countries having higher scores than the

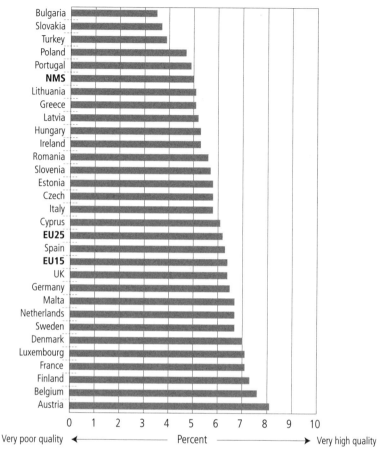

Source: EQLS (2003).

Figure 14.2. Quality of health services.
Response to EQLS question 54: In general, how would you rate the quality of each of the public services in (country)? Please tell me on a scale of 1 to 10, where 1 means very poor quality and 10 means very high quality health services.

NMS. However, as in other research (Alber and Köhler, 2004), some EU15 countries, notably Greece and Portugal but also Italy and Ireland, are below the mean score for the EU25, while the ratings of people from Cyprus and Malta put their countries in the top half for health services. There is a striking similarity in the top countries rated according to 'satisfaction' with services in the 2002 survey (Alber and Köhler, 2004) and now in terms of their 'quality' in 2003. There was no consistent pattern of differences between urban and rural areas.

There are no marked general differences by gender in assessments of health services. This might be considered surprising, as women report more ill health and are likely to be greater users of health services in their role as carers for children and older people. Within countries, nearly all the gender differences are small.

Older people are much greater users of health services; quality ratings tend to be higher specifically from people aged 65 and over. There is no clear trend for age; rather the mean score for health services is 6.4 among people aged 65 and over compared with 5.8 for younger people; the difference is more pronounced in the thirteen acceding and candidate countries (ACC13), specifically in Poland and Turkey. Differences in assessment of health services show a tendency for retired people to rate the service somewhat higher than employed people, but the differences were small in most countries. There was no consistently lower rating of health services by unemployed people.

The disadvantages experienced by lower income groups in access to medical services did not translate into lower global assessment of the quality of the health services. Although a lack of income-related differences in the assessment of health care was found previously (Alber and Köhler, 2004), it is nonetheless somewhat surprising—perhaps income groups lack awareness of their relative advantages and disadvantages or accommodate different expectations of the services. There are a few countries, such as Ireland, where those with high income rate the health service more highly (5.9 for people in the highest quartile compared with 5.1 among lower earners), but the general picture is of weak relationships between income and quality assessment.

14.6   The Future of Care Provision

The Eurobarometer survey (Alber and Köhler, 2004) asks a series of questions about care, who provides it and preferences for the future of care provision. It reveals a remarkably high level of informal caregiving throughout Europe: one in four respondents in the NMS and CC3 and over one in five in the EU15 reported that they had 'extra family responsibilities because they look after someone who has a long-term illness, who is handicapped or elderly' (Alber and Köhler, 2004, p. 56) (see *Figure 14.3*).

Looking at individual countries, there is no sharp distinction between reports from old and new member states; there are no clear signs that the expansion of services in the EU15 has eroded family care.

A closer inspection reveals a significant difference between the NMS and EU15 in where care is given: care in the respondent's home is given more frequently in the NMS and CC3 (17 percent report this compared with 10 percent in the EU15); care to a person not living in the same household is more frequent in the EU15.

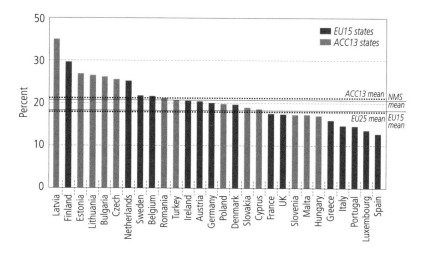

Figure 14.3. Prevalence of informal care activities.
Response to Eurobarometer 51.0, question 37 and Candidate Countries Eurobarometer 2002.2, question 22: Some people have extra family responsibilities because they look after someone who has a long-term illness, who is handicapped or elderly. Is there anyone living with you who has a long-term illness, who is handicapped or elderly, whom you look after or give special help to? And do you provide some regular service or help to such a person NOT living with you?

Throughout Europe, informal care predominantly goes to family members. In the NMS and CC3, care is much more heavily concentrated on the family than in the EU15. In the former, family care is six times more prevalent than extra-family care, whereas in the EU it is roughly twice as prevalent. Alber and Köhler (2004) argue that this suggests that the scale of family care in the new member states is not merely a response to a lack of public services but an indicator of the strength of adhesion to family values. Similarly, they propose that the distribution of care activities in the EU15 countries contradicts the idea that informal care and publicly provided community care are opposites or replace each other. In the EU15 informal care outside the home is most frequent in those countries where formal community services are most developed.

The Eurobarometer survey asked whether people would consider it a good or a bad thing if, in future years, working adults would have to look after their elderly parents more than nowadays. In the NMS and CC3, about four out of five respondents would consider it 'a good thing' to strengthen family responsibility for looking after elderly parents; only four countries report less than 70 percent who share this view. In contrast, more citizens in EU member states express skepticism about extended family responsibilities. On average, only 59 percent of EU citizens advocate more family support in the future. Hence, there is a tendency for western and eastern European countries to stand apart and to have rather different views concerning the desirability of working adults in future providing more family care for the elderly (see *Figure 14.4*). Within the EU15, Greece and Italy, and to a lesser extent Ireland and Portugal, are the countries that most clearly share the pattern of widespread support for extended family responsibilities, whereas among the NMS, only the Czech Republic resembles the western and northern European pattern of greater skepticism.

Within the current EU15, family support is favored by more than 60 percent of the respondents only in the Catholic countries of Ireland and southern Europe. In six other countries of western and northern Europe (Belgium, Denmark, Finland, France, The Netherlands and Sweden), less than half of the population advocates strengthening the responsibility of working adults to look after their parents. This supports the argument that the EU15 already has a care-policy divide that separates a secular and Protestant northwestern culture of care from a Catholic culture of care in Ireland and southern Europe. An enlarged Europe will supplement this cleavage, with a related divide between western and eastern views on family responsibilities for care of the elderly.

To assess the prospects for future developments of care policies, it is important to know the extent to which there is consensus or cleavage among different generations. Furthermore, a comparison by age is interesting because it allows us to at least approximate a solution to the problem of whether respondents see themselves in the role of 'care-giver' or 'care-taker' when giving their answers. In a question about future scenarios, it is likely that those who are already above the age of 60 perceive themselves as recipients, whereas those below 35 see themselves as potential providers of care.

The results are in line with the idea that respondents at different ages see themselves in different roles when answering the question. Throughout Europe, those in the highest age group are more in favor of extended family support than those in the youngest age group and those in the middle of the life cycle. This average tendency is repeated in the great majority of countries, with only a few notable exceptions. Differences between the generations tend to be greater in the EU15. However, the basic similarity between generations is more noteworthy than the differences. Thus, the proponents of extended family support usually outnumber its opponents by large margins, even in the youngest generation. This is remarkable because the younger generation is likely to be the future supplier of informal care. (The same results were found among female respondents.) In the NMS and CC3 there is not a single exception to the majority of younger people favoring family care in the future; indeed, in two countries (Cyprus and Slovakia) the youngest respondents had slightly larger majorities in favor of family responsibilities than

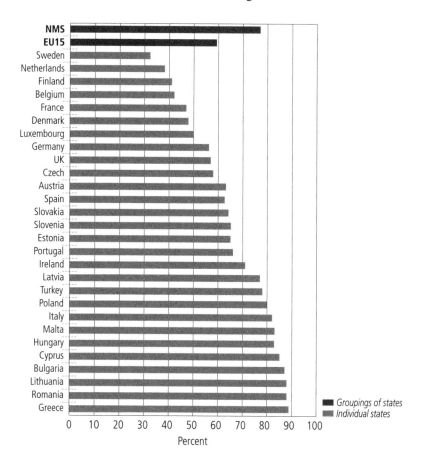

Figure 14.4. Perception of future family responsibilities for elderly care (percentage of respondents advocating that working adults should look after their elderly parents).

Response to Eurobarometer 50.1, question 33 and Candidate Countries Eurobarometer 2002.1, question 18: If in the future, working adults would have to look after their elderly parents more than they do nowadays, would you say that this would be rather a good thing or rather a bad thing?

the older generation. Slovenia is the only case where the margin of victory for the proponents of family care is markedly smaller in the younger generation.

In the EU15, four countries—Denmark, Finland, The Netherlands and Sweden—deviate from the general pattern of majority support for family care across generations. In Denmark, The Netherlands and Sweden, the elderly seem to champion the idea of 'intimacy at a distance,' as opponents of extended family support have an edge over its proponents even in the older generation. Finland and

Sweden stand out as the only EU countries where a majority of the younger generation are against extended family responsibilities. In contrast, the southern European
nations stand out with a strong advocacy of family support among the younger generations as well. In general then, Europeans across the generations usually tend to
be united in favor of extended family support. In most countries, there is no indication of a coming generational conflict between the likely recipients and providers
of care.

Finally, it seems clear that, across Europe, the idea of sending elderly people to
residential care facilities is highly unpopular. In 12 of the 13 candidate countries,
more than 80 percent of the respondents prefer social services that allow elderly
people to remain in their own homes. Only Slovenia has a somewhat more sizable minority of proponents of residential care. On average, the advocates of home
care outnumber those who favor residential care by a margin of 88 to 12 (see *Figure 14.5*). The citizens of EU member states prefer home care over residential care
to an almost identical degree.

The preference for home care over residential care and for family support models rather than formalized help became even stronger when respondents are asked
to think about the best way of caring for their own parents should they become
dependent.

In general, attitudes about appropriate care arrangements are most diverse
within the EU15. Even though the exact composition of the groups may occasionally vary, there are basically three preference patterns. The major dividing line
distinguishes a southern and central European culture of care from a northern and
western European culture. The Catholic countries of Ireland and southern Europe
favor family support, while the Protestant nations of The Netherlands and northern
Europe advocate state-provided formal care. The other continental European countries tend to be somewhere in between these two poles. The marked heterogeneity
of care preferences in the EU15 will make any attempts to arrive at a coordination or convergence of care policies in Europe extremely difficult, and there is little
doubt that the family support model will become stronger after enlargement.

It is not clear if the NMS citizens have a preference for family support because
they want to or because they have to, in view of the limited range of available
opportunities. Beyond this uncertainty, the findings suggest that the strength of
family care can continue to sustain the welfare state. However, it will also put
a heavy dual burden on working people—especially in the NMS and candidate
countries who already have to struggle to make ends meet—as they face a growing
challenge to combine paid and unpaid work.

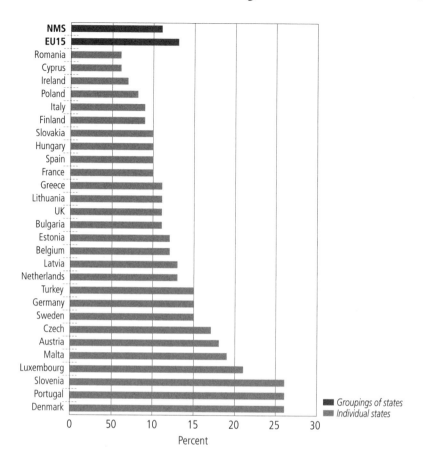

Figure 14.5. Proportions in favor of residential care for elderly people.
Response to Eurobarometer 51.0, question 36 and Candidate Countries Eurobarometer 2002.1, question 19: Which comes closest to your own opinion? Elderly people needing personal care should go into residential/nursing homes—or—The social services should help the elderly to remain in their homes for as long as possible.

14.7 Conclusions

The main findings in this chapter on health status are generally consistent with
previous research. They tend to underline the importance of social inequalities in
health, particularly in the new member states and the candidate countries. Thus,
the 'new' EU will demand intensified attention to social and economic conditions
as factors influencing health—and therefore to the role of policies beyond health.

The health status of people in the new member states and candidate countries
is generally less good than in the EU15, with the notable exceptions of Cyprus and

Malta. Particular challenges are posed by the poor health of people with low educational attainment in the new member states and candidate countries, especially when so many strategies to improve health emphasize effective communication and information—as well as opportunities to use that information. The health situation in the new member states gives no grounds for comfort regarding the challenges of meeting the health needs of an aging population; indeed, the prevalence of chronic illness and disability among older people in the new member states and candidate countries is striking.

The analyses of questions about access to and quality of services emphasize the need for more detailed investigation. These have become subjects of central importance to European-level debates about health and social protection and are related to major economic and employment concerns. It appears from both surveys that social inequalities in access are greater in the new member states and particularly the candidate countries.

The country rankings of quality of services revealed a remarkable similarity in the two surveys, reinforcing confidence in these data and the relevance of asking citizens directly for their views. While the general picture of the quality of the systems highlights differences between the different country groupings, there are also EU15 countries that are clearly not meeting the expectations of their populations. There is a great deal to be done to increase the confidence of citizens in the quality of their health services.

Family care of the dependent adult population remains impressively vital in Europe. In some cases this is no doubt because of a lack of attractive alternatives, but it also reflects enduring commitments to family support. Preferences for the future of care tend to emphasize measures to support families rather than to replace them with residential care. Even so, needs and demands for mobility and participation in the labor market will put increasing pressures on some groups of carers, particularly those who are employed.

There is much discussion of the principles underlying access to quality health services—support, equity, affordability, universality. The results show that social inequalities in access nevertheless prevail—specifically to the advantage of higher income groups. In many instances, older people still reported problems with physical access to services, and affordability was a real barrier for many people, especially those on low incomes in the new member states and the Mediterranean and accession countries. Enlargement will, in the short term, increase some of the challenges that remain to be overcome across the EU.

References

Alber, J. and Fahey, T. (2004) *Perceptions of Living Conditions in an Enlarged Europe*, Luxembourg: Office for Official Publications of the European Communities, See http://www.eurofound.eu.int/publications/htmlfiles/ef03113.htm/ accessed in February 2006.

Alber, J. and Köhler, U. (2004) *Health and Care in an Enlarged Europe*, Luxembourg, Office for Official Publications of the European Communities, See http://www.eurofound.ie/publications/EF03107EN.htm / accessed in February 2006.

Berkman, L. and Kawachi, I. (2000) *Social Epidemiology*, Oxford, UK: Oxford University Press.

European Commission (2003) *The Social Situation in the European Union 2003*, Brussels, Belgium: The European Commission.

European Foundation (2004) *Quality of Life in Europe*, Luxembourg: Office for Official Publications of the European Communities.

European Parliament (2004) *Report on the Communication from the Commission on Health Care and Care for the Elderly: Supporting National Strategies for Ensuring a High Level of Social Protection* (A5-0098/2004), Brussels, Belgium: Committee on Employment and Social Affairs.

Grammenos, S. (2003) European Foundation for the Improvement of Living and Working Conditions, *Illness, Disability and Social Inclusion*, Luxembourg: Office for Official Publications of the European Communities.

Robine, J.-M., Jagger, C. and the Euro-REVES Group (2003) 'Creating a Coherent Set of Indicators to Monitor Health across Europe: The Euro-REVES 2 Project,' *European Journal of Public Health*, **13**(1): 6–14.

World Health Organization and European Commission (2002) *Health Status Overview for Countries of Central and Eastern Europe that are Candidates for Accession to the EU*, Brussels, Belgium: European Commission: Health and Consumer Protection.

Part VI

Challenges Ahead for the European Union

Chapter 15

Civic Society and the Family: On the Formation of Social Capital in Europe

Jan H. Marbach

15.1 Introduction

As Wolfgang Lutz points out in Chapter 5, demographers have so far searched in vain for theories that can explain fertility trends in Europe today and make plausible predictions for the future. This lack of any overarching framework applies just as much to the other dimensions of demography. One possible approach that is showing promise within sociology and that could throw new light on demographic change is social capital theory. In this chapter we focus on the relationship between civic society and the family and how the two work together to shape patterns of social capital. The ideas and methods used here might be of use for future research in demography.

The concept of social capital has been presented as the social counterpart of human capital—the latter being considered an individual good. According to Loury (1977), social capital emerges from family relations and the social organization of small communities and is a resource upon which human capital can capitalize. Similarly, Coleman and Hoffer (1987) detected social capital in the number of persons interested in a child's school success. Initially, therefore, social capital was understood as an individual resource emanating from interpersonal relations that unfolded within the process of human-capital building. As Portes and Landolt (1996) pointed out, however, the concept of social capital has since been expanded in three directions:

1. The term social capital has been applied not only to individuals but to groups, regions and whole states, thus widening its meaning from 'individual resource' to 'collective good.'
2. As sources of social capital were often described in terms of their utility, it became a convention to infer the existence of social capital from its benefit to an individual or group.
3. As only the positive virtues of social capital were highlighted, the concept was stripped of any of the possible negative connotations of social relations.

The core elements of how we actually understand social capital can be summarized as follows: becoming involved in social relations and maintaining them has an intrinsic benefit that stimulates further investment. Socializing thus creates social capital as a by-product that may be useful on different occasions and in differing contexts. From that point of view, social capital is an inadvertent outcome of the fostering of contacts and of sociableness. The intrinsic gain is a common good, as the common interest aims at the maintenance of cooperation.

On the other hand, social capital is a personal resource that can be applied profitably. This view tacks an instrumental purpose on to socializing that carries with it an incentive to invest in social relations in order to accumulate social assets, namely, the commitments of others to ego. As such commitments are based on mutual trust, they achieve a social rather than a private good.

Trust becomes economically efficient, as it reduces the transaction costs that emerge if individuals trade using asymmetric information and experience monitoring problems. Prosocial motives can be a source of trust, as society gratifies prosocial behavior, but trust can also emerge among egoists if, in the course of repeated trading, they learn that noncooperation yields losses. Trust can nevertheless be exploited, rendering social relations asymmetric, detrimental or harmful. Hence, scaling social capital should allow negative values.

When using social capital as a public good, nonexclusivity and nonrivalry are the rule, which may encourage the problem of free riding. Social capital, however, has special properties that prove punitive to free riders. Social relations are cultivated through a potentially indefinite number of iterations, making cooperation a stable strategy (Axelrod, 1984; Taylor, 1987). Free riders are at risk of losing their social capital altogether, especially in networks that are dense and not very large and where they are less protected by anonymity. To benefit from social re-

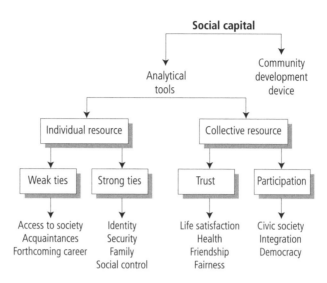

Figure 15.1. Social capital overview.

lations, one must be obedient to the rules of social exchange (Blau, 1964), that is, one must make a continuous investment that strives for a balance of give-and-take. Neglecting the fostering of social relations will mean losing them in the long run.

The value of social capital as a public good is not diminished but rather increased by the number of users, unlike the distribution of its payoff, as there is a loose bond between an actor's investment and his or her output. If ego ceases to invest in a network, that network ceases to be ego's social capital.

The concept of social capital has furthered both scientific research and public policy, having proven its worth as an analytical tool as well as a community development device (see *Figure 15.1*). In this chapter I will concentrate on social capital as a research tool.

Social capital as an analytical tool addresses two main levels of analysis that correspond with two types of social capital as sources of potential payoff. Social capital may serve as an *individual resource*, where social relations of ego or an individual actor, respectively, establish an ego- or actor-centered network. The effects will depend on the number and resources of network members, the structure of their connections with each other and the interplay of trust and commitment within dyads of ego and single others. The bulk of research on social capital, particularly if it makes use of social network analysis, can be subsumed under the individual perspective (Granovetter, 1973; Fischer, 1982; Lin, 1982; Coleman, 1988; Coleman, 1990; Burt, 1992; Flap, 1995).

Social capital, on the other hand, is handled as a *collective resource* where certain properties of groups, regions or whole societies are regarded as pivotal to the maintenance of social cohesion and trustworthiness. As social capital is considered a collective resource, empirical analysis is focused on aggregate data. Many authors prefer two distinct indicators of social cohesion—*trust*, representing a feeling of fairness and security, and *frequency of association* among people, delivering an objective measure of social and/or political participation (Dasgupta, 1988; Anheier *et al.*, 1995; Paxton, 1999; Sampson *et al.*, 1999; Torsvik, 2000; Paxton, 2002). Some authors, however, have stressed social values and norms as reflecting solidarity and cooperation, using indicators that are more or less halfway between a subjective view and an objective measure (Putnam, 1993; Portes, 1995; Putnam, 1995; Fukuyama, 1995a; Fukuyama, 1995b; Knack and Keefer, 1997; Paldam and Svendsen, 1998; Narayan and Prichett, 1999).

It should be added that other authors, in particular, Bourdieu (1983 and 1986), try to combine both levels of social capital in their analyses. Bourdieu's term 'field structure' is close to concepts of positional network analysis as 'structural equivalence' or 'regular equivalence' that combine (i) individual views of actors within a network and (ii) global views on the structure of the network (White *et al.*, 1976; Arabie and Boorman, 1982; Burt, 1990; Boyd, 1996; Batagelj *et al.*, 2002). Yet data requirements are high and include multiple complete networks that are usually confined to local case studies or collective actors within selected areas or boundaries.

15.2   Social Capital as a Collective Resource in Europe

My presentation of selected results in terms of social capital as a collective resource is as follows. *Figure 15.1* shows trust and participation as often-used indicators. To justify the actual results, I make use of the European Social Survey (ESS), 2003. ESS Round II ultimately included data based on national random samples of 20 European countries plus Israel. Respondents were persons aged 15 years or older, resident within private households, regardless of nationality and citizenship or language. The data set provides several indices that express social capital in terms of either trust and participation or items of well-being, the latter representing the possible output of social capital use (see *Box 15.1*).

Table 15.1 displays the correlation matrix of all indicators. Correlations represent the individual level of analysis across all 20 European states that took part in the study.

On the individual level, the social capital indicators, trust, fairness and helpfulness, are highly correlated. Correlations between this 'basic-trust' block and legal trust remain modest, indicating that there is a difference between trust among people and trust in legal institutions. Moreover, correlations between all sorts of

Box 15.1. European Social Survey (ESS) 2003: Items of social capital and well-being.

Social capital items

Trust:	*Most people can be trusted/you can't be too careful*
Legal trust:	*Trust in the legal system*
Fairness:	*Most people try to take advantage of you/try to be fair*
Helpfulness:	*Most of the time people are helpful/mostly looking out for themselves*
Membership:	*Number of voluntary associations where respondent is a member*

Well-being items

Life satisfaction:	*How satisfied are you with life as a whole?*
Happiness:	*How happy are you?*
Health:	*'Very good' = 1 to 'very bad' = 5*

Table 15.1. Correlation matrix of social capital and well-being indices.

	F	HF	L	LS	H	HS	M
Trust	0.59	0.48	0.28	0.30	0.17	0.26	0.23
Fairness (F)	–	0.51	0.24	0.30	0.13	0.29	0.21
Helpfulness (HF)		–	0.23	0.27	0.12	0.25	0.19
Legal trust (L)			–	0.23	0.14	0.19	0.15
Life satisfaction (LS)				–	0.31	0.68	0.19
Health (H)					–	0.33	0.14
Happiness (HS)						–	0.18
Membership (M)							–

Source: European Social Survey, 2003.

trust and the 'objective' measure of social capital, membership, are modest. Membership is considered to prove horizontal contacts among the members of a community, thus testifying to their civic engagement (Torsvik, 2000, p. 454). Figures in *Table 15.1* show only a modest correlation with trust and even less significant associations with the rest. Hence, membership seems to feature as a rather independent dimension of social capital. A second cluster of higher correlations shows up among well-being indices, especially between life satisfaction and happiness.

What about relationships between social capital and human capital indicators? As mentioned above, it was this very question that originally triggered scientific interest in social capital. Let us continue by looking first at the individual level, displayed in *Table 15.2*.

The cluster of high correlations on the upper left-hand side is the same as in *Table 15.1*. There is also, of course, a high correlation between level of education and

Table 15.2. Correlation matrix of social capital and human capital indices.

	F	HF	M	A	Y
Trust	0.59	0.48	0.23	0.19	0.19
Fairness (F)	–	0.51	0.21	0.16	0.15
Helpfulness (HF)		–	0.19	0.10	0.10
Membership (M)			–	0.29	0.30
% Academics (A)				–	0.80
Years of education (Y)					–

Source: European Social Survey, 2003.

years spent in full-time education. More interesting, however, is a medium correlation between membership and the human capital indices. It is at least stronger than correlations with the 'trust complex.' As membership normally reaches its highest peak after education has finished, a possible causal influence points from education to membership rather than in the opposite direction.

Yet, this is not a question that we should be answering at this stage. What else is at issue? Do aggregations of social capital have rankings similar to those on the individual level? If this is the case, the effects of social capital visible on the individual level are mediated or buffered by collective settings, such as cultural norms or traditions, habits or customs and the like, that exist within the settings. If, for example, Spaniards rank higher on trust than Italians, it may be that interactions between people in Spain rely less on mutual control than those between people in Italy, despite variations in trust among individuals running parallel in both countries. If, additionally, Spaniards on average have the edge over Italians in terms of helpfulness, evidence of nonaccidental differences between national shapes of social capital would be strengthened.

Similarly, Putnam (1993) has explained differences in the effectiveness of public administration in Italy by an unequal distribution of 'civic virtues' rather than by unequal degrees of modernization. He found reasons for differences in the domestic allocation of civic virtues in the history of Italy. During the late Middle Ages, republican city states founded on horizontal networks emerged in the north, while during the same period the south remained controlled by Catholic kingdoms that fostered hierarchical networks and—as Putnam (1993, pp. 88, 92 and 144) calls it—'amoral familism,' that is, a dichotomization of the world between the moral sphere existing within kinship boundaries and the rest of the world with its negligible moral rules. How could these differences remain stable over seven hundred or more years when political conditions changed completely? Because, Putnam (1993) writes, both civic virtues in the north and amoral familism in the south worked like infernal cycles.

We now return to the actual figures of social capital in Europe. *Table 15.3* shows the trust and fairness rankings of the 20 countries that took part in the Euro-

Table 15.3. Rankings of ESS countries according to trust and fairness (percentages above 75 percentile).

Rank	Country	Trust	Rank	Country	Fairness
1.	Denmark	67.5	1.	Denmark	74.2
2.	Norway	62.3	2.	Norway	69.2
3.	Finland	60.1	3.	Finland	68.5
4.	Sweden	52.7	4.	Sweden	63.2
5.	Netherlands	44.1	5.	Netherlands	52.5
6.	Switzerland	42.2	6.	Switzerland	51.4
7.	Ireland	40.8	7.	Ireland	47.9
8.	Israel	33.7	8.	Germany	42.6
9.	United Kingdom	31.1	9.	Belgium	40.7
10.	Luxembourg	30.6	10.	Luxembourg	39.4
11.	Belgium	30.4	11.	United Kingdom	38.3
12.	Spain	28.4	12.	Israel	37.8
13.	Germany	25.3	13.	Spain	33.0
14.	Italy	22.6	14.	Czech Republic	31.6
15.	Czech Republic	21.3	15.	Slovenia	28.2
16.	Slovenia	20.1	16.	Portugal	28.0
17.	Greece	17.2	17.	Hungary	25.3
18.	Hungary	17.2	18.	Italy	23.2
19.	Portugal	15.8	19.	Poland	22.7
20.	Poland	13.6	20.	Greece	16.2
GM		34.7			42.6
Cramer's V		33.2			32.9
N		36,058			36,815
Missing		2,541			1,784
Rank Correlation (Spearman)		0.93			

Source: European Social Survey, 2003.

pean Social Survey(ESS). ESS data from Austria and France had not been released at the time of writing, but it can be assumed that Austria's rankings would be scattered over the upper half while France's rankings would be persistently close to those of Spain.

There is a very clear association between a high correlation on the individual level ($r = 0.59$) and an even higher correlation ($r_S = 0.93$) among countries with respect to the social capital indicators, trust and fairness. Northern European states excel, having equal rankings in both dimensions. Middle European states and Israel are distributed in the midfield, while the bottom of the table is occupied by eastern European and Mediterranean countries. We have to face up to the fact that social capital, as measured by trust and fairness, is unequally distributed over Europe in a systematic manner that resembles, to a certain degree, the findings of Putnam

(1993) in Italy. One may object that thinking in terms of trust or fairness and using related items in the questionnaire are flattering the cultural customs of the north because they are uncommon in the south and the east, but—even if that were true—it would merely confirm the finding.

Table 15.4 presents an overview of all ranks in all indicators of all countries that took part in the ESS. The ranking below the heading 'country' mirrors average ranks across all indicators. There are only minor ranking shifts compared with *Table 15.3*. It may be more interesting to compare the profiles of countries in terms of inconsistencies in status. The Scandinavian countries are widely consistent in their ranks, yet Finland has a negative outlier with its health status. The opposite is true of Greece which has a low ranking in most indicators but excels in health, something that is consistent with Eurostat data on the health status of Greeks (European Commission, 2003, p. 34). Luxembourg has medium rankings in most social capital indicators, except for membership, and enjoys high life satisfaction and happiness, yet has only a modest health status (also consistent with Eurostat data on health). Italy, which has a mainly lower-midfield ranking, comes bottom in happiness. Belgians' low trust in their legal system seems to mirror the upheaval accompanying recent criminal cases that reflected adversely on the police and justice system. And, last but not least, Israelis' high trust in their legal system is worth highlighting.

Yet, all in all, a remarkable consistency prevails among country rankings across social capital and well-being indices, revealing three regional layers that combine a north-to-south and a west-to-east direction. Coinciding with those layers are distinct civic cultures, each at variance with a European policy that is set to foster integration by strengthening civic structures all over Europe.

Table 15.5, which parallels *Table 15.1* on the aggregate level of country ranking, demonstrates the ranking consistency of countries by much higher correlations than in *Table 15.1*, although the overall distribution of highs and lows resembles the individual-level distribution. There is a cluster of high correlations inside the complex of social capital indices relating to trust, with the exception of trust in the legal system. Membership plays a similarly abnormal role on the aggregate level. The high correlation between life satisfaction and happiness, as seen in *Table 15.1*, also shows up. There are nevertheless some special features worth highlighting on the aggregate level. Output indicators such as life satisfaction, health and happiness are, relatively speaking, more associated with basic trust indicators here than on the individual level. Hence, the relationship between social capital and people's well-being seems to show up more clearly at the country level than at the individual level of analysis.

Table 15.6 displays some conspicuous inconsistencies between ranking by percentage of academics versus years of education. Denmark comes only nineteenth

Table 15.4. Summary of ESS country rankings in indicators of social capital and well-being.

Country	Trust	Fair	Helpful	Legal trust	Life satisfaction	Happy	Health	Member-ship
Denmark	1	1	1	1	1	1	1	2
Norway	2	2	4	5	6	7	5	3
Sweden	4	4	2	7	5	6	7	1
Finland	3	3	5	3	4	3	11	8
Ireland	7	7	3	11	7	4	2	6
Luxembourg	10	10	13	6	2	2	10	5
Switzerland	6	6	7	8	3	5	8	*
Netherlands	5	5	8	14	9	10	12	4
Israel	8	12	11	2	11	11	4	11
UK	9	11	6	13	10	8	6	9
Belgium	11	9	12	16	8	9	9	7
Germany	13	8	9	9	12	13	15	10
Spain	12	13	14	17	15	12	13	13
Slovenia	16	15	10	15	14	14	16	12
Greece	17	20	20	4	18	16	3	17
Italy	14	18	17	12	13	20	14	14
Hungary	18	17	15	10	19	18	19	16
Czech Rep.	15	14	16	19	17	15	18	*
Portugal	19	16	18	18	20	17	20	15
Poland	20	19	19	20	16	19	17	18

Note: *Did not survey membership in associations.
Source: European Social Survey, 2003.

in terms of percentage of academics but ranks second in terms of years of education. The opposite holds true for Finland, which is fifth in terms of percentage of academics but twelfth in terms of years of education. Similar inconsistencies show up in Belgium, Greece, Hungary, Luxembourg, The Netherlands and Slovenia. There is, of course, a great deal of variation among the national education systems, and this may explain some of the inconsistencies; and we also have to factor in the close proximity among countries in years of education that is artificially expanded by ranking. Thus, inconsistencies must not be dramatized. Still, it seems worthwhile to examine associations between social and human capital indices by comparing their ranks on the aggregate level. This is done in *Table 15.8*.

The entries of interest are found in the furthest two columns to the right. One of the most striking deviations from correlations on the individual level (*Table 15.2*) is the low-ranked correlation between the percentage of academics and years of education ($r_S = 0.31$ versus $r = 0.80$). This is partly due to a different scaling. Individuals who spend more time in education normally reach higher grades. On the aggregate level, however, we compare only the share of the highest classification,

Table 15.5. Rank correlations (Spearman) of social capital and well-being indices by countries.

	F	HF	L	LS	H	HS	M
Trust	0.93	0.89	0.62	0.88	0.69	0.86	0.75
Fairness (F)	–	0.91	0.51	0.85	0.86	0.52	0.76
Helpfulness (HF)		–	0.49	0.79	0.59	0.82	0.75
Legal trust (L)			–	0.58	0.68	0.56	0.44
Life satisfaction (LS)				–	0.63	0.92	0.70
Health (H)					–	0.67	0.54
Happiness (HS)						–	0.70
Membership (M)							–

Source: European Social Survey, 2003.

Table 15.6. Rankings of ESS countries according to percentage of academics and years of full-time education completed.

Rank	Country	% Academics	Rank	Country	Years
1.	Israel	48.0	1.	Norway	13.3
2.	Luxembourg	38.3	2.	Denmark	13.2
3.	Ireland	29.8	3.	Ireland	13.0
4.	Norway	28.1	4.	Netherlands	12.9
5.	*Finland*	*25.4*	5.	Germany	12.8
6.	United Kingdom	23.5	6.	Israel	12.8
7.	Sweden	22.1	7.	United Kingdom	12.7
8.	*Germany*	*21.7*	8.	Czech Republic	12.4
9.	*Slovenia*	*14.8*	9.	Belgium	12.2
10.	Greece	14.0	10.	Luxembourg	12.1
11.	Czech Republic	13.7	11.	Sweden	12.0
12.	Poland	11.7	12.	Finland	12.0
13.	Switzerland	10.4	13.	Hungary	11.7
14.	Spain	9.6	14.	Poland	11.4
15.	Belgium	9.3	15.	Slovenia	11.4
16.	Portugal	8.9	16.	Switzerland	10.8
17.	*Italy*	*8.4*	17.	Italy	10.7
18.	Netherlands	7.3	18.	Spain	10.2
19.	Denmark	7.2	19.	Greece	9.7
20.	Hungary	5.8	20.	Portugal	7.4
GM		19.6	GM		11.8
Cramer's V		22.3	Eta squared		10.8
N		36,816	N		38,035
Missing		1,783	Missing		564

Note: Countries in italics are calculated from the transnational measure of education as the national measure is unavailable.

Source: European Social Survey, 2003.

Table 15.7. Summary of ESS countries' rankings in indicators of social capital and human capital.

Country	Trust	Fair	Helpful	Member-ship	% Academics	Years of education
Denmark	1	1	1	2	19	2
Norway	2	2	4	3	4	1
Sweden	4	4	2	1	7	11
Finland	3	3	5	8	5	12
Ireland	7	7	3	6	3	3
Luxembourg	10	10	13	5	2	10
Switzerland	6	6	7	*	13	16
Netherlands	5	5	8	4	18	4
Israel	8	12	11	11	1	6
UK	9	11	6	9	6	7
Belgium	11	9	12	7	15	9
Germany	13	8	9	10	8	5
Spain	12	13	14	13	14	18
Slovenia	16	15	10	12	9	15
Greece	17	20	20	17	10	19
Italy	14	18	17	14	17	17
Hungary	18	17	15	16	20	13
Czech Rep.	15	14	16	*	11	8
Portugal	19	16	18	15	16	20
Poland	20	19	19	18	12	14

Note: *Did not survey membership in associations.
Source: European Social Survey, 2003.

Table 15.8. Rank correlations (Spearman) of social capital and human capital indices by countries.

	F	HF	M	A	Y
Trust	0.93	0.89	0.75	0.29	0.65
Fairness (F)	–	0.91	0.76	0.23	0.69
Helpfulness (HF)		–	0.75	0.31	0.67
Membership (M)			–	0.28	0.65
% Academics (A)				–	0.31
Years of education (Y)					–

Source: European Social Survey, 2003.

namely, academics, with years spent by people of a country in the national education system. This shifting view creates different results, as *Table 15.6* has shown: there are countries with a high percentage of academics and a moderate level of time spent in education, such as Finland or Luxembourg, and countries with the opposite situation, such as Denmark and The Netherlands. More interesting may be that correlations in rank between social capital indices and years of education are more than twice as high as the percentage of academics. As years of education cover the whole spectrum of classifications, the sizable correlation of ranking with the trust complex and membership reveals a systematic association between social and human capital moderated by national educational usages and civic cultures. Countries with a longer average education tend to have a higher amount of social capital—or vice versa, as we know nothing about causal influences. These are more easily detected on the individual level to which we now turn.

15.3   Social Capital as an Individual Resource in Germany

On the individual level the concept of social capital posits that 'social relationships form a resource that individuals can draw upon in their personal and professional lives' (Hofferth *et al.*, 1999, p. 79). The basic idea, as Lin *et al.* (2001) put it, is that people invest time and money in building and maintaining social ties because they consider them a source of immediate or future return.

There are two different approaches to dealing with social capital as an individual resource. I label these two approaches by the surnames of the outstanding authors who defined the decisive steps: James S. Coleman and Mark Granovetter. Before I continue describing my operational applications, we must quickly look at the database I use to support these concepts. In the absence of a European survey or panel with an explicit focus on social network data across a decade or more, I rely on the German Family Survey.

15.3.1   Database

The German Family Survey was launched in 1986 at the behest of, and sponsored by, the German Federal Department of Youth and Family. The first wave of interviews started in 1988 and comprised 10,000 standardized face-to-face interviews conducted by professional polling companies. Respondents were Germans aged 18 to 55 living in the then West Germany. After German reunification in 1990, this first wave was complemented by an additional 2,000 interviews addressing East Germans of the same age.

The second wave of the family survey in 1994 involved about 11,000 interviews comprising both West and East Germans. In West Germany the bulk of interviews (5,000) readdressed respondents of the first wave who were then aged 24 to 61. All other respondents were newly sampled, thus making this a mixed panel-and-repeated-survey.

The third wave of the family survey was finished in 2000 using Computer-Assisted Personal Interviewing (CAPI). It includes, as another panel ingredient,

Box 15.2. Name generators.

The following name generators jointly applied in the Germany Family Surveys 1988–1990, 1994 and 2000 were used to build indicators of social capital:

1. With whom do you discuss things that are personally important to you?
2. To whom do you have a close emotional attachment?
3. From whom do you occasionally or regularly receive financial aid?
4. To whom do you occasionally or regularly give financial aid?
5. With whom do you spend most of your leisure time?
6. What persons, excluding you, reside in your household?
7. Whom do you count as a member of your family?

about 2,000 interviews with respondents of the first wave, then aged 30 to 67. The bulk of about 8,000 interviews meets the repeated-survey design with people aged 18 to 55.

An item that distinguishes the German Family Survey from comparable studies in Germany and elsewhere is the continued retrieval of ego-centered network data in all waves. Network information was gathered using an open-choice format with a set of 12 name generators and roughly six name interpreters (gender, age, residential distance, frequency of contact, relationship to respondent, evaluation) (*Box 15.2*).

15.3.2 Social capital measures

According to Coleman (1988 and 1990), social capital is highest in relations characterized by:

1. The easiest possible spatial availability;
2. The highest frequency of contacts;
3. A great multiplicity of things done with the same person; and
4. A tight density within the network linking each member to each other.

Hence, social capital relies essentially on 'strong ties' connecting people who tend to be similar to each other.

According to Granovetter (1973), the social efficiency of a network rises if relations:

1. Are focused merely on distinct purposes (weak ties);
2. Addressing a maximum of different people;

3. Who tend to be dissimilar to each other; and
4. Who are connected to each other only by chance.

Social capital based on 'weak ties' grants access to a larger range of society with less social control and social fragmentation than strong ties.

The indices presented in *Boxes 15.3, 15.4* and *15.5* are directly based on these divergent ideas.

Let us first look at social capital indices serving as independent variables.

Box 15.6 illustrates the explanatory power of social capital indices using loneliness as an example. Loneliness was measured using the loneliness scale of De Jong-Gierveld and van Tilburg (1999). In network literature, loneliness is an often-addressed item, and, as authors often confess, their data prevent them from deciding whether lonely people have smaller networks or whether smaller networks render people lonely. What is the finding of the logistic regression in *Box 15.6*?

1. The dominant protective factor against loneliness is, of course, a partner, be it a spouse or an unmarried intimate.
2. Nearly equally effective as a shield from loneliness, and ranked second, are the 'strong ties' of the Coleman index. Commanding a dense network seems to be more important for the absence of loneliness than having weak ties.
3. 'Weak ties,' according to Granovetter, also have a significant influence; but they rank only fifth and have the opposite effect, namely, a network consisting of weak and loose ties boosts the risk of loneliness. Hence, as regards loneliness, two indices of social capital produce effects in opposite directions.

Three dynamic influences deserve special attention: the fluctuation of both 'strong ties' and 'weak ties,' and of health, between 1994 and 2000. As the dependent variable dichotomizes respondents into lonely or not lonely over time, one may conclude that the influence goes from loneliness to growing or waning networks. Yet regressions of social capital indices on loneliness in 1994 do not reveal any effect of this sort. Rather, there are independent effects of both the 'stock' of social capital at a given time and its fluctuation over time:

1. Both 'strong ties' and their possible growth independently prevented non-lonely people in 1994 from becoming lonely in 2000.
2. Both 'weak ties' and their possible growth independently made people who were lonely in 1994 stay lonely in 2000.

While the effects of stock and growth coincide in the case of social capital, the effects of health and regaining one's health do the opposite. Enjoying stable

Box 15.3. Index of social capital following the Coleman tradition: Coleman capital.

1. Availability: Nominee resides in the same household, same house or close neighborhood.
2. Frequency of contact: Nominee is contacted at least once a week.
3. Intensity: Nominee shows up at least once in an *expressive* name generator (attachment, shared leisure time) as well as in an *instrumental* name generator (discussion on personal matters, financial aid given and/or received).
4. Density: Nominee is perceived as member of respondent's family and/or is sharing his/her household.

Coleman capital (strong ties)
is equal to
the sum of each nominee's scores meeting the five criteria
over all the respondent's nominees

Box 15.4. Index of Qualitative Variation (IQV).

This index is a building block for a Granovetter index of social capital, based on a network's heterogeneity. Heterogeneity is measured by the

Index of Qualitative Variation (IQV)

Technically, the IQV gauges the extent to which a potential amount of heterogeneity (given by the number of values of a categorical variable) is realized by a population. The IQV is normalized to the range between 0 and 1.

Criterion of qualitative variation within the ego-centered networks sampled by the German Family Surveys is the *relationship* between respondents and their nominees:

1. Partner (spouse or mate);
2. Consanguine kin;
3. In-law kin;
4. Friend;
5. Colleague (work place or voluntary association);
6. Neighbor;
7. Other person.

Qualitative Variation of Network Members
is equal to
the IQV based on seven classes of relationship
between a respondent
and all of his/her nominees

Box 15.5. Index of social capital following the Granovetter tradition: Granovetter capital.

This index is simply the IQV weighted with the size of the respondent's network.

A small but heterogeneous network may attain the same social range as a large network consisting of widely homogeneous people. In general, however, high qualitative variation is prevented by a very small network and facilitated by a large one, as it needs a minimum of seven network members to the full range of heterogeneity measured by the IQV here. Hence:

Granovetter capital (weak ties)

is equal to

IQV * NETWORK SIZE

Box 15.6. Logistic regression of reported feelings of loneliness (panel).

Dependent variable: 1 =   Felt lonely in 1994 and 2000 (n = 99)
                   0 =   No feelings of loneliness in 1994 and 2000
                        (n = 1457)

PRE: 18.4 %
Nagelkerke: 22.1 %

Ranking of Significant Standardized Effect Coefficients exp(B * StdDev)

1.	Has partner, 1994 and 2000	=	0.31	(3.23^{-1})
2.	Strong ties (Coleman), 1994	=	0.32	(3.15^{-1})
3.	Healthy, 1994 and 2000	=	0.33	(3.02^{-1})
4.	Became healthy in 1994–2000	=	2.61	
5.	Weak ties (Granovetter), 1994	=	2.45	
6.	Strong ties grown in 1994–2000	=	0.42	(2.39^{-1})
7.	Weak ties grown in 1994–2000	=	2.12	
8.	Age	=	0.67	(1.49^{-1})
9.	Thoughts of divorce, 1994	=	1.45	
10.	Male	=	1.33	
11.	Number of not-liked persons, 1994	=	1.26	

Source: German Family Survey (Panel 1994–2000).

---

health is a strong protection against loneliness, but recuperation from illness is the opposite, which simply means that a disease, especially a long-lasting one, scales up the risk of loneliness. The data in general suggest that the arrows of influence point from social capital to loneliness rather than in the opposite direction.

15.3.3 Social capital in postunification Germany

Having explored the explanatory power of social capital, we now turn to social capital as a dependent variable. Did the social changes that occurred in Germany in the wake of reunification in the late 1980s impact the social capital of German families? For inhabitants of the former German Democratic Republic, the process of inclusion in the societal system of the Federal Republic carried with it much of what some German authors call 'transformation stress.' In a short time, people had to adapt to a new institutional system marked by deregulation of the labor market and social security system. Afflicted by an economic slowdown in 1993 that ended a phase of catching up to the West German standard of living, East Germans had to face unfamiliar challenges such as an unemployment rate that was double even the high West German level.

So what would we expect regarding a possible association between a country's or region's economic development and the social capital of its inhabitants? In particular, is there any evidence that different political, social and economic circumstances in West and East Germany had different impacts on Germans' personal network relationships in either part of the country? Three alternative hypotheses have been formulated in the literature (Nauck and Schwenk, 2001, pp. 1866–1867):

No-Effect Hypothesis

As families in functionally differentiated societies are widely disintegrated, following their own living patterns and protected by moral firewalls against the public sphere, no effect is assumed.

Transformation Hypothesis

Times of social crisis trigger anomic reactions. A general erosion of any types of social ties is likely to follow.

Segmentation Hypothesis

There is a graduated vulnerability of different family types to external crisis. Hence, transformation stress will be socially segmented, with urban families or single-headed families or families with economic problems being more exposed than rural families, double-headed families or families without economic problems.

Table 15.9 displays covariates and factors included in the equations of variance analyses, with two indicators of social capital, one representing the Granovetter index 'weak ties' and the other representing the Coleman index 'strong ties.' Significant effects of covariates are indicated by regression coefficients B; factor effects are specified by levels of significance. Explained variances displayed in the bottom line are either high or at least sufficient. Note that the percentage of non-kin is

Table 15.9. ANOVA[1] (all sweeps).

ANOVA (all sweeps)	Weak ties *Granovetter capital*	Strong ties *Coleman capital*
Covariates (B)		
network size		1.702
% non-kin	0.0411	-0.0525
Main effects (significance)		
West versus East Germany	0.000*	0.000
gender	ns	0.000
age group	0.000	0.000
education	0.000	ns
size of community	0.003	0.000
lives with a mate	0.000	0.000
has child/children	0.000	0.000
jobless	0.005**	ns
healthy	ns	0.000
Alternative effects (significance)		
sweeps	ns	0.000
West–East split 1994	0.000	0.000
interaction 'sweep*WestEast'	0.000	0.000
R-squared	0.294	0.582
N = 20316		

Notes: [1] Analysis of variance between groups.
*not significant if 'West–East split 1994' applies.
**not significant if 'West–East split 1994' or interaction 'sweep*WestEast' applies.
Source: German Family Survey (1988/90, 1994, 2000).

positively associated with 'weak ties' and negatively with 'strong ties.' Note also that education and unemployment are significant factors of 'weak ties' but not of 'strong ties.' Both results are in accord with a vast body of literature on associations between human and social capital (Majoribanks, 1991; Valenzuela and Dornbusch, 1994; Leonardi, 1995; Hagan *et al.*, 1996) and the strength of 'weak ties' in finding a job or achieving a better occupational status (Lin *et al.*, 1981; De Graaf and Flap, 1988; Marsden and Hurlbert, 1988; Boxman *et al.*, 1991; Meyerson, 1994). Health, on the other hand, is associated with 'strong ties' but not with 'weak ties.'

Factors under the heading 'alternative effects' are—for technical reasons—included in the equations on an alternate basis and are meant to test different assumptions regarding the following effects:

1. Social change (influence of sweeps);
2. A unique split between West and East German respondents in 1994; and
3. An interaction between 'sweep' and 'West–East split.'

While social change and the interaction term do their job on the same level of explained variance, the split factor causes marginal augments. It is especially useful in determining whether societal and economic conditions in 1994 caused significant differences between West and East Germans. Results and conclusions rely on multiple classifications based on equations with the interaction term. The findings describe net effects controlled for all concurrent influences presented in *Table 15.9*. Scarcity of space forces me to omit figures of distinctive effects and to confine myself to a textual summary of results:

1. Social change lacks any statistical influence on Granovetter capital, as average levels remain the same over the whole period. The index shows a significant lozenge-like split in the mid-1990s, indicating different reactions of West and East Germans to different political and socioeconomic settings. The no-effect hypothesis can hence be rejected for 'weak ties.' Evidence strongly confirms the transformation hypothesis that predicts an erosion of social ties in the wake of a social crisis such as that which happened in East Germany. Confirmation of the transformation hypothesis, however, remains limited to 1994. In 2000 differences between West and East Germans disappeared.

2. Curves of Coleman capital indicate a rise in both parts of Germany triggered by social change, as covered by the three waves of the Family Survey. The curves of both East and West Germans show a nearly steady upsurge without hints of a crisis reaction in 1994. There is only a small but stable edge for West Germans as regards the strength of their Coleman capital. We may conclude that the no-effect hypothesis definitely applies to the Coleman index in both parts of Germany, thus rebutting the assumption of the transformation hypothesis that all kinds of ties are affected by the impacts of societal transitions.

3. Partial confirmation of the transformation hypothesis does not preclude transformation stress hitting vulnerable types of families more severely, as the segmentation hypothesis holds. Testing was confined to single- and double-headed families. Neither the Granovetter index nor the Coleman index reveal a special vulnerability of East German single-headed families beyond a general shortage of social capital exhibited by single-headed families as compared with double-headed families. The segmentation hypothesis is therefore not confirmed.

15.3.4 How transformation stress impacts social capital: Preliminary results

Some evidence for the transformation hypothesis may raise the question as to how transformation stress—or its absence in West Germany—impacted the social capital of Germans.

East German respondents had a depth of network size in 1994 that translated into a depth of 'weak ties.' We may conclude that as unemployment was nearly unknown in the former German Democratic Republic, East Germans reacted defensively, that is, an attenuated 'qualitative variation' induced by social change was not compensated for by expanding the network size but complemented by reducing it. The economic crisis triggered a personal crisis, for example, joblessness, and this translated into a derogation of 'weak ties.'

If Granovetter capital is sensitive to economic crisis, Coleman capital is not. The main reason is that unemployment has no influence on 'strong ties.' There was hardly any attenuation in the unemployment increase in East Germany during the whole decade.

The waning of differences between the development of 'weak ties' in West and East Germany in the second half of the 1990s suggests a gradual adaptation of East Germans to a formerly unfamiliar social setting. The no-effect hypothesis fails to capture that phenomenon, but the transformation hypothesis eventually does no better work as it is unable to explain how East Germans managed to close up to West Germans in the second half of the 1990s. East Germans, as seen before, reduced their network size when crisis sharpened in 1994, but even then strengthened their 'strong ties.' Transformation stress thus weakened East Germans' 'weak ties' but not their 'strong ties,' which seemingly allowed East Germans to recover once the crisis lost its initial impact.

15.4 Summary and Conclusion

1. Social capital was initially understood as an individual resource emanating from interpersonal relations and revealing its benefits within the process of human capital building. The concept was later expanded from individuals to groups, regions and whole states, with social capital widening its meaning from 'individual resource' to a 'collective good.'

2. In a first step we investigated social capital as a collective good, using the data of the European Social Survey (2003). Here, we found trust and participation in horizontal networks to be the preferred indicators of social capital as a collective good. By comparing correlations on the individual level with ranking correlations on the aggregate level of single countries, we learned how collective settings, such as cultural norms, traditions, habits and customs moderate or buffer the effects of social capital that are visible on the individual level. There is some evidence that social capital is unequally distributed over European countries in a systematic way, with northern European states often in the

lead, central European states and Israel in the midfield, and predominantly eastern European and Mediterranean countries occupying the bottom of the table. Comparing social capital and human capital indices reveals a sizable association between trust and participation on the one hand and years of education on the other, again moderated by national educational usages and cultures. Countries with a longer average education tend to have a higher amount of social capital.

3. In a second step we turned to social capital as an individual resource. Using the data of the German Family Survey we applied two measures of social capital with distinct profiles, one representing the concept of weak ties developed by Mark Granovetter, the other standing for the concept of strong ties in the tradition of James Coleman. In the application, social capital was factored in as an explanatory variable as well as a dependent variable. The case of Germany after reunification provides a 'natural' experiment of how social change impacts the social capital of families, given the situation in East Germany which had so many of the elements of a socioeconomic crisis. Three hypotheses on social networks of families that are exposed to societal transformation were tested. 'Strong ties,' as conceptualized by Coleman, remained unaffected in West and East Germany during the observation spell, thus confirming the no-effect hypothesis. Transformation stress, however, impaired East Germans' 'weak ties,' at least temporarily. The transformation hypothesis thus seems to hold for Granovetter capital, yet fails to explain its recovery in the second half of the 1990s, when socioeconomic conditions in East Germany continued to lag behind the West German standard of living. There is no evidence supporting the segmentation hypothesis. We have to acknowledge that the no-effect hypothesis—in the long run—seems to work, thus highlighting a high level of resilience that allows families to maintain or reconstruct their social capital in the face of economic crisis and social stress.

This chapter has, we hope, shown the potential of social capital as an investigatory and explanatory framework. Our understanding of Europe's diverse demography may well be significantly enhanced through its wider application.

References

Anheier, H. K., Gerhards, J. and Romo, F. (1995) 'Forms of Capital and Social Structure in Cultural Fields: Examining Bourdieu's Social Topography,' *American Journal of Sociology*, **100**(4): 859–903.

Arabie, P. and Boorman, S.A. (1982) 'Blockmodels: Developments and Prospects,' in Hudson, H.C. (ed) *Classifying Social Data*, San Francisco, CA, USA: Jossey-Bass Publishers, pp. 177–198.

Axelrod, R. (1984) *Die Evolution der Kooperation*, Munich, Germany: Oldenbourg [in German].

Batagelj, V., Ferligoj, A. and Doreian, P. (2002) *Generalized Blockmodeling of 2-Mode Networks*, Paper presented at the Sunbelt XXII International Social Network Conference, held in New Orleans, LA, USA, 13–17 February.

Blau, P. M. (1964) *Exchange and Power in Social Life*, New York, USA: John Wiley and Sons.

Bourdieu, P. (1983) 'Ökonomisches Kapital, kulturelles Kapital, soziales Kapital,' in Kreckel, R. (ed) *Soziale Ungleichheiten, Soziale Welt*, Sonderband 2, Göttingen, Germany: Schwartz, pp. 183–198 [in German].

Bourdieu, P. (1986) 'The Forms of Capital,' in Richardson, J. (ed) *Handbook of Theory and Research for the Sociology of Education*, New York, USA: The Greenwood Press, pp. 241–258.

Boyd, J.P. (1996) *Fibrations and Regular Equivalence of Social Relations*, Paper presented at the Sunbelt XVI International Social Network Conference, held in Charleston, SC, USA, 22–25 February.

Boxman, E.A.W., De Graaf, P. M. and Flap, H.D. (1991) 'The Impact of Social and Human Capital on the Income Attainment of Dutch Managers,' *Social Networks*, **13**: 51–73.

Burt, R. (1990) 'Detecting Role Equivalence,' *Social Networks*, **12**: 83–97.

Burt, R. (1992) *Structural Holes: The Social Structure of Competition*, Cambridge, MA, USA: Harvard University Press.

Coleman, J.S. (1988) 'Social Capital in the Creation of Human Capital,' *American Journal of Sociology*, **94**: 95–120.

Coleman, J.S. (1990) *Foundations of Social Theory*, Cambridge, MA, USA: Harvard University Press.

Coleman, J.S. and Hoffer T.B. (1987) *Public and Private High Schools: The Impact of Communities*, New York, USA: Basic Books.

Dasgupta, P. (1988) 'Trust as a Commodity,' in Gambetta, D. (ed) *Trust: Making and Breaking Cooperative Relations*, Oxford, England: Blackwell, pp. 49–72.

De Graaf, P.M. and Flap, H.D. (1988) 'With a Little Help from My Friends: Social Resources as an Explanation of Occupational Status and Income in West Germany, the Netherlands, and the United States,' *Social Forces*, **67**: 452–472.

De Jong-Gierveld, J. and van Tilburg, T.G. (1999) *Manual of the Loneliness Scale*, Amsterdam, The Netherlands: Department of Social Research Methodology, Free University of Amsterdam.

European Commission (2003) *The Social Situation in the European Union 2003*, See http://europa.eu.int/comm/employment_social/publications/2003/keag03001-en.html/ accessed in January 2006.

European Social Survey (2003) See http://www.europeansocialsurvey.org/ accessed in January 2006.

Fischer, C. (1982) *To Dwell Among Friends. Personal Networks in Town and City*, Chicago, ILL, USA: The University of Chicago Press.

Flap, H.D. (1995) *No Man Is an Island. The Research Program of a Social Capital Theory*, Paper presented at the workshop 'Rational Choice and Social Networks,' held 26–28 January, Wassenaar, The Netherlands.

Fukuyama, F. (1995a) 'Social Capital and the Global Economy,' *Foreign Affairs*, **74**(5): 89–103.

Fukuyama, F. (1995b) *Trust: The Social Virtues and the Creation of Prosperity*, New York, USA: The Free Press.

German Family Survey (1988/90, 1994, 2000) Munich, Germany: German Youth Institute.

Granovetter, M.S. (1973) 'The Strength of Weak Ties,' *American Journal of Sociology*, **78**(6): 1360–1380.

Hagan, J., Macmillan, R. and Wheaton, B. (1996) 'New Kid in Town: Social Capital and the Life Course Effects of Family Migration on Children,' *American Sociological Review*, **61**: 368–385.

Hofferth, S.L., Boisjoly, J. and Duncan, G.J. (1999) 'The Development of Social Capital,' *Revista Rationality and Society*, **11**(1): 79–110.

Knack, S. and Keefer, P. (1997) 'Does Social Capital Have an Economic Payoff? A Cross-Country Investigation,' *Quarterly Journal of Economics*, **122**: 1251–1288.

Leonardi, R. (1995) 'Regional Development in Italy. Social Capital in the Mezzogiorno,' *Oxford Review of Economic Policy*, **11**(2): 165–179.

Lin, N. (1982) 'Social Resources and Instrumental Action,' in Marsden P.V. and Lin, N. (eds) *Social Structure and Network Analysis*, Beverly Hills, CA, USA: Sage Publications, pp. 131–145.

Lin, N., Burt, R. and Cook, K. (eds) (2001) *Social Capital: Theory and Research*, New York, USA: Aldine de Gruyter.

Lin, N., Vaughn, J.C. and Ensel, W.M. (1981) 'Social Resources and Occupational Status Attainment,' *Social Forces*, **59**: 1163–1181.

Loury, G. (1977) 'A Dynamic Theory of Racial Income Differences,' in Wallace, P.A. and LeMund, A. (eds) *Women, Minorities, and Employment Discrimination*, Lexington, MA, USA: Lexington Books, pp. 153–186.

Majoribanks, K. (1991) 'Family Human and Social Capital and Young Adults' Educational Attainment and Occupational Aspirations,' *Psychological Reports*, **69**(1): 237–238.

Marsden, P.V. and Hurlbert, J.S. (1988) 'Social Resources and Mobility Outcomes: A Replication and Extension,' *Social Forces*, **59**(4): 1038–1059.

Meyerson, E.M. (1994) 'Human Capital, Social Capital, and Compensation: The Relative Contribution of Social Contacts to Managers' Incomes,' *Acta Sociologica*, **37**: 383–399.

Narayan, D. and Prichett, L. (1999) 'Cents and Sociability: Household Income and Social Capital in Rural Tanzania,' *Economic Development and Cultural Change*, **47**(4) 871–897, July.

Nauck, B. and Schwenk, O.G. (2001) 'Did Societal Transformation Destroy the Social Networks of Families in East Germany?' *American Behavioral Scientist*, **44**: 1864–1878.

Paldam, M. and Svendsen, G.T. (1998) *Is Social Capital an Effective Smoke Condenser?* Working Paper for University of Aarhus, Denmark, See 'wopaarhec 1998-8' in: http://www.econ.au.dk/afn/working_papers.htm/ accessed in January 2006.

Paxton, P. (1999) 'Is Social Capital Declining in the United States? A Multiple Indicator Assessment,' *American Journal of Sociology*, **105**(1): 88–127.

Paxton, P. (2002) 'Social Capital and Democracy: An Interdependent Relationship,' *American Sociological Review*, **67**: 254–277.

Portes, A. (1995) 'Economic Sociology and the Sociology of Immigration: A Conceptual Overview,' in Portes, A. (ed) *The Economic Sociology of Immigration: Essays on Networks, Ethnicity, and Entrepreneurship*, New York, USA: Russell Sage Foundation Publications, pp. 1–42.

Portes, A. and Landolt, P. (1996) 'The Downside of Social Capital,' *The American Prospect*, **94**: 18–21.

Putnam, R. D. (1993) *Making Democracy Work. Civic Traditions in Modern Italy*, Princeton, NJ, USA: Princeton University Press.

Putnam, R. D. (1995) 'Bowling Alone. America's Declining Social Capital,' *Journal of Democracy*, **6**: 65–78.

Sampson, R.J., Morenoff, J.D. and Earls, F. (1999) 'Beyond Social Capital: Spatial Dynamics of Collective Efficacy for Children,' *American Sociological Review*, **64**: 633–660.

Taylor, M. (1987) *The Possibility of Cooperation*, Cambridge, UK: Cambridge University Press.

Torsvik, G. (2000) 'Social Capital and Economic Development. A Plea for the Mechanisms,' *Rationality and Society*, **12**: 451–476.

Valenzuela, A. and Dornbusch, S.M. (1994) 'Familism and Social Capital in the Academic Achievement of Mexican Origin and Anglo Adolescents,' *Social Science Quarterly*, **75**(1): 18–36.

White, H.C., Boorman, S.A. and Breiger, R.L. (1976) 'Social Structure from Multiple Networks. I. Blockmodels of Roles and Positions,' *American Journal of Sociology*, **81**: 730–780.

Chapter 16

Europe's Future Generations: Closing Thoughts

Landis MacKellar

Asking an American to comment on the European social situation, especially these days, is an act either of faith or recklessness. Whichever it is, I thank the editors of this publication for giving me the chance to review the contributions and attempt a synthesis.

Many, indeed most, of the chapters take care to point out that Europe is not a homogeneous region, and is even less so now that the EU15 have become the EU25 through absorption of the new member states (NMS) and more candidate countries (CCs) are waiting in the wings. Viewed from afar, however, these differences blur. If a hypothetical observer in outer space were to look at the globe and attempt to describe Europe's distinctive demographic characteristics, that description would doubtless consist of three main points:

- *Slow population growth, especially slow labor force growth.* Europe's share in world population is shrinking and, without extraordinary increases in labor productivity, its share in world economic activity will also shrink. The basic cause of slow population growth in Europe is subreplacement fertility.
- *Population aging and aging of the labor force.* The ratio of the elderly to the working-age population is rising and, given the enormous inertia of demographic development, must continue to rise far into the future. Put differently,

even if fertility were suddenly to increase, substantial population aging would
still occur. Unless there are compensating changes in retirement ages and labor
force participation rates, the ratio of pension system beneficiaries to pension
system contributors will increase dramatically. The systems that provide health
care, long-term care for the chronically ill elderly and elder support more generally will come under growing stress. While longevity increases play a significant role, the main driving force that has 'locked in' European population
aging is subreplacement fertility.

- *Substantial immigration and the consequent growth of distinct ethnic and religious subpopulations.* The need for immigrant workers, the humanitarian im-
  pulse to reunite families and give asylum seekers a fair hearing and the apparently limitless supply of potential migrants have transformed Europe into
  a region of immigration. Moreover, with the notable exception of the United
  Kingdom, the European policy stance toward immigrants has been one of integration, not assimilation.

All three of these features could be argued to follow ineluctably from fertility
that has been low enough for long enough. Therefore, it makes sense to begin
this overview by looking at this phenomenon. I will then review changing family
formation trends and immigration and their consequences for pension and health
systems. I will close with some thoughts about the future of the European social
model. Throughout, I make references to other contributions to this volume.

16.1   Subreplacement Fertility

The European 'second demographic transition' manifested itself around 1960 with
an accelerating decline in marriage. Births outside marriage rose, as did the prevalence of cohabitation, but not by enough to offset the accelerating decline in marital
fertility. Since 1985 virtually all the EU15 European countries have been characterized by subreplacement fertility and declines in formerly high-fertility countries
such as Italy and Spain have been nothing short of spectacular. Fertility in many of
the NMS is even lower. Many commentators regard much of this as a temporary
result of disruptions following the collapse of Communism. However, the longer
the trend continues, the less plausible that viewpoint becomes.

There is so much gloom about European fertility that some perspective is in
order. Low fertility is hardly unknown outside Europe; something like half the
world's population lives in countries characterized by subreplacement levels. Europe itself experienced very low fertility during the 1930s. It is a common argument
that current trends mark not a break with the past but the continuation of a long-term
fertility decline that was briefly interrupted by the postwar baby boom. Moreover,

currently low total fertility rates (TFRs) may reflect in part delayed childbearing (i.e., an indeterminate number of today's women aged 15 to 45 will start to 'catch up' as they age).[1]

However, as Cordón points out in Chapter 3, Peter McDonald (2002) has advanced an argument that a TFR of 1.5 marks a danger point. His logic is that, even if fertility rises, populations with current TFRs below 1.5 are almost certainly destined to contract dramatically (demographic inertia, again). Compensating increases in immigration, labor productivity and labor force participation are exceedingly unlikely to be sufficient to avoid dramatic social consequences. If we label TFRs below 1.5 'radical subreplacement fertility,' then *most of the countries in the world with radical subreplacement fertility are European.* Whatever is going on in Europe is, to some degree, uniquely European.

It is particularly frustrating that the causes of this phenomenon are largely unknown. In the Europe of the 1930s and China today, the causes of low fertility are reasonably well explained by simple models (the first case) or policy interventions (the second case). To the extent that the economy is cyclical and government policies can be reversed, subreplacement fertility in these situations was (the first case) and is (the second case) bound not to last indefinitely. But, as the chapters in this publication make clear, we really do not understand why fertility in Europe is currently so low. The 'second demographic transition' model of van de Kaa (1987), Lesthaeghe (1995) and others offers a distinctly more modest, postmodern narrative than the 'first demographic transition' model of Notestein (1945), even in the latter's more baroque recent forms. The first demographic transition, Ansley Coale (1973) argued, is essentially irreversible. What about the second?

One of the oddities of the situation is that what people say is often at variance with what they do.[2] In Italy, with one of the lowest TFRs in Europe, young adults (18–34) respond that they expect their completed fertility will be about two children. Most have a negative view of childlessness, disapprove of the growing number of children who are only children and of the growing number of children born outside marriage. In the NMS, where marriages and fertility have both dropped dramatically since 1989, most survey respondents nonetheless express the view that they will end up having about two children.

One possibility for this dissonance is that fertility ideals are running up against material realities, for example, a shortage of housing and income. The latter, and to some extent the former, can be addressed by government policy. It is well known that fertility in Estonia has recently soared as family allowances were increased. But it is equally true that in Sweden much the same happened, but only temporarily, in the 1980s; after a few years, fertility began to decline again. Perhaps, just as central bankers can move currency markets only for a few days, social policy makers can reverse deep-set fertility trends only for a few years.

Another possibility is that the material resources for childbearing are there, but current family paradigms are not suited for childbearing and rearing. Cordón (Chapter 3) argues that employment practices, business hours, school hours and social expectation have not adapted to the new reality of the dual-earner family, and the result has been declining fertility.

Once again, policy responses are possible. Sgritta (Chapter 6) points out that in northern Europe, where government support for mothers and families is strong, female labor force participation increases with age, in other words, new mothers drop out of the labor force temporarily but quickly return to it. In southern Europe, by contrast, where support for mothers and families is weak, the labor force participation of married women declines sharply with age. Recognition of the dual-earner couple and the shifts in the family paradigm that accompany it are clearly one policy choice.

But as Wallace points out in Chapter 8, policies such as these represent choices. Policy makers can explicitly promote sexual equality (as they have in Nordic countries); they can explicitly reject it in favor of traditional norms (as they have for the most part in southern Europe) or they can grudgingly incorporate elements of egalitarianism while expressing clear preference for traditional roles (as they have in France and Germany). But such policy choices have political consequences needing to be worked out in the political process, which means confronting voters' values. Both the right and left in Europe are deeply reluctant to recognize the growing reality of two-earner families. For conservatives, the full-time mother is the ideal. For social democrats, generous time off for mothers is a matter of social justice. Even on an apparently trivial matter—extending store-opening hours to accommodate dual-earning households—progress has been painfully slow, with both left and right finding reasons to support small shopkeepers who oppose liberalization.

One indication that it is the nature of the family, not material scarcity, that is the main factor driving low fertility is the strong increase in the number of births out of wedlock. Births out of wedlock have increased from well under 10 percent of EU15 births in 1960 to very nearly one-third in recent years. Not unexpectedly, there are large regional differences, with figures ranging from single digits in some southern European countries to over half in Sweden. But there are some surprises—births out of wedlock represent over 20 percent of all births in Spain and over 30 percent in Ireland.

One point that emerges from Cordón's contribution is the important role of nonmarital fertility in driving overall fertility trends and patterns. Trends in out-of-wedlock births are difficult to analyse because they depend on two variables—the number of single persons involved in stable consensual unions (not a group that is easy to define) and the fertility of those couples. However, it seems clear that most variation in the level of fertility across European countries is explained by differences in out-of-wedlock fertility. Similarly, trends in fertility over time have been largely driven by fertility out of wedlock: there has been a convergence of European marital total fertility rates to the 1.0–1.5 range while the out-of-wedlock TFR has diverged. This mirrors experience in Japan, where marital fertility has long been stable but marriage rates have declined. In Japan, however, out-of-wedlock fertility is extremely rare and there is not the slightest indication that attitudes toward it are changing.

16.2 Delayed Family Formation and 'Alternative' Living Arrangements

The fertility trends described above cannot be understood outside the context of life transitions and living arrangements. All across Europe, both in the north where state support for the family is high and in the south where it is meager, family formation has been delayed and alternatives such as cohabitation have increased. As Wallace points out in Chapter 8, trends in family formation are really the amalgamation of trends in many other areas, among them the labor market, education and tolerance for nontraditional modes of life such as cohabitation. The average young European spends longer in university (or equivalent training), longer living at home, longer in casual or unstable employment and longer in nonmarital personal relationships than formerly, and certainly longer than young people in America.

I would frame Wallace's argument somewhat differently. What is happening in education is, I believe, mostly a reaction to the weakness of the market for young workers. And I am enough of a functionalist to believe that the tolerance for cohabitation (and other forms of stable or quasi-stable relationships), rather than being a cause of delayed family formation, is merely recognition that when marriage is delayed, there is need for an alternative arrangement under which sex is sanctioned.[3] Parenthetically, even though out-of-wedlock fertility in Japan is almost unknown, that country has experienced a very similar increase in acceptance of nonmarital sexual unions. At the bottom of it all, then, I see a weak youth labor market making it increasingly difficult for young people to marry, establish independent residence and begin reproduction. Sgritta writes in much the same spirit in Chapter 6 when he describes the inextricable links between changes in the European family economy and changes in the labor market behavior of women. Procreation has, according to him, become a rational, calculated choice; marriage, cohabitation and divorce are increasingly subjected to an economic assessment of the labor market for young workers.

Wallace sets up the counterfactual of a 'golden age': (i) full employment for men, (ii) full (and happy?) dedication of women to home production and (iii) a

strong state guarantee of income in old age. During the golden age, family formation was fast (no need for extended schooling because a good job was waiting),
fertility was high and retirement was early.

All these are things of the past. Again, I would seek explanations in structural
economic changes. Globalization and post-Fordism have all but eliminated full
traditional male industrial employment. Changes in technology and the structure
of output have strengthened women's position in the labor market; in combination
with the weakening of men's labor market position, this has translated into a shift
in the balance of power between the sexes. Women are increasingly reluctant to
specialize in home production for the account of a wage-earning male. As wage-
linked state pension guarantees have weakened, the need for women to establish a
strong independent source of old-age income has increased.

Extended education is, in part, a response to the increasing value of human
capital and the difficulty of obtaining attractive employment without proper qualifications. The explosion of specialized university and postgraduate degrees in the
United Kingdom is an attempt to exploit niches of the labor market where job
seekers (and holders) are willing to invest time and money to obtain a competitive
edge. However, this is a phenomenon largely limited to the United Kingdom. On
the continent, public universities are starved of resources yet, unlike in the United
Kingdom and the United States, do not commonly charge fees, even to students
who would be willing to pay. The cause of this reluctance are deeply held views on
universal access to learning. Laudable though the goal may be is, there have been
adverse consequences, including deteriorated infrastructure, crowded classrooms
and ultimately brain drain. In Austria, where I live, it is not rare to meet a student
who has been forced to delay completion of a degree for one or more years because
of his/her inability to gain access to a required seminar.

This is a clear inefficiency and would, it might be thought, elicit a strong policy
response. Yet policies related to higher education have, on the continent, done
nothing to encourage rapid transition into the workforce; quite the opposite. As
Samuel Brittan has often written in the *Financial Times*, too many policy makers
are still operating under the 'lump of labor fallacy,' according to which one way to
fight unemployment is to keep young persons out of the labor market and pension
off the old as fast as possible. The 'lump of labor fallacy' assumes that there is a
given amount of work to be shared out, so that every job taken by a young person
entering the labor market or an old person remaining in it will be a job unavailable
for a middle-aged worker. One worker's gain is another's loss. The problem with
this view, recognized as long ago as the late nineteenth century, is that the amount
of work to be done is not fixed; it is an endogenous variable.

Wallace points out in Chapter 8 that, to the extent that the entire labor market is rigid, flexibility and precariousness are displaced from established workers

on to beginning workers. 'Credentialism' and labor laws that discourage firms from hiring temporary and part-time workers are designed to protect consumers and workers, but they also act as a massive disincentive to employing the young. For example, it is common (France is a good example) for European employers to be required to grant a permanent contract to a 'regularly hired' new worker after only a few months. Faced with the inevitable risks of hiring a new labor force entrant, it is hardly surprising that many employers choose to hire someone older and more experienced or to forego hiring altogether.

For young Europeans, the result is an extended period, often extending to the end of their twenties or even longer, of (inefficient) education, travel, informal-sector work and internships or *stages*. Fortunately, the result is not all negative. It provides young people with a period of reflection and experimentation to sort themselves into occupations and functions according to what they are best at and enjoy most. Kovacheva, in Chapter 7, cites research by Ulrich Beck (1999) in which flexible work offers the opportunity for identity construction in a postmodern world. She also has a good point to make regarding the lengthening period during which young Europeans are dependent on their parents for housing and income security, namely, that this increase in material dependence has, paradoxically, been coupled with increasing independence from parents in terms of values. Also in partial compensation, Europe's young persons begin life as an independent consumer much earlier than their parents did.

16.3 Population Aging 1: Pensions

The trends described above, combined with demographic inertia, mean that Europe's future population will be much older than ever before. Population aging in Europe is already well under way. The elderly dependency ratio (60+ : 20–59) in the EU15 has increased from 29.3 percent in 1960 to 40 percent in 2003. As Cordón relates in Chapter 3, even under the most optimistic Eurostat population projection, which has fertility rising to near-replacement level and the recruitment of one million net migrants per year, the elderly dependency ratio will still reach nearly 75 percent by mid-century. The extent of increase in the elderly dependency ratio is quite insensitive to the choice of demographic parameters that go into the population projection.

The most direct impact will be an endemic European pensions crisis. At current labor force participation and employment rates, each worker will need to pay social contributions sufficient to support nearly twice as many retired elderly as are alive today. In Japan, where the demographic outlook is even worse and the labor market just as rigid (or perhaps more so), there is considerable scope for enabling more women who want to work to do so. In Europe, however, only in some of the southern European countries is there much scope for increasing the participation of women. Worse yet, greater female attachment to the labor force is one of the elements favoring continued low fertility. Reducing unemployment rates is often mentioned (especially by trade unions) as a win–win approach to pension system problems, but experience over the last 30 years does not give much cause for hope. The way to reduce European unemployment is greater flexibilization of the labor market, precisely what trade unions do *not* want. It would seem inescapable that the balancing item in the equation will be higher elderly labor force participation. The policy slogan for this is 'Active Aging'; but this is really a euphemism. What it means is older workers staying in the labor force longer than they thought they would have to. Moreover, again invoking the example of Japan (and also the United States), the key to keeping older workers in the labor force is a high degree of flexibility at this end of the labor market (inter alia, part-time work, flexible wages and peak-season employment).

So much has been written about the outlook for European pensions that the authors of this volume can perhaps be forgiven for having paid relatively little direct attention to it. However, a few basic generalizable points deserve to be mentioned. Three are crucial:

1. In the final analysis, the method chosen to finance pensions (pay-as-you-go [PAYG] versus capitalization or 'funding') is irrelevant. Whichever the method chosen, the members of the working-age population will still have to forego consumption in order to transfer resources to the elderly. At present, they do this by contributing to PAYG pension systems, thereby acquiring an implicit claim that the next generation will be forced to support them as well. If they do this by contributing to a funded pension system, they are implicitly purchasing a financial asset (i.e., a claim on the profits of a firm) from a member of the aged population who has annuitized his assets in order to generate income. Arguments abound regarding which type of claim is more reliable (let alone more virtuous), but they are of limited interest. Income of the young will still need to be transformed into income of the old.

2. Most of the economic inefficiencies that arise from ill-conceived pension systems have to do with workers being encouraged to retire too early. When general-equilibrium-model simulations of pension reform are done, the big gains to pension reform invariably arise in the labor market. Correcting labor market distortions does not require structural pension reform, but it does set off tremendous political disputes when the parameters of existing pension systems are adjusted. The obvious parameter to adjust is the retirement age. 'Active aging' will continue to be the byword, but it is certain to lead to bitter controversies. Its slogan sounds appealing, but who is in favor of the policies

it implies? Not old people, who want to retire; not employers, who want to offload expensive older workers on to the public pension system; not young people, who are waiting their turn in the job queue.

3. In an aging society, it is practically inevitable that pensions will need to be based on prices, not wages. This may sound like a technical issue, but the social implications are large. The first option means defining a socially acceptable fixed consumption basket for the elderly and financing it out of productivity gains; that way, increases in the old-age dependency ratio will not automatically translate into increased social contribution rates.[4] The second option means that, even if productivity growth raises wages by X percent, pensions will rise by X percent *pari passu*; hence, any increase in the old-age dependency ratio will translate automatically into a proportional increase in social contribution rates. A few years ago, calculations by David Blake (City University, London) and Michael Orszag (Watson Wyatt) came up with an astoundingly simple conclusion: at current levels of real benefits, all European pension systems are actuarially sustainable; at wage-indexed levels of benefits, none are (Blake and Orszag, 1998). Closely related to this are decomposition analyses which have shown that the main source of increase in pension spending has not been population aging, but increases in real benefits.

The implication of the last two points is that a deep social dialog on the role and position of the European elderly is needed; the implication of the first is that technical disputes about pension system financing are largely a red herring. The sooner the debate shifts from the latter to the former the better.

16.4   Population Aging 2: Health Care, Long-Term Care and Home Support

16.4.1   Health care

Health is an important issue regardless of population aging, but aging brings it to the fore. While average health-care spending differs drastically across countries, there is great consistency in relative health-care spending by age. Typically, health-care expenditure per person over 65 is six to eight times total health-care spending per capita in age groups corresponding to the prime of life—the twenties, say. Model age profiles of health-care spending underlie most existing projections of the health sector resources needed.

Nonetheless, two important qualifications need to be made to the link between population aging and health-care spending:

1. Most lifetime health-care expenditure occurs during the final months of life, the so-called 'terminal drop.' One consequence of this is that the demographic index most relevant to health-care costs is not the proportion of the population aged over x, but rather the proportion of the population within one year of dying. As far as I know, this subtlety has yet to be worked into systematic projections and analyses of health-care spending. Ever-greater robustness of the elderly population, as hypothesized by Fries (1980), might allow for substantial aging without increasing the proportion of the population at death's door.

2. Demography has been and will continue to be a secondary source of increase in health sector resources needed. It is technological progress—new treatments and improvements in old ones—that has dominated increases in health spending.[5] Most new interventions, even the ones that give rise to the most fiscal handwringing (e.g., hip replacements, cardiac bypass surgery) have astronomical benefit–cost ratios. Policy makers may call loudly for 'evidence-based' medicine (as they do in the United Kingdom), but their enthusiasm may falter when evidence emerges that costly new treatments are, for the most part, worth every penny.

Not related to demography, but equally important, it is well known from World Health Organization (WHO) statistics that health outcomes at the national level are unrelated (in international cross-sectional regressions) to health spending per capita. They are also unrelated to the share of that health spending accounted for by the public sector. This suggests that individual-level health behaviors are far more important determinants of health than the kind of health-care system. As Schulze brings out in Chapter 12, many of these behaviors, such as eating, drinking, smoking and exercise, are family-based.

Schulze (Chapter 12) asks what kind of health system delivers the most health for a price. I would ask the question differently. Despite the cost-cutters' rhetoric, health policy is rarely made on a cost-effectiveness basis. If it were, there would be far less neonatal heart surgery performed, governments would not be supporting antiretroviral treatment for HIV/AIDS sufferers and alcoholics would not receive liver transplants. Two fundamentals, it seems to me, are insufficiently appreciated by almost all writers on health policy. First, like it or not, health policy is decided, in the final analysis, by physicians. Second, physicians' world view is based, in the final analysis, on treatment protocols—if a patient presents with X, you do Y. Taken together, these fundamentals are fatal to the vision of an ideal health sector based on cost-effectiveness.

A more general way of phrasing the question would be, 'What kind of health system delivers needed health care while keeping costs to a reasonable level?' One approach, essentially the same as that used by Schulze (Chapter 12), is to separate health-care delivery and its financing, each of which can be public or private.[6] This is not a place for a systematic journey through the four cells of the implied matrix, each of which has its advantages and disadvantages, or to list the schemes and devices (for example, 'gatekeeper' approaches, capitation payments, approved treatment lists, patient copayments) that have been invented to correct problems that lurk, in varying degree, in each cell. Sowada's detailed description of the Polish health system in Chapter 13 gives a good overview of these in one European health system.

I would argue that, provided administration is reasonably efficient, any of the four approaches can deliver a reasonable standard of care, at a reasonable cost, the results to be determined largely by the health behaviors of the citizenry. Health-care systems, when you think of it, actually work remarkably well.

Consider the case of the United States, which is almost universally regarded as having a poorly functioning health sector. Spending, at 14 percent of GDP, is twice that of most other countries of its income level, yet life expectancy is lower. Large portions of the population are without any insurance coverage at all. Health gaps between black and white, rich and poor, are enormous. Yet, even in America, poor people with serious medical conditions receive care after a fashion, and the protocol approach means that the care provided is of a reasonable standard. Even the rich are unlikely to receive heroic medical care at the end of their lives, when the marginal benefit is small. The amount of money consumed by medical tort lawsuits would be unthinkable in Europe, but partly as a result of that, the American medical system is more responsive to patient demands than the European. Arguably, the United States does not have a health problem, it has a poverty/precarity problem.

And it also has an inequality problem. One of the few variables systematically related to health at the national level is the degree of income inequality. Intriguingly, wide social gaps appear to worsen the health both of the wealthy and of the poor. The European social model, with its emphasis on social inclusion and a relatively even distribution of income, gives policy makers on this side of the Atlantic a clear advantage.

16.4.2 Long-term care and home support

Far more worrying than the health outlook, in my view, is the outlook for (i) long-term care for the chronically ill elderly (such as those suffering from Alzheimer's) and (ii) home care for those elderly who need help but are not ill in the classic sense. My pessimism springs from several observations.

1. The Eurostat high variant projection summarized by Cordón shows that, while the population over 60 is expected to increase by 50 percent between 2000 and 2050, the population over 80 will increase by a factor of three. The 'aging of

the aged' is quite insensitive to the demographic assumptions that go into the projection. These 'oldest old' disproportionately suffer from chronic conditions or need help around the house. We can only hope that James Vaupel and his collaborators (1998) are correct; that the years of life added by the longevity revolution will be healthy, not disabled, ones.

2. Whereas demography plays second fiddle to technology where health-care costs are concerned, the roles are reversed when it comes to long-term care and home support. The rapidly rising number of oldest old will likely translate directly into rising demand for care. Despite occasional articles that find their way into the press about robots bathing nursing-home patients (in Japan) and the like, the technology associated with care is unlikely to change much.

3. The sorts of moral considerations that prevent (either informally or through the operation of hospital ethics committees) heroic expenditure to cure the very elderly do not operate to ration long-term institutional care and home support.

As statistics cited by Anderson in Chapter 14 show, a staggering number of Europeans—one in five in the EU15, one in four in the NMS and CCs—provide some degree of informal care. But this is mostly home support of an elderly person who just needs help with some of the activities of daily living. After a certain point on the impairment scale, home care is inappropriate both for the patient and the carer. As few governments regard themselves as purveyors of nursing institutions (although there are exceptions, like Austria), the real question is how institutional care will be financed and how the availability of beds in such institutions can be expanded.

In the United States, long-term care insurance, more often called 'nursing home insurance,' has proven immensely popular among the wealthy. Premiums on a policy purchased at the age of 65 run into hundreds of dollars a month, even when the deductible (the patient copayment) is high. One cannot blame the insurance companies for this, as the problem of moral hazard is acute—those who feel they will live to the age of one hundred buy nursing home policies; those who feel confident that they will be dead by eighty do not. The solution to adverse selection is to force all persons to participate, which is what Germany has sensibly done in mandating long-term care insurance for all its citizens. As population aging proceeds, I am confident that something along the lines of the German model will become increasingly popular.

Home support of the elderly, of the sort reported by Anderson (Chapter 14), is an even harder nut to crack. Home care may tug at the heartstrings, but in economic terms it is a low productivity, low value added activity. If it were not, the social assistants who help the elderly to wash and care for themselves would be receiving salaries far higher than they do.

Despite a rich mosaic of caregiving constellations—spouses caring for spouses, neighbors looking after each other—one of the most common configurations is that of a middle-aged woman caring for her own or her husband's parent. But this mode of operation is on a collision course with itself. As those requiring care become older and older, many caregivers themselves will be old and at least partially disabled. Middle-aged women are increasingly in the workforce and reluctant to forego needed income to look after a parent. It is also by no means to be assumed that parents wish to be cared for by their children. Schulze (Chapter 12) cites figures that 17 percent of parents of adult children reported feeling distant from their children and another 27 percent were ambivalent. Admittedly, Anderson (Chapter 14) reports survey data from the EU15 that 59 percent of citizens think it would be a good thing if families were to provide more support for the elderly themselves, but the range of estimates is large. There is a clear north–south or Protestant–Catholic divide, with the strongest support for family involvement being observed in countries such as Italy. Interestingly, differences in attitude between generations are much smaller than differences between countries—when people in a country approve or disapprove of greater family responsibility, all generations approve or disapprove of it.

Thus, we have rising demand for home care, a limited and indeed declining capacity on the part of families to provide it and a substantial proportion of the elderly who would prefer to obtain care through the market rather than the family. Based on these considerations, I have no hesitation in forecasting that a significant migration stream into Europe will consist of low-skilled immigrants working within this specific niche of the health sector. This is already happening informally (and illegally) as Romanian and Moldavian women travel to Italy in hopes of attaching themselves to an elderly pensioner who needs assistance.

16.5 Migration

Europe, for two centuries a major region of origin for migrants (mostly to the New World) has become, over the last 30 years, one of the principal global zones of attraction for international migrants. A few statistics collected from various contributions to this volume put the picture in perspective:

1. According to Cordón (Chapter 3), in the EU15 net immigration has steadily increased from 0.6 per 1,000 in 1960 to 3.3 per 1,000 in 2001, thus accounting for over 80 percent of all population growth in the EU15.
2. Net migration in 2000 was estimated to be 700,000 persons per year. That implies a rate of growth of the immigrant population of 3.5 percent per year,

even before natural increase is taken into account. Sixty percent of nonnationals on European soil have been present for over ten years.
3. In 2000, according to the information provided by Wihtol de Wenden (Chapter 11), 5 percent of the population of the EU (20 million out of 380 million) consisted of nonnaturalized foreigners. This figure is, however, highly variable, with nearly 10 percent of the population of Austria, Belgium and Germany being foreign as compared with below 3 percent in other countries such as Italy, Spain and Portugal. About one-third of these 'foreigners' are European Community (EC) citizens living in countries other than their country of birth (i.e., Italians in Germany and so forth). Three main areas of origin dominate: the Mahgreb, Turkey and former Yugoslavia.

Europe's transformation from an exporter to an importer of migrants started with the recruitment of *Gastarbeiter* in the 1960s, which in turn set off, with a lag, a wave of family reunifications. As Pflegerl points out in Chapter 9, European policy makers had no legal obligation to accommodate the demand for family reunification, especially at a time of high unemployment at home. That they did so is a credit to their attachment to humanitarian principles. Immigration accelerated sharply in the 1990s, as asylum seekers and refugees were displaced from the Balkans, Africa, the former Soviet Union and other regions. Clandestine migration, always significant, also increased and well-developed criminal networks arose to exploit opportunities for profit. Also contributing to the increase in the stock of the foreign-born on European soil was the massive increase in transborder mobility for study and temporary employment.

The 'European preference' in hiring means that classic labor migration into Europe—an immigrant showing up looking for a job or with an offer in hand—is rare. Family reunification is the driving force. A drawback of the priority given to family reunification is that it gives policy makers little control over the human capital profile of immigrants. Nothing could be further from the case of Australia, Canada and the United States, where potential immigrants are 'scored' on, among other things, their level of skills and qualifications. To implement a selective approach, however, European policy makers would be forced to admit that Europe has, in fact, become a continent of immigration in which migrants play a key role in society and in the labor market.

For many years, and most recently in the Barcelona Declaration covering European Community relations with the Middle East and Mediterranean (MEDA) region, 'codevelopment' has been proposed as a means of putting a brake on migration. In the Barcelona Declaration, there is explicit discussion of substituting flows of goods for flows of human beings (i.e., using the fruits of free trade and targeted investment to stimulate development and employment). More generally, the European Commission has expressed interest in assisting partner countries in 'managing' migration to maximize its contribution to development, which is much the same thing as saying to ensure it is a self-limiting phenomenon. To the extent that traditional EC policy toward migration was more interested in border control and other security-related activities, this is a welcome development. However, one of the main impediments to movement, from the potential migrants' point of view, is the lack of resources or opportunities to establish a beachhead in Europe. The impact of policies to accelerate development is likely, in the short run, to stimulate rather than discourage migration. Only in the long term, when partner countries have reached a substantially higher standard of living, will migratory pressures slacken. That long term is far beyond the horizon of any European policy maker.

Given the presence of substantial numbers of ethnically and religiously distinct subpopulations in Europe, with every likelihood that these will grow in importance, what should be done? The best approach is promote assimilation, yet the European political right (and more on the left than would admit it) are adamantly opposed to such a policy. 'Integration' is the policy of choice, but discussion of integration reveals that there are problems integrating even existing migrants, let alone more.

The situation has become especially tricky following 9/11. Current security responses, including tougher immigration controls, have been based on the assumption of a many-tentacled radical Islamic conspiracy. Most experts have thoroughly debunked this view. The new face of Islamic terrorism is likely not to be dirty nuclear bombs and weapons of mass destruction but the actions of largely autonomous cells (the Madrid train bombing) or low-tech outrages (the murder of Dutch film director Theo van Gogh). The profile of too many young European Muslims—urban, lower middle-class, educated and afflicted by strong feelings of exclusion and injustice—precisely fits the ideal terrorist type. There is an urgent need to address the problem of social exclusion of immigrant populations, especially Muslim ones.

One of the worst aspects of marginalization is the high unemployment rate of non-EU nationals. Data presented by Pflegerl (Chapter 9) show that on the continent, unemployment rates for non-EU labor force members are consistently two and three times higher than for EU nationals. Even in the United Kingdom, with its relatively liberal labor market, the unemployment rate for foreign males is three percentage points higher than the rate for nationals (8.4 percent versus 5.3 percent in 2002). This reflects the fact that immigrants are overrepresented in sectors characterized by high unemployment and in lowskilled and semiskilled jobs. That said, they are also overrepresented in sectors (such as construction) where the black economy is ever-present and taking advantage of generous unemployment benefits is a long tradition. This is changing, however, as immigrants increasingly take low-paid service jobs, often in the health and education sectors.

In addition, EU nationals have higher labor force participation than non-EU nationals. This might be expected for females, given the persistence of traditional roles. However, it is also true for men. In countries like Belgium and The Netherlands, the gap is an astounding 20 percentage points and more; even in the United Kingdom, national males are six percentage points more likely to join the labor force than nonnationals (Germany, 82.7 percent versus 76.4 percent). Some of this difference is because the population of working age (15–64) is younger among nonnationals than nationals, but this is only a small part of the observed difference. My interpretation is that failure to enter the labor market is yet another sign of social disaffection and the failure of the 'integration' model.

It has long been known that immigration can have only a slight impact on the long-term age structure of a population. In the near term, the inertia of population age structure means that a substantial amount of aging is inevitable. In the long term, immigrants themselves age. Thus, calculations such as those presented by the United Nations several years ago show that the number of immigrants needed to 'correct' deteriorating age structure measures is astronomical. Pflegerl (Chapter 9) summarizes simulations by Lutz and Scherbov (2003) showing quite convincingly that immigration cannot have any significant effect on old age dependency ratios in Europe. Parenthetically, a moratorium on such simulations should be declared: Didier Blanchet (1988) established this result, generally, elegantly, and using only very simple mathematics, years ago.

That said, however, to portray immigration as the answer to Europe's age structure problems and then debunk the myth is to set up a straw man. Immigration can fill specific gaps in the labor market, particularly gaps that are made worse by population aging. Such practices are already well established, as witnessed by the large annual inflow of skilled nurses from the Philippines, South Africa and other countries. The growing need for domestic care is, as I mentioned, already inducing significant migration, much of it illegal. As the demand for such labor associated with the increase in the aged population grows, it is inevitable that migration of this type will be tolerated and even encouraged. This is already seen in the rising share of women in total immigration and in the fact that, as pointed out by Pflegerl (Chapter 9), over 10 percent of immigrant workers in Greece, Spain and Italy are employed in household services.

Moreover, failure to shift old-age dependency ratios should not be confused with fiscal insignificance. Debates on the fiscal impact of immigrants typically bog down on the assumptions made regarding, for example, how many children they have or how much additional demand they place upon public services. The simplest case to analyse is legal temporary labor migration, referred to in World Trade Organization (WTO)–speak as 'Mode 4' movement of natural persons. Typical of such a program is the recruitment of Commonwealth nurses into the United Kingdom. Based on reasonable assumptions about incomes, taxes and remittances, and assuming that the nurses place no significant demand on public expenditure, a net fiscal benefit in excess of £3,000 per year per nurse can be estimated. This is insignificant relative to the broad fiscal picture but, for example, it represents £250 per year for every elderly person who is completely dependent on the state pension.

Asylum seeking represents a special form of immigration. The peak year for asylum seekers was 1999, coinciding with the Kosovo crisis. Major sources of asylum seekers in recent years have included Afghanistan, Iraq, Kosovo and Turkey (mostly Kurds). In actuality, host countries have shown considerable flexibility in how they deal with asylum seekers. Thus, the United Kingdom tightened eligibility rules in 2003 and reported a 40 percent drop in applications the next year. There is also an extraordinary range in refugee recognition rates, from 29.6 percent in Austria in 2003 to less than 10 percent in France, Germany and the United Kingdom.

Asylum seekers are regularly denied access to the labor market and highly restricted in their access to basic benefits. As often as not, they are 'ghettoized' in dormitories and accommodations that are little better than prisons. Thus, not surprisingly, all the possible social pathologies that can be associated with immigration are present in spades when it comes to asylum seekers. While variable and subject to control, the number of asylum seekers has continued to be of the order of 300,000 per year, compared with 700,000 legal net migrants in 2000. The policy challenge is to respect human rights while exerting legitimate control over immigration. To date, European policy makers have not succeeded.

It is practically by definition impossible to find reliable data on illegal or clandestine immigration, which can take many forms, from overstaying a student visa to being smuggled across the border. However, undocumented immigration is doubtless on the rise. This reflects developments at both ends: growing desperation in countries of origin and tighter limitations on legal migration in countries of destination. Increasingly, countries are recognizing that the stock of illegal residents has reached such proportions that some form of regularization is necessary. At the time of writing, Spain is engaged in a major regularization program, but this is only the latest in a series. France and other countries have also had extensive regularization programs. Germany and the United Kingdom, significantly, have not. On the one hand, regularization recognizes reality and rationalizes the situation. On the other hand, it holds out an inducement to yet more illegals to come on the gamble that, should they establish themselves securely in the black economy, they will eventually be forgiven and accorded regular status.

16.6   Europe's Future Generations

Given the above, what sort of world will Europe's future generations inhabit? Clearly, a world of their own choosing, because policy regimes and decisions will continue in force. It is probably a safe bet that something close to the European social model—priority given to equity over growth, ample provision of public goods and amenities and a commitment to social solidarity, even when it proves costly—will continue to increase. But there are at least three dilemmas to be resolved.

Dilemma Number 1: The status of the young must rise, but the voting power of the old is strong.

Much will depend on decisions affecting the distribution of income and wealth between the young and the old. In the period of economic challenge that followed the first oil shock, as Sgritta mentions in Chapter 6, European policy makers protected the old at the expense of the young, continuing to expand pension benefits even as the foundations of strong economic growth were collapsing beneath them. This is consistent with trends throughout the Organisation for Economic Co-operation and Development, where support for the elderly grew as support for children fell; old-age poverty declined relative to child poverty. It is a disturbing fact that in most developed countries, elderly suicide rates have declined while youth suicide rates have increased.

Reform of European pension systems will happen one way or another. Retirement age will be higher, disability pension rules will have to be tightened, social contribution rates (effectively, tax rates) will be higher and real pensions will perhaps be lower. But these adjustments need to be negotiated between the generations. An integral part of this process must be an increase in the economic status of the young relative to the old. If it helps to think of this in simple supply–demand terms, then go ahead and do so: the increase in the number of nonworking elderly relative to working young must raise the level of wages relative to the value of capital (chiefly apartments and houses owned by the old). Within the labor force, the wages of the young trained in the latest technologies must be raised relative to the old whose human capital is less up-to-date.

The problem is that, precisely when the economic status of the young should rise, the voting power of the old will hold sway. Public choice models have long suggested that middle-aged workers form an electoral alliance with elderly persons to protect the entitlements of the elderly at the expense of the young. If the European social model is to adjust smoothly to population aging, something must be done to ensure that gridlock of this sort does not occur. In some countries, it may prove easy: in Sweden, the key to pension reform was simply explaining to elderly people that they would have to accept a small sacrifice in order to ensure the welfare of the next generation. Just try that in Italy!

Dilemma Number 2: The Lisbon Commitment is on a collision course with the European social model.

In Lisbon in 2001, European policy makers committed themselves to becoming the most productive economic bloc in the world. The paradox is that the only way for European states to accelerate economic growth is to liberalize: deregulate the labor market; stop trying to pick winners in the market for corporate control. But labor market flexibility, and the uncertainty that comes when capital markets are shifted to an Anglo-Saxon basis, are inconsistent with the European social model. They also risk exacerbating the low fertility problem. Mothers who stay at home to care for children and aged parents, children and young persons who refuse to leave their home communities because of their deep emotional attachment, fathers who forego stressful careers to spend more time at home—these are all anathema to capitalism. The Romantic poets were acutely aware of this; one can only assume that the policy makers gathered in Lisbon had never read them. These sorts of paradoxes are by no means limited to European policy making; it is the height of irony that in the United States, those loudest in the defense of the traditional family are also loudest in singing the praises of turbocapitalism.

Dilemma Number 3: Europe needs immigrants, but it doesn't want them.

It is perfectly possible to adapt to population aging and labor force shrinkage with no immigration at all, let alone rising immigration. One need look no further than Japan for an example. The problem, in addition to the ethical issue of what to do about family reunification and asylum seekers, is that a low-immigration future is by definition a high-labor-cost future. Japan prepared itself for such a contingency by accumulating massive assets abroad, effectively transforming itself into a nation of coupon clippers (like the Swiss). Europe does not have the same cushion, and anti-immigration policy advocates should 'come clean' about the economic consequences of their prescription.

Immigration has proven to be a particularly bitter pill for European policy makers to swallow. Over the years, policy makers have insisted that migrants were present only temporarily in their capacity as workers, that development in partner countries would eventually lead to a slackening of migratory pressures and so on, even when facts were clearly showing them to be wrong. In fact, as Wihtol de Wenden points out in Chapter 11, official EU immigration policy has been a disingenuous tissue of self-deception. Whether they like it or not, as Pflegerl (Chapter 9) argues, many EU member states are now, by any reasonable definition, established countries of immigration. Saying it is not so will not make it not so.

16.7   Conclusion

This volume began with a quote from American author Jeremy Rifkin's book *The European Dream*, so it seems appropriate to return to it to end. Rifkin argues in his book that in the long run, it is the European social model that will survive and flourish, not American *laissez-faire* with its sharp elbows and overflowing prisons. He may be right; in fact, as an American living in Europe, I half-hope he *is* right. But in order to flourish, the demographic challenges described above need to be addressed.

After reading these chapters, I decided that if I were allowed three wishes for Europe, they would be the following: (i) flexibilize the labor market, (ii) rationalize university systems and (iii) get serious about assimilating immigrant communities. That is a big policy agenda, but the problems are big, too.

Notes

1.   For example, total cohort fertility in Germany and Italy is of the order of 1.5–1.6. However, TFRs of 1.2–1.3 (due to the low fertility of younger women) make it very likely that total cohort fertility will continue to decline. Recent slight upturns in European TFRs do not essentially modify this prognosis.

2.   To take just one example, the proportion of females aged 18–34 who report that complete happiness/satisfaction can be obtained only via children and home is reported by Sgritta in Chapter 6 to be 79.4 percent in Italy, 54.8 percent in Austria but only 29.9 percent in Finland. Yet, among these three countries, the ordering of TFRs, from lowest to highest, is Italy, Austria, Finland. As David Coleman (1996) has pointed out, it is in the most postmaterialist European societies (e.g., the Nordics) that fertility is high and in those apparently bogged down in modernism (e.g., Spain and Italy) that fertility is low.

3.   Admittedly the distribution of cohabitation is quite skewed; it has become the rule in northern Europe but remains rare in Italy.

4.   And more than productivity gains. Population aging goes hand in hand with labor scarcity, which should drive up wages and, *ceteris paribus*, reduce the proportional tax rate necessary to support the elderly population. If pensions are indexed to wages, this virtuous adjustment process arising from basic supply–demand forces is short-circuited.

5.   Note, in passing, that this point parallels nicely the point made about pensions (i.e. that it was rising benefit levels, not population aging, that had accounted for most spending increase). Do not underestimate, as well, improvements in health-care *quality*. The experience of having a tooth pulled in 2004 is very different from what it was in 1954.

6. Polar extremes are the United Kingdom and the United States. In the United States both delivery and financing are private, the latter through employee-sponsored health insurance plans (an arrangement that leaves the unemployed and those in nontraditional occupations out in the cold). In the United Kingdom the celebrated National Health Service is a network of public hospitals and practitioners whose fees are paid out of general government tax revenue. In most countries on the European continent, the bulk of health care is delivered by private physicians, but the bill is paid by the government. While most countries try to maintain the façade of adhering to social insurance principles, in fact, the government subsidies required to keep the health-insurance fund afloat have effectively broadened the financing base to include all taxpayers.

References

Beck, U. (1999) *World Risk Society*, Cambridge, UK: The Polity Press.

Blake, D. and Orszag, J.M. (1998) *The Simple Economics of Funded and Unfunded Pension Systems*, Pensions Institute Discussion Paper PI98-02. City University, London: The Pensions Institute.

Blanchet, D. (1988) 'Immigration et rgulation de la structure par âge d'une population,' *Population*2: 293–309 [in French].

Coale, A.J. (1973) 'The Demographic Transition,' in *International Population Conference*, Liège, 1973, vol 1, Liège, Belgium: International Union for the Scientific Study of Population, pp. 53–71.

Coleman, D. (ed) (1996) *Europe's Population in the 1990s*, Oxford, UK: Oxford University Press.

Fries, J.F. (1980) 'Aging, Natural Death, and the Compression of Morbidity,' *New England Journal of Medicine*, **303**: 130–135.

Lesthaeghe, R. (1995) 'The Second Demographic Transition in Western Countries: An Interpretation,' in Mason, K.O. and Jensen, A.-M. (eds) *Gender and Family Change in Industrialized Countries*, Oxford, UK: Clarendon Press, pp. 17–62.

Lutz, W. and Scherbov, S. (2003) *Can Immigration Compensate for Europe's Low Fertility?* Interim Report IR-02-052, Laxenburg, Austria: International Institute for Applied Systems Analysis.

McDonald P. (2002) *Low Fertility: Unifying the Theory and the Demography*, Paper prepared for Session 73, Meeting of the Population Association of America, held 9–11 May, Atlanta, GA, USA, See http://eprints.anu.edu.au/archive/00001113/ last accessed in December 2005.

Notestein, F. (1945) 'Population: The Long View,' in Schultz, T.W. (ed) *Food For Thought*, Norman Wait Harris Memorial Lectures.

Rifkin, J. (2004) *The European Dream*, New York, USA: Penguin Books.

van de Kaa, D.J. (1987) 'Europe's Second Demographic Transition,' *Population Bulletin*, **42**(1): 1–58.

Vaupel J.W., Carey, J.R., Christensen, K., Johnson T.E., Yashin, A.I., Holm, N.V., Iachine, I.A., Khazaeli, A.A., Liedo, P., Longo, V.D., Zeng, Y., Manton, K.G. and Curtsinger, J.W. (1998) 'Biodemographic Trajectories of Longevity,' *Science*, **280** (5365): 855–860.

Index

About the Authors

Robert Anderson is coordinator of the 'Living Conditions' research program at the European Foundation for the Improvement of Living and Working Conditions, a European Union (EU) agency charged with providing information for policy making, specifically at EU level. His current research activities include: monitoring the quality of life and living conditions in the EU; projects on aging and changes in employment over the life course; measures to promote the social inclusion of people with chronic illness; and creation of employment in care services. He formerly worked with the European office of the World Health Organization, developing and implementing its health promotion program. He is the author of several books and edited volumes on health services, health promotion, chronic illness and family care.

Juan Antonio Fernández Cordón is Director-General of the Statistical Institute of Andalucia in Seville, Spain, and prior to that, Head of the Institute of Demography at the Spanish National Council for Scientific Research. He has been Professor of Demography at the Universities of Algiers, Algeria, and Montreal, Canada. His research interests are fertility, family structures, family and demographic policies and population projections. He is now a member of the Scientific Council of the *Institut national des études démographiques* (INED) in France and acted for many years as national expert at the European Observatory for the Social Situation, Demography and the Family.

Dušan Drbohlav is Associate Professor of Social Geography at Charles University in Prague, teaching international migration. He has researched international migration issues at California State University, Los Angeles, and the Catholic University, Leuven, Belgium, and has worked on migration-related issues with the government of the Czech Republic, the European Commission, Council of Europe, International Organization for Migration, the United Nations High Commissioner for Refugees, Organisation for Economic Co-operation and Development and the North Atlantic Treaty Organization. He has published numerous book and journal articles about migration and immigrants' inclusion in a host society.

Constantinos Fotakis is advisor at the General Directorate of Employment and Social Affairs of the European Commission in charge of research coordination. He joined the European Commission in 1981 and since 1985 has worked on employment and social policy issues. From 2000 to 2005 he was head of the Social and Demographic Analysis Unit, charged with the preparation of the Commission's annual report, *The Social Situation in the European Union.* He has produced many contributions on the implications of demographic trends for the labor market and social welfare systems.

Siyka Kovacheva is a lecturer in Sociology at the University of Plovdiv and head of New Europe Centre for Regional Studies in Bulgaria. Her areas of expertise are youth transitions to adulthood, civic participation, unemployment and self-employment, family life, including gender and intergenerational relations and youth policy. Her publications include *Exploring the European Youth Mosaic, The Social Situation of Young People in Europe* (with L. Chisholm), *Keys to Youth Participation in Eastern Europe, and Youth in Society. The Construction and Deconstruction of Youth in East and West Europe* (with C. Wallace).

Wolfgang Lutz is leader of the World Population Program of the International Institute of Applied Systems Analysis (IIASA). His work focuses on family demography, fertility analysis, population projection and the interaction between population and environment, and he has conducted in-depth studies on population–development–environment interactions in Mexico, several African countries and Asia. He is the author of the IIASA series of world population projections and has developed approaches for projecting education and human capital. As well as being principal investigator of the Asian MetaCentre for Population and Sustainable Development Analysis, Professor Lutz is author and editor of 28 books and over 150 articles (including some in *Science* and *Nature*). He is a director of the African Population and Health Research Center in Nairobi, Kenya; the Max Planck Institute for Demographic Research in Rostock, Germany; and the Population Reference Bureau in Washington, D.C., USA.

Landis MacKellar is an economist specializing in economic demography. His research has covered population and development, population and the environment and, most recently, the economics of population aging. Since 1998 he has been leader of the Social Security Reform Project at the International Institute of Applied Systems Analysis (IIASA). Prior to joining IIASA in 1994, he worked for the International Labor Organization in Geneva and Africa and was Assistant Professor of Economics at Queens College of the City University of New York and an economist at Wharton Econometric Forecasting Associates.

Jan H. Marbach is a sociologist and has been head of the Family Survey of the Deutsches Jugend Institut since 2001. His personal research areas are social networks and the development of social capital in a lifelong perspective, with a special focus on intergenerational exchange.

Fritz von Nordheim is a social protection expert specializing in policies related to older workers, pensions and societal aging. After a decade of comparative welfare state research, he joined the division for economic and statistical analysis of the Danish Ministry of Social Affairs in 1992, where he worked in the areas of retirement, old age care and child policy, serving as an occasional consultant to the welfare ministries of Latvia and Lithuania. In the General Directorate of Employment and Social Affairs of the European Commission, where he worked from 1998 to 2005, Mr. von Nordheim played a leading role in the development of active aging as a paradigm for EU policy responses to aging. Since June 2005 he has served as head of the European Commission Representation in Denmark.

Johannes Pflegerl worked at the Austrian Institute for Family Studies in Vienna, Austria, from 1995 to 2005, and from 2000 to 2004 was a member of the coordination team of the European Observatory on the Social Situation, Demography and Family. Since October 2005 he has been a lecturer in sociology at the University of Applied Sciences in St. Pölten, Austria, carrying out research into family and migration. Several of his articles have appeared in international publications.

Rudolf Richter is Professor of Sociology at the Institute of Sociology of the Faculty of Social Sciences, University of Vienna, and was formerly chair of the coordination team of the European Observatory on Social Situation, Demography and the Family. His main areas of research are the sociology of family, sociology of the life course, political sociology and interpretative sociology.

Hans-Joachim Schulze holds a special chair for parental child rearing and the effects of family policies in cooperation with the Netherlands Family Council. His teaching covers family theories, family processes and the interplay between the family and its environment. His research area is directed toward the perception of the parental role by women and men, the relation between partnership and parenthood, intergenerational relations and the relevance of community for family development.

Giovanni B. Sgritta is Professor of Sociology at the University of Rome *La Sapienza* and was the Italian representative to the European Observatory on the Social Situation, Demography and the Family. He has participated in many comparative projects and research programs and is author and editor of books and articles on social policy, family, childhood and generational issues.

Christoph Sowada has been Assistant Professor at the Institute of Public Health of the Jagiellonian University Medical College in Krakow, Poland, since 2000 and is a researcher in the fields of health economics and the economics of health insurance. He was a member of the research team on the ACE Research Projects (1993–1994 and 1997–1999), CASE-Warsaw Project (2002–2004), GVG/European Commission Project (2002) and many others. He is a member of the German Economic Association (*Verein für Sozialpolitik*) and the Polish Public Health Association.

Zsolt Spéder is Director of the Demographic Research Institute of the Hungarian Central Statistical Office and a member of the editorial board of *International Sociology*. His primary fields of research are status changes in the life course, structural and ideational determinants of fertility and partnership, differences in demographic behavior, social inequalities and poverty, the interrelation of demographic behavior and well-being and longitudinal panel research methods. He is editor of the collection *Hungary in Flux*, author of *The Changing Faces of Poverty: Facts and Meanings* (in Hungarian) and co-author of *Fertility and Family Issues in an Enlarged Europe*. He is currently directing a large-scale panel survey in Hungary and is a coordinator of the Generations and Gender Survey.

Claire Wallace is Professor of Sociology at the University of Aberdeen. She has worked in the field of youth studies, family and work for many years, and her most recent book in this field is *Youth in Society* (with S. Kovacheva). She is editor of the journal *European Societies* and a contributor to the *Journal of Youth Studies*.

Catherine Wihtol de Wenden is Director of Research at the *Centre d'études et de recherches internationales* (CERI) of the *Centre nationale des recherches scientifiques* (CNRS) and a Doctor of Political Science. As both a political scientist and a lawyer, she has worked for 20 years on various topics relating to international migration, leading many field studies and directing collective research on comparative topics, mostly European. She has been a consultant for the Organisation for Economic Co-operation and Development, the European Council, the European Commission and an external expert for the United Nations High Commissioner for Refugees.

Chris Wilson joined the World Population Program of the International Institute of Applied Systems Analysis (IIASA) in November 2004. His research interests range from historical population trends to demographic theory. He is one of Europe's most widely cited demographers, with one of his papers (written with John

Cleland of the London School of Hygiene and Tropical Medicine) being the most cited article ever in *Population Studies*, Europe's premier demographic journal. His current research focuses principally on the causes and consequences of global demographic convergence and the future of Europe's population.

Join our
online community
and help us save paper and postage!

www.earthscan.co.uk

By joining the Earthscan website, our readers can benefit from a range of exciting new services and exclusive offers. You can also receive e-alerts and e-newsletters packed with information about our new books, forthcoming events, special offers, invitations to book launches, discussion forums and membership news. Help us to reduce our environmental impact by joining the Earthscan online community!

How? – Become a member in seconds!

>> Simply visit **www.earthscan.co.uk** and add your name and email address to the sign-up box in the top left of the screen – You're now a member!

>> With your new member's page, you can subscribe to our monthly **e-newsletter** and/or choose **e-alerts** in your chosen subjects of interest – you control the amount of mail you receive and can unsubscribe yourself

Why? – Membership benefits

✔ Membership is free!
✔ 10% discount on all books online
✔ Receive invitations to high-profile book launch events at the BT Tower, London Review of Books Bookshop, the Africa Centre and other exciting venues
✔ Receive e-newsletters and e-alerts delivered directly to your inbox, keeping you informed but not costing the Earth – you can also forward to friends and colleagues
✔ Create your own discussion topics and get engaged in online debates taking place in our new online Forum
✔ Receive special offers on our books as well as on products and services from our partners such as *The Ecologist*, *The Civic Trust* and more
✔ Academics – request inspection copies
✔ Journalists – subscribe to advance information e-alerts on upcoming titles and reply to receive a press copy upon publication – write to info@earthscan.co.uk for more information about this service
✔ Authors – keep up to date with the latest publications in your field
✔ NGOs – open an NGO Account with us and qualify for special discounts

Join now?
Join Earthscan now!
name
surname
email address

Earthscan Member
[Your name]

Click to Change

My profile
My forum
My bookmarks
All my pages

www.earthscan.co.uk

The Natural Advantage of Nations
Business Opportunities, Innovation and Governance in the 21st Century

Edited by Karlson 'Charlie' Hargroves and Michael Harrison Smith

Forewords by Amory B. Lovins, L Hunter Lovins, William McDonough, Michael Fairbanks and Alan AtKisson

'I am particularly pleased with the new book, *The Natural Advantage of Nations,* which will, in effect, follow on from *Natural Capitalism,* and bring in newer evidence from around the world'
AMORY B. LOVINS, Rocky Mountain Institute

'This is world-leading work, the team deserves the loudest acclamation possible'
BARRY GREAR AO, World Federation of Engineering Organisations

'A seminal book, a truly world changing book... As part of the process of pulling together the people whose ideas they wanted in the book, [the editors] have pulled together a whole movement'
L. HUNTER LOVINS, Natural Capitalism, Inc

This collection of inspiring work, based on solid academic and practical rigour, is an overview of the 21st century business case for sustainable development. It incorporates innovative technical, structural and social advances, and explores the role governance can play in both leading and underpinning business and communities in the shift towards a sustainable future.

The team from The Natural Edge Project have studied and incorporated key works from over 30 of the world's leaders in sustainability. The book is also supported by an extensive companion website. This work takes the lessons of competitive advantage theory and practice and combines them with the sustainability paradigm, in light of important developments in economics, innovation, business and governance over the last 30–50 years.

Far from being in conflict with economics and business practices, this book demonstrates how we can improve the well-being of society and the environment while driving innovation in an increasingly competitive world.

Hardback 1-84407-121-9 Published January 2005

HOW TO ORDER:

ONLINE www.earthscan.co.uk
CUSTOMER HOTLINE +44 (0)1256 302699
EMAIL book.orders@earthscan.co.uk

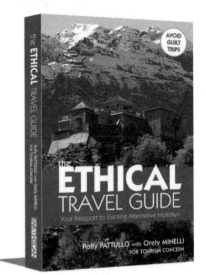